About the Author

Peter Saunders has been a practising obstetrician and gynaecologist for thirty years and a consultant in the National Health Service since 1974. He is a Fellow of the Royal College of Obstetricians and Gynaecologists and Director of Postgraduate Education at University College London Medical School.

He has lectured widely, is the author of over thirty medical publications and two books – *Birthwise: Having a Baby in the 80s* and *Womanwise: Every Woman's Guide to Gynaecology*. A frequent contributor to the media and woman's health journals; he is a strong supporter of informed choice and believes that caring for the pregnant woman is as much an art as a science.

Oct 20, 2000.

For D.

With you   o far
away to give you helpful advise
in these most important months of
your life, I thought I should
give you this book so you can
compare notes with Isabelle!
     all the best for the three
of you!
          Amar Mrs. Floiyn

This book could not have been written without invaluable advice from medical and midwifery colleagues, helpful criticism from patients and friends, and the tireless energy and patience of Veronica Evans who produced the entire manuscript.

I dedicate the book with grateful thanks to the mothers, past and present, in whose care I have participated and without whom my professional life would not have been possible.

Peter Saunders
London 1996

YOUR PREGNANCY

MONTH-BY-MONTH

Revised Edition

Peter Saunders FRCOG

Hodder & Stoughton

Copyright © 1996 by Peter Saunders
Illustrations © 1996 by Rodney Paull

The right of Peter Saunders to be identified as the Author of the
Work has been asserted by him in accordance with the Copyright,
Designs and Patents Act 1988.

First published in 1996 by Hodder and Stoughton
A division of Hodder Headline PLC
Revised edition published in 1998
10 9 8 7 6 5 4 3 2

A CIP catalogue record for this title is available from the
British Library

Saunders, Peter, 1937–
    Your pregnancy: month-by-month
    1. Pregnancy–Popular works 2. Prenatal care–Popular works
    1. Title
    618.24

    ISBN 0 340 71724 6

Design and computer page make-up by
Tony and Penny Mills

Printed and bound in Great Britain by
Mackays of Chatham PLC
Chatham, Kent

Hodder and Stoughton
A division of Hodder Headline PLC
338 Euston Road
London NW1 3BH

Contents

Abdominal Pain; Travel; Immunisation; Bathing and Douching; Carpal Tunnel Syndrome; Bleeding from the Nose and Gums; Muscle Cramps; Headaches; Fainting Attacks; Shortness of Breath; Heartburn; Backache; Insomnia; Libido; Mood Changes; Rest.

Foreword

Fifty years ago, as a medical student and awed spectator, I was introduced to the miracle that is childbirth. Despite a lifetime in obstetrics, the drama and the pleasure of involvement in this profound event remain. Yet so much else has changed in obstetric and midwifery practice.

In the 1940s and 1950s we still relished the immense benefits of blood transfusion and antibiotics that all but eliminated the twin scourges of haemorrhage and infection. The 1960s and 1970s saw at last the application of scientific method to childbirth which enabled physicians to address the problems of fetal welfare and establish the baby as a patient in pre-natal life. The 1980s and 1990s, however, showed signs of reaction to scientific or 'mechanistic' medicine which seemed to have diverted obstetric physicians from caring, compassion, consideration and towards clinical dialogue. So it appears we must learn again the language of communication.

Peter Saunders has undertaken this task – and a massive one it is – to inform in depth in language that women can understand and to be comprehensive yet bright and digestible: in effect to achieve the ultimate goal of medicine for the 'lay' – balance.

In this book he has I believe been successful. It will offer knowledge and understanding, and will contribute to making childbirth less fearsome and more joyful.

Sir Stanley Simmons
President of the Royal College of
Obstetricians and Gynaecologists
(1990–1993)

About the Book

Having a baby in the 1990s is an exciting prospect. Advances in medical knowledge have made obstetrics safer than ever before for the mother and her unborn child, pain in labour can be minimised with epidural anaesthesia and continuous electronic monitoring of the baby's heartbeat can accurately predict distress and indicate the need for early delivery. The risks to the baby of a number of conditions, such as German measles and Rhesus disease, have been reduced and sophisticated techniques exist for diagnosing certain abnormalities so that termination may be offered as an alternative to the birth of a malformed baby.

Yet alongside this high technology has come disquiet. Some women believe that birth has become too passive, with liberal interference. Certain procedures have become routine, such as induction of labour and episiotomy, while monitoring techniques in labour limit the mother's movement and her choice of position whilst giving birth.

Modern women are aware and enquiring and want to be involved in decisions affecting their health and future, and never more so than in pregnancy. The expectant mother is sometimes baffled by the vast array of tests and investigations, and may feel that her choice of medical attendant or where she can have her baby is limited. Because time is often short when seeing the doctor or midwife, she may not be adequately prepared for what to expect, what is normal and can be safely ignored, and what is relevant and may need attention.

Why Month by Month

When we talk about pregnancy and childbirth there is a logical progression from fertilisation and conception, through the antenatal period leading to delivery and beyond.

Pregnancy is traditionally divided into trimesters, or three-monthly stages, because certain events in pregnancy are more common at certain times. We know, for example, that miscarriage is less common after the first trimester and that problems arising from raised blood pressure rarely occur before the middle of the second trimester.

This book breaks pregnancy down even further into a monthly guide, so that each month the expectant mother may trace the progress of both her baby and herself, and be aware of the changes and complications that may occur.

Some chapters will inevitably overlap and there are also a number of medical conditions which have a bearing on the management of pregnancy, such as diabetes and heart disease, which do not have an obvious monthly slot, so these have been discussed at the stage in pregnancy which is particularly relevant.

Sections on family planning, sterilisation and the infertile couple complete the story.

The incentive for this book has come from you, the reader, and my purpose is twofold: to present a comprehensive account of all aspects of pregnancy and labour and to clarify the implications of alternative treatments so that the choices are better understood, in the hope that childbirth will be both a safe and memorable experience.

Introduction

The aim of the obstetric practitioner is to deliver a healthy woman of a healthy baby. A greater proportion of babies are now being born alive and well in the United Kingdom than ever before, and yet there is still much to learn.

Nature can and all too often does falter. In about ten to fifteen per cent of pregnancies there is a significantly increased risk of a problem and in as many as thirty to forty per cent there may be some exception to the usual course of development and delivery. Rarely is the mother herself in danger: the life at stake is usually that of the unborn child. The possible risks to a fetus include genetic disorders, exposure to harmful chemicals, poor nutrition, infection, disease of the mother, and complications during pregnancy and delivery.

Until quite recently not much was known about life before birth or what could go wrong in pregnancy and so very little could be done to prevent these problems, but in the last ten years a new approach to diagnosis has emerged in perinatal medicine – the study of the world of the unborn and the complex changes occurring in the first few hours of life.

For statistical purposes, the death rate of babies from twenty-eight weeks of pregnancy until the first week of life per thousand total births is known as perinatal mortality and there has been a significant and consistent downward trend in this rate over the years (see diagram on page 4). One major factor in accounting for this downward trend is the dramatic improvement in the survival of babies with very low birth weight, mainly resulting from the paediatricians' expertise and intensive care in the first few hours and days of life. Indeed, some babies born as early as the twenty-fourth or twenty-sixth week of gestation and weighing under 454gms (1lb) are now surviving to go home fit and well. This downward trend has also continued for deaths occurring after the first week of life, and the encouraging factor is that it does not seem to be accompanied by an increase in long-term handicap.

Premature birth is one of the two major contributors to perinatal

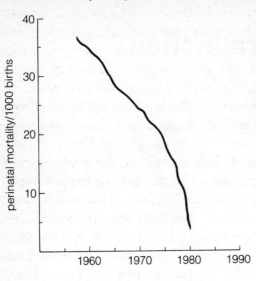

Perinatal Mortality in England and Wales (1958-80)

Graph showing a decrease in perinatal mortality.

mortality and, in spite of all efforts, its incidence has not altered over the past decade. The other common cause of peri-natal death is congenital deformity. The day is still far off when most defects can be detected before birth, let alone prevented, but many new develop-ments provide us with the hope of early diagnosis and, ultimately, of pre-vention.

The concept of caring for a baby *before* birth represents a major change in medical thinking. Previously, doctors concentrated on the patient they could see, touch and treat. An improved understanding of how pregnancy affects a woman's health has helped greatly to reduce problems with the mother, but the baby, sometimes viewed more as a passenger than a patient, remained a biological mystery. How could physicians attempt to treat an unborn baby which they couldn't examine, and how could they meet the needs of both patients without creating risks for either the mother or the baby?

Less than a generation ago medical scientists developed a technique called amniocentesis (see pages 141–47) that could provide the answer to some of the questions. This is a method of sampling the amniotic fluid surrounding the baby in order to obtain clues about its well-being. Other diagnostic procedures for the unborn child include ultrasound (sound waves that produce images of the baby which make possible an accurate prediction of its size and normality); biochemical tests of proteins in the mother's blood and urine to detect the efficiency of the placenta in providing essential oxygen to the baby; and the still experimental method of peering directly into the womb (see page 148).

4

With these pioneering achievements, obstetricians today can find out more about an unborn baby than would have been thought possible thirty years ago. As doctors have learnt more about life before birth, the baby has emerged as a patient in its own right. It has become clear that the nine months of pregnancy can determine whether a baby is healthy at birth, develops normally as a child, and reaches full potential as an adult. It is also clear that the time to save lives and prevent impairment is before as well as after a baby is born.

At birth the most vulnerable babies of all are the smallest, those who weigh less than 2000gms (under 4½lbs). At one time all babies this small were thought to have been premature but doctors soon discovered that as many as forty per cent are in fact mature. Nevertheless, because of growth retardation in the womb, these babies are at considerably greater risk of having problems before birth and afterwards. New methods can detect this condition during pregnancy and a scheduled delivery before term may give the poorly growing infant its best possible chance of survival.

Other methods of protecting the unborn baby are less dramatic but equally significant. Ever since the 1960s, when the birth of thousands of babies with limb deformities alerted the world to the dangers of the drug thalidomide, there has been greater restraint in the use of drugs in pregnancy. More prescription and non-prescription medications, as well as alcohol and nicotine, have been added to the list of suspected threats to a baby's health and doctors are very aware of the need to weigh the potential benefits of any drug given to the mother against its possible risk to the developing fetus.

As the relevance of the mother's state of health and her environment before and throughout pregnancy become increasingly apparent, greater emphasis is being placed on pre-pregnancy counselling. This is not confined to discussing genetic or acquired disease but also seeks to emphasise the importance of all-round good health, a balanced diet, suitable exercise, stopping smoking, avoiding alcohol, and losing weight where appropriate.

Deformities caused by chromosome abnormalities are better understood now than ever before and genetic counselling by experts offers the facts and understanding that parents need in order to make an informed, responsible decision about having a further pregnancy if there was a problem before, or continuing with the present pregnancy. For couples who fear that their genetic make-up may jeopardise the well-being of their unborn children, counselling may be one of the most important experiences of their lives. They can find out exactly what has gone wrong in the past and why, what the odds are of the same error occurring again, if they are at risk for any future problems, and what pre-natal tests are available.

Increased medical knowledge and sophisticated techniques have inevitably caused a radical change in the pattern of antenatal care and supervision of the mother and her unborn child in labour. While there is an attempt to separate low and high risk pregnancies – with more of the mothers at low risk of developing problems being cared for in a community environment – hospital antenatal clinics are time-consuming, overcrowded and sometimes understaffed.

Some mothers feel that the choice of where and how they can have their babies is limited, and to a certain extent this is true. This problem has recently been highlighted by the Department of Health in response to a Select Committee of the House of Commons whose remit was to investigate modern aspects of maternity services. This report has pointed out some of the deficiencies in the present system and has emphasised the importance of the mother being able to choose for herself where she would like to have her baby, whom she would like to be her attendant and how she would like to deliver. The concept of team midwifery has been introduced, where a select number of midwives attempt to give one-to-one care to a woman throughout her pregnancy, thereby reducing the risk of conflicting advice when the mother is seen by a number of different attendants. Hospitals around the country are busy putting these suggestions into practice.

So perhaps the 1990s can be thought of as the era of the unborn child. While there is an urgent need for continuing medical research into the many less well understood aspects of childbirth, practitioners looking after pregnant mothers need to understand women's expectations and the need for explanations suited to an educated generation.

PART 1

CHAPTER 1

Preparing for Pregnancy

Pre-conception Care

While some women find themselves pregnant almost by accident, many choose a time that feels right to go ahead and try for a baby and plan a pregnancy well in advance. This chapter is aimed at anyone who is considering becoming pregnant at some time in the near future and gives some suggestions about what to do to prepare for the pregnancy.

A visit to the doctor will give an opportunity for a general health check, counselling about fertility and conception, antenatal care and different aspects of birth and parenthood. Many family doctors and some hospitals run pre-conception clinics where psychological preparation for pregnancy, diet, health and fitness are discussed, and steps can be taken to prevent some of the hazards in pregnancy, for example stopping smoking and having a rubella vaccination. This is also a good time to check that a cervical smear has been performed within the previous three years and to arrange genetic counselling if applicable (see table on page 137).

Age

The number of women in Western societies who had their first baby between the ages of thirty and thirty-nine more than doubled between 1970 and 1986, and there is clearly a tendency towards postponing the first pregnancy. Many women want to develop careers after university and can use reliable contraception to postpone pregnancy. The increasing number of older women wanting to have a child may also be related to the increased divorce rate, with a new couple considering a child as the fulfilment of their relationship.

Although many women are seeking to postpone their first pregnancy until their mid-thirties or even later, delay in becoming pregnant does carry with it certain disadvantages. It becomes more difficult to become pregnant; fertility declines; there is a greater need for assisted conception such as IVF; and there is an increased incidence of certain abnormalities in the fetus, notably Down's Syndrome (see pages 389–390). Fertility probably starts to diminish after the age of thirty-one. This is gradual and at the age of thirty-five, for example, the monthly chance of a pregnancy that has the potential to produce a viable child is only half what it was at the age of thirty, and at thirty-eight the chance is only half what it was at thirty-five. This does not of course imply that half of all thirty-five-old year women are infertile but it does mean on average that the development of a pregnancy leading to the birth of a viable child takes longer after this age.

Although there is no theoretical age limit for conception, women in their mid-thirties and early forties also have an increased chance of miscarriage, may develop some blood pressure problems during the pregnancy and there is certainly a greater incidence of forceps deliveries. There is also an increased Caesarean section rate.

Weight before Pregnancy

Overweight Women

Conception problems are usually associated with being overweight, and obese women are also at higher risk of heartburn arising from pressure on the stomach, and from varicose veins, tiredness and breathlessness. Strict dieting is not recommended during pregnancy but careful attention to nutrition will reduce excessive weight gain. Babies born to overweight women tend to be slightly larger than average. Women who are not very fit or mobile may find it hard to move about in labour or change position, and epidural or general anaesthesia are technically more problematical.

Underweight Women

A woman starting pregnancy very underweight is potentially a far greater problem than a woman who is overweight. If she is grossly underweight or even anorexic, ovulation and menstruation may cease –

this is Nature's way of reducing fertility during periods of starvation. Poor diet before pregnancy is associated with an increased incidence of miscarriage and also a baby that may be smaller than it should be during pregnancy (see pages 206–207). Although the baby is a parasite and will take whatever nutrients are needed from the mother, starvation before or very early in pregnancy can influence the baby's growth.

Smoking

Happily there is no clear evidence that smoking before pregnancy for whatever length of time will harm a developing baby. But it is now well documented that continuing to smoke during pregnancy can increase the chances of a variety of complications. The sorts of things associated with smoking during pregnancy are vaginal bleeding, miscarriage, premature labour and early delivery. There is also strong evidence that an expectant mother's smoking adversely and directly affects her baby's development in the womb. The most widespread risk is low birth weight. In industrialised nations such as the United States and the United Kingdom smoking is blamed for as many as a third of all the babies who are born too small, and this does not just mean small in size but also small in development.

There are other potential risks as well. Babies of smoking mothers are more likely to suffer from breathing difficulties at birth; they are twice as likely to die of a cot death as babies of non-smokers; and babies of smokers are generally not as healthy at birth as those of non-smokers. There is also evidence that on average they may never catch up to the child of non-smokers in their long-term physical and intellectual achievements. In effect the baby is confined to a smoke-filled womb. Its heartbeat speeds up and, due to insufficient oxygen, it cannot always grow and thrive as it should.

The effects of tobacco, like alcohol, are probably dose-related. Tobacco use reduces the birth weight of babies in direct proportion to the number of cigarettes smoked. So cutting down on the number of cigarettes may help. The news, however, is not all bad. There are also studies to show that women who stop smoking in early pregnancy, no later than the fourth month, can reduce the risk of damage to the baby to the level of the non-smoker. The sooner the better, but stopping even in the last month can help preserve some oxygen flow to the baby during delivery. Some women find it easy to stop smoking in early pregnancy because they develop a distaste for cigarettes.

A survey which followed the progress of 17 000 children in the UK from birth compared the mental abilities of eleven-year-old children whose mothers smoked during pregnancy with those of a similar group whose mothers were non-smokers. Children of mothers who smoked up to ten cigarettes were some five to five and a half months behind in school progress and those of mothers who smoked ten or more cigarettes a day five and a half to seven months behind in comparison with children of the same age who had non-smoking mothers. In addition, the survey showed that children of smoking mothers tended to be shorter than the children of non-smoking mothers.

What does all this mean? Basically that you should not smoke during pregnancy. If you do, you run a considerable risk of having a smaller baby after a difficult pregnancy with some impairment in the child's subsequent mental and physical growth, and the risks seem to increase with the number of cigarettes smoked. Cutting down or stopping smoking can solve the problems because the baby grows most rapidly in the last three months of pregnancy and will have a good chance of attaining a normal birth weight if you stop smoking as late as the final three months.

Passive Smoking

It is becoming more and more apparent that smoking does not just affect the person who is puffing away; it affects everyone around, including a developing fetus whose mother happens to be nearby. Studies show that parental smoking can cause respiratory problems in their children and can impair development even into adulthood, and it also increases the odds that the children themselves will become smokers.

Alcohol

The Old Testament admonished women to drink no wine or strong drink before bearing a child and newlyweds were forbidden to drink on their wedding night for fear that they might conceive a defective child!

In a report that may represent the earliest medical study of alcoholism in pregnancy, British physicians in the late 1800s noted a high incidence of stillborn or very sick babies among women jailed for drunkenness in Liverpool. Yet, despite such long-standing concern, only in the last decade have several large scale studies shown that excessive alcohol can indeed cause disorders such as learning difficulties, growth impairment, brain and nervous system abnormalities, and occasionally even death.

On the other hand one of the concerns that can be put aside is that a few drinks early in pregnancy will prove harmful to the developing embryo. In a recent study women who had two or three such drinking episodes early in pregnancy were no more likely to have babies with structural defects or growth retardation than teetotallers. Since the majority of women go off alcohol anyway at the onset of pregnancy the problem may not arise, but if you wish to continue drinking alcohol during pregnancy you should keep it to a minimum.

Alcohol is a particularly dangerous drug because it passes freely across the placenta until the concentration in the baby's blood is as high as in the mother's, and its effects are proportional to the amount drunk. The babies of women who are chronic alcoholics face a thirty to fifty per cent chance of being born with the condition known as 'fetal alcohol syndrome' in which they show certain abnormalities including short eyeslits, a prominent nose-bridge, and ridges running between the nose and mouth. Their eyelids droop, they may be cross-eyed, they suffer an increased incidence of abnormalities of the joints and genital organs, and some have heart defects. Babies of alcoholic mothers are shorter and smaller than most newborns, irritable as infants and often grow up to be hyperactive children.

Heavy drinking, i.e. the consumption of five or six glasses of wine, beer or distilled spirits a day throughout pregnancy, should be avoided, whereas light drinking during pregnancy, i.e. one glass of wine at night, will cause no problems whatsoever. The fact that many women spontaneously give up drinking in early pregnancy is probably related to the nausea and vomiting that they often experience at the time. However much more needs to be known about the motivation behind this change in behaviour.

Caffeine

Caffeine belongs to the chemical family of xanthines which includes compounds found in tea, coffee, cola and, to a small degree, chocolate. When you drink coffee while pregnant you expose your baby to the same concentration of caffeine as that in your own blood. Excessive caffeine consumption, the equivalent of five or six cups of coffee a day, has been shown to increase the risk of birth defects in laboratory animals, although it is unclear whether the same effect occurs in humans. It has been suggested that caffeine may increase the risk of stillbirth, miscarriage and premature labour. One study of pregnant women who were heavy coffee drinkers found a higher incidence of these complications, but another study found no clear link.

Narcotic Drugs such as Marijuana and Cocaine

While no studies have been done to prove that they are all harmful, there is no evidence that they are safe and to avoid potential risks they should not be taken at all. Research into the effects of LSD suggests some increased risk of limb and nervous system defects in the children of women who have taken it while pregnant. There is no evidence of chromosome damage in women who used LSD prior to conception.

Narcotics, however, are known threats to an unborn child. If a pregnant women is a morphine or heroin addict the baby is at much greater risk of growth impairment and premature birth. In addition, sixty-five per cent of these babies may become addicted in the uterus and suffer withdrawal symptoms within twenty-four hours of delivery. The baby becomes irritable and overactive, develops tremors and cries with a peculiar high-pitched note. The addicted newborn must be given an opiate at regular intervals in gradually decreasing doses over the first several weeks of life. Some of the less severely addicted babies can be successfully treated with mild sedatives such as phenobarbitone. Methodone usually only causes mild withdrawal symptoms, though fatalities are not unknown. Cocaine and 'crack' can cause profound effects on the developing fetus including certain congenital abnormalities.

Opiate Dependence

Addicts not attending drug dependence clinics tend to jeopardise their health because of the necessity to spend all their emotional and financial resources to obtain supplies of opiates (heroin). Injecting drugs also runs the risk of HIV or Hepatitis B infection. Addicts who are known to the medical services are more likely to take advice to withdraw from opiates slowly during the pregnancy. In later pregnancy even cautious reduction of opiates may cause withdrawal symptoms in mother and fetus and therefore the lowest dose which prevents this may have to be continued. Hospital admission may be advisable to assess and monitor true opiate needs.

If you are addicted to any of these drugs you should contact your doctor as soon as possible so that their quantity can be monitored and withdrawn gradually during the pregnancy.

Drugs for Pain Relief in Labour

This will be further discussed in Chapter 12. Suffice it to say that the administration of hypnotic, analgesic or anaesthetic drugs during labour is very carefully controlled because most of these drugs cross the placenta if they are given too often and at incorrect intervals and may cause breathing difficulties in the baby at birth. There are two types of anaesthesia: local and general. In local anaesthesia an injection is given to freeze an area of skin so that painless surgical treatment is possible. This is usually completely harmless in pregnancy. General anaesthesia induces an unconscious state, and pain relief with epidurals has no effect on the unborn baby.

While non-urgent operations are usually better avoided during pregnancy, if a general anaesthetic becomes necessary for an illness such as appendicitis which demands surgery, there should be no worry as the anaesthetic drugs and the techniques used are specifically adapted so that the baby is unaffected. Obviously if you are to have a non-urgent anaesthetic your doctor should be informed if there is a chance you may be pregnant so that the operation may be deferred.

Specific Drugs for Pre-existing Disease

There are of course many drugs which the physician may need to prescribe because of associated illness in pregnancy. Examples include women who have become pregnant with known conditions, such as epilepsy, diabetes, and thyroid or heart problems. In the majority of cases drugs given in the right way, in the right dose and at the right time will not affect the pregnancy.

Aids to Fertilisation

Pregnancy will result if spermatozoa of sufficient quantity and quality are deposited by the male in the woman's vagina and move upwards through the cervix and the uterus into the Fallopian tube. Once in the tube they then have to swim some distance upward against the normal current. If the arrival of a single sperm in the tube coincides precisely with the arrival of an egg (which has been received from the ovary by the tentacles of the tube and wafted down to meet the sperm) fertilisation may occur.

In humans conception always happens in the Fallopian tube and the fertilised egg then passes along the tube into the uterus within three to four days. Once there it sinks into the prepared lining of the uterus and begins to grow and form an embryo. The best time to have intercourse in order to conceive is the day before ovulation so that the sperm will have time to travel into the Fallopian tube and be ready and waiting when the egg is released. Women who have a regular twenty-eight-day cycle usually ovulate around day fourteen and those with a longer cycle ovulate later. What is constant is the time interval of about twelve to fourteen days between ovulation and the onset of the next menstrual period. Women who get no symptoms of ovulation quite simply predict when ovulation is likely by the calendar method. This consists of noting the first day of the last menstrual bleeding over two or three cycles in order to work out the length of the cycle. Assuming that most women ovulate about fourteen days before the next period, ovulation can be predicted by working back fourteen days from the first day of a period.

An even better method entails taking the temperature every

morning on waking, starting on the first day of the period, because it is known that the body temperature rises after ovulation and stays up until the next period comes. If the temperature is plotted over twenty-eight days, the day or two on which the rise occurs is a guide to ovulation.

A blood test taken in the week preceding a period, at around day twenty-one, measuring the hormone progesterone will also confirm ovulation as there is a rise in level of this hormone in the second half of the menstrual cycle. Kits are also available from chemists detecting another hormone called the luteinising hormone (LH) which comes from the pituitary gland and rises rather dramatically after ovulation.

How Long Does it Take to Achieve a Pregnancy?

Even if intercourse takes place at exactly the right time pregnancy may not occur immediately. It is quite usual for a couple to take a few months or even longer to conceive. It is reassuring to know that ninety per cent of couples with no abnormalities may expect to

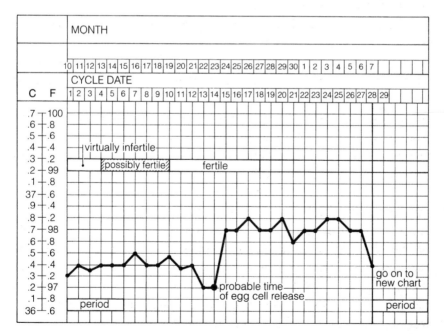

Specimen chart of a 28-day cycle, showing body temperature variation.

achieve a pregnancy within a year of trying, though some women are more anxious than others about their failure to conceive. There is generally no need for fertility tests or investigations before this time, although a visit to the doctor and an examination may do much to reassure the couple that there is no problem. Failure to conceive is much more commonly the result of over-anxiety, tiredness or tension rather than any physical cause such as failure to ovulate, blockage of the tubes or insufficient sperm. The doctor is often able to give advice without referral.

Choosing the Sex

There has been much publicity recently about choosing the gender of a child prior to conception and, while many women who have two children of one sex would dearly like the third to be different, to date there is no convincing evidence that it is possible to predict the sex before fertilisation with one hundred per cent certainty.

Much research is being done into sex prediction, particularly to benefit those couples with sex-linked diseases (where a congenital condition passes through generations carried by one or other sex, e.g. haemophilia). Sophisticated techniques for ensuring the likelihood of a particular sex are being evaluated and it may be that it will be possible to choose the sex of an unborn child within the next ten years, although it is likely that this will be governed by legislation. Suffice it to say that the age-old remedies of making the vagina less acid, having intercourse at high altitude, and timing sex to take place before ovulation have not been proved to be significant.

When to Stop Contraception

Two or three months should preferably elapse between stopping the pill or having an IUCD removed before conception. This is mainly to allow ovulation to regain its regular pattern and to make it easier to calculate when the baby is due. Women who come off the pill often do not ovulate straight away and therefore a confusion may arise in calculating the estimated date of delivery. If you inadvertently become pregnant while taking the pill, no harm will come to the developing baby. Likewise with the coil, unplanned pregnancy generally causes no problems, though the risks of miscarriage and ectopic pregnancy (see pages 105–113) are somewhat higher.

If you become pregnant with an IUCD in place and wish to continue with the pregnancy, then it is normal practice for the coil to be removed if that is possible by gently tugging at the string. This does not usually interfere with the pregnancy. Some women become pregnant with a coil which cannot be removed, either because the string gets hidden or because firm tugging is needed on it. It is very rare that there is an associated problem in this case and the coil is usually retrieved at the time of the birth of the baby (see pages 427–428).

Cervical Smears

The cervical smear, also called the Pap test after the doctor who invented it, Dr Papanicolaou, is a basic screening test designed to detect a pre-cancer of the cervix. It can also diagnose some vaginal infections. Usually performed at the pre-pregnancy counselling examination or booking clinic, it can be left to the postnatal visit but the pregnancy period is an ideal time to do a cervical smear and it is quite surprising how often pregnancy is the first opportunity for a woman to have this test.

What is a Cervical Smear?

The procedure consists of scraping the outside of the cervix lightly with a wooden spoon or spatula. The invisible scrapings are transferred to a microscope slide which is suitably prepared and sent to the laboratory for examination. The whole procedure is painless and takes a few seconds to perform.

What Does the Pathologist do with the Smear?

Once in the laboratory the pathologist will examine the cells of the cervix to see how they are arranged. Essentially these cells lie in a number of ordered layers invisible to the naked eye, but sometimes the cells are jumbled up in a haphazard way. The smear is graded from Class 0, which is absolutely normal, to Class 5 when the cells are completely jumbled up, and the importance of the result depends on the degree of order observed in the cells. For example, an abnormal smear may mean that there are changes on the cervix which could lead to a cancer formation in years to come. Therefore an atypical smear does not mean that there is a cancer present: it merely gives the doctor a clue as to whether changes might occur in later life and repeat cervical smears need to be performed at more frequent intervals than usual.

When Should the First Smear be Done?

Medical opinion varies considerably. Some suggest that the first smear test should be taken once intercourse is occurring regularly, however young the girl may be, as there is evidence to suggest that the incidence of cervical cancer in later life may be related to frequent intercourse occurring in youth. Others suggest that the first smear should be done if and when the contraceptive pill is used.

How Often Should a Smear be Done?

Again there are no hard and fast rules but most doctors agree that smears should be done every three to five years until the age of thirty, every two years until the age of forty, and yearly until the periods stop or the menopause arrives.

What is a Positive Smear?

If on routine examination a cervical smear test shows the presence of abnormal cells, then the smear is usually repeated after a short interval. If the second test confirms the findings, further invest-igation is necessary. This usually involves an outpatient examination of the cervix by a very powerful microscope (a colposcope) that can see down the canal of the cervix which is impossible with the naked eye. Colposcopy enables the specialist to look at many layers of cells on the surface of the cervix and differentiate between a cervix which is merely inflamed and one which might have an early pre-malignant condition.

Cone Biopsy of the Cervix

If colposcopy does not yield sufficient information, then the woman may be admitted to hospital so that a small piece of the neck of the womb can be removed for pathological examination (biopsy). If the microscope examination shows that there is no active cancer but the appearance suggests that the cervix is at risk of developing cancer in years to come (pre-cancer) then often no further treatment is undertaken apart from frequent reviews by repeating cervical smears. On occasions the abnormal area is treated using heat or a laser.

One of the problems with cone biopsy is that the cervix may become incompetent (see page 200) which could be a predisposing factor in late miscarriage. More recently a refined method of cone biopsy as an outpatient has been developed which does not involve cutting and reduces the risk of incompetence.

Abnormal Smears in Pregnancy

If a smear taken at the booking clinic is abnormal, then colposcopy is undertaken. In the great majority of instances no further treatment other than observation is required until after the baby has been born, when a further smear will be done at the postnatal clinic to see if any definitive treatment is needed.

Cone biopsy is possible during pregnancy without causing any problems with the pregnancy but this is only done using special techniques and with a very light anaesthesia. Some doctors advise inserting a cervical stitch (see page 200) in a subsequent pregnancy to prevent the possibility of miscarriage.

The Role of the Father

The attitudes and expectations of the pregnant mother and her partner, his interest and involvement in the pregnancy, and helping with the inevitable problems that occur once home with a newborn baby, have dramatically changed in the last decade. Whereas previously it was unusual for the male partner to attend antenatal classes or be present at delivery, now it is very much the rule rather than the exception.

Pre-conceptual Care

Dr David Haslam, writing in the fertility magazine *Novum* in the spring of 1994, makes a plea for more emphasis to be placed on the man in fertility counselling. 'Perhaps it's time,' he says, 'that we started caring for men and their sperm in the same way that many general practices offer pre-conceptual care for their female patients. After all it takes two to tango. It cannot be right to put all our ova in one basket when it comes to pre-pregnancy counselling.' He goes on: 'After all we nag women enough about not drinking this, not smoking that, and avoiding liver pate and camembert. Isn't it time for men to get more involved?'

There is plenty of evidence of course that fathers-to-be should be advised to cut down on smoking and drinking, should probably avoid excess heat and need to take care in particular occupations. It is possible that some illnesses and virus infections can be damaging to sperm and it probably makes sense if the man has a chronic illness to wait until things are on the mend before trying for a baby.

A recent report in the *British Medical Journal* warned that the average sperm count has been falling significantly over the last few decades, although the reasons are not fully understood. It would seem sensible for the couple to see their family doctor together before embarking on a pregnancy, not only to share the thoughts and problems, but also for the man to have a brief examination of blood pressure, blood count and blood group. This may on occasions pick up an undiagnosed illness and allow the doctor to treat a condition which may cause some problems with fertility.

Antenatal Care

Though it rarely happens, one wonders why more partners do not attend the first (booking) visit early in pregnancy. This is the time when a plan is made for the sort of care the woman will need, and when anxieties can be discussed regarding abnormalities that may occur and what tests might be necessary in pregnancy to ensure that the baby is growing satisfactorily. All these matters involve both the mother-to-be and her partner.

Wherever the woman has her baby, antenatal preparation classes are available and fathers are encouraged to attend, if not all, at least some of these sessions. Evidence shows that it increases involvement and makes for a much better understanding of the support that the mother needs when she is in labour.

Sharing the Experience of Labour

One of the questions that the mother-to-be is asked early in pregnancy is whether she would like her partner to be present at the delivery, so that by the time labour starts he may be involved in what has happened during the antenatal period and be looking forward with some anticipation to the event. Just as it was rare for the partner to be present at birth twenty years ago, it is now pretty unusual for the mother not to have his support.

Few fathers enter the delivery room without fear. Even obstetricians who have assisted at the births of thousands of other people's babies can experience a sudden loss of confidence when confronted with their own baby's delivery. Yet very few of these fears of 'freezing' or 'falling apart' or fainting or becoming sick are ever realised and, being prepared by childbirth education classes, the experience becomes more satisfying. Even most unprepared fathers come through labour and delivery far better than they thought they would.

It is important for the partner not to feel that they are on stage and must perform perfectly at the delivery. Midwives and doctors won't be evaluating the partner's every move and comparing him with the husband or partner next door. More importantly, neither will the mother-to-be. It is more a question of being beside her, holding her hand, urging her on, providing the comfort of a familiar face, and perhaps assisting in some of the active components of labour which have been taught in the antenatal classes.

Just because it is currently in vogue for fathers to attend births does not mean it is mandatory. There are studies that have shown that fathers who don't attend births do not have less meaningful relationships with their offspring than fathers who do. Just as fathers who don't bond with their babies immediately after birth don't seem automatically to become less loving parents.

What is important is that the father does what his partner would like and what feels right. If it doesn't feel right for the father to attend the birth for whatever reason, it would probably do more harm than good to all concerned for him to be there.

Another point for fathers to remember is that labour wards and delivery suites are not as they were twenty years ago. With modern methods of pain relief, and particularly with epidurals, labour does not necessarily imply severe, unremitting pain for the mother. Moreover, the labour room often has a calm and pleasant atmosphere.

Bonding

Until the 1960s few fathers ever witnessed the birth of their children and, since the word 'bonding' originated in the 1970s, none was even aware that the possibility of bonding with their offspring ever existed. Such a lack of enlightenment did not stop generations of loving father/son and father/daughter relationships from developing. Conversely, every father who attends the birth and is allowed to hold his child immediately isn't automatically guaranteed a lifetime of closeness with his offspring.

Being with the partner during delivery is very special and being deprived of that opportunity is reason for disappointment, particularly if several months were spent training together for childbirth. There is, however, no reason to expect a less than fulfilling relationship with the baby if, for instance, the labour ends in a situation where the attendants suggest you do not stay. What really bonds the father with the baby is daily loving contact, changing nappies, giving baths, feeding, cuddling and lullabying. The child will never know that the father didn't share in the moment of birth but will know if he wasn't there when they needed him from then on.

The Sexual and Reproductive Organs

The Female External Sex Organs

Unlike the sexual and reproductive organs of a man, the woman's are almost entirely hidden by the pubic hair which starts on the front of the body near the legs at a soft pad of fatty tissue called the mons, or little hill, which overlies the pubic bone. In a woman the pubic hair on the abdomen stops in a straight line, while in a man the hair can stretch up the abdomen to reach the navel. The quantity and texture of the pubic hair varies with each woman and with racial background. Women from Mediterranean countries tend to have thicker and coarser body hair than Western women.

Apart from an obvious protective function, the pubic hair serves to retain the aroma produced by the small glands in the pubic area

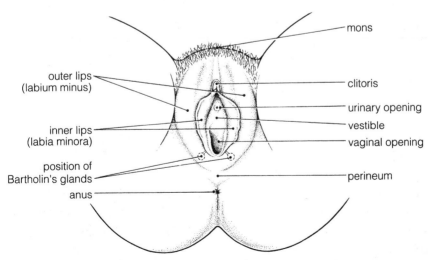

The female external genitalia.

during sexual excitement. Hair appears at the time of puberty when the ovaries first become mature and produce their hormone oestrogen. After the menopause, when the ovaries degenerate and the amount of oestrogen decreases, the hair becomes thinner and straighter. Another substance which is responsible for the female growth of hair is a hormone called testosterone. This is a male hormone, present in very small amounts in all women, and comes from a small organ called the adrenal gland that sits above the kidney.

The external female genital organs consist of several structures which surround the entrance to the vagina, collectively known as the vulva. The outer lips (labia majora) of the vulva are two folds of skin joined together at the mons. These lips act as a protective cushion for the vital structures and keep the inner area moist. The size of the lips again varies with age: in the very young and old the lips are small and thin, whereas during sexual reproductive life they are larger and thicker as fatty tissue is present under the skin.

Running along the inner edge of the outer lips are two elongated folds of tissue called the inner lips (labia minora). The inner lips are much thinner and contain no fatty tissue. They fuse together just below the mons but also surround the clitoris to form its foreskin.

The clitoris is a small bud-shaped organ which is the exact equivalent in the female of the male penis and it is the most sensitive area of the female body. Although most of the clitoris is usually hidden from view, its tip can be recognised as a small, pink, fleshy projection at the point where the two inner lips meet. Just as the male penis can become erect following sexual stimulation, so the clitoris, which is extremely sensitive to touch enlarges in response to stimulation by the finger or the penis, ultimately producing the orgasm.

Just below the clitoris and between the labia minora there is a cleft called the vestibule, which contains two openings: a small urinary opening which connects by a short tube to the bladder, and a larger vaginal opening which is the entrance to the vaginal canal. Because the urinary opening is so close to the vaginal entrance, irritation and infection of the urine can occur occasionally after prolonged or vigorous intercourse.

In women who have not had sexual intercourse the vaginal opening is covered by a thin membrane called the hymen. This membrane is thin and very stretchy and has several very tiny openings through which the blood from menstruation flows. The shape and size of the hymen varies with each woman and it is usually stretched or torn during the first attempt at intercourse. Often the hymen has already been stretched, either by the use of tampons or during certain recreational activities. Young girls who do a lot of horse-riding often find it relatively easy to use tampons as the hymen may stretch with this sort of exercise. The tearing of the hymen that occurs during the first act of intercourse usually causes a little discomfort and perhaps some bleeding which normally stops very soon. Even today women in some parts of the world must satisfy their husbands that they come to the marriage bed as virgins, and the presence of blood after intercourse on the wedding night may still be regarded as proof that the hymen was intact before marriage and that previous intercourse had not taken place.

Just inside the vaginal opening on either side are two small bodies or glands called Bartholin's glands which are important because they may occasionally become infected and give rise to a tender swelling which may need surgical treatment. The natural function of these glands is to supply lubricating fluid during intercourse.

Finally, there is the external opening called the anus through which faeces are expelled from the rectum. Between the anus and the lower part of the vestibule of the vagina is a triangular area of skin covering muscles which are stretched and may be deliberately cut during childbirth in order to make more room for the baby to be born. This area is called the perineum.

The Female Internal Sex Organs

These comprise the vagina, the uterus or womb, the ovaries and the Fallopian tubes or oviducts.

The Vagina

The vagina is the passage leading from the vulva upwards towards the uterus. The adult vagina is about 10–12cms long and, because it is made up of muscle tissue, it is capable of great distension. Normally the walls of the vagina which are lined with folds of skin lie close together. During sexual intercourse, the vaginal wall stretches to accommodate the penis, and during childbirth it will distend enormously to allow the baby to be born.

During reproductive life the walls of the vagina are usually moist, particularly during sexual arousal, allowing the penis to slip easily into the vagina. The moistness is regulated by hormones and is the result of a constant shedding of very tiny cells from the vagina, and also a small and constant outpouring of fluid from the neck of the womb, or cervix. This fluid also serves as a protection against infection, lubricating the vagina and keeping it clean. This self-cleansing ability makes the once popular habit of vaginal douching unnecessary.

In the years before puberty and after the menopause when the influence of hormones on the vagina declines, the moistness disappears, the walls become dry and brittle, and the vagina is more prone to infection.

The Uterus, or Womb

The uterus is a hollow muscular organ, shaped rather like an upside-down pear, consisting of an upper part, the body, tapering down to its lower portion, the cervix or neck of the womb. The normal uterus is about 9cms long and 6cms across at its widest part and weighs about 50gms. During a pregnancy, under the influence of the female hormone oestrogen, the uterus stretches enormously and may weigh up to thirty times more than normal.

The cervix, or neck of the womb, projects about 10cms (4ins) into the vagina and is readily accessible for examination. It can easily be seen by using a torch inserted into the vagina (called a speculum) and can be located by the doctor's examining finger, allowing inspection for any abnormalities. A smear test is done by gently scraping the surface of the cervix with a wooden spoon so that cells from the cervix can be examined under a microscope (see pages 19–21).

Women can be taught to feel their own cervix by inserting their fingers into the vagina so that if, for example, they are using a contraceptive cap it can be fitted snugly around the cervix preventing access by the sperm, or they can check the thread of an intrauterine device (IUCD). The cervix feels rather like a nose with

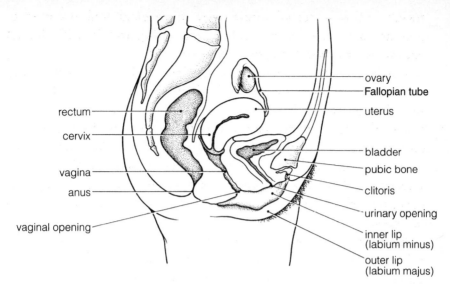

ovary
Fallopian tube
uterus

bladder
pubic bone
clitoris

urinary opening

inner lip
(labium minus)

outer lip
(labium majus)

rectum

cervix

vagina
anus

vaginal opening

Side view of the female pelvic organs.

a small dimple in its centre through which the menstrual fluid emerges. This entrance through the cervix into the uterus is usually very small, about the diameter of a fine straw, so there is no danger of a tampon slipping through the cervix into the womb. In pregnancy, however, and particularly during childbirth, the cervix is able to expand to such an extent that a baby's head can pass through.

The remainder of the uterus, the body, usually lies bent forward at an angle of ninety degrees to the vagina and is made up of thick, stretchy muscle on the outside and a hollow cavity which connects with the cervix below and the Fallopian tubes on either side at the top. It is along this cavity that the sperm pass in order to gain entrance into the Fallopian tube. The cavity is lined by very special cells which are frequently shed and rebuilt during menstruation.

The uterus is kept in its position by a sling of muscle tissue and ligaments spread to the side of the bony pelvis, rather like a fan. These supports have great stretchability, allowing the uterus to expand and grow during a pregnancy. With advancing age and after repeated childbirth, the supports lose some of this elasticity and become so weak that the uterus sags, resulting in a dropping or prolapse. It is important to realise that the uterus is merely a cradle for the baby and has no hormone function of its own. This is why removal of the uterus, or hysterectomy, does not cause any alteration in femininity, sexuality, or cause hair to grow on the face or body. The only change that occurs after hysterectomy is that periods no longer exist.

Some women are born with a double uterus due to an error in the way growth occurs in the very early stages in the life of an embryo. The uterus may be split into two at its upper part only, or completely separated into two distinct parts with no inter-communication. Occasionally two separate cervices are present and there may also be two separate vaginal entrances. In such cases, menstruation, ovulation and conception occur normally. The abnormalities often go unnoticed and cause no complaints. They are most often only diagnosed incidentally on routine examination or in pregnancy. There is a slightly higher risk of miscarriage, or premature labour, and during later pregnancy the baby may be forced to lie in such a position as to make normal delivery difficult so that Caesarean section may be necessary.

Extremely rarely, the uterus and other internal genital organs may be so immature that normal growth is never achieved, and it is also possible for an individual to be born with part-male and part-female sexual organs. The true sex at birth can be accurately determined only by blood and chromosome tests so that the child is reared in its correct sex. It may be necessary to remove some of the genital organs of the wrong sex and stimulate those of the correct sex with hormones. Treatment is directed to restoring anatomy so that physical and physiological normality is achieved in the correct sex. Plastic surgery later in life may permit satisfactory sexual intercourse but fertility is never achieved.

The Ovaries

The ovaries are the female egg cells equivalent to the testes in the male. They are about the size and shape of an almond and are located on either side of the uterus. The ovaries have a dual function: first to form eggs, and second to produce the female sex hormone oestrogen. In a child the ovaries are small, delicate structures but after puberty they enlarge to the adult size of about 3.5cms (1.4ins) long and 2cms (0.75ins) wide.

After the menopause, or change of life, they shrink to become half the normal adult size. The ovaries are enclosed in a very fine membrane or capsule and sometimes this swells forming a fluid filled cavity, or cyst. Cysts can enlarge considerably and may need surgical removal. It is the oestrogen formed by the ovaries that is responsible for all the feminine attributes of the mature woman, i.e. fullness of the breasts, feminine contour of the hips, and normal growth of the sexual organs. The functions of the ovaries are described in more detail later in the chapter.

The Fallopian Tubes

These are two small hollow tubes extending outwards and backwards from the sides of the upper end of the uterus. The outer ends are funnel-shaped and consist of a number of finger-like projections which lie close to and surround the ovary. The egg which is shed from the ovary passes along one of these tubes once it has been sucked up by the 'tentacle' end of the tube. Human fertilisation can only take place in one of the Fallopian tubes. Should conception occur, the fertilised egg is helped along the way by very fine hairs, called cilia, inside the lining of the tube which are constantly moving in one direction.

The lining of the tubes is very fine, about the width of the lead in a pencil, and the cells bordering the lining are extremely delicate. If the tubes are damaged by infection from bacteria that swim through the neck of the womb into the body and hence to the tubes, the very thin channel may become blocked, preventing the egg from gaining entry to the tube and causing subsequent infertility. Sometimes the egg and sperm meet in the tube and fertilisation may occur but the fertilised egg may not be able to pass back into the womb to grow as an embryo, becoming lodged in the tube to grow as a tubal or ectopic pregnancy (see pages 110–113).

As well as being a pathway for the sperm and egg, the lining cells of the tubes form nourishing substances which are essential for the growth of the fertilised egg during the first few days of its life in the tube. There is no need for both Fallopian tubes to be present for conception to occur: some women are born with a single tube only or have had one tube surgically removed because of infection or an ectopic pregnancy. Providing the remaining tube is healthy, pregnancy can occur just as easily.

The Bony Pelvis

The mechanism of labour is usually a process of accommodation between the baby and the passage through which the baby must pass. A description of the anatomy of the bony pelvis and of the soft parts connected with it is therefore important.

In both sexes the pelvis forms a bony ring through which the body weight is transmitted to the lower extremities, but in the female it assumes a particular form which adapts it to the process of childbearing. The cavity of the pelvis is round and smooth in the female, whereas in the male it tends to be more heart-shaped and distorted by several bony protuberances. The normal pelvis (see diagram below) is composed of four bones: the sacrum at the back, two innominate bones on either side, which are united by strong articulations with the sacrum and with one another at the symphysis pubis, and the coccyx, which is the rudimentary tail at the lower end of the sacrum. Obviously the size of the cavity of the pelvis has to be sufficiently large for the baby's head to pass through unimpeded and

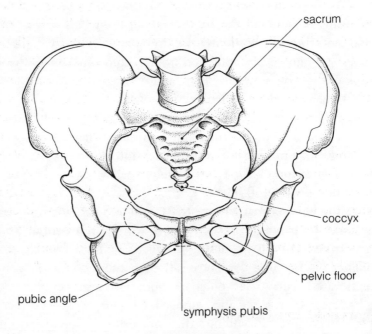

The bony pelvis.

at the same time to accommodate the pelvic organs (see diagram on page 34).

The sacrum is a curved bone which forms the rear part of the pelvic girdle. It actually consists of five vertebrae which have been fused together, joining with the spine itself above and the coccyx below. The size of the inlet, or brim, of the pelvis depends on the breadth of the sacrum which should be broad, well curved and tilted backwards. If it is unduly narrow, then the size of the brim of the pelvis is restricted.

The symphysis pubis is a joint in front of the pelvis which is small and fairly narrow. It is composed of cartilage and is able to open slightly in the pregnancy as ligaments relax, enabling the bones to move. In labour the bones actually separate by as much as 1.5 cms (0.5 ins). There is an angle, called the pubic angle, formed by the branches of the pubic bones which unite at an angle of ninety degrees. Sometimes this arch is narrower than that (which can be detected by your doctor's examining fingers) and this may prevent engagement of the head (see pages 217–219).

The joints of the pelvis are supported by a number of strong ligaments and there is a large layer of muscle and fat tissue extending across the lower parts of the bony pelvis from the lower edge of the symphysis to the tip of the sacrum. This is sometimes called the pelvic floor and this predominantly muscular tissue allows the passage of urine and faeces. It is perforated in front by the urethra leading down from the bladder and behind by the rectum and anal canal. The vagina perforates the pelvic floor roughly in the middle. There is an important pair of muscles called the levator ani which stretch from either side of the pelvis, joining together in the midline to form a sort of hammock or sling across the pelvic outlet. These are the muscles that flex during coughing. When the baby's head passes through the pelvic floor, the levator ani are folded sideways against the walls of the pelvis and usually come back to their normal position after delivery. It is these muscles that often need toning up by postnatal exercises after the baby's birth.

Is my Pelvis Large Enough?

This is a question that often crops up, but the pelvis that is abnormally small or abnormally shaped, thus preventing a normal birth, is comparatively rare. Remember that the bony pelvis is roughly funnel-shaped. The baby enters the circular mouth of the funnel (inlet) and emerges from the spout (outlet). If any diameter of the pelvis is below the limit of normal variations, the pelvis can be regarded as a little small or contracted. In reality, of course, a normal birth will depend not only on the size and shape of the pelvis but the size and position of the baby's head (disproportion – see page 295). Disproportion is very difficult to judge before the onset of labour unless the baby is absolutely huge and the pelvis tiny. The obstetrician can get an idea of pelvic size from a woman's history by looking at her height and shoe size. Some doctors like to examine every pregnant woman at the first antenatal visit and one of the reasons is to assess the size of the bony pelvis. This is, however, pretty inaccurate because of course there is no baby's head to compare it with. Other medical attendants like to examine the pelvis internally about a month before the baby is due, i.e. at thirty-six weeks, and get an idea as to whether the head will actually press down through the rim. Many obstetricians, however, feel that, unless there are gross problems, the only arbiter of whether there is disproportion is labour itself.

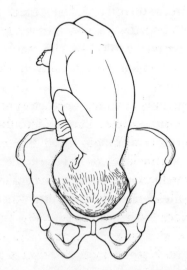

Suspected disproportion. Note the widest diameter of the baby's head has not passed through the brim of the pelvis.

Occasionally an X-ray, called an erect-lateral picture, can measure the various diameters of the pelvis, but as I have already said, it is extremely rare nowadays, and certainly in Western societies, for a woman's pelvis to be so small as not to allow a baby's head through, in which case the baby will of course be delivered by Caesarean section. If the obstetrician considers that the pelvis may be a little small but reasonably satisfactory, then labour will be allowed to proceed normally, with the reservation that Caesarean section can be performed if there is any undue delay or difficulty.

The Testes and Sperm Production

Throughout a man's reproductive life, which in rare cases continues after the age of eighty, spermatozoa are constantly being formed by the two testicles suspended in the scrotum, a thin-walled sac of skin. The scrotum is a highly specialised structure which, because of its external location and its large area of skin surface, constantly maintains the testicles at a temperature of about six degrees Fahrenheit below that of the interior of the body. In warm weather the scrotum is large and flaccid, exposing a large skin area for heat loss through evaporation, while in a cold temperature the scrotum is small and contracted to conserve heat. The scrotal pouch is therefore a highly effective air conditioner. The sperm-making cells of the testicles are extremely sensitive to heat and, within twenty-four hours of being exposed to a temperature as high as that of the body's interior, cease producing spermatozoa. This is why in some instances when production of sperm is not very satisfactory it is recommended that a man wears loose-fitting underpants. Also, there are occasions when bathing in cool water daily can allow the temperature of the sperm to remain at the fertile level.

In the early life of the fetus, the testicles are situated high up in the abdomen. They gradually migrate downwards reaching the scrotum at about eight weeks before birth but occasionally boys delivered full-term are born with undescended testicles. The condition usually corrects itself within the first few months or years of life but, if not, the child may be given injections of a hormone or may require a surgical operation to guide the testes into the scrotum.

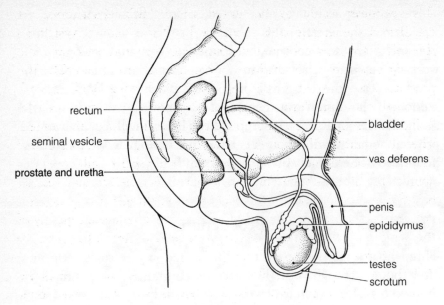

Side view of the male pelvic organs.

In the human adult the two testicles have the shape and size of plums. Their function is the production of sperm cells and the manufacture of the masculinising hormone testosterone, accomplished by separate types of cells.

The word 'spermatogenesis' means the creation of sperm cells. This is a continuous process commencing in early adolescence and usually not ceasing until death. Each testicle contains hundreds of thousands of little round chambers, lined with cells called spermatogonia from which the forerunners of spermatozoa are derived. When the formation of a spermatozoa has been completed, it is delivered into a collecting duct that interconnects with larger ducts through which it finally passes into a narrow coiled tube called the epididymis lying above each testicle. The canal of this coiled tube is continuous with the canal of the vas deferens, which runs from the upper scrotum through the body to the outside of the penis from which the sperm cells are ejaculated.

At the upper end of each vas, near the point where it empties into the urethra, is a collecting sac called the seminal vesicle which contains a small amount of viscid fluid. Millions of sperm cells enter this repository daily to be stored there until ejaculation. At ejaculation the muscle cells in the walls of the seminal vesicle go through a series of contractions, expelling the fluid, swarming the spermatozoa into the urethra. Other glands, most notably the prostate, also contract during orgasm expelling their fluids as well. All these secretions form the semen. Because of their tiny size, the millions of sperm cells make up a negligible amount of the semen. Therefore male sterilisation (i.e. tying or severing each vas tube near the testicle to obstruct the upper journey of the sperm cells) does not appreciably diminish the amount of ejaculate. The seminal vesicle, prostate and other glands still discharge their fluids during orgasm, precisely as they did before the operation. The volume and quality of the semen are the same, whether ejaculated during intercourse or masturbation.

The second type of testicular cell, the interstitial cell, produces the hormone testosterone which is absorbed directly into the blood-stream from its place of origin in the testicle. Carried in the blood, it affects such masculine characteristics as body form, libido, sexual potency, voice register, and body and facial hair. These cells are not sensitive to heat unlike spermatogonia and they continue to function normally wherever the testicle is. That is why men with undescended testicles are completely masculine except for the absence of sperm. However, in the castrated male, or eunuch, removal of the testicles causes profound modification of masculine characteristics because of the lack of testosterone in the bloodstream.

Eggs and Spermatozoa

The eggs of all mammals are alike in both size and appearance – round, with a clear, thin, shell-like capsule, and rigid as firm jelly. The capsule encloses liquid in which are suspended hundreds of fat droplets, protein substances and other materials including the nucleus or centre. The egg, the largest cell in the whole body, is about two-hundredths of an inch in diameter, about a quarter as large as the full stop at the end of this sentence. The eggs of mice, rabbits, gorillas, dogs, pigs, whales and humans are all about the same size and it is incredible but true that the whale's tons and the mouse's ounces

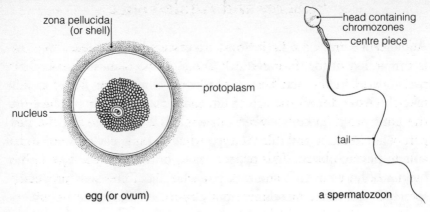

Eggs and spermatozoa.

develop from round specks of matter of relatively the same diameter and weight.

The spermatozoa of various species show greater differences in form than do the eggs. The human sperm consists of an oval head, about a six-hundredth of an inch in diameter, mostly occupied by the central nucleus. With the aid of additional magnification one can see that the head is loosely enveloped by a thin membrane and it is attached by a short neck to a cylindrical middle piece that terminates in a thin tail which is about ten times as long as the head. The tail, which consists of several hair-like fibres, resembles a horse's tail and is capable of rapid side-to-side lashing movements by means of which the sperm are propelled. The motor which moves the tail is located in the middle piece and a single sperm can swim an inch in four to sixteen minutes depending on whether it is crossing the watery fluid secreted from the uterus or the Fallopian tube, or the relatively thick fluid coming from the cervix.

When ejaculated the sperm is suspended in seminal plasma or a fluid which is thick and produced by the male during sexual orgasm. Semen, which arises from the prostate gland and the seminal vesicles, is full of white mucous lumps which make it rather sticky, with an acrid odour. These dissolve within five minutes of ejaculation. The amount of semen ejaculated depends in part on the interval between successive ejaculations. In humans the normal quantity varies from about a half to one and a half teaspoons.

Puberty and Adolescence

Adolescence, from the Latin word 'adolescere' which means to grow, is the period of life during which the child becomes an adult. This period varies in duration from one individual to another, but is usually taken to extend from the age of ten to eighteen. Puberty, again from the Latin word 'pubertas' which means adulthood, is really the first part of adolescence and it is the time when a young person starts to be able to have children. This happens in a girl because the eggs in her ovaries begin to mature and in a boy when his testes start producing sperm. Probably the most important physical development of puberty is menstruation, though there are a number of other very important physical and mental changes also taking place around this time.

During childhood the all-important pituitary gland in the brain is concerned mostly with physical growth. At puberty the gland's activity increases and this is usually manifested by a sudden spurt in stature. In girls, this happens just before or after the periods start. Some sexual differentiation does start in childhood: the nipples of the breast are usually more obvious in girls than boys, even by the age of three, and the limbs become plump and round between the ages of six and eight. The bones of the pelvis widen between the ages of seven and eleven in girls and definite signs of puberty are usually present by the age of nine or ten, when the breasts develop even more and become enlarged. Hair growth begins and usually appears first around the vulva; body contour changes because fat is laid down in the tissues; and there is usually some evidence of dark skin pigmentation on the vulva and even around the eyes, mouth and nipples.

The time when a girl's first period occurs, called the menarche or onset of menstruation, varies between different cultures and civilisations. In Western societies, puberty has been starting earlier and earlier but there is still a very wide variety of ages at onset and the first period may occur at any time between ten and sixteen. The average age in the UK is about eleven and among the factors contributing to an early puberty are better living conditions, nutrition, and improved standards of general health, borne out by the fact that menstruation tends to occur earlier in the higher social classes and in urban surroundings.

As well as the physical development that takes place around puberty, there are great emotional and psychological changes as childish innocence is replaced by self-consciousness and modesty. As a girl begins to grow up, she becomes increasingly interested in her own appearance; she may be aggressive and rebellious as she becomes imaginative and curious; she finds it more difficult to obey orders and may challenge the authority of her parents and teachers. She is looking for independence, and will perhaps start confiding in others rather than her mother. She is often embarrassed by lankiness and awkward movements that occur as growth rate spurts. She may get pimples and blackheads and put on quite a bit of weight. She becomes aware of her sex for the first time and her impulses are often homosexual, manifesting themselves in passions for an older girl or woman and gradually being replaced by interest in the opposite sex.

Delayed Puberty

It is important to emphasise that, although the average age of puberty in this country is eleven, the general changes in the appearance of a girl and the onset of menstruation may be delayed until sixteen, or even later, and this should give no cause for concern.

If, however, menstrual bleeding has not started by the age of sixteen and especially if there is no obvious breast or hair growth, then the family doctor should be consulted. Very rarely, puberty fails to occur because of a hormone imbalance.

Precocious Puberty

This term is arbitrarily defined as the onset of menstruation, accompanied also by the other changes in puberty such as breast development and body hair, before the age of ten. In the majority of instances this is just an individual characteristic and there is no particular abnormality. What happens is that the pituitary gland in the brain, which orchestrates the balance of hormones in the body, merely matures earlier than usual.

If a child has any bleeding from the vagina before the age of ten, a visit to the doctor is advisable, although there is usually a simple explanation and no abnormality is found. Occasionally the doctor will want to perform certain tests to ensure that the hormone system is normal.

Menstruation and Ovulation

Menstruation

During the reproductive stage of a woman's life, from puberty until the menopause, two complicated but precisely timed events occur at regular monthly intervals. The first is ovulation, or the release of an egg by the ovary, and the second involves the changes in the tissue lining of the womb as a result of that ovulation. When a girl is born each ovary contains thirty to forty thousand immature egg cells called follicles. Of these not more than four to five hundred are destined to develop into mature eggs. All the other follicles never manage to ripen properly and shrink to a minute size, becoming lodged in the ovary itself.

All the secondary sexual characteristics which appear around the time of puberty, such as breast growth, hair over the pubis, and changes in the distribution of body fat, which mark the transition to womanhood, are under the control of the pituitary gland. At around the age of puberty, it is this gland which is responsible for sending a chemical messenger or hormone to the ovary, which in turn is responsible for maturing the egg follicles into their adult form. This hormone is called follicle stimulating hormone (FSH). Once mature, this follicle itself puts out another chemical messenger from the ovary called oestrogen and the very first sign of oestrogen being present shows itself in the development of breast-buds, soon followed by other signs of puberty.

Each month during the reproductive years one follicle matures and as it grows it moves towards the surface of the ovary, under the influence of a second hormone coming from the brain called luteinising hormone (LH). The egg follicle bursts and expels its egg. This process is called ovulation and usually occurs around the fourteenth day before the onset of menstruation. Once released, the egg is attracted to the tentacles of the Fallopian tube by a remarkable

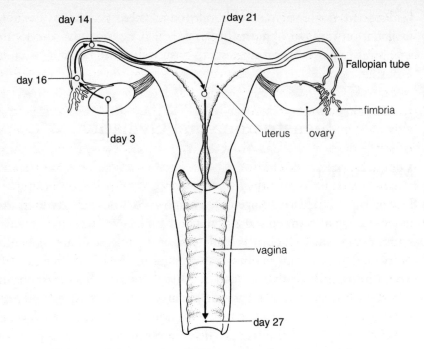

Journey of the egg during the menstrual cycle. Note the position of the egg on different days.

chemical process. The egg travels down the tube and waits there for the sperm to fertilise it. Although ovulation takes place roughly midway between the periods, the precise timing varies in any individual. Thus some women ovulate around day nine of their menstrual cycle and others as late as the twenty-first or twenty-second day. Because fertilisation can only occur within thirty-six hours of ovulation, it is important for those who wish to conceive and those who are using the temperature method of contraception to have precise knowledge of when ovulation occurs.

It is important to remember that ovulation always occurs twelve to fourteen days *before* the next period. Thus, if a woman has a twenty-eight day cycle, she will ovulate around day twelve to fourteen. If she has a thirty-five-day cycle, she will ovulate around day twenty. If she has a three-week or twenty-one-day cycle, then she will ovulate around day seven.

Ovulation can often be recognised as a crampy pain on one or other other side of the abdomen, occasionally accompanied by a discharge from the vagina which may be bloodstained. Many women have no outward sign of ovulation and, if it becomes important to establish when it occurs, certain tests have to be carried out.

Ovulation may occur infrequently, or perhaps not at all, in the first year or two after menstrual bleeding has commenced. It is common for ovulation to occur infrequently until the hormone processes in the body have matured sufficiently. This is why periods take a few months to settle into a regular rhythm at first and why true fertility is not achieved at the start of puberty. Because ovulation is infrequent in early reproductive life, the first few periods are usually quite painfree. Similarly, older women beginning the menopause tend to get irregular periods as ovulation becomes infrequent with declining fertility.

Once the egg has been released, the remainder of the ruptured follicle collapses and changes into a small yellow body called the corpus luteum. It now acquires a new function, producing a second important hormone called progesterone which is extremely important in preparing the lining of the womb for the fertilised egg, should pregnancy occur. Progesterone makes the lining of the womb juicy so that the egg may implant in it and be fed. Regardless of whether a pregnancy occurs in any particular cycle, progesterone is always secreted after ovulation occurs, causing the womb lining to change in preparation for the fertilised egg. Examination of the lining of the womb is therefore a simple and convenient way of detecting whether a woman is ovulating. Progesterone also raises the temperature very slightly so, if ovulation has occurred and progesterone has been produced by the fading follicle, the temperature will remain slightly elevated in the latter fourteen days of the menstrual cycle. This is the basis of the temperature test for ovulation.

Just as the presence of both Fallopian tubes is not vital, so one ovary works as well as two. Ovulation usually occurs from alternate ovaries each month but there is no absolute pattern. If one ovary is removed, the remaining organ takes over completely and ovulation should occur every month from the same side with no reduction in potential fertility. This seems to be one way in which the body protects itself against diseases of the reproductive organs.

I have described how, under the influence of follicle stimulating hormone from the brain, the ovarian follicle grows and the ovary produces the female hormone oestrogen. Apart from producing the egg, oestrogen also affects the lining of the womb, causing it to thicken and proliferate and grow. This change occurs on a monthly basis before ovulation, that is to say for the first twelve to fourteen days of the menstrual cycle. After ovulation the hormone progesterone is produced and this causes the lining of the womb to change in consistency as nourishing substances necessary for the implantation of the fertilised egg are produced.

If conception does not occur, these hormones, oestrogen and progesterone, gradually dwindle away, the lining of the uterus stops becoming thick and receptive, its cells shrink and shrivel, and gradually disintegrate and this causes the discharge of blood known as menstruation, or the period. Once the period is over, the whole cycle is repeated and a new follicle starts growing, forming its own oestrogen, and the lining of the womb again becomes thick and receptive. On the other hand, if fertilisation does occur, the two hormones continue to be produced in large amounts, enabling the fertilised egg to grow and implant in the womb. The ovaries then stop forming new follicles and produce less oestrogen and progesterone, a function taken over after the fourth week by the placenta, or afterbirth.

Menstruation continues until the age of forty-five to fifty, when the ovaries gradually shrink with age and become ineffective at producing oestrogen. The result is that the periods will cease and this is called the menopause. The amount of blood lost during menstruation varies enormously. On average four to six tablespoons of blood, equivalent to roughly half a teacup, is lost each period. The amount of blood lost will depend on the thickness of the lining of the womb being shed. For example, a girl on the pill usually has very scanty periods as the pill prevents ovulation and consequently the lining of the womb never becomes thick and juicy, always remaining rather thin.

Menstrual flow consists of a mixture of blood coming from the shed lining of the womb, degenerate cells, and a sticky fluid that is an outpouring from the cervix. Menstrual fluid has a particular odour which is not due to the blood itself but is formed by the action of small bacteria that live in the vagina when the blood trickles to the outside. Though it may pass unnoticed, it is important to reassure the young girl who starts to menstruate that any odour is absolutely normal and has nothing to do with hygiene.

Women experience at least some discomfort during menstruation and for some the pain can be quite severe. No one really knows why menstruation causes discomfort, though there are many theories. It has been suggested that the pain is really a spasm or cramp of the womb which contracts during a period under the influence of certain chemical messages. It used to be thought that the pain was worse in girls whose external opening to the cervix was particularly tight. Probably menstrual cramp is a result of several factors under hormone control and its severity is influenced by emotional factors and cultural attitudes.

The most common method of absorbing menstrual fluid is either sanitary towels or tampons that are introduced into the vagina. Sanitary towels are normally used in the early years of puberty but by the age of sixteen or seventeen most girls can be taught how to introduce internal tampons without discomfort. It is not necessary to have had intercourse prior to using a tampon as the small opening in the hymen that is usually present is large enough to accommodate a small-sized tampon.

Myths and taboos surrounding menstruation are legion. Throughout history the menstrual process has been surrounded with mystique and ritual. In primitive cultures menstruation was regarded as evil and dangerous, and even today in some parts of the world it is believed that a menstruating woman can damage crops, turn milk sour, and even cause animals to abort! For this reason it is common for women to be completely isolated from the rest of the community during a menstrual period.

There is of course no basis for any of these assumptions and it is perfectly safe for a woman who is menstruating to take part in any activity she likes. She can lead an absolutely normal life, including recreational activities, sports, bathing, swimming and sexual intercourse.

Ovulation

Two weeks before the onset of the next menstrual period the follicle containing the egg is ripe. At this stage it measures about two centimetres and, as well as serving as a container for the egg, has also itself become a tiny hormone-producing gland. Suddenly the follicle

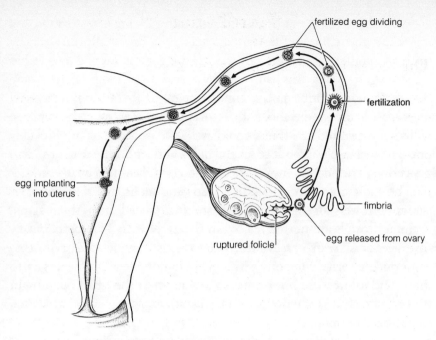

fertilized egg dividing

fertilization

fimbria

egg released from ovary

ruptured folicle

egg implanting
into uterus

The passage of the fertilised egg along the tube
21 days after the last menstrual period.

ruptures, exactly why is as yet unknown. The egg is now discharged to
the surface of the ovary where it is caught by the Fallopian tube and
for about twenty-four hours it awaits possible fertilisation by a sperm
but, if this does not occur, the egg begins to disintegrate and dies.
Once the follicle has ruptured it is transformed into a structure known
as a corpus luteum which forms large quantities of the hormone
progesterone for the next two weeks. As the progesterone enters the
woman's bloodstream it alters the lining of the uterus, preparing it like
a bed to receive the fertilised egg, and this happens every month. If
fertilisation does not occur, then the outer layers of the lining of the
uterus are shed and this is when bleeding recurs at menstruation.

So menstruation can be seen as the final phase in a series of
changes that take place in the woman's body each month, repeating
themselves broadly speaking from when the periods start in the early
teenage years until the last period at the time of the menopause, at
around the age of fifty. Altogether, then, the woman ovulates and
menstruates about four hundred times in her life.

Fertilisation

The Release and Capture of the Egg

Several hours before the actual ovulation the tube has probably received signals as to the site on the ovary surface where the rupture will take place and the fimbria, or finger-like projections of the tube, position themselves to catch the egg and prevent it from disappearing. The fimbria move back and forth across the ovary's surface like tentacles of a sea anemone, tasting the chemical messenger substances and wafting the egg into the tube.

Sometimes the tube, if it is long and mobile, can reach the opposite ovary and it then begins to compete, trying to draw in the egg and on occasions actually succeeding. The fact that the egg can jump across to the opposite tube is known for certain because a high proportion of women who have had a tube removed, for instance due to ectopic pregnancy, can get pregnant in this way. The mobility of the tube can be impaired if the woman has had an inflammation of the tube, salpingitis, or adhesions around the end of the tube, so that sometimes the tube is blocked and the woman is unable to conceive.

The Egg's Journey down the Fallopian Tube

After ovulation the egg, having passed from an ovary into the tube, travels down the five-inch tube, and this process takes from three to five days. The muscle walls of the tube encircle a canal which is wider at the end where the egg is caught and gradually narrows to the size of a fine straw. The egg is propelled down the tube towards the uterus by a mechanism which seems to be a combination of fluid currents and rhythmic contractions, together with little hair-like projections in the tube.

The Upward Journey of the Sperm

The egg and sperm meet in the mid-portion of the tube. Explanations of how the sperm ascends from the vagina into the uterus and from the uterus to the meeting point in the tube have shifted as knowledge of the subject has increased. It used to be thought that the sperm was endowed with certain qualities which directed it somehow along the proper path to ensure fertilisation. Today it is known that the fate of several hundred million sperm depends at least in part on the phase of the woman's menstrual cycle.

During intercourse the sperm are catapulted into the upper vagina near the neck of the uterus. The sperm cells swim haphazardly in all directions: some into the vagina, some towards the outside and others away from the middle of the vagina far to one side or the other. Most of the sperm never reach the protective confines of the cervical canal but remain in the vagina and are exposed to a hostile environment of vaginal secretions, which are quite acid. Sperm cells are sensitive to this acid and those remaining in the vagina usually die off within a few hours. A few, by sheer accident, gain the sanctuary of the cervical mucus which is weakly alkaline and the sperm cells thrive in it. Some swim straight up the inch-long mucus filled canal while others get bogged down on the way, becoming hopelessly stranded in small bays and coves.

A small proportion of the total number actually reach the cavity of the uterus and begin their upward excursion. Whether this progress results solely from the swimming efforts of the sperm or whether they are aided by fluid currents and contractions of the uterus is unknown. The undaunted ones reach the openings of the two Fallopian tubes, one on each side of the cavity of the uterus, and continue their journey up from the uterus into one of the tubes. Only a few thousand of the four hundred million cells ejaculated ever reach the middle of the tube where the egg lies waiting and the one sperm that achieves its destiny has won against gigantic odds, several hundred million to one, and the baby it engenders has a far greater mathematical chance of becoming Prime Minister than the sperm had of fathering a baby!

The Moment of Fertilisation

The moment the sperm and egg fuse and a new individual begins to form is shrouded in mystery. A couple of hundred sperm out of the four hundred million reach the egg and, like a well co-ordinated team, they penetrate the outer layers of the egg one after another. While they are trying to do this many sperm perish but after a few hours at least some of the outer layers have been removed and the surface of the egg is becoming exposed.

Like a bird's egg, the human egg has a kind of shell which is tough and elastic. At the moment when a small number of sperm are on their way through the egg, suddenly a single one breaks all the way through, penetrates the inner lining of the egg and at that moment the composition of the ovary changes, immediately shutting out all the other sperm even if they have almost pierced it. This makes it impossible for any further sperm to fertilise the egg but, if this should happen, further development will sooner or later be arrested. The excluded sperm continue to jostle around the egg for several days and gradually die.

Fertilisation is the process of fusion of a male seed, or spermatozon, with a female egg, or ovum and in humans fertilisation must take place in one or other Fallopian tube. The egg, which has been shed from the ovary, is attracted to the tentacles at the outer end of the tube by certain chemical substances, enters the lining of the tube and is transported along the tube by the wafting action of minute hairs and by the rhythmical contractions of the tube itself.

During intercourse about four hundred million sperm are ejaculated into the vagina to start the hazardous journey through the neck of the womb into the cavity, and then along the Fallopian tube towards the egg. Each sperm, which is about 0.05mm long, consists of a head and tail and propels itself quite quickly, possibly covering 2.5cms (1in) every eight minutes. Many millions of sperm die on the way and only a few hundred actually manage to find their way into the tube. The remainder disintegrate and die without any harm to the woman.

Only one single sperm is capable of burrowing its way through the shell of the egg. As soon as this happens the head of the sperm separates from the tail and fertilisation has occurred. The fertilised egg now forms a barrier which prevents any further sperm from gaining entrance. Very soon after fertilisation the egg begins to divide, first into two, then four and so on, forming a clump of cells called the morula or mulberry which begins to move slowly from the tube into the uterus where it will grow to form an embryo. It is suggested that the time taken for the fertilised egg to reach the uterus is probably from three to five days.

One of the real mysteries is why the male's vast production of sperm is not seen as wasteful. Assuming that a man produces 10^8 million sperm a day, during an average reproductive life of sixty years, he would produce well over two trillion sperm. Assuming that a woman ripens one egg per lunar month, or thirteen per year, over the course of her forty-year reproductive life, she would total five hundred eggs. But the word 'waste' implies an excess. Assuming two or three offspring, for every baby a woman produces she wastes only around two hundred eggs. For every baby a man produces, he wastes more than one trillion sperm. The average human ejaculate contains almost half a billion sperm, which is pretty extravagant as only one sperm can fertilise the egg!

The essential step in the initiation of a new life is fertilisation or the penetration of the egg by the sperm and the fusion or mating of part of the two cells to form a single cell. From this united parent cell originate all the billions of cells which will form the baby. The most important part of the cell is the nucleus which is not a solid mass of tissue but is made up of a network of tiny rods called chromosomes. These chromosomes contain a substance called DNA which is the constituent of the body's cells, carrying the blueprint of the offspring. When the two sets of blueprints, one from the father and one from the mother, unite, they produce a unique individual. In any particular case there is one chance in four hundred million that that particular individual could be you! If any of those other four hundred million sperms had fertilised the egg from which you were created, you would certainly have been a strikingly different person, perhaps of the opposite sex. The selection of parents is absolutely fortuitous. If your father and mother had not been who they were, you would not be who you are.

There is a specific number of chromosome characteristics for each species and every cell in the body of each individual belonging to the particular animal species contains this number of chromosomes. Chromosomes are paired: one species has its genetic material divided into forty pairs of chromosomes; while in another species, like the rodent, it may be divided into seventeen pairs.

The fruitfly, which has contributed to man's knowledge of genetics, possesses only four pairs of chromosomes. In humans, there are forty-six single chromosomes but each has a counterpart. Thus there are twenty-three different pairs.

Before fertilisation the chromosome number of each human parent cell, sperm and egg, has been halved from forty-six to twenty-three.

One member of each pair remains in the fully mature sex cell. Thus, when the two mature sex cells fuse each brings twenty-three chromosomes to the process of fertilisation and when they come together the human species number of forty-six is restored.

Chromosomes are really chains of small genetic units called genes and the total number of genes in our twenty-three pairs of chromosomes is estimated at between ten thousand and fifty thousand. Since the individual genes are the ultimate determinants of genetic inheritance, the almost infinite variety of combinations explains why all humans differ so markedly, unless of course they are identical one-egg twins. One-egg twins have exactly the same chromosome gene make-up since the egg divides after fertilisation and an independent embryo develops from each half.

The Continued Growth of the Embryo

Twenty Hours

The head of the victorious sperm with its genetic blueprint now lies inside the tiny nucleus in the egg. Roughly twelve hours after fusion of the chromosomes the first cell division takes place and these divisions continue at intervals of twelve to fifteen hours.

Thirty Hours

Now the fertilised egg moves slowly towards the uterus, propelled by millions of little hairs called cilia and it is at this stage that there may be risks for the growing cells. For instance, if the passage along the tube to the uterus is obstructed or blocked, then the fertilised egg will continue to grow in the tube which results in a tubal or ectopic pregnancy (see pages 110–113).

Three Days

The egg remains in the tube for about three days after fertilisation, repeatedly dividing during its slow journey towards the uterus. Once inside the uterus one of the most critical phases of development is over. Now the fertilised egg, which is called a blastocyst, has to face two new tasks: it has to attach itself to the lining of the womb and it has to signal its presence to the mother.

Eight Days Old

The lining of the uterus, called the endometrium, has been prepared by hormones from the ovary to receive the fertilised egg and when the blastocyst has finally come to rest and has established contact with the lining of the uterus intensive chemical changes take place between it and the mother.

Eight days after fertilisation the blastocyst secretes a mucus that proclaims its presence in the uterus as a new developing individual with a different genetic make-up from that of the mother in whose body it lives. The blastocyst now sinks into the top of the uterus and as it does so the uterus expands enormously and becomes soft.

Implantation

Proteins and hormones formed in the blastocyst enter the woman's bloodstream, and these can be detected by a blood test, hence the blood pregnancy test using HCG (see page 61). In this way it is possible to verify a pregnancy with a high degree of certainty before the first menstrual period has actually been missed.

Eleven Days Old

The blastocyst now swells, with the cells dividing roughly twice a day, so that on the twelfth day they number a couple of thousand, and now the blastocyst is securely anchored in the uterus. Protuberances like cables develop which will ultimately become the amniotic sac, the umbilical cord and the placenta.

Sex Determination

Will it be a boy or a girl? Probably no other question is asked of an obstetrician more frequently than what sex an unborn baby will be. However the doctor's guess is just as good as yours and without special tests such as amniocentesis, chorion sampling or sophisticated ultrasound (see pages 149–157) no one can predict the sex of an unborn child.

Sex is determined at the moment of conception. The mature female egg contains one sex chromosome called X and the male sperm has a fifty–fifty chance of containing either an X or a Y chromosome. If a sperm bearing an X chromosome unites with the egg, the child is a girl; if a Y one does, it is a boy. Since the sex of the offspring depends on which sperm fertilises the egg, the sex of the child is therefore determined by the male.

SOME INTERESTING FACTS
ABOUT THE SEX RATIO

* The percentage of male births is slightly higher than female.

* The percentage of male births rises during and after wars.

* The percentage of female births increases directly with the age of the parents.

* The percentage of female births increases with birth rank; that is first births are more likely to be male than subsequent births.

* A higher number of sons are born to couples of a higher socio-economic status.

* The ratio of sons to daughters is higher for couples with higher sexual intercourse rates.

* Sex ratio varies with the seasons, and the ratio of male to female births has been lower after certain natural disasters such as floods, earthquakes and epidemics.

CHAPTER 2

The First Month
(0–4 Weeks)

The Duration of Pregnancy: Due Date

The duration of pregnancy, from fertilisation to full-term delivery, averages 265 days but, since the day of fertilisation is not always known, it is customary to use the first day of the last normal menstrual period as the marker because that day is more easily pinpointed and because only four per cent of women give birth on their due date.

A normal full-term pregnancy can last anywhere from thirty-eight to forty-two weeks. That is why the medical term for due date is EDD (estimated date of delivery) and the date your doctor gives you is only an educated estimate. It is usually calculated by taking the first day of the last normal menstrual period, adding seven, and from that date counting back three months. For example, say the last menstrual period began on 11th April, add 7 to 11, giving 18 and count back three months. The EDD will be 18th January the following year.

If the periods come predictably every twenty-eight days, the date of delivery is more likely to be close to the estimated due date. If the cycle is longer than twenty-eight days, the date of delivery will be later than the EDD, earlier if the cycle is shorter.

If the menstrual cycle is irregular, the dating system may not work. Say there has been no period in three months and suddenly a pregnancy is confirmed: when did conception take place? The very first clue, the size of the uterus, will be noted when the initial internal pregnancy examination is confirmed. Later on there are other milestones which together can more accurately gauge the length of the pregnancy. The first is when a fetal heartbeat is heard with a special stethoscope device at about ten to twelve weeks; and the next is when the first flutter of life is felt at about twenty to twenty-two weeks with a first baby, or sixteen to eighteen weeks with subsequent pregnancies (see pages 159–160). The height of the fundus (the top of the uterus) at each visit, and ultrasonic examination, are also useful gauges in estimating the due date. Most pregnant women in the UK have an ultrasound dating examination at about nineteen to twenty weeks which can accurately predict the due date (see page 149).

Although each chapter will give a detailed description of fetal development, the chart on pages 56–58 is a brief account of the baby's growth during the first three months.

Development of the Placenta and Amniotic Fluid

Small sponge-like protrusions called villi surround the newly embedded embryo, rapidly increasing in number and size. At about twelve weeks these villi develop with immense speed to form the placenta, or afterbirth. A complete placenta is normally formed between twelve and fourteen weeks and this takes over the basics of nourishment and hormone production. This is why many of the unpleasant side effects of early pregnancy, such as nausea, vomiting and fatigue, gradually disappear as the mother's hormones are no longer responsible for maintaining the pregnancy. As the placenta develops and becomes mature it takes over these functions, and the mother's hormone levels therefore go back to normal.

Amniotic Fluid

While the baby is growing it is surrounded by a sea of liquid known as the amniotic fluid contained within the amniotic cavity. This fluid gradually increases until at term there is just about one litre (two pints) present. After the thirty-sixth week the amount of fluid gradually decreases.

This fluid provides a liquid environment in which the fetus can develop and move about freely. It helps to provide a constant temperature for the baby to grow, it allows certain substances (particularly urine) to be excreted from the fetus, and of course it acts

THE GROWTH OF
THE EMBRYO

Three Weeks

Three weeks after conception the human embryo is barely two millimetres long. Already the rudimentary brain, heart, and gill arches (which will later become the face and throat and inner ear) are forming.

Four Weeks

The embryo is some six millimetres long now and already the brain and backbone are being formed. The heart is beginning to pump blood to the liver and the ribs are starting to grow around the rudimentary lungs.

Five Weeks

The fertilised pregnancy is now visible to the naked eye. The fetus within the newly formed sac of fluid is beginning to take shape.

Six Weeks

The head is being formed, rapidly followed by the chest and abdominal cavity. A rudimentary brain is present and the spinal column is properly formed. The heart is forming in the chest cavity and by the end of the sixth week the first rudimentary heart circulation is beginning to function. The arms and legs are as yet extremely short but hands and feet are already starting to take shape. By this time the spinal cord shimmers through the thin skin and much of the skeleton can be seen. It is now just over fifteen millimetres long.

Seven Weeks

The heart has now started to beat with sufficient force to circulate cells through the blood vessels. The liver and kidneys have

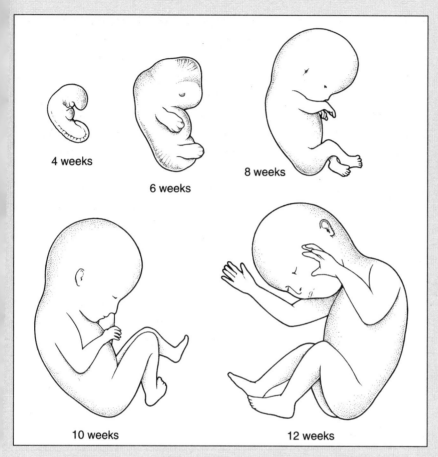

Diagramatic representation of early development of the fetus.

developed but are small and incapable of functioning. The eyes and ears are starting to form though the skin over them remains completely intact. The umbilical cord, the link between the placenta and the embryo, forms as one large blood vessel conveying oxygenated blood to the embryo and two vessels taking de-oxygenated blood and waste products back from the embryo to the placenta.

Eight Weeks

By this time the embryo is still only four centimetres, about one and a half inches, long but inside this tiny body all the organs are already in place. Everything to be found in a fully grown adult has now been formed. It weighs about thirteen grams, less than half an ounce.

Ten Weeks

The eyes have grown and are recognisable, the inner part of the ears has formed and the face is much clearer.

Eleven Weeks

The fetus can be clearly identified as a small human baby, although the head is relatively large for the body and the limbs are rather short. The eyes are completely formed and the ears are developed. The limb buds have grown rapidly, though the fingers and toes are still joined together. The ovaries and testicles are formed within the body and the external genitalia are developing.

Twelve Weeks

Most of the essential organs of the fetus are now formed and the majority of them are beginning to function. It is of course at this time that congenital abnormalities may occur if some factor has been introduced that has the ability to interfere with the formation of a particular organ at a critical stage in its growth. Once an organ has been properly formed it cannot really come to much harm whatever happens to the mother or the fetus. The embryo is now fixed well into the uterus and it is very unusual for miscarriage to occur after this time. All the hormones needed for the rest of the pregnancy are being produced in the placenta, which is also responsible for the entire interchange of nutrients and the removal of waste products from the fetus.

What can the fetus do? Its body jerks and moves, it hiccups and it flexes its arms and tiny legs, practising its new-found abilities.

as a shock absorber to protect the growing fetus from the rigours of pregnancy. Many women fear that their baby may be damaged by a fall or a direct blow to the uterus or abdomen during pregnancy, but this is extremely unlikely since the amniotic fluid protects the baby.

When the membranes rupture, amniotic fluid leaks out of the uterus through the vagina and this is usually followed by contractions of the uterus and labour. Sometimes leakage of fluid may occur early in pregnancy and if this occurs it does not necessarily mean that labour will ensue as the amniotic fluid is not a stagnant pool and the fluid is re-formed every three hours or so.

Much is now known about the composition of the amniotic fluid and withdrawal of a sample of fluid in early pregnancy can be used to diagnose certain conditions in the developing fetus such as chromosome abnormalities and Down's Syndrome (see pages 389–390).

The Umbilical Cord

This structure extends from the umbilicus of the fetus to the surface of the placenta and carries the blood from the baby to the placenta via two arteries whilst returning the blood via a single vein. The umbilical cord is about twenty inches long and is about the thickness of an index finger.

The Diagnosis of Pregnancy

The following symptoms are common signs of early pregnancy:

- **Missed Period**
  Failure of your period to come at the right time is generally the first sign of a pregnancy although there are other causes for a delay or even a missed period, including stress, psychological upsets, medical diseases, changes of climate and occupation, and certain drugs, notably the Pill. It is quite possible to become pregnant and still appear to menstruate during the early months but on close observation the periods are different, usually shorter, scantier and infrequent.

- **Breast Changes**
  Engorged and tender breasts are the commonest early complaints of pregnancy and are due to changes that occur in the breast tissue in preparation for their use later when the baby is born. Sometimes veins stand out underneath the skin and the nipple enlarges and becomes darker. Occasionally stretch marks occur in the area of the breasts as well. After the first few months a sticky, yellowish, watery fluid called colostrum can be expressed from the nipples by gently squeezing the breast.

- **Digestive Problems**
  Nausea and vomiting are not uncommon. Certain foods may repel you and changes in appetite often occur. You may experience a distaste for alcohol and a craving and desire for strange foods. Feeling sickened by cooking and other smells, perfumes and even washing-up liquid is not uncommon, and some women lose their taste for tea and coffee.

- **Tiredness**
  It is common to feel exhausted earlier and more frequently, and this is not because of anaemia but because of the hormone changes.

- **Frequent Need to Urinate**
  Because of local congestion, the bladder feels full and you will need to urinate much more frequently during the day and night.

- **Emotions**
  You may experience moments of depression and irritability in early pregnancy.

- **Darkening of Line from Navel to Pubis**
  Later in pregnancy, at about the fourth or fifth month, a dark line can appear in the centre of the abdomen. This has no significance whatsoever and is purely the result of certain hormone changes.

Pregnancy Testing

In ancient cultures all manner of tests were devised to determine pregnancy. The saliva from a pregnant woman would supposedly make a goat throw up! A golden ring suspended over a woman's abdomen would spin wildly if she were pregnant, in one direction if it was a boy and in the other if it was a girl.

Urine Testing

The simplest way of confirming pregnancy is by testing a fresh early-morning specimen of urine. The test depends on the fact that in early pregnancy there is a hormone called human chorionic gonadotrophin (HCG) in the mother's circulation, and this hormone is concentrated and excreted in the urine. HCG is secreted from the moment of conception but increases in amount, doubling every other day and reaching a peak at somewhere between sixty and eighty days of the pregnancy, after which it declines.

These tests are accurate in ninety-nine per cent of cases by the thirty-fifth day. A 'do-it-yourself' kit is available at most chemists with simple instructions and, although not quite as accurate as a specific early-morning test, it is about eighty-five to ninety per cent accurate.

Blood Tests

The blood pregnancy test, again using Beta HCG, is the most valuable diagnostic test. Beta HCG is a tiny spectrum of the HCG complex and is very specific for pregnancy. This blood test gives an accurate result in about ninety per cent of cases when done within a few days of a missed period.

Ultrasound

Ultrasonic techniques (see pages 149–157) are now commonly used in obstetrics and can confirm a pregnancy as early as the third week

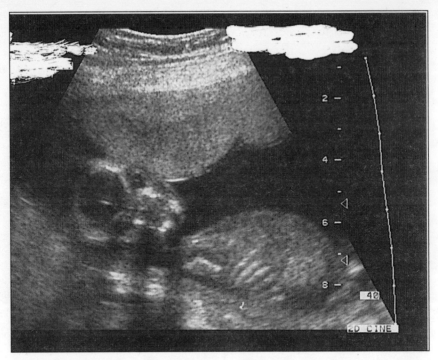

Ultrasound is usually performed on all pregnant women when they first attend the clinic and sometimes again later on to check how the baby is growing.

after the last missed period. More importantly, they can often predict the viability or otherwise of a pregnancy as the rhythmical pumping movements of the fetal heart can be seen from an early stage. Simple and easily portable machines (sonicaid or doptone) are available which employ a different principle, whereby reflected waves from the fetus can be detected and converted into audible signals which are surprisingly similar to the fetal heart sounds. With these machines the fetal heartbeat can be recognised at the tenth week.

Clinical Examination

Most doctors get a pretty shrewd idea that a pregnancy is present from the history, examination of the breasts and an internal examination which can usually suggest a pregnancy by six weeks after the last period. Certain changes take place in the pelvic organs; the uterus becomes soft and enlarged and has a different consistency; and a violet coloration is seen in the vagina when the cervix is inspected.

Early Pregnancy Assessment Unit (EPAU)

This is an outpatient service for women with early pregnancy problems, mainly bleeding, when scans make the dates uncertain, or for reassurance where there is a previous bad obstetric history. There is no time limit in pregnancy but most women are seen in the first three months. Previously women with bleeding in pregnancy were admitted to hospital, waited several hours for an ultrasound and were then fasted for longer periods in case surgery was needed.

EPAUs generally consist of a waiting area, an examination room, a scan room and private rooms for counselling, though this will very much depend on the numbers involved and the resources available to individual hospitals. Arrangements vary from hospital to hospital but usually units are open in the morning, with ward staff available to deal with telephone enquiries until late evening. The workload also varies but an average EPAU will see about thirty patients a week. Ultrasound assessment is the mainstay of diagnosis, with transvaginal examination giving clear images by eight weeks, together with a diagnosis as to whether or not the pregnancy is viable.

Medication in Pregnancy

Almost all chemical substances can cross the placenta and become concentrated in the fetus. Whether or not a drug causes harm depends on many factors, including the genetic make-up of the mother and fetus, the chemical structure of the drug, the month of pregnancy in which the drug is used and the total amount. There are a host of medicines that can damage the fetus only during early pregnancy when the organs and the limbs are being formed: others cause harm only during the last three months, while a third group appears to be most dangerous when given just before delivery.

Effects of medication on the baby do not end at childbirth since many substances can be transmitted from the mother to the nursing infant via the breast milk. Concentrations of the drug in the milk vary and they depend on the blood supply to the breasts, the amount of milk produced, and again the chemical structure and dose of the drug. While some medications appear only in tiny amounts, others are highly concentrated and potentially harmful to the infant, particularly during the baby's first month.

Most drugs, however, are simple chemicals which when given to the mother pass from her circulation to the baby's through the placenta, and many drugs taken by the mother have no effect on the baby at all. Problems only occur if the incorrect dose is taken or if it is taken at the wrong stage of pregnancy.

The whole question of prescribing drugs in pregnancy is extremely complicated. On the one hand an antibiotic given to the mother may cure the baby of an infection but, on the other hand, the same antibiotic given at the wrong time in pregnancy might cause minor malformations of the fetus.

Whether a drug given to the mother actually crosses the placenta and affects the baby depends on the size of the molecules. Chemicals with small molecules pass easily into the circulation of the baby whereas those with large molecules do not. Many drugs like aspirin, codeine and certain sleeping tablets do not cross over to the fetus and usually cause no damage. The antibiotics that do cross over the placental barrier enter the fetal circulation shortly after being given to the mother, and they may be needed to treat the baby if, for example, the membranes have been ruptured for longer than twenty-four hours, increasing the likelihood of infection in the unborn child.

Some drugs pose little threat in pregnancy, others become more hazardous. Aspirin, for example, which is not considered harmful in early pregnancy may, if taken in high doses in the final months, cause problems with the baby's circulation, prolong pregnancy, and possibly even cause bleeding during delivery. Again, the risks of a drug like alcohol differ according to the stage the pregnancy has reached.

The tragic effects on babies born to mothers who had taken thalidomide brought about a wide awareness of the potential dangers of drug administration during pregnancy and a new appreciation among doctors of the care needed in prescribing. The problem of knowing which drugs can safely be taken in pregnancy is complicated by the variety of remedies available for any one condition and, equally, the variety of conditions for which a single drug may be effectively given. The point is that drugs have to be used correctly, in the right dose, for the right reason and at the right time.

The risk that certain drugs may cause abnormalities in the baby is greatest during the third and eighth week – the period when the organs and the skeleton are being formed. The dangers of drug-induced abnormalities are reduced after that time as development of the baby becomes more and more fully established, a fact which has led doctors concerned with the care of pregnant women to think extremely carefully before prescribing any drug within the first three months of pregnancy.

The Effect of Different Drugs during Pregnancy

Painkillers

Medications to relieve pain are the most commonly prescribed class of drugs during pregnancy, labour and delivery, and in the postpartum period.

Aspirin

Aspirin is a member of a class of drugs known as salicylates and until recently aspirin and products containing salicylate were consumed by approximately eighty per cent of women at some time during pregnancy. Aspirin is an important ingredient of most pain relievers and it is generally safe to use soluble aspirin or Disprin in the early and middle stages of pregnancy. As pregnancy advances, however, aspirin can be more hazardous, both to the woman and her baby, and can cause alteration in blood clotting resulting in a higher incidence of anaemia in the mother and bleeding before and after delivery. As well as this there is a slightly increased risk of the baby bleeding once born. Although aspirin is excreted in the breast milk, in normal doses the effects on a nursing infant are minimal.

Alternatives to Aspirin

Codeine or Paracetamol or Panadol are often given for the relief of simple aches and pains or headaches and can be taken quite safely.

There are occasions when stronger painkillers than those in the aspirin group may be needed and there are a number of preparations which are safe to use in pregnancy. Your doctor will know which ones are suitable.

Anti-sickness Pills

Over half of all pregnant women experience some degree of nausea and vomiting in early pregnancy and for a woman who is pregnant for the first time the incidence can be as high as seventy-five per cent. While most cases of morning or evening sickness respond to a variety of conservative approaches, home remedies and helpful hints (see pages 75–77), these measures can prove inadequate for a certain number of women. Although doctors share the concern of pregnant women that medication may be taken only when absolutely necessary, it is also true that persistent vomiting can result in consequences far more detrimental to a woman and her fetus than those caused by careful use of drugs to relieve symptoms.

There are a number of commonly prescribed drugs that, as far as is known, are safe in pregnancy, including vitamin B6 which is available without prescription, and a group of antihistamines which are often used in travel sickness as well, such as Avomine, Dramamine and Meclizine. Again, it must be emphasised that self-administration of drugs is extremely unwise and advice must be given by the doctor.

Antacids

There are a number of antacids which can be used during pregnancy for the relief of indigestion or heartburn (see pages 192–193) and these can all be safely used. Examples include Maalox, Milk of Magnesia, Rennie's tablets, and a host of others. Alka-Seltzer should be used sparingly as it does contain quite a lot of aspirin. Stronger drugs such as Tagamet and Zantac (which are relatively new and popular drugs used for treating duodenal ulcers and other conditions where excessive acid is produced) are also believed to be safe.

Laxatives

For most women constipation is an annoying problem throughout pregnancy (see pages 78–79) and it happens because there is relaxation of the smooth muscle of the intestine which interferes with the forward wave-like movement called peristalsis. Certain supplements such as iron only serve to worsen this problem. None of the commonly used laxatives and stool softeners has ever been reported to have caused harm to the developing fetus. It is better, however, to drink plenty of fluids and eat high-fibre foods such as bran and fresh fruit which should keep the bowel action normal.

Breast-feeding mothers should select a laxative with care since some may increase bowel action and cause diarrhoea in the nursing infant. However, the general conclusion is that laxatives on the whole are safe to use if taken in normal doses.

Anti-diarrhoea Pills

Again, used sparingly, most of the anti-diarrhoea pills obtainable without prescription are safe in pregnancy. It is also useful to have some sachets of Dioralyte handy. This is a powder containing vitamins, minerals and other essential ingredients and replaces what is being lost through diarrhoea and vomiting and restores the normal fluid balance in the body.

Antibiotics

After pain relievers, antibiotics are the drugs most frequently used by pregnant women. There are so many new and powerful antibiotics on the market that it is extremely difficult to know categorically which ones are safe and which should be avoided. As a matter of principle, those most recently introduced are better not taken during pregnancy and any antibiotic must be prescribed by a doctor. We know, for example, that penicillin and its derivatives are completely safe, whereas Tetracyclines may affect the tiny buds which eventually become the baby's teeth, causing yellow discoloration if given in the first few months of pregnancy. Another antibiotic to be avoided is Streptomycin which can cause hearing loss and abnormally short or small limbs.

Apart from the penicillin group, safe antibiotics include Erythromycin, Cephalosporins and Sulphonamides such as Gantrosin, although these should be restricted to the early and middle part of pregnancy as significant levels can persist in the newborn for several days after birth and it is possible that the baby may become jaundiced or anaemic. Premature infants are especially susceptible to this complication so if a woman is at risk of premature labour or has premature rupture of the membranes (see pages 211–212) it is probably best to avoid Sulphonamides during the last few months of pregnancy.

Another drug worth mentioning is Trimethoprim, different Sulphonamides combined in a single tablet. The trade names of this popular combination are Bactrim or Septrin. Essentially, there is no evidence that these drugs cause any congenital abnormalities but they should be avoided for the first three months. As has already been stated, Tetracyclines should be avoided throughout pregnancy.

Thrush (monilia) (see pages 163–164) is a common vaginal infection in pregnancy and there are a number of safe pessaries and creams that can be used, including Canestan and Gyno-Daktarin. Metronidazole (Flagyl) is a very commonly prescribed drug for the vaginal infection Trichomonas (see page 165) and its use in pregnancy is controversial. While most case reports and reviews say that it is safe, there are a small number of studies which link its use to a higher incidence of spontaneous miscarriage and birth defects. It is probably therefore best to avoid it, certainly in the first three months of pregnancy.

Sleeping Pills and Sedatives

In small doses, and especially later in pregnancy when sleep may become a problem because of the enlarging and active baby, there are a number of completely safe sedatives that can be given for short periods. However, drugs containing barbiturates are probably best avoided.

Tranquillisers

There are so many tranquillisers that it is impossible to make accurate comments about their safety, but the more simple drugs such as Valium, Temazepam and Equanil can be given in the correct dosage during pregnancy with your doctor's permission for short periods, though they are probably best avoided as pregnancy proceeds since they may cause sleepiness in the unborn child.

Specific Drugs

There are of course many drugs which the physician may need to prescribe because of associated illness in pregnancy. Examples include women who become pregnant with known conditions such as epilepsy, diabetes, thyroid problems or heart conditions. If the pregnant woman is already taking drugs, then her doctor will take note of this and in some instances cease treatment and in others alter the dosage depending on various tests. She can be assured that the great majority of drugs, given the right way, in the right dose and at the right time will not affect her pregnancy.

At this point it is worth mentioning a vitamin called folic acid which has recently caused universal interest because of its supposed effects on preventing miscarriage and reducing the risk of certain abnormalities of the central nervous system. Folic acid is a naturally occurring vitamin present in vegetables which is partly responsible for the way in which the fetus grows. Some authorities recommend that every woman should take folic acid in a dose of 4mgs per day when contemplating a pregnancy and for the first three months into pregnancy. Certainly folic acid has no side effects and in our present state of knowledge this advice is very reasonable.

Environmental and Occupational Hazards of Pregnancy

Many pregnant women encounter serious problems relating to a wide variety of toxins in their home and work environments. Scientists have proved that certain pollutants can cause medical illnesses as well as reproductive failure. Insulating a house or painting and preparing a room for your baby brings with it questions about the effects of the chemicals used on your developing fetus. Misconceptions about the dangers of video display terminals and radiation released by microwave ovens and television sets can often add to your anxieties, as do fears that you must find a new home for your beloved pet cat, dog or bird to be sure that the potentially serious diseases which can be caused by these animals will not harm your fetus.

Exposure to fumes, chemicals, asbestos, noise pollution and

radiation poses definite hazards during pregnancy and knowledge of these hazards and the methods of preventing or minimising their effects is valuable to the outcome of a successful pregnancy. Here are a few of the commoner problems that women frequently enquire about.

Noise Pollution – Can Excessive Noise Affect the Outcome of Your Pregnancy?

There is increasing scientific evidence that exposure to noise, especially unexpected and uncontrollable noise, can be associated with hearing loss, high blood pressure, heart disease, insomnia and nervous disorders. As with other forms of stress, noise pollution may also decrease the amount of oxygen going to the fetus during pregnancy. Studies as early as 1941 showed that maternal emotional agitation induced by harsh sound decreased the fetal heart rate. It is known that fetuses hear some of the sounds to which their mothers are exposed but usually the protective uterine and amniotic fluid environment screens out most of this noise.

In 1991 some Finnish researchers exposed a group of twenty-seven pregnant volunteers to measure amounts of noise transmitted through headphones. All the women were in their third three months of pregnancy. All the relevant tests on the placenta and maternal circulation were normal, which is reassuring for pregnant women who enjoy listening to loud music on personal stereos.

Another study of 131 children, whose mothers were exposed to excess levels of industrial noise for a minimum of one month during pregnancy, showed hearing deficits in as many as forty per cent of those infants whose mothers were exposed to the highest noise levels over the greatest number of days. However, small amounts of environmental noise over short periods of time produce no problems.

Hair Dyes

Although much has been written about the potential for chemicals used in perms and hair dyes to cause cancer and birth defects, there has never been a published scientific study which supports this assertion.

Heavy Metals – Which Metals Pose the Greatest Threat to You and Your Baby?

Lead, mercury and cadmium give the most cause for concern. Until recently it was commonly believed that lead poisoning was limited to babies and young children who ate particles of lead paint pealing from walls in old buildings. Lead, which is commonly present in industries such as brass foundries, storage battery manufacturing, shipbuilding, paint manufacturing, printing, ceramics and pottery glazing, crosses the placenta and is present in the umbilical cord blood at nearly the same concentrations as in the mother. Excessive amounts of lead in the mother have been linked to high mortality rates, pre-term delivery and possible structural malformations. Fortunately there are simple blood tests which can detect signs of excessive lead, and women who fear that they may have been exposed to high levels can be tested.

Pesticides

There are no known studies linking normal use of household pesticides with an increased incidence of birth defects. Agricultural pesticides, however, have been associated with problems and it is probably best to protect yourself and your baby from the effects of pesticides by avoiding their use in the home or garden, lawn or greenhouse, and by wearing gloves and a disposal face mask where circumstances make this impossible.

A pregnant or nursing woman should try to avoid foods that are suspected of containing pesticide residues. It is best to peel and thoroughly wash fruit and vegetables, and it is probably best to wait until after the first three months to spray pests such as fleas or ants within the home.

Asbestos

Until its hazards were publicised in the 1970s, asbestos was widely used for insulating thousands of homes, public buildings and schools. Asbestos fibres released into the air can be inhaled into the respiratory tract and lungs over a long period of time and cause a debilitating lung disease. However, you need not fear that acute asbestos inhalation will adversely affect the outcome of your pregnancy as these fibres are too large to enter the bloodstream or cross the placenta.

House Painting

Essentially there is no danger associated with painting during pregnancy provided the room is well ventilated to dispel any fumes. In addition to paint, work with floor and furniture polishes can be associated with noxious fumes and it is probably better to leave a window open and feel uncomfortably cold than to inhale non-circulating air.

Lead-based paints are dangerous and should not be used to paint a baby's room.

X-rays and Irradiation

Everyone is exposed to what is referred to as 'background irradiation', the amount of radiation received from the atmosphere. Since its effect is cumulative, it must be considered alongside the radiation from man-made sources, i.e. X-rays. As a general principle no one should be subjected to an X-ray unless there is a valid reason, although X-rays used for ordinary diagnostic purposes are at such a low level that they do no harm to ordinary tissues.

It was Dr Alice Stewart in 1954, working at Oxford University, who suggested for the first time that diagnostic X-rays applied to the pregnant uterus might occasionally harm the baby. Until then they had been widely used to confirm pregnancy, to determine the size and position of the baby, to help decide whether the baby was alive or dead, and to confirm the presence of twins. However, during the last twenty years the use of abdominal X-rays in pregnant women and women of reproductive age has been largely replaced by ultrasound (see pages 149–157).

There are three theoretical risks from X-rays in pregnancy. First, it is possible to produce genetic mutation, i.e. an alteration in the smallest known genetic unit, the gene, or the larger unit, the chromosome. Experimental work has demonstrated that X-rays directed at the genital organs of fruitflies and other animals such as mice can induce physical or chemical changes in their genes which in turn result in anatomical or physiological changes in their offspring, and the offspring of subsequent generations. A second possibility concerns congenital abnormalities in the newborn. The risks of an abnormality will depend on the number of X-rays, their strength, and a number of other factors which need careful consideration. The third potential danger is an increased incidence of leukaemia or cancer of the blood before the age of ten in children whose mothers receive an abdominal X-ray during pregnancy, but the many studies all over the world show great disagreement regarding the outcome.

Sometimes specific treatment by X-ray or radium is carried out for certain conditions, and there is an enormous variation in the amount of radiation which reaches the fetus as a result of these treatments. Several hundred or even thousand times the diagnostic dose is sometimes necessary for so-called therapeutic irradiation and, if the patient who has been receiving this sort of treatment is found to be pregnant, occasionally abortion may be advised.

What does all this add up to? Admittedly there is uncertainty about the effect of X-rays on women in general and particularly during pregnancy, but the staff of X-ray departments are very aware of the possible problems and give protection by shielding the reproductive organs from X-rays in non-pregnant women, and carrying out X-rays just after menstruation to avoid the exposure to very early undetected conception.

Since the advent of ultrasound, there are few indications for X-rays during pregnancy and certainly this is to be avoided in the early months. Should an X-ray be required later in pregnancy, the mother can rest assured that the minimum dose will be used and that precautions will be taken to avoid subsequent problems. It is extremely difficult to give categorical advice to a woman with an unsuspected pregnancy who has had an X-ray examination or has been exposed to some radiation (if, for example, she happened to be present when her child was being X-rayed). The potential risks to the unborn baby depend on a number of factors, including the part of the body concerned, the number of X-rays used, the dose and the stage of the pregnancy. Ultimately a decision about whether the pregnancy can safely continue has to be made by the parents in consultation with medical experts.

CHAPTER 3

The Second Month

(4–8 Weeks)

Changes in Your Baby

By the fourth week of pregnancy the egg has settled into the womb lining. The outer cells reach out like roots to link with the mother's blood supply and the inner cells form into two and then later into three layers. Each of these layers will grow to be different parts of the baby's body: one layer becomes the brain, the nervous system, the skin, eyes and ears; another layer becomes the lungs, stomach and gut; and the third layer becomes the heart, blood, muscles and bones. At this stage the baby is still very small, about 2mm in length (less than one eighth of an inch), but it is beginning to take shape.

By the sixth and seventh weeks there is a large bulge containing the heart and a bump for the head where the brain is developing. The heart begins to beat and can be seen quite clearly on an ultrasound scan (see pages 61–62).

Dimples on the side of the head will become the ears, there is thickening where the eyes will be, and small swellings called limb buds where the arms and legs are growing.

Changes in You

At this stage your period is now due and you may already have begun to feel somewhat different from usual. There may be premenstrual symptoms, such as tender breasts, a fullness in the lower abdomen and decreased energy levels, but no period arrives. As the days pass you may suspect that you are pregnant and may notice changes in your appetite and a dislike of or preference for certain foods. Some nausea and occasionally vomiting can begin at about this time.

As the sixth and seventh weeks arrive you may have gained a

few pounds or even lost some weight and, although the abdomen is not really enlarging, you may notice your clothes are getting a little tight around the waist. At this stage changes are occurring gradually.

In early pregnancy one of the first symptoms is the need to urinate frequently and this can continue during most of the pregnancy. This is not really because the uterus is starting to enlarge but because the hormones circulating in the body increase the blood flow to the bladder. Another early symptom of pregnancy is tiredness, which is very common but lessens after the twelfth week of pregnancy when the placenta is fully formed. Constipation is another annoying feature (see pages 78–79).

Before pregnancy the uterus was about the size of your fist. After six weeks it is about the size of a tennis ball and as the uterus grows cramping or even pain, in the lower part of the abdomen or on either side is quite common.

Common Complaints in Early Pregnancy

Like most pregnant women you may suffer from a variety of physical discomforts at some stage during your pregnancy, often called minor complaints by the doctor mainly because they are usually self-limiting and rarely significant. They may be quite distressing to you and occasionally need treatment. Some, such as headaches, stuffy nose, tiredness and constipation, occur equally in non-pregnant women but their presence may cause worry and anxiety during pregnancy and it is for this reason that a rather lengthy list of such complaints follows, together with suggested remedies in the hope that you will be re-assured about their significance or their lack of importance.

Nausea and Sickness

A sensation of nausea and even vomiting is so common in the early weeks of pregnancy as to be normal. This complaint is very variable; it usually occurs in the morning but may occur at any time of day, though rarely at night unless you get out of bed suddenly. No one really knows why nausea and vomiting occur, although several theories have been put forward. The cause is probably a combination of the following:

- Hormone changes – in early pregnancy several hormones, notably oestrogen from the ovary and other hormones that come from the pituitary gland, circulate in excessive amounts which can disturb the normal metabolism of the body. This is why sickness almost always stops by about the twelfth week when the placenta is fully formed and takes over much of the hormone production.

- Vascular changes – blood pressure varies quite markedly in early pregnancy, particularly with changes in posture as the blood vessels in the body relax. This may cause a feeling of strangeness, nausea and occasional fainting.

- Alterations in the rates of secretion in the stomach and small intestine may upset your normal digestive system.

- Psychological changes – there is no doubt that nausea and vomiting may stem from anxiety. Your feelings about the pregnancy may have some bearing as excessive vomiting is more common in women with an unplanned or unwanted pregnancy. There is no truth, however, in the idea that unusually severe vomiting suggests that the baby may be abnormal, or increases the risk of miscarriage.

Nausea is one of the early symptoms of pregnancy and may begin when the menstrual period is only a few days overdue, gradually disappearing over the course of several weeks. In the beginning there may be a feeling of an 'unstable stomach' with uncertainty as to whether sickness will follow. The uncertainty may be replaced in a few days by vomiting which often occurs as soon as the head is lifted from the pillow. As the morning lengthens the nausea and vomiting decrease and usually by lunchtime an ordinary meal is possible. There are, however, many exceptions to this pattern. Some women vomit only in the evening, others at regular intervals all day long. Sometimes women who feel nausea are actually hungry and have a desire to eat whereas others have a marked dislike of food.

Irritants that may cause nausea in early pregnancy are kitchen odours, tobacco smoke or alcohol. It is not uncommon to notice flecks of blood in the vomit but this should not cause concern as any repeated vomiting may cause breakage of tiny blood vessels in the throat or gullet which heal spontaneously.

Management of Nausea and Vomiting

There are no hard and fast rules for the treatment of nausea and vomiting in early pregnancy but the following suggestions may help:

- Remember that some degree of nausea and sickness is very common in the early weeks of pregnancy.

- These symptoms will almost certainly disappear by the end of the twelfth week of pregnancy.

- Get up slowly in the morning and have some dry toast and a cup of tea.

- Take frequent small meals and small quantities of liquids.

- Avoid fats and fatty or spicy foods.

If these simple remedies do not help or if vomiting becomes excessive, then do not hesitate to contact the doctor as there are good treatments available which are safe. Although it is best to avoid medication during the early few weeks of pregnancy, drugs in the antihistamine group are perfectly safe and extremely effective. They are usually prescribed morning and evening and, because they have a mild, sedative action, they may cause drowsiness. An alternative treatment is vitamin B6 which can be obtained at the chemist without prescription.

If you experience vomiting which is so excessive and unresponsive to the usual treatments that you feel generally unwell, you will need to be admitted to hospital where a restricted diet together with one of the antihistamine drugs usually relieves the problem. If vomiting continues, feeding with intravenous fluids and a restricted intake of fluids by mouth are necessary until the vomiting and nausea cease. With this strict regime the symptoms usually disappear rapidly and you will be discharged after a few days.

Excessive Salivation

This is a most distressing symptom but is happily fairly rare. Saliva is produced in excessive quantities from the glands in the mouth, often becoming so profuse that you are unable to swallow it and are forced to spit out quantities into a handkerchief. It may seem as if you are constantly being sick but this is in fact not so and the difference between being sick and producing excessive saliva is important because the normal anti-sickness treatments will not be of any help.

Unfortunately there is not an absolute cure but the condition is self-limiting and will settle spontaneously. Occasionally treatment with one of the belladonna group of drugs (Atropine) helps to dry the secretions.

Appetite and Taste

We have already seen that women note a temporary diminution in appetite early in pregnancy and ordinary amounts of food often lead to a rather bloated feeling. You may develop a craving for a particular food, or occasionally eat one particular food to the exclusion of almost anything else. There is no need to be anxious about these cravings which usually settle spontaneously as the pregnancy advances.

Similarly an alteration in taste is quite a common symptom in early pregnancy and may persist for some time. Some women complain that everything tastes the same and others that certain foods that they used to like are unpalatable. Again there is nothing sinister about this complaint and normal taste sensations return after pregnancy.

Constipation

Some women become constipated only when pregnant and others who are prone to constipation find that pregnancy increases this difficulty.

One of the reasons why constipation occurs particularly in the first part of pregnancy is that the hormone progesterone makes the intestine relax and therefore reduces its power to propel the contents towards the rectum. Basically the hazards of constipation are greatly overrated, probably in part because of the emphasis on a daily bowel movement in pharmaceutical advertising in the popular media.

There is no evidence that it is harmful not to have a daily movement. However, an evacuation every twenty-four to forty-eight hours is preferable. The following are useful hints to avoid constipation:

- Take a moderate amount of daily physical exercise.
- Keep up fluid intake.
- Eat wholemeal bread rather than white.
- Have a coarse cereal such as oatmeal for breakfast.
- Eat plenty of salads and vegetables.
- Fruit at night before going to bed is worth trying.

If constipation becomes a problem and causes discomfort, your doctor should be able to prescribe a laxative. The correct amount will enable the bowel to open normally each day. Too large a dose will result in attacks of diarrhoea, inevitably followed by two or three days of constipation while the intestine fills.

Many women are frightened that if they have not had a bowel movement for a few days a strong movement will disturb the pregnancy or even cause a miscarriage, but it can safely be said that this will not happen. Occasionally iron tablets prescribed by the doctor may increase the constipation, in which case the doctor will normally change the brand or advise less frequent doses.

Abdominal Pain

Some degree of discomfort in the abdomen during pregnancy is very common. On the other hand persistent, severe abdominal pain may indicate a complication and should be reported to the doctor. There are many causes of pain in the abdomen and indeed the pain could be due to a condition that has nothing to do with the pregnancy, for example, acute appendicitis which, though rare, is just as common in pregnancy as at other times.

In early pregnancy many women experience a vague sensation of low abdominal cramp which is rather hard to locate and is usually of no significance, whereas the pain of an impending miscarriage is fairly severe and experienced in waves rather like labour pains. A pregnancy in the Fallopian tube (see pages 110–113) can cause severe pain localised to one side of the abdomen which almost always occurs before ten weeks and is often accompanied by vaginal bleeding.

As the uterus enlarges and grows out of the pelvis by the third month, the ligaments that hold it in place begin to stretch and this can lead to sharp twinges of pain usually in the groin on both sides, worse on exercise and better when resting. Constipation of course may also cause abdominal pain as the bowel distends, and this is often aggravated by abdominal distension and a desire to pass wind, which is due to hormone changes relaxing the bowel.

Infections in Pregnancy

Rubella or German Measles

The first and by far the most important infection which causes problems in the unborn child and is preventable is rubella or German measles. If you are exposed to the rubella virus, whether or not flu-like symptoms (headache, fever, swollen glands, a rash and a general feeling of illness and nosebleeds) are apparent, you develop antibodies that will protect you against another bout of infection. It is now routine for a blood test to be carried out at the first visit to an antenatal clinic which will detect whether these antibodies exist. If a woman with no rubella antibodies gets German measles in early pregnancy, there is a ten to twelve per cent chance that the baby may be born with some deformities. The risks are related not to the severity of the disease in the mother but to the timing of the exposure to the virus. Babies whose mothers contract German measles during the first eight to ten weeks of pregnancy may be born with severe defects of the heart, eyes and brain. The incidence and severity of the problems are much lower if the infection strikes after twelve weeks, and virtually non-existent after sixteen. A protective vaccine is available if you have not developed antibodies.

An immunisation programme for schoolgirls aged eleven to thirteen was introduced in the UK in 1970 to prevent congenital abnormalities occurring as a result of rubella infection in pregnancy

80

although, because of a low acceptance of vaccination and occasional vaccine failure, it has not provided immunity for all women before they embark on pregnancy. The best way of achieving this aim is through a screening programme centred on doctors' surgeries and family planning clinics. In some areas this is proving very successful.

If you are found to be susceptible to the condition, steps must be taken to avoid any person who has been in contact with German measles during the first three months of your pregnancy. It is not possible to administer the vaccine during this time for fear of affecting the unborn child. Vaccination, however, can safely be given after the birth of the baby. It is important to consult a doctor if you have been in contact with anyone who has recently had German measles or develops it within two or three days of meeting. An injection can sometimes be given to prevent German measles from developing but, as this is extremely expensive and is in short supply, it is usual for a blood test to be done to see if you are immune.

It is not always easy to tell from the first blood test whether you have had rubella in the past or have recently developed it, and further blood tests may be needed at intervals of two to three weeks to see if the antibody levels have increased. If the results show that there has been a recent infection and it is within the first twelve weeks of pregnancy, it is customary for the doctor to advise you of the risks of continuing. Under English law termination of pregnancy may be performed if in the opinion of two medical practitioners there is a substantial risk that the unborn child will be affected. You may not of course wish to consider termination but, if you do, your doctor will discuss it with you.

How Long does Immunity Last?

Antibodies from a prior infection or vaccination in childhood may persist for up to sixteen years. The girl who is vaccinated at thirteen but does not start her first pregnancy until the age of thirty may do so unaware that she is no longer adequately protected. Most antenatal clinics screen women for rubella antibodies at the first booking appointment but, although this provides valuable evidence on the efficacy of vaccination for future pregnancies, it is too late for the pregnancy in question.

In a small number of women vaccination fails to provide protection and for this reason as well as the limited duration of immunity it has been suggested that all women should be screened *before* starting a pregnancy.

What if Pregnancy Occurs Soon after Vaccination?

Women who have been given the protective injection are advised not to become pregnant for at least three months. If a pregnancy inadvertently occurs, the doctor should be immediately notified so that specialist advice can be sought. Contrary to what one might expect, a number of studies have shown that it is extremely unusual for the unborn child to be affected by the vaccine, although the decision on whether or not the pregnancy should continue is a very individual and delicate one which can only be taken after expert counselling.

Can Rubella Recur More than Once?

Re-infection with the rubella virus is extremely unusual, but possible. The immunity afforded by vaccination may be temporary in certain circumstances or the vaccine may be too weak to produce the desired effect. If you are in any doubt, your degree of protection should be confirmed by a further blood test.

Other Viral Infections in Pregnancy

There are a number of conditions similar to rubella which may produce no symptoms at all, or they may cause vague flu-like illnesses with a fever, fatigue, swelling of glands and a sore throat, and sometimes a rash. If contracted in the first few weeks of pregnancy, some of these conditions may have an effect on the developing baby. They are discussed in more detail below.

Measles

Unlike rubella the measles virus does not appear to cause birth defects, though it can be linked to increased risk of miscarriage or premature labour and is quite a severe illness if it is contracted during pregnancy.

If you contract measles near your due date, there is a risk of infection to the newborn which could be serious, and an injection to lessen the risk can be given.

Chickenpox (Varicella)

Eighty-five to ninety-five per cent of the adult population are immune to chickenpox as they have probably contracted it in childhood. If contracted for the first time in pregnancy, there is a slight risk of damage to the fetus but this is very small. Even if the fetus is exposed when at its most vulnerable, during the first half of pregnancy, there is only a two to five per cent chance of its developing any defects. If exposure occurs in the second half of pregnancy, then damage is very rare.

Chickenpox once again becomes more of a threat if you contract it close to term, when infection can lead to your baby being born with chickenpox. The risk is reduced if delivery does not occur until you develop antibodies and pass them to your baby through the placenta, which may take one to two weeks, but if you develop chickenpox within four or five days of delivery there is a twenty per cent chance the newborn will arrive infected and will develop a characteristic rash within a week or so, which can be extremely serious.

The risk of the newborn being infected is small if you contract chickenpox between five and twenty-one days before delivery, and serious consequences from the disease at that point are rare.

In general terms, however, chickenpox is more severe during a pregnancy and you should go to your general practitioner if you develop a rash and generally feel unwell. If you are pregnant and chickenpox has been confirmed, then some doctors like to give an injection of ZIG (zoster immune globulin), or possibly another drug called aciclovir, which lessens the severity of the condition. It is as well not to go to the antenatal clinic until you have been fully checked and are not contagious.

Mumps

Mumps in pregnancy is rare because most young adults again have had the disease or were immunised against it in childhood. Occasionally developing mumps in pregnancy triggers uterine contractions and thus can lead to miscarriage in early pregnancy or to premature labour later. There is no evidence that mumps can harm the developing fetus.

Toxoplasmosis

This condition is a rare silent infection with the parasite toxoplasma and occurs either from contact with infected cats' faeces or from eating or handling undercooked meat. Most women have no symptoms, though sometimes it causes symptoms similar to flu or glandular fever.

It is often called the 'French disease' because of the incidence of commonly eaten raw meat. If you develop this condition in early pregnancy and you are not immune, certain complications can occur including miscarriage, stillbirth, premature labour, and low birth weight. Occasionally the fetus is affected by the virus as it crosses the placenta and the baby can be born with certain handicaps. Many women may become infected during pregnancy without knowing it and the baby is usually unharmed, but it is important to inform the doctor if you develop flu-like symptoms in early pregnancy or a rash in the first three months.

There is no known vaccine for toxoplasmosis but, if the condition is suspected, a blood test can tell whether you are already immune, i.e. have developed toxoplasmosis at some time in the past. If there is any doubt as to whether this is a first infection, or if the blood test is high, then it may need to be repeated a week or two later. If the antibody level in the blood rises, it may be necessary to test the blood of the baby by fetal blood sampling (see page 149) to make sure that the virus has not crossed the placenta and entered the bloodstream of the baby. If this does happen in the early few weeks of pregnancy, then a decision may have to be made as to whether pregnancy should continue or not. If there is a risk that the baby may be infected with the toxoplasma virus and after counselling the couple have elected to continue with the pregnancy, then a course of a specific antibiotic (spiramycin) may lower the incidence of problems with the developing baby.

In some countries, e.g. France in particular, toxoplasma blood tests are routinely performed, either before pregnancy or in the early weeks. In the UK at present this is not the policy, largely because the incidence of toxoplasmosis causing problems with the fetus is very small, and the precise diagnosis of whether a fetus may be affected may not be apparent until several blood tests and blood samples from the baby have been repeated at regular intervals. Sometimes an accurate answer cannot be given until twenty or twenty-four weeks into the pregnancy. If you are worried about toxoplasmosis, talk to the doctor and, even if a particular hospital policy does not include toxoplasma as a routine blood test, it can always be arranged.

Uncooked or raw meat should be avoided. Cats can pose more of a problem, especially if they are hunters who will pick up the organisms from the animals and birds they catch. It is probably wise to make sure you keep away from cat litter trays, or at least wear rubber gloves when handling them. If you wear gloves while gardening you should be reasonably safe.

Cytomegalovirus (CMV)

This condition may cause a mild general illness and may actually reside in the cervix for long periods of time. It may well be, and probably is, sexually transmitted and is more common in lower socio-economic groups. Unfortunately not much is understood about this virus or how to control it and occasionally an unborn child may acquire the virus at birth or across the placenta. This can cause growth problems, hearing defects and a low IQ. There is unfortunately no way of testing for this disease in any regular laboratory, and vaccines as yet do not exist. A blood test can tell you whether the virus is or has been in your body.

Hepatitis (Liver Infection)

The virus responsible can be transmitted in many ways, for example by blood transfusion, needle puncture, tattooing, ear piercing, contamination by human faeces or blood, or occasionally by sexual intercourse. The later in pregnancy that hepatitis is acquired the greater the risk of the child acquiring it and thus possibly becoming a carrier. The symptoms may be specific, as in the case of yellow jaundice, or you may develop a flu-like illness similar to a number of other viral conditions. Fortunately a vaccine is available now to protect susceptible and exposed individuals. Screening is usually a part of antenatal care and if you are at risk you will be advised to be vaccinated if you test negative before the onset of pregnancy. If you are a hepatitis carrier, then the baby should be vaccinated at birth with gamma globulin.

Listeriosis

This is an uncommon virus infection in early pregnancy which can occasionally cause miscarriages and stillbirths. The organism may be contained in certain soft cheeses or unpasteurised dairy products. Some authorities suggest that processed meat products such as pate are also a possible source of the condition. Pre-cooked chilled foods and ready-made dishes found in cold cabinets in foodstores are a recognised cause of the listeria bacteria and, if you are reheating food of any description, make sure it is well heated right through.

Sexually Transmitted Diseases

The incidence of serious sexually transmitted diseases has increased dramatically in recent years and a greater number of women of child-bearing age are acquiring these infections, thus putting a greater number of unborn children at risk. There are a number of mild conditions such as moniliasis (thrush – see pages 163–164) and trichomonas (see page 165), which may be acquired or transmitted through sexual activity but there are also some more serious conditions such as syphilis, gonorrhoea, herpes and the HIV virus and these will be discussed separately.

Syphilis

In the past syphilis played the role now taken over by AIDS. It destroyed king and commoner alike and produced millions of deformed infants. Only the advent of penicillin arrested its ravages. It seems, however, that syphilis is making a comeback, certainly in parts of the United States, and it is still common to give a blood test for this condition at the first visit to the antenatal clinic.

Syphilis is notoriously difficult to diagnose and is caused by a thin corkscrew-like organism which thrives in a warm, moist environment. It enters the body through any tiny break in the skin and burrows its way into the bloodstream. Sexual contact is the usual source of infection. Syphilis produces a painless ulcer that normally appears at the site where the organism enters the body, i.e. mouth, throat or vagina, and it takes anything from ten to ninety days for the swelling to appear after the initial contact.

One of the problems in diagnosis is that the ulcer may not be noticed since it causes no pain and tends to disappear whether treated or not within three to six weeks. However, the organisms remain in the body so that at any time from six to twelve months after the appearance of the ulcer new symptoms may arise, such as a skin rash, temporary baldness, low-grade fever and swollen glands. These complaints may last for a few days or months but eventually they, too, disappear. Syphilis loses its infectiousness as it progresses. After the first two years a person rarely transmits the condition through intercourse and after four years it is not contagious.

Until then, however, a pregnant woman can infect her unborn child. A fetus infected early in pregnancy may die or be disfigured. If infected later, the child may show no sign of infection for months or years after birth. It is for this reason that a routine blood test is performed at the first booking appointment in early pregnancy in order to detect either a previous or more recently acquired infection. With a recent infection, treatment is by antibiotics, which normally halt the spread of syphilis to the unborn baby.

Gonorrhoea

Gonorrhoea is much more common and potentially more dangerous than syphilis. In men the symptoms, which are both painful and obvious, include a burning sensation on urination, or discharge from the penis, but in as many as nine out of ten infected women there are no symptoms at all. The organism responsible for gonorrhoea can live undetected in the vagina, cervix or tubes for months or even years, but eventually women develop complications, such as chronic pelvic infection, as the organism spreads.

If symptoms do arise in women there is usually pain in passing urine, with a foul-smelling discharge from the vagina or abdominal pain from infection of the pelvic organs. If a woman with gonorrhoea becomes pregnant, her disease infects the unborn baby, increasing the risk of premature labour, growth impairment and illness in the newborn. It can also cause a serious form of eye disease or conjunctivitis which may lead to blindness in the baby.

Treatment for gonorrhoea in pregnancy is the same as at other times, by penicillin or a similar antibiotic. It is important that, if you experience any of the symptoms mentioned, or have been having sexual intercourse with a partner who develops either a sore penis or a discharge and urinary pain, these facts are reported immediately to your doctor so that appropriate tests can be made and treatment instituted.

Herpes

Genital herpes is currently enjoying almost as much media exposure as advertisements for cigarettes and alcohol. The reason for this wide coverage is that the disease is spread by sexual intercourse, cannot be cured easily, may cause cancer, and may be passed to new partners without either being aware of the risk. And (final horror) may be passed to newborn babies threatening them with death or brain damage. To round off this catalogue of doom, a substantial proportion of those infected may suffer over a period of years from recurrent attacks which effectively prevent some of them from enjoying a regular sex life.

In comparison syphilis and gonorrhoea appear to be relatively mild. So severe has been the shock of this disease that some members of the permissive society wish they had never joined! Certainly the illness is occurring more frequently and causing much more trouble than it did in the past. However, while it can be most unpleasant and dangerous for some sufferers, many of the dangers have been grossly exaggerated for the great majority of those infected.

Herpes is often referred to as a new disease although the name has been used for a variety of skin conditions. The word 'herpes' is derived from a Greek verb meaning 'to creep'. The first descriptions of a genital disorder that was probably herpes date from the early eighteenth century when the sexual mode of its transmission was soon appreciated. It was not until 1990 that it was suggested that herpes might be a virus infection, but in the early 1960s two main strains of the virus were identified: type 1 causing most non-genital infections, and type 2 causing genital infections. However, the two forms often mix and type 2, the only significant venereal disease which is proved to be caused by a virus, may appear both on the mouth and on the genitals.

Genital herpes appears as a series of very painful blisters on the lips of the vagina, the cervix, the pubic area and occasionally the buttocks and thighs. The first blisters persist for two to four weeks and then disappear, recurring for periods of a week or a fortnight, often during times of stress. In men the outer covering of the penis and the outer layer of the foreskin are more commonly attacked than the shaft of the penis, while the scrotum is rarely affected.

Herpes ulcers are often difficult to diagnose. They usually start as small groups of reddish blisters about 2–3mm in diameter which begin to discharge clear, yellowish fluid within one to two days and then leave behind a series of painful ulcers. These usually heal fairly quickly forming crusts or scabs within four to five days and the healing is usually complete within three weeks. Herpes tends to recur in forty to sixty per cent of patients and, although subsequent attacks are far less severe, they can prove to be more troublesome. The events that initiate recurrent herpes vary widely, though they can be annoyingly constant for an individual. They include attacks of fever, exposure to ultraviolet light, trauma, menstruation and stress.

If genital herpes occurs during a pregnancy, there is a small risk of miscarriage as in a number of viral illnesses. However, a much greater risk occurs later in pregnancy. If there is an active crop of blisters in the last few weeks, then there is a serious danger that the infant will acquire the disease while passing through the birth canal during delivery. The percentage of babies who develop herpes after such exposure is not known but the consequences for those who do are devastating. The death rate for newborns with visible herpes is as high as sixty per cent and those who survive suffer severe damage to the eyes and nervous system. The effect on the newborn is much less severe if the mother is exposed to recurrent attacks rather than developing herpes for the first time. Much controversy rages around the safest method of delivery in a mother who presents with herpes vesicles. Some authorities believe that a Caesarean section prevents any spread of herpes through the vaginal canal. Certainly, if vesicles are obvious and the membranes have ruptured within four hours, then Caesarean section is almost always indicated.

It must be stressed that vaginal delivery is quite safe if there are no active blisters in the last few weeks of pregnancy. In the past swab tests were taken from the vagina or ulcer area to see whether the infecting organism had gained access to the body and if so Caesarean section was indicated. In fact this is not necessary and it must again be emphasised that the only danger is with active blisters occurring at the time of delivery.

Treatment of Herpes

If you notice a painful blister around the vulva or vagina during pregnancy you should report this immediately to your doctor because there are good and safe treatments. The best is a substance called Acyclovir which comes in the form of cream or tablets and a local application of cream often makes the ulcer disappear and takes away the discomfort. Alternatively a course of tablets can be given over a five-day period and your doctor will advise you which is best. Remember that there is a danger of spreading the virus from the genital region to the eyes and, although the risk of inadvertently touching the genitals and then eyes during sleep is remote, it is a good idea to wear pants or pyjama trousers in bed to make sure of avoiding genital–hand–eye contact.

Herpes sufferers should avoid sexual intercourse when genital sores are present and ideally avoid sexual activity as soon as they experience the infection, and intercourse should always be with a condom.

Prognosis

It must be emphasised that it is common for herpes blisters to occur once or twice and then not again, although sometimes there are recurring attacks which can be quite distressing. There is little danger to the unborn child if herpes occurs in pregnancy and the only dangers exist if there are active ulcers present during the latter stages of pregnancy and then only if delivery is by the vaginal route.

If no blisters are present in the last few weeks of pregnancy then there is every reason to anticipate a normal vaginal delivery. Sufferers from herpes may obtain much support from self-help groups which exist in several parts of the country, for example, the Herpes Association.

AIDS (Acquired Immune Deficiency Syndrome)

This is caused by the human immune deficiency virus (HIV). The incubation period may be as long as ten years. Most women acquire AIDS through intravenous drug use and rarely by heterosexual contact with an infected partner. The presence of other sexually transmitted diseases, particular herpes and syphilis, increases the risk of HIV infection. There is practically no risk of contracting the disorder by casual contact.

The symptoms of early AIDS are many and varied and difficult to classify. If it is suggested that fatigue, weight loss and flu-like complaints are characteristics, then half of those reading this book will think they have AIDS. If in fact there is any significant reason to suspect or fear AIDS, your doctor can give you a blood test.

Infection in pregnancy by the virus is a threat not just to the expectant mother but to her baby as well. A large proportion of babies born to mothers who are HIV positive will develop the infection within six months and it is suspected that pregnancy itself could speed up the process of the disease in the mother. For this reason some infected women choose to terminate their pregnancy. Most infants born of infected mothers will carry the mother's HIV antibodies for as long as fifteen months after delivery and this makes the diagnosis of AIDS in these youngsters much more difficult. If AIDS does not exist, then these antibodies disappear without doing any harm.

The current question is whether there should be a screening process which would routinely test all pregnant women, as there is for syphilis, or whether the test should simply be available to all women as it is at present. The argument against routine screening is that it would present the mother with a problem which could not be solved. There is as yet no treatment for the disease which would prevent the baby becoming infected or the mother seriously ill. Termination of pregnancy of course is offered to all mothers who are infected.

Screening for AIDS should ideally take place before conception, when the information derived can help women to make important decisions in their lives. The availability of good counselling, both before the AIDS test and following a positive result, is imperative and many authorities have trained midwives to provide this service. There is now good evidence that triple therapy, i.e. using three specific drugs, will improve the maternal condition and postpone the onset of infection. This is one good reason why women should be screened in early pregnancy as the outcome for mother and baby can be altered. Many antenatal clinics in the country offer HIV testing at patients' request.

CHAPTER 4

The Third Month

(8–12 Weeks)

Changes in Your Baby

By eight weeks the embryo is still only 4cms (about 1.5ins) long but inside this tiny body all the organs found in a fully grown human are already in place. The fetus now weighs about 13gms, less than half an ounce. The face is slowly forming, the eyes are more obvious and there is a mouth with a tongue. There are the beginnings of hands and feet and the major internal organs are all developing.

By twelve weeks, sexual differentiation has taken place and the embryo has developed the organs which will show whether it is male or female.

The placenta, which is rooted to the lining of the womb, is growing and it is here that oxygen and food from the mother's bloodstream pass across into the baby's bloodstream, being carried to the baby along the umbilical cord. Inside the womb the baby begins to float in a bag of fluid called the amniotic sac or amniotic liquor. This sac breaks before or during labour and the fluid drains out.

The umbilical cord is the baby's lifeline and is the link between mother and baby. Blood circulates through the cord, carrying oxygen and food to the baby and waste products away.

Changes in You

Changes are still gradual and you may not yet 'show' much at this time, but you will probably be thinking about looking at maternity clothes even though you don't really need them yet. The breasts become even fuller and they may tingle or become quite heavy. There is a sense of fullness in the lower abdomen as well, although the uterus is still only a little larger than a grapefruit.

As the twelfth week approaches unpleasant features such as nausea, vomiting and constipation diminish. This is mainly because the placenta has now fully formed and has taken over the function of maintaining the pregnancy which your own body and your hormones have done up until now. This is the stage of stability where misfortunes such as miscarriage become remote.

Again, as the uterus enlarges in the abdomen, it is not unusual to get twinges of pain or discomfort low down on either side. This is normally due to the stretching of the ligaments that support the uterus and is very common. If the pain really becomes troublesome or is located towards one side or the other, then consult your doctor.

When to See Your Doctor

If a pregnancy is suspected, then an appointment with your family doctor should be made, who will confirm the pregnancy either by examination or by one of the pregnancy tests previously discussed (see pages 61–62). Once the pregnancy is confirmed your doctor will discuss the antenatal care and your options regarding labour and delivery. The maternity services in the UK have expanded enormously in the last twenty to thirty years to allow you a choice as to who looks after you during your pregnancy and labour, and where you actually have the care and delivery. There are a number of different options which your doctor can discuss and advise on.

After the first consultation with your doctor, who will outline the sort of care available in the area, it may be that you will want to think about the options, discuss with friends and perhaps read the various pamphlets that are available explaining the choices. Many family doctors enjoy and are trained in antenatal care and some can actually look after you during delivery in your local general hospital, but it is important at this consultation that there is good communication as you may well have your own strong ideas about the way in which the antenatal care is to be carried out and where and how you will have your baby. Some family doctors do not do obstetric work, in which case referral will probably be made to another doctor in the same practice.

The type and place of antenatal care you receive is linked with the choice of where your baby is to be delivered, but often the first antenatal consultation and booking clinic will be at the local consultant's unit where the sort of care you would like can be discussed further.

Shared Care

The most common option if you choose to have your baby in hospital is a scheme whereby you see the hospital staff two or three times during the pregnancy while your family doctor and/or the community midwife undertake the rest of your care. You will normally be seen at the hospital for a booking appointment at around ten to twelve weeks, again at about thirty-four or thirty-six weeks, and then probably once more when the baby is due.

Hospital-based Antenatal Care

You may decide that you would prefer all the visits to be carried out at the local hospital where you will probably have your baby, in which case your family doctor will arrange this for you.

Family Doctor/Community Care

You may feel that you would like to have your antenatal care in the familiar surroundings of your doctor's surgery, particularly if you have decided to have your baby at home. Again, this can be discussed with the consultant team at your first booking appointment.

Domino Scheme

Domino stands for 'Domiciliary – In/Out' and this scheme was introduced many years ago. It consists of a community midwife who shares your antenatal care with the hospital and your family doctor, often visiting you at home to do the antenatal checks. The same midwife will look after you at home, will take you into hospital, deliver your baby and arrange for you to go home very soon after the birth, say within forty-eight hours. You can of course stay longer in hospital if you wish.

Midwife Delivery

If you choose a midwife to deliver your baby, then the community midwives will care for you throughout the antenatal and postnatal periods and you will be delivered by a midwife, possibly not seeing a doctor at all. The opportunity for you to see a midwife throughout your antenatal care and be delivered by her or one of the midwifery team, and only seeing a doctor if the midwife is concerned about the pregnancy, varies from one region to another. In some units you would be seen for your first visit by the doctor and then once or twice during the pregnancy, or not at all unless complications arose. Other units have midwifery care only, where you could choose solely to see a midwife for antenatal care and delivery.

Whatever choice you make you can be assured that there will be full back-up by hospital staff should problems arise.

Team Midwifery

Practitioners concerned with maternity care are continually looking for better methods of helping you prepare for pregnancy, not only in terms of physical fitness but also comfort and continuity of care. Certain hospitals are now setting up team midwifery units whereby a group of about four to five midwives work together to care for you and your baby through the pregnancy and the postnatal period. The principle here is that you get to know the team of midwives, building up a rapport with them, and you will also be able to discuss with them the plans you have for the labour and delivery, knowing that you will be in contact with one of these midwives throughout labour.

This plan, which is relatively recent, is a very welcome addition to the maternity services and has great advantages for both mothers and midwives, who gain a great deal of job satisfaction from caring for women and their families right through the maternity period.

Where to Have Your Baby

Many years ago the scarcity of hospital beds only permitted women in certain categories to have their babies in hospital, and they were selected on the grounds of being possibly at risk of having complications. As the hospital building programme thirty years ago developed, more and more women had their babies in hospital as it was thought this was the safest place to be and that any emergency treatment for the mother or baby was readily available.

Over the last ten years there has been a different approach to maternity care, prompted by pregnant women themselves, who felt that the choices of where to have antenatal care and delivery were limited. There seemed to be dissatisfaction with the traditional patterns of care and a Health Committee Report on Maternity Services was published in 1992. This investigated a number of issues and made several recommendations as to how maternity services might be managed in the future. The principal findings were:

1. The policy of encouraging all women to give birth in hospitals could not be justified on grounds of safety, given the absence of conclusive evidence.

2. There was a strong desire among women for the provision of continuity of care throughout pregnancy and childbirth, and many regarded midwives as the group best placed and equipped to provide this.

3. There seemed to be a widespread demand among women for greater choice in the type of care they received.

4. A home birth or birth in a small maternity unit were options which had not been available to the majority of women in this country and many were unhappy about this.

5. Many interventions during labour, such as epidurals, episiotomies, Caesarean sections and monitoring, should be subject to detailed

and accurate research, thus preventing many women having to undergo such procedures as routine.

6. The experience of the hospital environment often deterred women from taking control over their own bodies and left them thinking that they had not had the labour and delivery they had hoped for.

7. It seemed that many women preferred the atmosphere of their local doctor's surgery and that community-based antenatal care should replace many of the hospital visits, provided there was ready access to specialist assessment.

8. Within hospital women should be able to exercise choice as to the personnel who would be responsible for their care.

9. The relationship between the woman and her care-giver was recognised as being of fundamental importance.

These recommendations led to a document called *Changing Childbirth*, emphasising the importance of choice for pregnant women in all aspects of their care.

Consultant Maternity Unit

If you choose to have your baby in hospital under a consultant you will be seen by one of the team of doctors during your antenatal visits and your overall care will be supervised by the consultant's team.

When you go into hospital to have your baby you will be attended by the hospital midwives on the labour ward and, should any problem arise, one of the medical team will be there to assist. Consultants lead the team and set the policies and you should see your consultant at least once or twice during your antenatal care, but you may not actually come into contact during delivery if things are straight-forward. The hospital will probably have two or three consultants and it may be that you will want to be referred to one that you know or have heard about.

The two main disadvantages of entire hospital care are the waiting time in the clinics and lack of continuity. Because the average hospital looks after two to three thousand women having their babies every year and at an average antenatal clinic perhaps eighty to ninety women are seen, there is a certain amount of waiting around in the clinics, which can be annoying. Also, because hospital doctors are changing and the nature of their job demands that they must be available for emergencies elsewhere in the hospital, it may also be that the same doctor is not often seen at each visit. It must be remembered, however, that if any complications or problems arise the consultant in charge of the team will automatically know about them and will be there to make decisions.

You may for some reason wish not to be referred to a particular hospital close at hand. You should discuss this with your family doctor who should be able to refer you to a neighbouring hospital.

GP Unit Delivery

The idea here is that your family doctor and midwife will look after your antenatal and postnatal care and either the midwife or the doctor will actually deliver you in a unit in a local hospital, where the atmosphere is much less rushed than in a large hospital. This scheme was first introduced about twenty years ago and for a number of reasons has not been developed. It is still possible for your family doctor or local midwife to deliver you within the confines of the consultant based unit and this has the advantages of providing continuity of care whilst having expert medical attention in the hospital setting if needed.

'Stand-alone' Midwifery Units

The midwifery profession in this country has been working for some time towards a system of midwifery-only care, both in the antenatal period and during delivery. It has recently been suggested that a situation might be possible where midwives had their own caseload and took full responsibility for women under their care. The natural progression from this would be for midwives to be given the opportunity of establishing and running maternity units, both within and outside hospitals. There are a number of units in the country where this does in fact already occur.

WHO'S WHO IN MATERNITY CARE

Consultant Obstetrician: The senior specialist in overall charge of maternity care in the hospital. The number of consultants in each hospital varies from three to six or more, depending on the size of the unit. You will be allocated to a particular consultant, usually at the request of the doctor who refers you, and will remain under his or her care for the duration of pregnancy.

Consultants work with a team of trained staff. You will probably meet your consultant at the first booking clinic and at varying stages during subsequent clinics. Do remember that, because of the number of women attending each clinic, it may not always be possible to see the consultant or the same member of the team at each visit. If you have not seen the consultant and are anxious to do so, then talk to the sister in charge of the antenatal clinic.

Consultant Paediatrician: A senior specialist in overall charge of newborn babies and children. Paediatricians work in teams just like obstetricians, though you may not see a paediatric doctor until the baby is born. Paediatricians do not routinely attend births but will examine the baby soon afterwards.

A paediatrician is usually present at a Caesarean section and will attend during a normal birth if it is anticipated that breathing difficulties could occur in the baby, for example, due to a known complication in pregnancy in the mother such as diabetes, or fetal distress (see pages 304–305).

Registrar: The doctor, immediately junior to the consultant, who is in the advanced stages of training in their career. This grade of doctor is always resident in the hospital and available to come to the Labour Ward at a moment's notice if help is required with delivery.

Senior House Officer: A junior hospital doctor doing his early obstetric training. The SHO will be present at delivery if things are not absolutely straightforward and is immediately below the registrar in the line of command. Most SHOs are capable of performing routine forceps deliveries (see pages 288–292), episiotomies (see pages 263–265) and surgical repair of a cut or episiotomy.

If delivery is complicated or needs different expertise, the registrar will be contacted who will, in turn, inform the consultant.

Midwife: A specialist in the management of normal pregnancy and labour. Some midwives work in hospitals and others in the community. If the labour and delivery are straightforward the midwife will probably deliver the baby. Midwives also staff the lying-in wards in hospitals. Like the hierarchy of the consultants and the junior team of doctors, the nursing staff consists of senior and junior midwives and many hospitals have student midwives attached to the unit who assist the senior staff.

Family Doctor: Many family doctors play a large part in looking after pregnant women in the antenatal period but few actually supervise delivery. Community-based antenatal clinics usually take place in local surgeries and are run by the doctor and the midwife together. Some family doctors like to see their patients all the way through pregnancy and others intermittently. The doctor will have received training in maternity care recognised by a diploma from the Royal College of Obstetricians and Gynaecologists (DRCOG).

Health Visitor: A nurse, usually attached to a Health Centre. She will visit you from the time the midwife care finishes – about ten days after the baby is born. She is there to help and advise in the care of the baby and will be introduced at some time during the antenatal period. Health visitors are mainly based in the community and care not only for new mothers but also elderly and other patients.

Anaesthetist: A specially trained doctor in giving general anaesthesia and local anaesthesia (epidurals – see pages 274–281). These doctors work in a team in much the same way as obstetricians, i.e. there are consultants and junior staff. In almost every hospital in the country there is a resident, or living-in, senior anaesthetist whose main job is to cover emergencies on the Labour Ward.

Radiologist: The radiologist is a doctor specifically trained in imaging techniques, i.e. taking X-rays, performing ultrasound and other more sophisticated procedures. You may come across a radiologist in the Ultrasound Department, though the majority of scans are done by the radiographers.

Radiographer: The radiographer is not a doctor but is a health professional trained in performing imaging techniques such as X-rays and ultrasound, and it is likely that the radiographer will be the operator of the scanning machine.

Physio-therapist: The physiotherapist encourages and teaches antenatal care and exercises, helps to combat the pain of labour, looks after women who have delivered in the lying-in period, and is skilled in teaching muscle strengthening activity and dealing with other ligament and joint problems that may occur in or after pregnancy.

Many obstetric units have a physiotherapist particularly skilled in maternity care, whom you will probably meet conducting preparation courses during the antenatal period, as well as after the baby is born.

Social Worker: Formerly called an almoner, this professional assists with social problems that may occur during or after pregnancy. The social worker has special counselling skills for women who have emotional or social problems and bridges the gap between your family doctor and the health visitor. There is usually a medical social worker attached to each maternity unit with a special interest in maternity care.

Medical Students: Many hospitals have undergraduate medical students attached to them for the purposes of training. These students learn about antenatal care, labour and delivery with the medical team and may be involved in your care on the Labour Ward. Students are required to undertake a certain number of normal deliveries under supervision. Their training also consists of learning how to repair a cut or episiotomy.

If you don't like the idea of medical students being present during delivery, make your feelings known to the Labour Ward sister.

While there is broad acceptance that midwives are professionals in their own right, there remains a difference of opinion in the profession as to whether a pregnant woman needs to be seen by a doctor at any stage providing the pregnancy proceeds quite normally. There must obviously be close co-operation between midwives and emergency services so that women or babies who develop complications can be referred.

It remains to be seen over the next few years how many women prefer midwifery-only care and, just as importantly, the outcome for the mother and baby will need continual review and assessment as compared with more conventional methods.

Delivery at Home

Although at present in the UK about ninety per cent of women are delivered in a hospital maternity unit, home delivery, which was feared as a poor second best by most women twenty-five years ago, is now considered desirable by their daughters. Some women perceive obvious advantages in delivering their babies in their own surroundings and feel better able to cope in this situation. However, the high percentage of hospital confinements has come about for several reasons.

Modern obstetric care is designed not only to prevent complications but also to recognise and treat them promptly and, as it is impossible to be sure that pregnancy, labour and delivery, as well as the progress of a newborn infant, will be absolutely normal until after events have occurred, most obstetricians prefer to look after their patients where all the facilities and extra services that may be required in an emergency are to hand.

Some women prefer hospital delivery because they have complete confidence that everything is prepared for them and only in hospital can they be assured of adequate rest after delivery. There has recently been a resurgence of interest in delivering babies at home and many women rightly feel that the place to have their babies is in their own surroundings where they will feel relaxed and comfortable and where the medical attendants are invited guests. If you have strong feelings about having your baby at home, you should discuss this with your family doctor or consultant when you first visit the booking clinic. Because the interest in home births is reasonably recent, you may find that there is some opposition to your views, but most doctors and midwives will be sympathetic to what you want and will explain fully the advantages and disadvantages.

There may be situations where you will be advised strictly not to have your baby at home. This may be because certain complications develop during the pregnancy or it may be that a past history of a medical disease may increase the likelihood of a problem with delivery and in this case it is as well to listen carefully to the medical advice. If, however, risks of having your baby at home are minimal, then this can be arranged appropriately through the hospital and your local doctor's surgery. Preparations for a home confinement will be carried out and everyone concerned will be made aware of this in case an emergency situation arises which may mean that you need to be transferred to hospital at a later date.

Possible Problems in the First Few Weeks of Pregnancy

The two main serious conditions that occur in the first two months that may result in loss of the pregnancy are miscarriage and ectopic pregnancy. Although both may start with some bleeding from the vagina, this symptom is common and not necessarily significant. However, once pregnancy has been diagnosed any bleeding from the vagina should be taken seriously and reported to the doctor. Although there are many minor causes of bleeding that will not interfere in any way with the pregnancy, sometimes it can be more dangerous.

Decidual or Implantation Bleeding

A small amount of blood loss often occurs without pain around the expected time of the next period and this is because small fragments of the lining of the uterus can be dislodged while the early pregnancy sinks into its wall. This shows itself as vaginal spotting which can be red or brown, small in amount and usually clears within a few days. Occasionally there can be some mild cramp-like feelings as well.

Bleeding in Early Pregnancy

This can occur from anywhere in the lower genital area just as in the non-pregnant woman. One of the causes of this is a cervical erosion. This term is used to describe the appearance of the outside covering of the cervix which looks rather like an inflamed ulcer because of increased congestion in pregnancy. Bleeding here often occurs after intercourse or for no particular reason and no treatment is necessary as the bleeding tends to be mild, clears up of its own accord, and leads to no problems. Occasionally small polyps or harmless warts grow in the uterus or cervix. Again, they usually cause no problem to the pregnancy; the doctor should be able to diagnose this and no treatment is necessary.

Other causes of bleeding include varicose veins of the vulva, infections of the vagina and, very rarely, cancer of the cervix.

Miscarriage

Painless vaginal bleeding can, however, be an impending sign of a miscarriage and it is not always easy when examined at the first consultation for the doctor to decide whether the bleeding is coming just from a harmless cause or whether it may prove to be one of the first signs that a miscarriage may occur.

The words 'miscarriage' and 'abortion' describe exactly the same thing, i.e. the interruption and loss of a pregnancy before the end of the twenty-fourth week. In British law, which has recently changed, a baby born after the twenty-fourth week is considered to be viable (capable of survival), which is of medico-legal importance as pregnancies must not be terminated after this time. Estimates vary but approximately fourteen to eighteen per cent of all pregnancies (one in six) end in a miscarriage and the great majority of these occur before the twelfth week of pregnancy. Unfortunately many miscarriages occur for no obvious or demonstrable reason. A miscarriage is more likely to occur in the woman over thirty-five who requires six months or longer to conceive or who has had a previous miscarriage.

Known causes include general medical diseases such as diabetes, heart problems, kidney disorders, abnormalities of the pelvic organs (e.g. fibroids – see pages 251–252) or malformations of the uterus, a cervix torn during a previous birth, or an acute infection causing a high fever. Miscarriage is also more common in women who have certain vaginal infections.

Probably the commonest reason for miscarrying is a fault in the chromosomes or in the make-up of the cells of the baby which results in some structural abnormality. Because Nature tends to discard what is not normal the human uterus is then more likely to expel its contents. Unfortunately this is not always the case as not all deformities are incompatible with life. Other incidental happenings in the first few weeks of pregnancy – minor accidents, overwork, mental strain, excessive exercise, travel, stomach upsets and so on – are often blamed for causing a miscarriage but the fact is that the embryo that is destined to stay inside the uterus clings very strongly to its new bed.

A miscarriage after twelve weeks is much less common, though a well-recognised cause is incompetence of the cervix (see pages 200–201).

Signs of a Miscarriage

The first signal of an impending miscarriage may be bleeding from the vagina which often occurs after the first or second period. If the bleeding is slight and there is no pain, the outcome for the pregnancy is good and in most instances the bleeding will stop and the pregnancy will proceed normally.

If bleeding occurs in the first few weeks your doctor should be informed and you will probably be told to take things easy and rest in bed until the bleeding stops. It is usually all right to get up for toilet purposes but you should keep housework to a minimum, avoid heavy lifting and refrain from sexual relations. If no further bleeding occurs, there should be no worry and this early stage is no more than a threatened miscarriage which indicates that the uterus is trying to decide whether or not to expel its contents.

When the doctor carries out an examination, if it is only a threatened miscarriage, the cervix or neck of the womb will be tightly shut and there will be little pain. As it would be impossible and probably not necessary to hospitalise every woman who bleeds in the early stages of pregnancy, admission to hospital is usually reserved for those in whom the pregnancy is particularly precious, such as those with a history of recurrent miscarriages.

One of the problems with a threatened miscarriage is the time taken in deciding whether the pregnancy is all right or not, and whether miscarriage is likely to occur. Unfortunately this is a bit of a waiting game as there is no easy way to make a definite diagnosis straight away and, provided the doctor believes that the pregnancy is still intact, no interference is the rule.

An ultrasound scan (see pages 149–156) may be helpful in detecting whether a pregnancy is still alive or not as early as four weeks after the last missed period, and nowadays it is common for women who do bleed to have an ultrasound for this reason. If the pregnancy is too early, then the ultrasound will be repeated ten to fourteen days later to see whether there has been normal growth of the fetus or not.

If the bleeding persists, becomes heavier and bright red, and there is pain, then the prognosis is more in doubt and admission to hospital may be necessary for observation and further tests to see whether the pregnancy can survive. If the pregnancy is not viable, i.e. alive, then the bleeding will only stop when the uterus has been emptied spontaneously or by a small operation known as a D & C whereby the products are scraped out of the uterus.

Missed Abortion

By this term we mean that there are no outward signs that anything is wrong, no bleeding occurs, but the baby in the very early stages of pregnancy may have died within the womb. The mother may often say that the feelings of pregnancy that were present early on, such as tingling of the breasts and nausea may subside, and the woman may just say that she doesn't feel pregnant any more. Sometimes the doctor may find at a routine antenatal visit that the uterus has failed to grow in size since the previous attendance.

If there is doubt as to whether the baby is growing or not, an ultrasound scan will be performed which should clearly show absence of the fetal heart beating if the pregnancy has succumbed. Sometimes repeated ultrasound tests need to be performed at regular intervals and urinary pregnancy testing also repeated.

Some doctors suggest that, if there is definite evidence that the baby is not alive in the first three months, then it is best to do a D & C and evacuate the uterus so that the pregnancy can be finished and another one tried for again in a few months. If there is doubt as to whether the pregnancy is alive or not, then it is advisable to take no action. No harm will come to the mother even if nothing is done and the baby is not alive as she will almost always start to miscarry on her own and surgical interference may not be necessary.

No one really knows what causes missed abortion except to say that for some reason the early developing fetus does not cling into its bed in the uterine wall or perhaps the early developing placenta has not managed to oxygenate the developing baby adequately. Suffice it to say that this is a very common occurrence and one that usually has little significance later in terms of the ability to conceive again.

Recurrent Miscarriage

Unfortunately some women have a tendency to repeated mis-carriages. Sometimes a cause can be found after blood and urine tests, X-rays of the womb, and measurement of the couple's chromosome count. Known causes include medical diseases such as untreated diabetes, thyroid disorders, certain infectious diseases, abnormalities of the womb such as fibroids, or an incompetent cervix (see pages 200–201). Some of these abnormalities may be treated successfully but for others there is no obvious cure.

If the doctor has performed these tests after repeated miscarriages and has found no abnormalities referral may be made to a special recurrent miscarriage clinic of which there are a number around the country. One of the most significant advances in the causes of recurrent miscarriage is that there may be some rejection process going on between the mother and her baby. Rather like a patient who receives a transplanted organ from someone else rejects it, so the uterus of the mother rejects the fetus. Recently much research has been centred on women who recurrently miscarry and in some instances blood tests on the mother and the father can demonstrate whether this rejection process is occurring and, if so, the woman can be treated with a special blood transfusion containing certain blood cells which prevent rejection. Unfortunately this particular theory has not turned out as satisfactorily as once was thought. There is, however, hope in another interesting area. This concerns the development in the mother of certain antibodies called anti-phospholipids and anticardiolipins. These can be detected by a routine blood test and, if positive, treatment with low dose aspirin may help prevent a miscarriage. These conditions are associated with blood clotting in early pregnancy loss and slow growth of the fetus. Possible beneficial effects of treatment with an anticoagulant called heparin are being investigated. It is worth asking your doctor for referral to one of these recurrent miscarriage clinics if you have experienced more than three miscarriages for no obvious reason.

One of the questions often asked by women who have had a miscarriage is whether any abnormality was found at the time. Unfortunately, apart from very obvious abnormalities, there is often no apparent cause and, although it is possible for the pathologist to examine the fragments removed from the uterus, the results are often not helpful.

Women frequently feel guilty about miscarriage, asking themselves whether they did anything or ate anything specific that might have promoted the problem. The answer inevitably is no: miscarriages are not caused by physical exertion, lifting, painting ceilings, and only rarely by falling off a bicycle or skiing.

When to Try Again?

How long should you wait after a miscarriage before you try to become pregnant again? Opinions vary enormously but, in the absence of any known cause, it is usually safe to try again after two or three menstrual periods and there is certainly no need to wait the often quoted six months. Talk to your family doctor and gynaecologist, however, because if there are recurrent causes for this then it is wise not to get pregnant before these have been sorted out.

What Can be Done to Prevent Another Miscarriage?

The best advice is to let your doctor know as soon as you feel pregnant or miss a period next time. Taking care at the time when periods are due, avoiding intercourse and strenuous exercise during the first few weeks are sensible precautions. Remember that if you have miscarried once you have practically as good a chance of continuing with the next pregnancy as a woman who has never had a miscarriage. If you have miscarried twice in succession, the chances are somewhat reduced.

Some doctors like to prescribe the vitamin folic acid while trying to become pregnant and during the early weeks of a new pregnancy because there is some evidence that deficiency in this vitamin can lead to certain types of abnormality and miscarriage, and an adequate amount of folic acid helps early implantation of the fertilised egg.

Finally, two points to emphasise. If bleeding in pregnancy settles, further development of the pregnancy will be normal and the baby unharmed. The commonest cause of a miscarriage in the early weeks of pregnancy is a chromosome abnormality which causes a problem in fetal development and is usually a one-off situation, and miscarriage occurs in this case because the uterus tends to discard what is not normal.

Ectopic Pregnancy (Tubal Pregnancy)

The word 'ectopic' means misplaced and an ectopic pregnancy is one that grows somewhere other than in the uterus, its normal site. To all intents and purposes the only place for a pregnancy to grow other than in the uterus is in the Fallopian tube where fertilisation of the egg by the sperm takes place. Exceedingly rarely a pregnancy could form in an ovary. Cases have been reported in medical literature of pregnancies which have actually grown to a fairly advanced stage free in the abdomen, outside the uterus.

How Does Ectopic Pregnancy Occur?

Three or four days after fertilisation in the Fallopian tube the egg passes down the tube towards the uterus where it sinks into the prepared lining and starts its growth as an embryo. Although the distance between the tube and the uterus is not great, the journey of

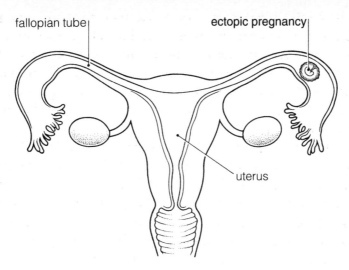

Ectopic or tubal pregnancy. Fertilisation has occurred normally, but the egg cannot pass along the tube to the uterus so it grows in the tube.

the fertilised egg can be quite perilous and migration along the tube can occur only if the tube is absolutely healthy, the hairs inside the lining that waft the fertilised egg along are not damaged, and there is no obstruction to its passage.

If a blockage prevents the fertilised egg from reaching the uterus, the three-day-old pregnancy will start to grow in the tube itself. Such a pregnancy is doomed to failure because in growing it distends the outer wall of the tube which is only relatively thin, and the pregnancy will eventually burst out of the tube causing acute pain, bleeding and sometimes shock.

Why does this happen? There is often no known cause for an obstruction but the tube may sometimes be kinked or damaged by previous pelvic infection or scarred from previous operations and for some reason there is a higher incidence of ectopic pregnancy in women who have been using the IUCD.

Diagnosis

This can be notoriously difficult, especially in the early stages, but the diagnosis is suggested by a history of a missed period, low abdominal pain, usually on one side or the other, followed by some bleeding from the vagina which is often dark brown in colour and hardly ever fresh or profuse. If these symptoms occur then the doctor should be consulted immediately. The doctor may perform an internal examination but that may not necessarily make a diagnosis possible and an ultrasound scan may be helpful.

Transvaginal scanning is the most useful method and may show an empty uterus with a possible swelling in the region of the tube, or occasionally blood in the abdominal cavity. These signs are significant of an ectopic pregnancy. If in doubt, serial blood tests of a hormone called HCG (human chorionic gonadotrophin) may be helpful, as in a normal pregnancy the levels are doubled over forty-eight hours.

If an ectopic pregnancy is suspected, the only sure way of making a diagnosis is by the insertion of a torch through the navel into the abdomen under anaesthetic (laparoscopy). The whole of the pelvic organs can be visualised and a pregnancy in the tube can be seen quite clearly. Obviously, the earlier the diagnosis the better because a ruptured ectopic pregnancy may have serious consequences. The woman may complain of acute abdominal pain, faintness and pain in the shoulder, and this will necessitate an immediate operation to deal with the situation.

Treatment

In the past, if a pregnancy in the tube was diagnosed then the whole tube with the pregnancy in it was removed, provided of course that the tube on the other side had first been inspected and found to be normal. Nowadays some units are performing more conservative measures where the pregnancy can be removed from the tube and the tube reconstituted surgically. This can be done either by a formal operation or by keyhole surgery using the laparoscope or torch if the tubal pregnancy is unruptured. A newer approach is to inject the tube with a special drug which can destroy the fetus in the Fallopian tube (methotrexate).

However, if the tube has to be removed completely, it is important to realise that, provided one healthy tube remains, there is little alteration to future fertility and the majority of women who have had one tube removed are able to conceive and have a normal pregnancy.

A second ectopic pregnancy occurring in the remaining tube is extremely rare.

The important message is to report pain and bleeding in the early few weeks of pregnancy.

Molar Pregnancy (Hydatidiform Mole)

This uncommon condition is a rare cause of bleeding in early pregnancy which occurs frequently in women in the Eastern countries, particularly Hong Kong, China and Malaysia, and rarely among Western women. The name 'hydatid' means grape-like and describes the appearance of the placenta, which grows rapidly and abnormally at the expense of the baby and resembles a bunch of grapes in shape and consistency. Usually no embryo develops but occasionally a mole can occur together with a fetus.

What essentially happens is that instead of the baby developing normally the placenta grows very abnormally and very quickly and eventually bleeding will occur which can be quite profuse. Occasionally there is no bleeding at all and the diagnosis is suspected only if the uterus becomes a little larger than it should be, the mother has felt no movements, and no heartbeat can be heard with the stethoscope. The diagnosis is usually made by special hormone tests and ultrasound scans as the mole gives a characteristic appearance which is easily recognised, together with the absence of a fetus.

Treatment

It is important to empty the uterus by a surgical D & C so that all the fragments are removed. Because fragments of the abnormal placenta stick to the lining of the uterus, the D & C may need to be repeated three months later. The tissue removed at operation is always examined microscopically and a diagnosis obtained.

If a molar pregnancy is confirmed there is no specific management other than routine urine and blood testing at two- to three-monthly intervals. The reason for this is that the abnormal placental tissue can secrete high levels of hormones which occasionally remain in the woman's body for up to a year and it is important to make sure that the hormone level is not rising.

Very occasionally the tiny bits of tissue remaining may form themselves into an early malignant tumour called a chorion carcinoma and this is why repeated testing is necessary. Should this occur, treatment is by special drugs which usually effect a cure. Even if the pathological examination reveals a simple mole, follow-up by repeated D & Cs and hormone testing is usually advisable for one to two years as very small fragments of tissue can remain in the uterus undetected and can grow again. Therefore, women who have had a molar pregnancy are advised not to become pregnant until the repeated tests have become clear for at least a year, and to use barrier methods of contraception as the pill can interfere with the reading of hormone results. A normal pregnancy will usually follow a molar one as it is extremely unlikely that this abnormality will recur.

Because of the rarity of this condition every mother who has a molar pregnancy is registered with a central agency of the Royal College of Obstetricians and Gynaecologists, and management and treatment of the condition is carried out by one or two large centres who have experience in the problem and will help to advise the mother and her doctor when it is safe to proceed with another pregnancy.

Pain in the First Trimester

It is not uncommon for mild lower abdominal pain or aches to occur in the early few weeks of pregnancy. If the pain is localised to one side or other, or becomes severe, and especially if associated with any vaginal bleeding, this must be reported straight away to the doctor. Urinary tract infections are quite common in early pregnancy and there may be pain either in the lower abdomen on passing urine or sometimes in the flank area.

As we have seen, pain that comes and goes in waves, rather like contractions, is one of the signs of an impending miscarriage and, if this does not settle, then it should be reported.

Just occasionally acute pain may be experienced, together with an inability to pass urine. This is due to the uterus growing in a downward position which is not uncommon and has no significance, but it may press against the water channel thereby causing acute retention of urine, in other words the inability to pass urine. This is called a retroverted gravid uterus and is easily cured by the passage of a catheter to relieve the overfull bladder.

In early pregnancy the ovaries sometimes swell (ovarian cyst) and this can give rise to pain. usually on one side or the other which is usually only mild to moderate and settles spontaneously. Please remember that abdominal pain may be due to causes unrelated to the pregnancy: for instance acute appendicitis is just as common in the pregnant woman as the non-pregnant one.

CHAPTER 5

The Fourth Month
(12–16 Weeks)

Changes in Your Baby

By fifteen weeks the baby is about 10cms, or 4ins, long. The facial features are being modelled, the forehead is growing, and the thread-like blood vessels are fully visible under the transparent skin. The eyelids have closed and probably will not open again until the fetus is seven months old. The nail-buds are appearing on the fingers and the arms have grown long enough for the hands to grasp each other. It weighs about 20gms, just under an ounce, at the age of twelve weeks and about 50gms, or one and three quarter ounces, by sixteen weeks.

The range of movements the baby makes becomes more intricate and it can now grasp the cord, suck its fingers, or even make complex facial expressions. It begins to breathe properly and from now on the baby will inhale and exhale amniotic fluid. The tiny sacs in the lungs are not expanded and the baby obtains oxygen and nutrients from the bloodstream.

The baby also rehearses the functions of digestion and excretion by swallowing the amniotic fluid and passing it out through its bladder. At this stage there are about 180ml (6fl.oz) of amniotic fluid in which the baby is floating.

Changes in You

The uterus has grown and can now sometimes be visible to the external eye. In fact by sixteen weeks the uterus has reached halfway to the umbilicus (see the diagram on page 118) and you are getting bigger too, although there are huge variations in weight in the first four months of pregnancy. Some women put on half a stone while others actually don't put on any weight at all and this is again because the placenta has only just taken over the function of feeding the baby. After sixteen weeks, however, what is eaten does make a difference to your own weight as we will see later in this chapter.

In a second or third pregnancy you may appreciate the movements of the baby by now, but in a first pregnancy, because you don't know what to watch for, movements are not obvious until about twenty to twenty-two weeks.

By the sixteenth week your energy should have totally returned, although you may feel tired after a full day. Your skin may be slightly blotchy, stretch marks may appear, and it is not uncommon for little skin tags, or moles, to occur (see pages 167–169).

Most doctors will have suggested that you have an ultrasound scan at about twelve weeks or before to date the pregnancy (see pages 149–156) and you will have had all the blood tests that need to be performed by this time. Another reason for having a scan between ten and twelve weeks is the recent knowledge that there are certain features that can be detected on a scan which can help to predict Down's Syndrome (see pages 389–390). The most important one is an excessive fold of fat in the neck region called a nuchal pad. Not every ultrasound department will have the expertise for detecting this pad of fat but this procedure is becoming more common. It has to be said that the finding of excessive fat in the neck region is not diagnostic of a Down's Syndrome baby, it is only suggestive, and follow-up tests may need to be done to make a definite diagnosis (see pages 139–147).

Measuring the Growth of the Uterus

This is often measured to keep track of the baby's growth and the doctor does this either by finger breadth or with a tape measure. Measurements are usually made from the symphysis pubis to the top of the uterus, which is about level with the navel, but not every doctor measures in the same way. The size of the uterus varies, as does that of the baby, and the abdomen can therefore differ considerably in appearance. The 'bulge' is not so apparent in a first pregnancy because the muscles of the abdomen and the uterus are unstretched, but in a subsequent pregnancy the abdomen feels very much more prominent as the muscles are looser.

Measuring the size of the baby on a regular basis helps the doctor

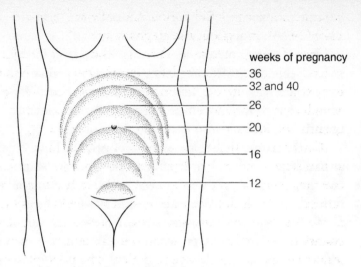

weeks of pregnancy
36
32 and 40
26
20
16
12

Measuring the growth of the uterus.

to ensure that growth is occurring normally. If the measurements are smaller or larger than normal, there may be a very simple explanation (perhaps the dates have been miscalculated) but sometimes this may indicate delay in the growth of the baby (see pages 206–207).

Weight

In the opinion of most doctors, weight control is an important aspect of antenatal care. Excessive weight gain in pregnancy can lead to complications but, on the other hand, the mother and her unborn child need proper nutrition. At first glance these two ideas may seem contradictory but in fact they are not. Studies have been made of nutrition in relation to childbirth and they conclude that on average women who are well nourished have fewer complications in pregnancy than poorly nourished women, and produce healthier babies.

All women will gain some weight in pregnancy but the amount varies not only from woman to woman but also between pregnancies in an individual woman. It is extremely difficult to make rules about the amount of weight that any given woman should or should not gain during a pregnancy because of the many variable factors, but a woman of average build eating normally will gain in the region of 11kg (24lbs) throughout the pregnancy.

One of the problems is that the increasing weight stems from several sources: the unborn baby, the placenta, the fluid in which the baby swims, the uterus, the breasts, the blood circulating in the body, as well as the tendency for a pregnant woman to retain an additional quantity of fluid and also to accumulate some fat.

Weight in the first three months of pregnancy is very variable and at this stage is not really dependent on what you eat. This is because the pregnancy is being supported by your hormones, which are in turmoil, and it is not unusual for some women to put on half a stone in the first three months while others put on no weight at all. By the twentieth week, however, what you eat and how you eat starts to influence the amount of weight put on. The principles are:

- Don't skimp on eating.

- Eat three times a day with enough at each meal to keep you going until the next.

- Don't nibble between meals and don't go to the fridge thinking that an apple or an orange or some cheese will do no harm. Everything that you eat outside of normal hours has the tendency to increase your weight.

- Eat sensibly.

- Don't diet.

- Avoid unnecessary things such as sugar, starch, biscuits, chocolates, etc.

Until 1990 the standard advice offered by most nutritionists and doctors was that a woman's optimum weight gain during pregnancy was about 24–28lbs. This, however, is far too simplistic and does not take into account variations in the woman's pre-pregnancy height, age, background and socio-economic status, but as a rough guide it can be useful. Some women put on a lot of weight and others very little in pregnancy, and wide variations in weight still manage to produce overwhelming numbers of healthy babies. However, total disregard for sensible eating habits should not be encouraged.

Most of the baby's weight gain takes place during the last three months, while that of the mother is more evenly distributed throughout pregnancy. The effect of weight loss in the first three months on the growth of the baby and development is unclear but there is probably little influence. This is of course Nature's way of protecting the baby against the common occurrence where the woman does not put on weight because she is being sick and nauseous.

Of greater concern is the woman who gains little weight, or loses weight, during the third three months despite an adequate intake. This may signify a poorly functioning placenta and a distressed infant. Equally disconcerting is the woman who has a sudden and marked weight gain over a short period of time during the last part of pregnancy. This may be an early indication of pre-eclampsia (see pages 203–206). This is one reason why you are weighed every time you come to the clinic.

Often a woman's greatest concern about gaining weight is that she will be unable to shed her excess pounds following delivery. In fact, weight is quickly lost. Approximately 12–14lbs disappear at the moment of delivery, if one adds together the average weight of the baby, the placenta and the amniotic fluid. Over the next six to eight weeks there is a reduction in the size of the uterus accompanied by the loss of excessive body fluids. Several studies have found that breast-feeding women tend to lose their pregnancy fat at a faster rate than women who do not nurse their babies. The most pleasant surprise for many women at their six-week check is that they have no more than 5–10lbs to lose in order to return to their normal pre-pregnancy weight.

Medical and Obstetric Complications Associated with Obesity

We have already seen some of the disadvantages of starting a pregnancy overweight and, indeed, overweight women do have a greater likelihood of pregnancy related diabetes (see pages 246–249) and high blood pressure (see pages 201–206), as well as increased risk of a difficult labour and delivering a large baby. Also, anaesthetic complications associated with a Caesarean section are increased.

Swelling of the Ankles, Legs and Fingers

About a quarter of the normal weight gained during pregnancy results in an increase in the amount of water held by the tissues. This excess fluid tends to collect in the lower part of the body so that the feet and ankles first show evidence of it. Many pregnant women complain of swelling of the feet, ankles and lower legs towards the end of the day. This is usually aggravated by long periods of standing and is worse in warm weather. It is useful to raise your feet whenever possible during the day by propping them up on a chair or bench or stretching out on a bed or sofa. Usually swelling of the legs and feet subsides and, by morning, the ankles are back to normal.

The fingers are the next commonest site of swollen tissues in pregnancy. This causes them to feel stiff and their puffiness frequently makes rings uncomfortable, tight and possibly difficult to remove. If a ring needs to be removed, simply soak your hand in cold water and then soap the finger and ring before attempting to remove it.

If the swelling is moderate, and confined to the legs and fingers, usually goes away at night, and is not associated with excessive or rapid weight gain, it has no special significance. Diuretic tablets are not popular as they can interfere with other systems in the body, notably kidney function, and are only rarely prescribed. Appetite suppressants are also to be avoided in pregnancy. If sudden or pronounced swelling and weight gain occurs, you should report this to your doctor as it may be one of the first signs of toxaemia of pregnancy (see pages 203–206).

Nutrition

Proteins

Proteins form the basic structure of every cell in the body and they are vital to the normal development of the fetus and placenta. An increase in the intake of protein is good during pregnancy to provide for the needs of the fetus and to allow for the necessary bodily changes that occur. While the recommended daily protein intake for a non-pregnant woman is 45gms, the normal daily amount in pregnancy is about 75gms. If a woman is breast-feeding, she will also require 20gms of protein above her pregnancy total.

Since protein is abundant in most diets, these requirements are attained by practically all pregnant women. Routine use of specially formulated high protein supplements, powders or beverages are usually unnecessary.

Proteins are made up of small elements called essential amino acids and these acids are found in greatest abundance in animal protein such as meat, fish, milk, cheese and eggs. Vegetables contain less protein than meat but they are also valuable because they supply the pregnant woman with iron, folic acid, vitamins and salt. Many pregnant women worry about salt intake because until relatively recently obstetricians believed that sodium had something to do with the cause of pre-eclampsia but this has been totally discredited. There is in fact no need to restrict your salt intake.

Vitamins

It is probably unnecessary to take multi-vitamin supplements if you have a healthy diet. There are, however, certain vitamins that are important, particularly folic acid which is necessary for the normal growth of the fetal cells, and if insufficient amounts are ingested anaemia can result. There is evidence to show that folic acid supplements can be instrumental in preventing miscarriages and also in lowering the incidence of certain abnormalities of the baby.

Iron Supplements

It used to be commonplace for all women to be given iron throughout pregnancy. In the great majority of instances this is probably unnecessary. It was thought that the woman's blood became diluted by the pregnancy with a loss of iron and that this was increased because of the transference to the breasts and the fetus. In fact many women do not need routine iron in pregnancy, though your iron level will be checked at the beginning and in the middle of your pregnancy and, if low, iron supplements are usually given.

Calcium

Calcium is necessary for the proper development of the baby's bones and teeth but, even if you have inadequate calcium, your baby is able to obtain sufficient amounts by extracting it from your bony skeleton. Recent laboratory studies have suggested that calcium supplements can be associated with a decreased incidence of blood pressure problems in later pregnancy and perhaps even in relaxing the uterus and preventing premature labour.

Milk is unquestionably the best source of calcium and two to three glasses a day will satisfy the entire pregnancy. Skimmed milk has slightly more calcium than whole milk or low fat milk. If you don't enjoy drinking milk, it can be added in liquid or powdered form to puddings, soups, cereals, casseroles, and other prepared foods. Other dairy products such as a cup of yoghurt, 1.5oz of unprocessed cheese, such as cheddar, 1.75 cups of ice cream, or 2 cups of cottage cheese, supply an amount of calcium equal to that found in one glass of milk.

Good non-dairy sources of calcium include salmon, sardines, dark green and leafy vegetables, and dried figs, dates, apricots, almonds and soya beans.

Fluoride

It is believed that fluoridisation of public water supplies is a safe, effective and practical way of preventing dental problems and thus reducing the cost of dental care in children and non-pregnant adults. There is some controversy, however, as to the advantages and safety of any fluoride preparations in pregnancy.

Artificial Sweeteners

There is some confusion among women and their doctors as to the safety of artificial sweeteners such as saccharin during pregnancy. Not much is known about the safety of saccharin, especially in the first three months of pregnancy, but there is some suggestion that it should be used sparingly before conception or in early pregnancy.

The Vegetarian Diet

There is some evidence suggesting that vegetarian diets can prove critical in the prevention of conditions such as heart disease, cancer, obesity and osteoporosis, but it has also been stated that the vegetarian diet may lack certain substances essential for the growth of the fetus. This is, however, not really substantiated and most babies born to vegetarian mothers are in excellent health, and the pregnancy outcome is normal.

The main concern is that the vegetarian receives adequate amounts of good quality protein, which is determined by the amount that is available to the body for use, and by amino acids. Cereals and leafy vegetables, if eaten together, give a good quantity of proteins of adequate nutritional value. The more liberal vegetarian diet can provide sufficient protein with two daily servings of egg and dairy produce and for the stricter vegetarian perhaps high protein nuts and peanut butter might be considered. Remember that protein is also available in cottage cheese, skimmed milk, low fat yoghurt and buttermilk.

It is true to say that the vegan diet may be deficient in calcium, iron and some vitamins and therefore these are the women who should take supplements in pregnancy.

The Veins

Varicose Veins

These are simply swollen veins which stand out under the skin and can be quite painful. They appear first as enlarged worm-like tubes beneath the skin or as a little spidery network in the skin itself around the ankles and knees. They can occur at any stage in pregnancy but, if they do appear during a first pregnancy, they will probably be mild and improve after delivery.

Veins become varicosed because the valves which are normally present in their lining become incompetent in pregnancy as the vein is stretched. If these valves do not work properly, pressure will be transmitted to the piece of vein below and the walls of the vein will be subjected to a strain which gradually stretches the vessel until it can be easily seen just under the skin. As pregnancy continues and the uterus grows there will be pressure on the veins in the pelvis tending to obstruct the flow of blood from the legs to the heart and therefore again raising the pressure in the leg veins. Excessive weight gain is an important factor in causing the veins to stretch.

Varicose veins may cause no symptoms but they sometimes give rise to discomfort. Once the veins become enlarged a feeling of heaviness or fatigue or a dull ache and irritation may occur along them and they may appear unsightly. Once present varicose veins usually become more noticeable with successive pregnancies. While mild varicosities can disappear after the pregnancy, severe cases will only partially improve and may need treatment after the pregnancy is over.

Varicose veins may be largely prevented, or at least their development can be kept to a minimum, by avoiding excessive weight gain and constant standing. When sitting it helps to raise the feet so that the heels are above the level of the hips: in other words, don't stand if you can sit and don't sit if you can lie. When lying down, lie with your legs raised on a pillow as this will assist drainage of the blood.

Sitting with crossed legs is not a good idea because it may block the main flow of blood behind the knee. Well-fitting support tights are helpful and should be put on each morning before getting out of bed and should stretch from the thigh right down to the foot.

If the veins cause pain or anxiety, then you should consult your doctor. Occasionally injections of a substance directly into the veins are helpful in preventing them from stretching further and it may be that surgery will be advised after the pregnancy is over. Usually, however, no treatment is indicated for at least three months after the pregnancy. In some cases veins develop around the vulval region, causing aches and irritation. Unfortunately there is very little treatment to be recommended as support for veins in the vulva is obviously difficult.

Thrombosis

The term actually means clotting of the blood in the vein, which obstructs the blood flow back to the heart. Clots can occur anywhere where there are veins but logically this will be commonest in the areas which have the most pressure on them, i.e. the leg veins or veins deep in the pelvis.

A clot may occur in those veins just under the skin which can easily be seen, or deeper in the connecting group of veins that are invisible. If a clot forms in a superficial vein, it will cause a tender swelling over the vein site which may be red and hot, or sometimes a red, streaky mark over the vein. These small clots do not usually have any serious significance, although they can be quite painful, and are best treated by wearing firm stockings from the thigh to the ankle throughout the day.

Thrombosis of the deep veins can be more significant and this usually causes pain in the calf, or behind the knee, with swelling of the leg. Because the veins are deep under the skin, there is often no redness. The importance of a deep vein thrombosis is that the veins are larger and therefore there is a wider area of blood which gets blocked off in the leg. More seriously, the clot can break off in the vein and be transported into the lung where it can lodge and can cause difficulty in breathing (pulmonary embolus).

If you notice discomfort in the leg, it is important that you report this to your doctor who may order specific tests which can determine whether or not there is a clot. If a deep vein thrombosis is suspected or confirmed, a course of blood-thinning injections (anti-coagulants) is given which usually dissolves the clot. For a fuller description of thrombosis and management, see pages 347–349.

Piles or Haemorrhoids

Piles are simply varicose veins around the rectum and anus and they are formed much in the same way as varicose veins in the legs, except that the pressure which causes the valves to become incompetent may be increased by constipation or excessive straining. During pregnancy the hormone progesterone is the culprit which relaxes the muscle of the vein wall. As pregnancy advances and the uterus gets bigger, the pressure on the veins will obviously increase.

The commonest symptom of piles is bleeding from the rectum, often noticeable only after the passing of a motion. Irritation around the anus and sometimes soreness and pain occur with bowel opening.

Occasionally the piles are large enough to protrude outside the anus and form a swelling which can be seen and felt, and can become quite painful.

The best treatment for piles is their prevention and, in turn, the prevention of constipation. Irritation, soreness and bleeding can be helped by ointments applied to the anal area after opening the bowels and going to bed, and suppositories may be just as helpful. If the piles are felt as a lump outside the anus they can often be pushed back with the finger but your doctor's advice should be sought. Treatment for a pile which is thrombosed is usually conservative, although occasionally the doctor may have to remove the little blood clot and this is quite easily done with a local anaesthetic.

Like varicose veins in the leg, piles usually get better after pregnancy and often disappear within six or eight weeks but, if they persist and give further trouble, treatment is usually by injection or operation. However, surgery may be deferred as piles tend to recur in subsequent pregnancies.

The Urinary System

Passing Water Frequently

This is one of the commonest signs of early pregnancy and occurs within the first few weeks because of an increased blood supply causing congestion within the bladder and in some cases because the bladder is compressed by the enlarging uterus. The symptoms usually improve as the pregnancy advances although towards the last few weeks of pregnancy it can recur as the baby's head goes down into the pelvis and the bladder becomes irritated.

As a rule no specific treatment is necessary but, if frequency persists, or if you have to get up at night, or passing urine becomes painful, then you should see your doctor to exclude a urinary infection.

Inability to Pass Urine (Retention of Urine)

In early pregnancy the uterus is sometimes tilted backwards

(retroverted). This is not important in itself but can cause pressure on the bladder which can block the urine flow. If this occurs then there is intense desire to pass urine but an inability to pass more than a few drops. The bladder consequently fills up and cannot empty, causing abdominal swelling and pain. If this should happen admission to hospital may be required so that the urine can be removed by a catheter.

Retention of urine may also occur after the baby is born, usually because of a reflex precipitated by anxiety in the mother that passing urine will hurt the stitches, or by bruising of the bladder as the baby's head pushes past it. Again, a catheter may be required.

Incontinence

It is not unusual in pregnancy for leakage of urine to occur, especially on coughing, laughing or sneezing, or even sometimes when turning over in bed. This rather frightening complaint is mainly due to hormone changes which relax the bladder and the urinary channels. Occasionally, and particularly in women who have had a number of pregnancies, it can be due to a lowering or dropping of the womb (prolapse). Usually no treatment is required because the condition improves as pregnancy advances. However, if a prolapse is present, the insertion of a pessary into the vagina will help.

Incontinence on exertion sometimes returns after pregnancy and may in fact continue for several weeks or months. Here the services of a skilled physiotherapist in the lying-in period are vital in order to teach the mother how to tone up her stretched pelvic muscles. Occasionally, if incontinence continues after the pregnancy despite conservative measures, then medical advice should be sought.

Urinary Infection

Partly because the urinary opening is close to the vagina and partly because of hormone changes in pregnancy, urinary tract infections are quite common. They are caused by bacteria that reach the bladder and sometimes the kidneys via the urethra, which is the tube through which the urine passes out from the body.

It is important that urinary infections are diagnosed early in pregnancy and, because urinary infection is sometimes present without the mother's knowledge, your urine is always tested at the first booking appointment in the antenatal clinic and subsequently on routine visits. If a laboratory specimen shows that there is more than a certain amount of bacteria in your urine, treatment with an appropriate antibiotic is advised. Common complaints include running to the 'loo', burning or stinging on urination, a recurrent urge to pass urine frequently, and occasionally difficulty in passing urine or even urine stained with a few flecks of blood. It is important to inform your doctor if you notice any of these symptoms.

Cystitis

This is the medical term for a bacterial infection of the bladder where the infection travels up from the urethral channel into the bladder itself. The symptoms are similar to the ones already described and antibiotics are effective in relieving discomfort and preventing an upward spread of infection to the kidneys.

Pyelitis (Pyelonephritis)

This term means infection in the kidneys. It is caused by bacteria which gain entry to the urinary channel through the bladder and pass via the ureter, through which urine empties, into the kidneys where the urine is actually made. Women who have recurrent urinary infections in pregnancy are more prone to pyelitis, as are those in whom there is a previous history of kidney problems.

The symptoms are severe pain in either flank area where the kidney is situated, almost always on the right, and usually there are urinary symptoms such as increased frequency, or occasionally the urine may be blood-stained. There is an intense desire to urinate but only small amounts of urine are passed which can be quite painful. In addition the mother may be running a fever and may generally feel unwell.

Treatment consists of taking the appropriate antibiotic once a specimen of urine has been sent to the laboratory for culture to see which bacteria are responsible for the infection; pain relievers while the discomfort persists; and drinking plenty of fluid. The symptoms usually subside over a few days, though the urine must be checked by a mid-stream sample to ensure that no bacteria remain.

Recurrent Urinary Infections

Sometimes urinary tract infections recur during pregnancy and it may be necessary to prescribe courses of different antibiotics over several weeks and occasionally for the remainder of the pregnancy to ensure that the urine remains sterile, or free from infection. Once the pregnancy is over the doctor may advise further investigation of the urinary tract to exclude causes which can be detected by a special X-ray of the kidneys known as an intravenous pyelogram. As it involves the use of X-rays this investigation is not usually performed during pregnancy.

Kidney Stones

Stones in the kidney or ureter channel are no more common in pregnancy than at any other time. They are caused by aggregation of small crystals which form themselves into 'stones' and result in severe pain in the kidney on the affected side, or in the loin if the stones have managed to pass down the ureter on the way to the bladder.

Kidney and ureter stones can be extremely painful and are more difficult to diagnose in pregnancy because the use of X-ray and imaging techniques to identify them have to be performed with caution. In fact ultrasound will show up the stones and avoid the use of X-rays. Small stones are usually expelled spontaneously but occasionally they may have to be dislodged by inserting a tube through the urethra and encouraging the stones to be passed. This involves a short anaesthetic but will not harm the pregnancy.

CHAPTER 6

The Fifth Month

(16–20 Weeks)

Changes in Your Baby

At this stage your baby weighs about 280gms (10oz) and is 17.3cms (7.2ins) long – about the size of a large banana. The rapid growth rate of the baby has now slowed down; however, it is continuing to grow and develop, and different organ systems are maturing and developing.

The Fetal Digestive System

The baby has developed sufficiently to swallow amniotic fluid. After swallowing, the fetus can absorb much of the water in it and pass unabsorbed matter as far as the large bowel. There are certain enzymes present in small quantities and, if an infant is born prematurely, there may be uneven amounts or deficiencies of these enzymes.

Fetal Swallowing

Swallowing by the baby at different stages of pregnancy can be observed by ultrasound and this can be seen as early as eighteen weeks.

It is believed that swallowing amniotic fluid helps growth and development of the digestive system. It may also condition the digestive system to function after birth. There have been studies to determine how much fluid a baby swallows and it seems that at full term the baby may swallow large amounts of fluid, even as much as 483ml (17fl.oz) in a twenty-four-hour period.

The amniotic fluid swallowed contributes only a small amount to the caloric needs of the fetus, but it is believed that the developing baby may obtain essential nutrients from it.

Meconium

During pregnancy you may hear the word 'meconium' and wonder what it means. It actually refers to undigested debris from swallowed amniotic fluid in the digestive system. It is a greenish-black/brown substance that the baby will pass from its bowels several days or weeks before delivery, during labour or after birth.

The presence of meconium can be important at the time of delivery. If a baby has had a bowel movement and meconium is in the amniotic fluid, the infant may swallow the fluid before birth or at birth and, if meconium is inhaled into the lungs, it can cause problems. For this reason, if meconium is seen at the time of delivery, it is important to remove it from the baby's mouth and throat.

The passage of meconium into the amniotic fluid may also be caused by a distressed fetus in labour.

Lanugo

A soft, downy hair called lanugo covers all of the baby's skin and the skin itself begins to thicken at this stage with little fat deposits, making it less transparent. Some scalp hair may also be present.

Changes in You

The sixteenth to the twentieth weeks of pregnancy are rather tranquil. Many of the minor discomforts such as nausea and vomiting and constipation have disappeared by now because the placenta has taken over producing the hormones that are essential for the continued growth of the baby. You may feel a surge of energy and there is often a sense of well-being and anticipation. Your mood improves and sleep patterns return to normal. You may be feeling more confident and secure in your pregnancy as the risk of problems such as miscarriage diminishes. Travel plans can be made because it is an ideal time to go away: you can play sports and swim and you won't be limited in any normal activities.

Your abdomen is starting to enlarge and may actually show at this stage. This is more common in a mother who is having a second or third pregnancy because the muscles are looser. At sixteen weeks the uterus is actually about the size of a cantaloupe melon or a little larger, and can be felt halfway between the symphysis pubis, or central bone of the pelvis, and the navel.

It is important to realise that women differ in their appearance, both to themselves and to others. Shorter and plumper women *show* more readily than those who are taller and slimmer, so don't worry about others' comments on how big or small you seem. There is also much more gas in the abdomen and this may give the impression of a larger swelling: again this varies from woman to woman. The important feature is that the uterus is growing normally and your doctor or midwife will be able to tell you this.

This month is also the time when special tests may be done, including blood tests, amniocentesis and an ultrasound scan. The twenty-week scan is important because at this stage the various parts of the baby's body are clearly seen and any abnormality can be noted. As well as this, accurate measurements of the head and the abdomen of the baby confirm its size and the due date.

Genetic Risks

'Will Our Baby be All Right?'

This question perhaps more than any other is the natural anxiety of all couples embarking on a pregnancy. In the majority of instances of course the answer is yes, but what concerns the couple is not perhaps the present but the past and the future: the genetic legacy that has been received from their parents and the genetic risks they might pass on to their unborn children.

All parents would like to peer into the future for reassurance that their babies will be perfect in every way. There are no crystal balls available but medical genetics, a relative newcomer among clinical specialties, has made great progress in identifying those parents at high risk of having a child with a genetic disorder and in developing pre-natal tests for detecting such problems early in pregnancy.

Genes and Chromosomes

The basic units of heredity that link past, present and future generations are genes, tiny molecules of DNA, the fundamental fabric of life that determines how we develop. Every cell in the body has a nucleus containing thousands of genes arranged on twenty-three pairs of rod-like structures called chromosomes. One pair, the sex chromosomes, determines the sex of an individual. A woman has two X chromosomes in every cell nucleus, a man has an X and a Y. The other twenty-two pairs of chromosomes which govern all other aspects of development are called autosomes and are usually identical in size and shape. Genes also

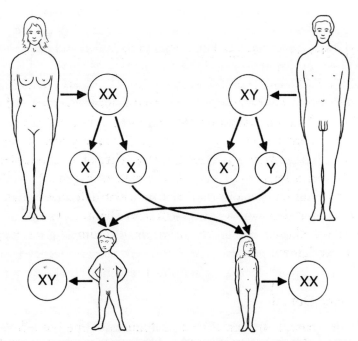

Normal chromosome arrangements.

134

occur in pairs, each gene occupying a specific site on a particular chromosome.

Not all genes have equal influence: some are 'dominant' and exert their influence, or in medical terms express themselves, even if carried in only one of a pair of chromosomes. Some are 'recessive' which are less influential and these genes are masked by dominant genes. They express themselves only if a child inherits two of the same recessive genes. If both parents carry the same faulty, recessive gene, each child they conceive faces a twenty-five per cent risk of inheriting a double dose of the defect, a twenty-five per cent chance of inheriting two normal genes and not being affected, and a fifty per cent chance of inheriting an abnormal gene from one parent and becoming a carrier of the defect.

The genes and chromosomes affect every conceivable aspect of an individual's appearance, well-being, likelihood of developing certain illnesses, and even longevity and behaviour. Medical genetics, the study of heredity, is one of the most complex of medical sciences as well as one of the most sophisticated, yet a great deal about how genes affect life is still unknown.

Genetic Errors – What Can Go Wrong?

The blueprints for life encoded in the genes are so detailed and intricate that it is not surprising that occasionally mistakes occur. What is surprising is that mistakes don't occur more often. Of every one hundred newborn babies, only two to four have any sort of genetic defect, yet all parents worry about the possibility of a genetic flaw. It is true that in a sense each of us is a carrier of a genetic problem. Every individual has an estimated four to eight defective genes, but the chances that they will affect the child are slight.

Geneticists classify hereditary problems according to the way in which they originate:

Single Gene Defects

A child of a parent with an abnormal dominant gene has a fifty per cent likelihood of inheriting it. The most common of these defects are minor, such as the growth of an extra finger or toe. However, some uncommon dominant problems can be fatal and may not be diagnosed for decades after birth. Huntington's Chorea, for example, is a degenerative disease usually not diagnosed until mid-life. There is no way of detecting this inherited problem until symptoms develop.

Far more common are autosomal recessive disorders, giving rise to conditions such as cystic fibrosis (see pages 138–139), or sickle-cell anaemia which is an anaemia or lack of blood occurring in certain races (see pages 161–162). Blood tests can identify carriers of some of the most serious diseases.

X-linked Problems

Only women are carriers of X-linked problems and only their sons are at risk. For example, a boy faces a fifty–fifty chance of inheriting a defective gene on his mother's sex chromosome. A daughter also may inherit the gene and become a carrier but she will not develop the symptoms because of the matching healthy gene on her other X chromosome. The most common X-linked problem is haemophilia, the bleeding disease.

Chromosomal Defects

A chromosomal flaw involves a much larger part of the genetic material than a single gene defect and has a much more devastating effect. While an abnormal gene might cause a problem similar to the misspelling of a word in this book, a chromosome error could be compared with leaving out an entire chapter or putting it in the wrong sequence. Chromosome problems occur in an estimated one in every two hundred conceptions – much less frequently than single flaws – and very often they result in miscarriage. An example of a chromosome problem is Down's Syndrome (see pages 389–390).

Genetic Defects Due to a Combination of Causes

There are many such conditions which include both familial inheritance and environmental factors, and there is no clear pattern as to why and when these defects occur. The most common ones affect the neural tube which is the precursor of the backbone, spinal cord and

WHO MIGHT BENEFIT
FROM GENETIC COUNSELLING?

* A woman over the age of 35.
  (The incidence of Down's Syndrome increases after this age.)

* Parents of a child with a known single gene abnormality, a neural tube defect or other form of physical impairment.

* Women who have a tendency to miscarry.

* Couples with known chromosome abnormalities.

* Women who may be carriers of X-linked disorders.

* Couples whose family members have a high incidence of certain diseases.

* Couples whose ethnic or racial backgrounds increase the likelihood of a particular problem like sickle-cell anaemia.

* If the mother has given birth to a baby with congenital abnormalities.

brain in the embryo. If the top end of this structure doesn't close in the first month of pregnancy, the unborn baby will not develop a normal brain. This condition, called anencephaly, is always fatal (see page 139). If there is a flaw in the formation of the lower part of the tube, the spinal cord and nerve will remain outside the body (spina bifida – see pages 403–404).

Parents at Risk

Some genetic defects occur in a random fashion, but much more often there is a pattern to their occurrence, and as geneticists have learned about the way one generation transmits a defect to another they have been able to counsel parents about the potential risks to their unborn children. Today there is a network of genetic counselling centres across the country staffed by physicians, or specially trained geneticists, who can provide immediate access to the facts and statistics about certain problems. Genetic counsellors cannot provide easy answers to all parents at risk. However, they can offer the facts and understanding that parents need to make informed, responsible decisions about having a child or continuing a pregnancy.

For couples who fear that their genetic make-up may jeopardise the well-being of their unborn children, counselling may be one of the most important experiences of their lives. They should be able to find out exactly what has gone wrong in the past and why, what the odds are of the same error occurring again, if they are at risk for any future problems, and what pre-natal tests if any are available. Whereas genetic counsellors may not be on the staff of every hospital in the country, there are centres in each region which can provide this service. If it is requested, your gynaecologist or midwife will be able to refer you.

Cystic Fibrosis

Cystic fibrosis is an inherited condition for which no cause is known, with an incidence of about one in two thousand babies. It is a generalised disorder affecting glands which secrete abnormal cells, resulting in excessive sweating, blockage of the bowel and chest complications. The pancreas, which is a gland sitting next to the liver, is affected in eighty per cent of cases, preventing proper digestion and absorption of fats and leading to malnutrition and failure to thrive in the young child. Often lethal, the average life expectancy is between twelve and sixteen years with a risk of recurrence in either sex of one in four.

The condition can be diagnosed pre-natally by amniocentesis or CVS if there is a family history or strong suspicion. Within twenty-four hours of the baby being born blood tests which measure the sweat electrolyte levels can give an indication. Ninety-five per cent of patients who survive infancy have chest complications, with a persistent cough, recurrent bronchitis, pneumonia and obstruction of the air passages.

No cure is known but health can be maintained and life expectancy improved by preventing chest complications and treating them promptly if they occur. Expert genetic counselling should identify the risks of recurrence. Gene mutation is now recognised and there are many possible different mutations. If parents are carriers, then there is a twenty-five per cent chance of a subsequent fetus being affected.

Special Tests

Alpha-fetoprotein Test

Alpha-fetoprotein is a substance found in the blood of a pregnant woman in varying levels throughout her pregnancy. Critically between sixteen and eighteen weeks the level is fairly constant in most women but at much before or after this time the results are too variable. A high level above normal can indicate that the baby could be suffering from a defect of the spine such as spina bifida or other abnormalities of brain development (hydrocephalus, a large head, and encephalocoele, a failure to develop a part of the brain properly). A low level may be found in Down's Syndrome babies.

The alpha-fetoprotein test has been largely replaced by ultrasound and this is one of the reasons why routine ultrasound is performed early in pregnancy.

Special Blood Tests to Exclude Down's Syndrome

Research findings that a low AFP might signify a baby with Down's Syndrome led to the development of a blood test called the Bart's Test, because much of the original research was carried out at St Bartholomew's Hospital in London. It again involves taking a blood sample from the mother at sixteen to eighteen weeks and measuring three hormones that are commonly secreted in the pregnancy – AFP; oestriol levels, which indicate the amount of the female hormone oestrogen circulating in the blood; and HCG (human chorionic gonadotrophin) levels, which is another hormone present in high doses in pregnant women.

This is a screening test for abnormalities of the baby that may be due to chromosomes, the commonest one of which is Down's Syndrome. For the test to be accurate the sample of blood must be taken between sixteen and eighteen weeks, and because this timing is critical the stage of pregnancy is first confirmed by an ultrasound scan. There is a range of normal results, but essentially a very high result indicates that you may be at risk of having a Down's Syndrome child and that you are more at risk than anyone else of your age. *It does not diagnose the condition and, again, it must be emphasised that it is only a screening test.*

Some hospitals offer this test as a routine service. Because laboratory space is limited, others may make a small charge if there is no indication for the test, but do not charge if there is a high risk of having a child with Down's Syndrome, i.e. a woman over the age of thirty-five or with a previous history of abnormalities.

The result of the test indicating the risk factor comes back in a percentage form and, if there is a high risk factor, the only way to be sure that there is an abnormality is to have an amniocentesis test.

The great value of this test is of course that it is completely safe and involves merely taking blood from the pregnant mother, but further countrywide evaluation will be needed to assess its overall usefulness and no decision as to whether every mother should have the test has yet been made.

Do remember to ask on your first visit to the antenatal clinic what the hospital procedure is concerning this test and whether your attendants feel that it is indicated. Even if the test is not routinely performed in your area, most hospitals will do the test for you for a fee, which is usually in the region of £50.

Other Tests in the Prediction of Down's Syndrome

There is good evidence that the skin thickness on the neck of the baby is much pronounced in children with Down's Syndrome. This skin fold can be measured by ultrasound (Nuchal Screening) which must be done between twelve and thirteen weeks of pregnancy. Current opinion suggests a pick-up rate of Down's Syndrome of around seventy per cent.

One of the problems is that more than one screening test may give contradictory results, but your doctor will be able to advise on which test to undergo.

Amniocentesis

Amniocentesis means the removal for analysis of a small amount of fluid from the baby's sac via a needle inserted through the mother's abdomen into the uterus. Because the baby drinks amniotic fluid and passes it out again the fluid contains cells from the baby's system which can provide a good deal of information. There are four main reasons for amniocentesis:

- To detect certain abnormalities of the baby in early pregnancy.

- To determine the sex of the fetus.

- To investigate the risks to the baby in a woman who is sensitised to the Rhesus factor (Rh disease – see pages 237–240).

- In rare cases, to determine if the unborn baby's lungs are sufficiently developed to function outside the womb: in other words whether the baby is mature enough to be delivered early if there is an indication to do so.

The Detection of Congenital Abnormalities

It must be emphasised that, although there are many abnormalities of the baby's chromosomes, only a limited number can be diagnosed by amniocentesis and it is not a test that can provide assurance that the baby will necessarily be completely normal in other ways.

The most important condition that can be diagnosed is Down's Syndrome. Children with Down's Syndrome have definite physical characteristics that make early recognition possible. They have limited intellectual capacity, some have severe learning difficulties, and there are often associated heart abnormalities. It appears that something goes wrong with very early cell division resulting in an abnormal number of chromosomes (see page 135), which can be detected by examining the amniotic fluid. We know how Down's Syndrome comes about but we still do not know why. However, we do know that there are certain predisposing factors, most important of which seems to be maternal age.

The incidence of Down's Syndrome in babies born to mothers below the age of thirty is the same as it would be in the normal population. With mothers over thirty-five there is a gradual increase, until at the age of forty the likelihood of giving birth to a Down's Syndrome child is at the rate of one in seventy pregnancies. In an ideal world it would seem reasonable to offer amniocentesis to any woman who wishes it after the age of thirty-five, but in practical terms this is not possible in the UK as the number of laboratories in the country capable of chromosome analysis is limited. Most units in the National Health Service recommend the test only to women who are over thirty-seven or who have a history of previous chromosome problems within the family.

Other conditions that may be screened by examining the amniotic fluid are spina bifida and hydrocephalus, and other rare familial diseases.

Sex-linked Conditions

There is a group of rare conditions which are sex-linked: in other words they occur only in one sex. If chromosomes can be measured, so obviously can the sex (see pages 52–53). Pre-natal sex determination is usually carried out if there is a high risk of a severe sex-linked congenital abnormality lethal to life, in which case termination of the pregnancy may be considered if the relevant sex is known. These conditions are fairly rare.

Couples with two or three babies of the same sex may desperately wish to have a baby of the other sex, and in some countries male offspring are considered more important! Gender determination purely on social grounds, however anxious the couple may be for this information, is not generally acceptable.

Rhesus Disease

One of the earliest uses for amniocentesis was in the prognosis and care of infants whose mothers had been sensitised to the Rhesus factor (see pages 237–240). In such cases it may be necessary to repeat the test on several occasions to measure the amount of a substance called bilirubin in the baby's blood. This will indicate whether the baby may be severely affected by anaemia and need delivery before term with a subsequent blood transfusion.

Fetal Lung Development

Examination of the amniotic fluid later in pregnancy may help to decide whether the baby's lungs are sufficiently mature to withstand being born, if there is a medical need for premature delivery.

This test has rather gone out of fashion lately but is used in some areas when a medical condition such as extremely high blood pressure makes it advisable to deliver the baby at an early stage, say thirty to thirty-two weeks. Examination of the fluid can give a clue as to whether the baby's lungs are mature enough to withstand birth.

When is Amniocentesis Done?

Other than in cases of Rhesus disease, where the procedure may need to be repeated throughout the pregnancy, the usual time for amniocentesis to be performed is between fifteen and seventeen weeks, though some units skilled in the procedure are performing the test at about fourteen weeks.

The reason fifteen to seventeen weeks is chosen is that technically it may be difficult to obtain a specimen of fluid in early pregnancy, as the amount of fluid is scanty and the chromosomes being measured may be insufficiently mature before this time.

How is Amniocentesis Performed?

The procedure is usually simple, relatively painless and quick, and needs no preparation beforehand. It can be done in the antenatal clinic, although normally it is carried out in the ultrasound scanning department. Before amniocentesis an ultrasound scan is performed in

WHO SHOULD BE OFFERED
AMNIOCENTESIS IN PREGNANCY?

* All women over the age of thirty-seven.

* Women with a history of a child born with Down's Syndrome, or with certain chromosome abnormalities.

* Women in whom a Down's blood test has shown an increased likelihood of chromosome abnormalities.

* In certain instances where women have had a previous child affected by spina bifida or hydrocephalus, although nowadays sophisticated ultrasound techniques are probably sufficient.

* Women with a history of a child affected by certain sex-linked diseases.

* In certain instances of rare inherited familial abnormalities following genetic counselling.

order to locate a pool of amniotic fluid that can be sampled and to avoid piercing the placenta with the needle. This is particularly important in women who are Rhesus negative as the procedure may cause mixing of the fetal and maternal circulation and sensitise the mother in future pregnancies. This is why a protective injection of anti-D immunoglobulin (see pages 238–240) is given at the time of amniocentesis to a woman who has a Rhesus negative blood group.

There are slight variations in the technique, but usually a small freezing injection of local anaesthetic is given into the skin a few minutes before the insertion of a longer needle through the anaes-thetised area of skin and the wall of the uterus into the amniotic sac. There is a small sensation of discomfort amounting to no more than a pinprick as the needle goes through the wall of the womb and about 10ml of fluid is withdrawn. It is advisable to rest for the remainder of the day so as not to irritate the uterus and to prevent leakage of fluid from the tiny hole.

Possible Complications

It may not always be easy to obtain the fluid and occasionally the laboratory will have difficulty in growing the chromosomes, but the only real problem with amniocentesis in early pregnancy is the possi-bility of a miscarriage. Simply withdrawing the fluid is sufficient to traumatise the uterus and it may then start contracting. The general figure for this complication is given at around one per cent, although in practice in experienced hands it is probably much less.

When counselling a woman for amniocentesis the benefits of diagnosis must be weighed against the possible risk. For example, a woman aged forty has a risk of one in seventy of having a Down's Syndrome baby which is higher than the risk of a miscarriage (one in a hundred) for the test, whereas in a woman of thirty-five the risks of amniocentesis are perhaps slightly greater than of having a Down's Syndrome child. These are all decisions that need to be carefully considered in consultation with your doctor.

You may wonder why the baby is not harmed or damaged by the needle and the simple answer is that it swims around in fluid and tends to move away from any object that approaches it. Also remember that the test is not done blind but in the ultrasound department so that the position of the fetus can be noted and a pool of fluid located.

Other very rare complications which have been recorded are infec-tion or minor positional abnormalities of the fetal limbs.

How Long Does it Take to Get the Results?

In order to detect chromosomes, the amniotic fluid needs to be incubated for two to three weeks and this is why the results take this length of time to come back. The pregnancy may therefore already have advanced to nineteen to twenty weeks before a diagnosis can be made.

What Happens if There is an Abnormality?

Before amniocentesis is performed your medical attendant will have discussed with you the possible options in case the results indicate that you are carrying a baby with Down's Syndrome, so that you may be fully informed when the time comes if a difficult decision has to be made such as whether to continue with the pregnancy.

If an abnormality has been found, you will want to discuss the various options with your doctor, of either terminating the pregnancy or continuing, so that at least you can prepare yourselves as a couple for the outcome.

How is Termination of Pregnancy Performed at Twenty Weeks?

At twenty weeks unfortunately it is inadvisable to terminate a pregnancy by the conventional vaginal method used in the first twelve weeks, because the fetus is too large and the procedure can be dangerous. The pregnancy is therefore usually terminated by inserting a small pessary or tablet into the vagina which starts the uterus contracting in a few hours, in the hope that it will spontaneously expel the fetus. Sometimes it takes four or five pessaries at three-hourly intervals before the uterus starts contracting because obviously it is not used to going into labour at this early stage of pregnancy. Usually, however, this works well and you will then unfortunately have to go through what is a mini-labour. On the rare occasions when this does not work the pregnancy is usually terminated by a further injection into the uterus which starts it contracting.

Availability of Amniocentesis

The availability of the test is usually limited by facilities in laboratories, which are normally reserved for certain at risk categories (see chart on page 144).

Even if you do not fall into one of the recognised at-risk categories, you may still wish to have amniocentesis for peace of mind. This should be discussed with the specialist at the booking clinic. Some laboratories accept social requests and each regional laboratory differs in this respect. It may be possible to obtain the test privately by payment to the laboratory in question. The consultant in charge of your care will be able to advise whether private testing is possible or advisable in view of the possibility that amniocentesis may cause miscarriage of a normal healthy baby.

Finally, it must be re-emphasised that the only indication for amniocentesis to sex the unborn child is in cases where there is a family history of hereditary disease linked to a male or female fetus: in other words, when there is a strictly medical reason. Amniocentesis is not generally acceptable in the UK when the couple wish to know the sex of their unborn child purely on social grounds.

Chorionic Villus Sampling (CVS)

Although this test is not done in the second trimester, usually being carried out at nine to ten weeks, it is convenient to discuss it in this chapter because it is an alternative method of diagnosing abnormalities such as Down's Syndrome. This test is more complicated than amniocentesis, not available in all areas, and its safety is still being assessed. It can be used to detect the same chromosome abnormalities as amniocentesis and also other genetic disorders such as the blood diseases thalassaemia (see pages 161–162) and sickle-cell anaemia (see page 161). It is also possible to detect the sex of the fetus and this again can be of value if there is a known sex-linked condition running through the family.

A narrow plastic tube is passed into the uterus through the cervix and some cells from the developing placenta are drawn off. Alternatively, some doctors prefer to put a needle through the abdominal wall rather like amniocentesis, using ultrasound control. The procedure takes a few minutes: it is uncomfortable but relatively painless.

The great advantage of this test is that results are obtainable between seven and ten days. This means that if there is a problem with the chromosomes, and Down's Syndrome, for instance, is diagnosed, termination of pregnancy, if requested, can be performed before twelve weeks by a safe, simple method. Unfortunately, on the down side, the risk of miscarriage is higher than with amniocentesis.

Amniocentesis versus Chorionic Villus Sampling (CVS)

Amniocentesis is the tried and trusted method and is available in most hospitals whereas CVS is a more specialised procedure and referral to an expert centre may be necessary. The obvious advantage of CVS is that it can be performed within the first ten to eleven weeks of pregnancy. Amniocentesis, on the other hand, cannot be done much before fifteen to sixteen weeks, it takes three weeks for the results to come back, and the pregnancy will have advanced to nineteen to twenty weeks before a decision can be made, at which time termination is a much more unpleasant procedure. The miscarriage rate after amniocentesis, however, is only a half to one per cent whereas with CVS it is nearer two to three per cent.

A sample of fluid from the amniotic sac will also give a wider range of results if you require additional information to the chromosome analysis. The decision as to which test is more suitable for you has to be made following full consultation with your doctor or geneticist.

Fetoscopy

This is a rarely performed procedure which involves a microscope camera being inserted into the uterus through the abdomen, in much the same way as in amniocentesis, so that a view can be obtained and a photograph taken of the fetus. By sampling tissue it may be possible to diagnose several blood and skin diseases that amniocentesis cannot. It has even been suggested and successfully proven in some centres that certain conditions suffered by babies in the womb can actually be treated before birth via fetoscopy. For example, babies with excess fluid of the brain can have a shunt inserted to drain the fluid. Occasionally other conditions such as urinary tract obstruction can also be treated.

Obviously this procedure is limited to very few centres and is only performed by expert hands for certain defined situations.

Fetal Blood Sampling (Cordocentesis)

By this we actually mean that, instead of inserting a needle into the amniotic fluid and withdrawing some of the fluid contents, a needle can be directed into the umbilical cord so that a sample of blood from the baby can actually be taken before birth. This is a procedure not without its risk, the main one again being promoting premature labour, and this test is usually reserved for those cases when it is vital to know the baby's blood group before birth, such as congenital forms of anaemia, or if blood testing of the baby is important to see whether the baby has developed an infection with, say, the toxoplasmosis organism (see pages 84–85). It can also be used for the diagnosis of chromosome abnormalities.

Ultrasound (or Scanning)

Ultrasound is probably the most significant advance in obstetric care, and has now been in use for some twenty-five to thirty years. It was the first safe procedure developed to visualise the baby inside the mother's uterus.

What is Ultrasound?

Ultrasound makes use of sound waves of such high frequency that they are just above the normal range of hearing. The sound waves pass through a transducer and focus on the mother's abdomen just above where the baby is lying. They then bounce off the various surfaces within the body and send back echoes which are translated as a picture on a television screen. The technique was first used in the early 1900s to detect submarines below the ocean surface and later in industry to expose construction flaws.

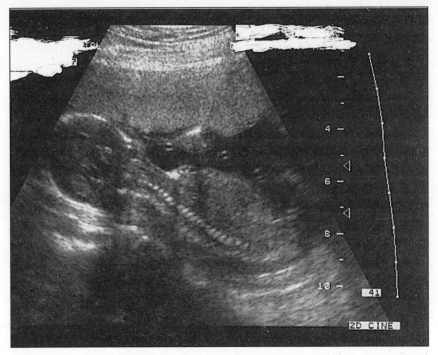

Ultrasound view of 20-week fetus.

How is Ultrasound Performed?

Ultrasound examination may be via the abdomen or the vagina. Sometimes, when there is a special need, the doctor may use both ways. It is a simple, painless procedure. For a clear scan you must have a full bladder, drinking two pints of liquid an hour before your scan. Your abdomen is painted with oil and a probe is moved slowly over the abdomen (or vaginally) up and down in a symmetrical way so that you may be able to differentiate the beating heart, the curve of the spine, the head, and arms and legs. Sometimes the baby can even be seen sucking its thumb.

Who Performs Ultrasound?

This varies from hospital to hospital and the procedure is either

150

performed by a doctor specialising in the technique, usually a radiologist (the same doctor who performs X-rays), or one of their staff, technicians or radiographers, who are specially trained personnel working in X-ray departments. Your consultant, or any of the medical staff specially trained in ultrasound, may also perform this test.

What Can Ultrasound Show?

The uses of ultrasound in obstetric practice are really limitless. New applications and special skills are being developed constantly, but in essence the whole of the inside of the uterus, the baby, the amniotic fluid and the placenta can be seen, and abnormalities noted.

What are the Main Uses of Ultrasound?

In Early Pregnancy

Within the first few weeks of pregnancy ultrasound can be used to diagnose whether a pregnancy is intact and proceeding normally. A small embryo and beating heart can usually be detected as early as four to six weeks of pregnancy. In some centres this procedure has replaced the urinary pregnancy test if there is any doubt whether the pregnancy is intact or if it is not known if the woman has miscarried. Ultrasound can suggest whether or not the pregnancy is alive, and can also be used in the early weeks to see if the pregnancy is misplaced, for example in the Fallopian tube.

Many hospitals now perform ultrasound on all pregnant women when they first come to the booking clinic, partly as a reassurance to the mother and partly so that the size of the baby can be measured. A scan between eleven and thirteen weeks of pregnancy can measure the distance between the top and the bottom of the fetus called crown/rump length. This is an accurate method of date of gestation and most hospitals will redate the pregnancy if the scan date of delivery is more than one week different from the date of delivery calculated from the last period.

It is always done in early pregnancy before amniocentesis or before the AFP test (see page 139), again to accurately date the pregnancy.

Mid-pregnancy Scan

It is now routine for pregnant women to have an ultrasound scan at nineteen to twenty weeks. This is the best time to examine the baby for any possible abnormalities, and also the most accurate time for dating the pregnancy. Some women may have forgotten the date of their last period, or there may be some discrepancy between the size of the uterus and the dates. At around twenty weeks the baby's head can be seen quite clearly in outline and its diameter can be measured on the screen and correlated with the known average.

Measurements to confirm the baby's age can also be carried out earlier in pregnancy but at about twenty weeks most babies' heads are the same size. Early in pregnancy it may be difficult to measure the head and later in pregnancy each baby is going to develop its own shape and size and so there are going to be inaccuracies. Once the diameter of the head is measured it is plotted on a graph and equated to a known value so that accurate dating of the EDD can be made.

This is also the optimum time for looking at all the baby's organs: the heart, the limbs, the spine, the head, etc. The machines are so sophisticated now that the amount of urine inside the baby's bladder can even be measured.

To Assess Fetal Growth

Sometimes repeated or serial tests are carried out to see how the baby is growing and once again the diameter of the head is measured on the screen and correlated with the various stages of pregnancy (see the graph on page 153). Apart from measuring the head, it is possible to measure the circumference of the abdomen which can also give useful information about the baby's size.

There are other criteria which are sometimes used for assessing the accurate growth of the baby. The thigh bone can be measured from top to bottom and the circumference of the head. An estimate can also be given of the amount of amniotic fluid present in the sac. This becomes important later in pregnancy in certain cases where the baby

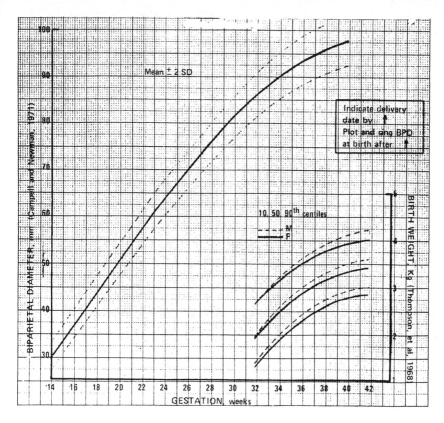

Chart used to predict size of developing baby.

is not growing very well as a diminution of amniotic fluid may be relevant in the assessment of a slow growing baby (see pages 206–208). This is particularly important if there is a suspicion that the baby is not growing as well as it should be, either because the mother has some illness which is known to cause lack of oxygen from the placenta and inadequate nourishment to the baby, or routine examination in the clinic suggests that the size of the uterus does not correspond to the dates of the pregnancy.

Position of the Placenta

It is sometimes important to determine the position of the placenta.

This is particularly so before amniocentesis is performed so that the needle doesn't pierce the placenta, or when bleeding has occurred later in pregnancy and the placenta is lying below the baby (placenta praevia – see pages 221–224).

Associated Problems in the Pelvis

Occasionally other swellings exist in the mother's pelvic organs which may be significant in terms of how the pregnancy proceeds and labour occurs. Examples are fibroids, cysts of the ovaries, or abnormalities of the bony pelvis (see pages 32–35).

Multiple Pregnancy

A twin pregnancy is often suggested by a uterus that is much larger than it should be, a family history, or excessive movements. Before the days of ultrasound twins were occasionally missed in the antenatal clinic, but now that everyone has an early scan the diagnosis can be made with certainty.

How Often Can Ultrasound be Performed and How Safe is it?

Since the crude initial studies in the 1950s the advent of ultrasound has overcome many of the diagnostic limitations of X-rays and has virtually eliminated the need for exposure of the baby to radiation. Like all diagnostic techniques concerned with forming images, some hypothetical risk should be presumed. Studies are continually being carried out in a number of countries to assess the complete safety of ultrasound as its application becomes more widespread.

At the time of writing it is true to say that many large studies tend to support the safety of diagnostic ultrasound exposure in humans, though in some animal studies it has been suggested that repeated ultrasound exposure can affect the way the embryo grows.

In twenty-five years of clinical use and study no known risks and a great many benefits have been associated with the use of ultrasound and recent research in the UK suggests that the benefits of routine ultrasound examinations in pregnancy outweigh any possible potential risks. In theory, therefore, it is possible to repeat the ultrasound examination a number of times in pregnancy.

The Use of Ultrasound in Predicting the Sex of the Baby

The routine ultrasound test done at nineteen weeks often is able to detect the presence or absence of a penis and can in ninety per cent of cases give an accurate prediction of the sex of the baby.

The radiographer or person performing the ultrasound will not as a general rule spend much time looking for the genitalia as there is much more important evidence to determine at this time. Reasonably enough many women want to know the sex of their baby and may ask at the time whether this is possible. Policy varies in different ultrasound units: some departments readily give the information while others do not routinely sex the baby, mainly because this can take up more time than is necessary in a busy department, and also because there is no hundred per cent guarantee that the answer is right. By and large the ultrasonographer will not bring up the question of the sex of the unborn baby unless requested to do so and it may be as well to ask your doctor in the clinic what the policy of the hospital is so that you are not disappointed.

Can You Have Someone with You at the Ultrasound Test?

Again, the policy varies from unit to unit but most ultrasound departments welcome the partner present, although more than one visitor can cause congestion.

What if an Abnormality is Found?

Remember that in many hospitals the test is performed by non-medical personnel who are trained to detect abnormalities but do not advise on the significance or management. What normally happens is that a member of the medical staff is immediately called to the ultrasound department and will discuss the findings with you.

Other Incidental Findings by Ultrasound

As ultrasound apparatus becomes more sophisticated as well as the expertise of the operator, minor changes from what are normal in the anatomy of the baby may be noticed and the true significance of these is not always known.

For instance, it is quite common for one kidney to be larger than the other, and sometimes the developing brain in early pregnancy has very small cysts called choroid plexus cysts. These are insignificant in the majority of cases but, if they persist, they may be associated with other abnormalities of the baby.

The problem is that some of these findings are significant and others not. Sometimes the radiographer and obstetrician are not absolutely certain of the significance of these minor abnormalities, which of course causes a lot of anxiety during the consultation. Although every hospital has an ultrasound department, there are certain centres dotted around the country which specialise in high-power resolution scanning with experts who can further elucidate the significance of minor findings, and it may be that your hospital will refer you to another centre for expert advice.

Doppler Ultrasound

This technique involves the use of ultrasound to diagnose more accurately the well-being of the baby if previous tests have shown that it is not growing well enough (see pages 152–153). The scanner can identify the veins and arteries through which blood flows and can detect the speed at which the blood is travelling. This can correlate directly with how much oxygen the baby is getting and is a more accurate predictive test of a failing placenta.

Colour Doppler

Using the same principle in a more sophisticated manner with colour techniques, the blood vessels can be highlighted more specifically. Most units have the availability of performing doppler ultrasound, although the colour doppler is still in its early stages and its uses have not been completely evaluated.

CHAPTER 7

The Sixth Month

(20–24 Weeks)

Changes in Your Baby

The baby is now growing quickly, the head and body are now more in proportion and the baby doesn't look so 'top-heavy'. Protective fat continues to be deposited under the skin which is less transparent but still very wrinkled. Eyebrows and eyelashes are clearly present and the skin covering the baby begins to grow from two layers, the epidermis on the surface and the dermis which is the deeper layer below. The epidermis is responsible for patterns of surfaces on fingertips, palms, and soles of feet, which are genetically determined. The dermis which lies below the epidermis forms little projections containing blood vessels and nerves. When the baby is born the skin is covered by a white substance that looks like paste. This is called vernix and is secreted by the glands in the skin at about twenty weeks of pregnancy. The vernix protects the growing baby's skin from amniotic fluid.

The baby's muscles and organs grow rapidly and the cells in the brain involving conscious thought mature from now on. A cycle of waking and sleeping is well established and during this time the growth of the baby increases quickly so that by the end of this month the baby may weigh about 570gms (1.25lbs).

Changes in You

Most women enjoy this month and there is often a feeling of well-being, energy and enthusiasm. By twenty weeks the uterus has reached up to the navel and measures about 21cms (8.5ins) from the pubic bone. Weight gain at this stage should be between 4.5 and 6.3kgs (10–14lbs) and by now your waistline has definitely gone and your pregnancy is pretty obvious.

Minor complaints such as increased vaginal discharge and abdominal itching are quite common and sometimes varicose veins can appear. Swelling of the legs is not uncommon at the end of the day and this is quite normal.

Movements of the Baby

Roughly halfway through pregnancy, eighteen to twenty weeks after the last period, a woman in her first pregnancy begins to notice the first fluttery movements of the fetus. She does not usually know how they are supposed to feel which is why, if you are pregnant for the first time, you will probably notice the motions a couple of weeks later than a woman who has previously given birth.

In a first pregnancy, movements of the baby are usually felt somewhere between the eighteenth and twentieth week but sometimes not until the twenty-fourth week. In subsequent pregnancies the movements are usually felt somewhere between the sixteenth and eighteenth weeks, though some mothers claim that they can be felt as early as the fourteenth.

What the Movements Feel Like

The first signs are difficult to explain but some liken them to bubbles or butterfly wings, or the twitching of a fish's tail. Other comments are that they are vague flutterings rather similar to the sensation caused by wind rumbling around the intestine. Gradually, however, these movements become stronger, more persistent and more obvious. As the baby grows the feelings change in character so that they produce thumping or kicking movements which become more powerful as pregnancy continues.

Don't expect to feel the baby moving or kicking constantly because it does go to sleep in the uterus and lies quietly without moving for periods of up to several hours. In early pregnancy the baby is nearly always quite quiet for up to twenty-four hours. This does not mean that your baby has come to any harm and movements usually start up again quite spontaneously. If definite movements are felt in the second trimester and these cease completely and abruptly for more than a day or so, then it might be helpful to visit the doctor who will be able to reassure you by listening to the baby's heartbeat with a small electronic machine in the clinic.

Anaemia

Anaemia means that there is a decreased number of blood cells and a low level of haemoglobin (the oxygen-carrying chemical contained in these cells). Women who are anaemic feel weak, tired and look pale but these symptoms can also be due to the pregnancy itself.

Ideally, you should arrive at term with a blood count in the region of 12gms which will allow you to withstand the normal blood loss during delivery and to cope with breast-feeding, which may make demands on your reserves of iron. Blood transfusion is only occasionally necessary during labour if the mother has a low iron level or if bleeding occurs during or after delivery. It is not unusual for a blood transfusion to be given during Caesarean section.

Women with twins need increasing amounts of iron and folic acid to meet the demands from both babies, and others who are anaemic throughout pregnancy are more prone to miscarriage, premature labour and other complications.

Iron Deficiency

Anaemia is caused by a lack of certain substances, the commonest of which is iron. A loss of iron always accompanies bleeding, hence the constant drain on the supply of iron in the non-pregnant woman due to menstruation. During pregnancy there is no bleeding but extra iron is needed for growth of the baby, the placenta and the breasts. Most women simply do not get enough iron in their diet to make up for these losses. This is why iron supplements are often prescribed throughout pregnancy.

There are a variety of different iron preparations. Some cause nausea or constipation and your doctor will change the prescription as necessary. If it is impossible for you to take tablets at all and you do have anaemia, then there are other ways of making up iron, such as intramuscular or intravenous injections.

Folic Acid Deficiency

Anaemia can also be due to a deficiency of this vitamin, which is widely distributed in green vegetables. It is needed for the formation of the baby's cells as it grows and, again, is in increasing demand as pregnancy progresses. Most hospitals prescribe tablets of folic acid in addition to the iron.

Sickle-cell Anaemia

Several other types of anaemia can occur in pregnancy and are hereditary: in other words they can be passed through generations. One such condition is sickle cell anaemia found almost exclusively in the Afro-Caribbean population. Here ordinary red cells are altered in shape to resemble a sickle and tend to be more fragile than the normal red cells so that they dissolve, causing the blood to become very dilute. The severity of sickle-cell anaemia depends on whether both parents have the condition, or whether the mother is not herself a sufferer but can carry the problem to the next generation.

Various complications can arise from the stress of pregnancy and labour in women with sickle-cell anaemia, notably attacks of fever, pain in the joints, blood clots in the legs, and in extreme circumstances collapse. Treatment is usually by blood transfusion, which corrects the anaemia, careful observation, and prevention of situations which may trigger an attack, such as lack of oxygen during a general anaesthetic.

The diagnosis of a sickle-cell problem is made by a special blood test which is why all women from the West Indies, African nations and parts of India are screened at the first visit to the antenatal clinic.

Thalassaemia (Mediterranean Anaemia)

There are other hereditary anaemias which can cause problems as

161

well. Thalassaemia, or Mediterranean anaemia, is found in people who come from countries of the Mediterranean basin such as Cyprus or Greece. Rather similar to sickle-cell anaemia, the red blood cells are more fragile and are easily destroyed.

Both sickle cell and thalassaemia have a carrier status and, if both parents are carriers. there is a one in four risk of an affected child. All 'at risk' parents are offered a blood test at the booking clinic.

Vaginal Discharge in Pregnancy

Vaginal discharges are of several kinds, some requiring treatment and others being perfectly normal and of no importance. Remember that the vagina, just like the uterus, is very strongly influenced by the female sex hormones: oestrogen and progesterone. Oestrogen stimulates the tissues to mature, and progesterone further develops them. This is most obvious in pregnancy, but changes occur in the lining tissues of the vagina and the cervix as well as the uterus during each menstrual cycle. These changes, which are caused by the hormone oestrogen, make the cells lining the cervix liberate a thin, slightly sticky mucus and this is most marked midway between the periods.

The cells which make up the lining of the vagina are arranged rather like bricks making up a wall. The top cells are thin and large and are constantly shed into the vagina, rather like leaves falling off a tree. In fact they are said to 'exfoliate' which means just that. In the vagina they are acted upon by the helpful bacteria which normally live there to produce a weak acid (lactic acid) and this prevents dangerous bacteria from growing in the vagina.

Thus the vaginal cells and the mucus add to the vaginal discharge. Some fluid also seeps between the cells of the vagina to join the secretions there and this seepage is often increased during sexual excitement, anxiety, or sometimes if you are ill or emotionally upset.

The amount of normal vaginal secretions varies considerably, just as the quantity of secretion in the mouth (saliva) varies. The secretions not only keep the vagina moist but also keep it clean. Sometimes, however, a vaginal discharge is a sign of infection.

Normal Vaginal Discharge in Pregnancy

A small quantity of thick mucoid vaginal discharge is usually present in early pregnancy and is often one of the earliest symptoms. It is usually clear, without an odour, non-irritating or bloody and is much like the discharge many women have prior to their menstrual periods. As pregnancy advances this discharge often increases and may become quite heavy. Some women are more comfortable wearing sanitary pads during the last months of pregnancy for this reason.

Other than offending aesthetic sensibilities, the discharge should be of no concern. It is important to keep the genital area clean and dry, to avoid tight pants, jeans and leotards, to rinse the vaginal area after soaping during a bath or shower, and to avoid exposing it to such irritants as deodorant soaps, bubble-baths and perfumes.

Abnormal Vaginal Discharge in Pregnancy

Sometimes vaginal discharge is caused by bacteria, which can cause infections. These infections are due to different organisms, but they are very common and can easily be treated. If the discharge has a strong odour, causes itchiness, has a yellow-green colour, or is blood-stained, then this should be reported to your doctor.

Types of Vaginal Infection Causing Discharge

The four main vaginal infections which can occur in pregnancy, and which are relatively minor, are:

- Yeast (monilia)
- Trichomonas
- Bacterial Vaginosis (BV)
- Chlamydia

Yeast Infections (Monilia or Thrush)

This is possibly the most common vaginal infection of all and one of the most irritating. It is caused by an organism called candida albicans. No one really knows why thrush occurs, although the fungus itself thrives because of the relatively high sugar content of the cells lining the vagina during pregnancy. It may be a new infection contracted during pregnancy or it may simply be a flare-up of a dormant infection which has not previously caused any symptoms, for the thrush organism lives in the vagina innocently and only causes a discharge due to some stimulus.

The main culprit is again the high levels of oestrogen. This is why monilia is common not only in pregnancy but also in diabetes, and sometimes is also caused by the contraceptive pill.

Monilia causes a thick, white, curdy discharge, often associated with intense irritation and redness around the vagina, and there is often a feeling of burning. This irritation may cause great distress and sometimes is so severe that it wakes the woman up at night or prevents sleep. Because the urethra is so near the vagina, it is not uncommon for urinary symptoms such as frequency or burning while passing urine to occur.

Thrush is easily recognised when the doctor examines the vagina because its appearance is quite characteristic. Sometimes, however, a swab test is done to confirm the diagnosis. Treatment is usually by a course of pessaries placed in the vagina and sometimes antibiotic cream as well which can be smeared around the entrance if there is soreness. Often a three- or four-day course clears this completely.

Unfortunately thrush infections tend to recur, especially after pregnancy, when the treatment can be more energetic and the cause, such as the contraceptive pill or inflammation of the cervix, will be treated. In the past treatment by mouth with a specific antibiotic has not been possible because this is not absorbed in the vagina, but lately there is a useful drug that can be used. This drug is called Diflucan but is not commonly prescribed in pregnancy.

Your partner may harbour thrush but rarely has symptoms. Sometimes thrush causes an irritation on the penis and if so treatment with a similar cream is all that is required. There is no need to avoid having sexual intercourse during treatment with the cream and pessaries, and in fact some doctors recommend this for the obvious reason that the partner will be treated at the same time.

Trichomonas

This is an infection, also mild, and usually sexually transmitted, caused by a little organism that sits in the vagina and the male prostate gland. The sort of discharge that this produces is thin and yellowish-green with a rather nasty fishy odour, though itching and irritation are not common. Again the diagnosis is fairly simple on inspection and confirmed by swab testing.

In most cases the infection will readily respond to a special antibiotic called Metronidazole (Flagyl) which should be given to the woman and her partner, though this treatment is not advisable in the early weeks of pregnancy. There are suitable alternative treatments which your doctor will advise on.

Bacterial Vaginosis (BV)

This is a relatively new term coined for an old bacterial infection of the vagina. This infection is bacterial, very common, and again accompanied by a fishy odour. It is rather difficult to diagnose accurately but responds to the penicillin drugs or Erythromycin which can be given in pregnancy.

This infection may cause concern if the membranes rupture prematurely in late pregnancy and it is therefore important to treat the condition early on.

Chlamydia

This is another bacterial infection which is sexually transmitted. The only symptom is a mild, irritating, usually yellow discharge. Often the discharge goes unnoticed. In the non-pregnant woman chlamydia can cause problems with the Fallopian tubes and is implicated in certain cases of infertility. Interestingly, this organism is also implicated when the membranes rupture prematurely, and some doctors feel there is an association between chlamydia infection and cot death babies. Two-thirds of babies born to infected mothers do contract the infection during vaginal delivery.

Chlamydia can be diagnosed both on inspection by the doctor and also by taking special swab tests. In the non-pregnant woman the antibiotic called Tetracycline is the best treatment, although this is definitely contra-indicated in pregnancy because it may cause discoloration of the baby's teeth and also has something to do with the way that the premature teeth develop. There are, however, other good antibiotics which can be used instead, notably Erythromycin.

Blood-stained Discharge

It is not uncommon to notice some blood-smearing in the vagina and generally this is of no significance but, if it becomes anything more than just a stain, it should be reported to your doctor. Blood-stained discharge can be caused by some of the previous vaginal infections we have discussed because the vaginal walls become a little dry and irritated and bleed on contact. Sometimes there are more important causes, such as the blood coming from elsewhere in the pelvis.

Cervical Erosion

One of the commoner causes of mild vaginal bleeding, especially after sexual intercourse or contact, is cervical erosion. As we have seen, the lining of the vagina is built up of layers of cells, and the same arrangement covers the cervix where it pokes into the upper part of the vagina. However, a sudden change occurs at the edge of the canal leading through the cervix. The cells which line this form a single layer and are thick; they are large, active, and secrete plain mucus. Sometimes in pregnancy the exact position of the change from the flat wall-like cells of the vaginal part of the cervix to the tall, single cells of the cervical canal moves, and in many women it moves outwards.

This means that the tall cells now appear around the entrance to the canal to look like lips. The same effect can be obtained if you close your mouth and draw in your lips. Your mouth now appears as a slit ringed by pink skin. If you now pout your lips, your mouth is ringed by red lip membrane. This pouting of the cells is called an erosion and is often a normal event precipitated by the hormone oestrogen. It is common after pregnancy for this appearance of the cervix to persist, though it does not need treatment unless a blood-stained or thick discharge continues. The treatment after pregnancy usually consists of touching the area with an acid stick or hot wire (cauterisation).

Just occasionally poking through the cervix can be a little polyp which is simply a little blood vessel on a stalk. Again it is of no consequence and usually does not need treatment, although it is useful for the doctor to know that it is present as it may be the cause of a blood-stained discharge. It must be emphasised that simple blood-staining is usually not significant but, if this turns into fresh, bright bleeding, this must be reported to your doctor immediately.

Later in pregnancy, or even as labour starts, a little blood-stained discharge is common and is one of the signs of impending labour (the 'show'). The little plug of mucus that sits within the cervix guarding the entrance to the canal and preventing infection is pushed out when mild contractions start causing a little discharge or blood-staining. It has no other significance.

Sometimes the discharge is watery as well and you may think that in fact your membranes have ruptured and the amniotic fluid around the baby has leaked through. Occasionally it is quite difficult to tell whether a watery discharge is due to a normal secretion from the cervix or the waters around the baby, or even a small leaking of urine which can occur quite commonly. The doctor or midwife will be able to tell the difference quite simply and you should report it if this worries you.

The Skin

Pigmentation of certain areas of the body is quite common in pregnancy. The breasts are a particularly good example. Some dark pigmentation around the breast tissue and nipple is common in all pregnant women but more marked in those who have dark hair. It usually starts about the third month of pregnancy and may involve most of the skin over the breasts.

The Black Line

You may notice a dark line which develops down the centre of your abdomen, usually starting around the third month. There is no particular significance to this pigmentation, which is caused by darkening of cells within the substance of the skin and usually fades after delivery.

Other Areas of Pigmentation

If you already have a mole or birthmark it is likely to become darker during pregnancy. Any scar on the abdomen may undergo quite marked pigmentation, and freckles may also enlarge.

Stretch Marks

What causes stretch marks, and why some women get them and not others, are two of the questions commonly asked by pregnant women, and it is undeniably irritating if your friend has no stretch marks at all whilst you are covered with them.

There are many theories as to the likely origin of stretch marks but probably their occurrence is again mainly due to hormones, notably progesterone and cortisone, which are produced in very high levels during pregnancy. If the hormone production in a particular woman is going to be a little above average then stretch marks will probably occur. Although it is commonly thought that oiling the abdominal skin will prevent the marks, this is not in fact so, but regular oiling may improve the texture of the skin. Avoiding excess weight gain will play some part in keeping down the number of marks but, once again, they will remain although they fade from a reddish colour to light silver after the pregnancy and become much less noticeable.

Skin Irritation and Rashes

A pregnant woman's skin is very susceptible to a number of stimuli which cause no problems at any other time. This is why some mothers complain of an unexplained rash with irritation, often around the middle of pregnancy. Sometimes allergies to food, plants, perfumes or soaps may cause rashes that disappear but can be worrisome at the time.

Any rash that does not disappear after two or three days should be reported to your doctor because there may be other causes. This is particularly important in the first three months of pregnancy because a rash may occasionally be one of the symptoms of German measles (rubella – see pages 80–82). Usually a mild sedative at night or an antihistamine drug which has no effect on the fetus cures the rash.

In an overweight woman a red irritating skin rash is sometimes present in folds of skin, often in the groin or sometimes under pendulous breasts. This is usually due to excessive sweat which cannot evaporate because of the contact between skin surfaces. The best treatment is frequent washing followed by an ordinary talcum powder. If these simple remedies do not help, your doctor should be consulted.

Vaginal and Vulval Warts

These are small swellings around the vulva or vagina which usually do not cause symptoms, although they may cause irritation. They look like pieces of excess skin on a little stalk and they are usually caused by a virus, though occasionally sexual intercourse can promote them. Most vulval warts have no significance, although they may grow somewhat in pregnancy and may be associated with trichomonas (see page 165). If they persist your doctor should be consulted, who will advise accordingly. If they become troublesome or multiply, especially in the area of the vaginal skin where a cut may be made to help the baby emerge (episiotomy – see pages 263–265), then occasionally they can be dabbed with an acid stick or even cauterised.

In rare cases, vulval warts are associated with some venereal diseases (see pages 86–92).

Other Swellings around the Vulva

From time to time women develop swellings around the vaginal and vulval area during pregnancy. One of the commonest is called a Bartholin's cyst which presents with an acutely painful swelling usually on the lower end of the inside lip. It often starts pea-size but can become quite large and frequently becomes infected, causing acute throbbing pain. These cysts should be reported straight away. Treatment is with a small surgical incision, making a pouch of the area, and this can be done without a general anaesthetic.

Sometimes polyps, or fatty lumps, appear around this area, and varicose veins, just like on the legs, can cause swelling around the entrance to the vulva. There is no treatment for these and they usually settle after the pregnancy.

Care of the Breasts

Whether you intend to breast-feed or not, wear a good bra during pregnancy. It should be a comfortable fit, with wide shoulder straps and a wide back to allow room for expansion with advancing pregnancy, and provide support for the breasts. If you are going to breast-feed, there are several types of nursing bra available which give good support and easy access for the baby, but do not buy one until after mid-pregnancy when the breasts will have reached almost their full size. It is better to have cotton rather than nylon as perspiration occurs frequently in pregnancy and a cotton bra will be much more comfortable.

At your first antenatal visit breast-feeding will be discussed together with the suitability of nipples for feeding. The breasts and nipples are usually examined again later in pregnancy and occasionally nipple shields can be worn to improve the shape of nipples that are retracted.

The breasts should be carefully washed and dried each day and the breast tissue gently massaged once milk or its precursor, colostrum, appears. Nipples of normal shape require no special care apart from washing and drying but gentle lubrication with baby oil once a day keeps the skin soft and pliable.

You may be anxious about whether your breasts are suitable for feeding, or you may have strong ideas about feeding your baby with milk from the bottle. Most antenatal clinics in hospitals and in the community have midwives who specialise in breast preparation and will help to answer any queries. (For a fuller explanation of breast- and bottle-feeding please turn to pages 350–366.)

Teeth

The care of teeth is extremely important as changes taking place during pregnancy tend to affect the teeth and cause decay. It is particularly wise to visit the dentist early in pregnancy so that attention can be given to any defects. Your dentist will advise on the correct dental care during pregnancy.

In the UK it is unusual to add calcium or fluoride to the diet although in the USA and other countries it is thought that the addition of these substances helps to strengthen the teeth and prevent mild infection. Don't be anxious if your gums bleed freely when you brush your teeth (see pages 190–191).

There is no reason to avoid a local freezing injection if your dentist needs to do some reparative work or even a short anaesthetic provided that you inform your doctor that you have been advised to have one. The best time to have a short anaesthetic is in the middle three months of pregnancy.

Clothes

Clothes should be comfortable, not too tight and if possible hung from the shoulders to prevent constriction of the waist. There are now so many specialist maternity shops providing pretty clothes that there is no reason to feel dowdy and unattractive.

Girdles and Abdominal Supports

Whether you find that an abdominal support is comfortable or not depends mainly on whether you are used to wearing one when you are not pregnant. Women who are used to wearing a support find it more comfortable to continue during pregnancy, especially if the abdomen becomes saggy after the second or third child. Otherwise, wear a support for comfort if you think it relieves backache and the muscular aches and pains that so commonly accompany the later stages of pregnancy. Obviously a girdle should not be too tight, but no harm can come to the baby from an abdominal support of any kind.

There is a specially designed pelvic belt for women who suffer from backache during pregnancy (see pages 193–194). This is shaped to provide firm support for the pelvic bones and lies under the abdomen in the front so that no pressure is put on the uterus. Your chemist or antenatal clinic should be able to obtain the belt for you.

Shoes and Stockings

Shoes with broad toes and low rubber heels are usually the most comfortable to wear during pregnancy. Low heels are sensible as the extra weight carried in later pregnancy sometimes disturbs the sense of balance, thus making you more liable to trip and fall.

There is no reason not to wear tights or stockings but garters can cause difficulty by interrupting the blood supply to the legs, thus increasing the risk of varicose veins.

CHAPTER 8

The Seventh Month

(24–28 Weeks)

Changes in Your Baby

By twenty-four weeks of pregnancy the baby weighs roughly half a kilo, a little over one pound, and it measures from about 21cms (8.4ins) from top to bottom. It is now moving about very vigorously and responds to touch and to sound. The baby is surrounded by vibrations and noises which it can begin to perceive as early as the fifth month: blood swishing and pounding in the mother's blood vessels, the rumbling of her stomach and intestines, and her voice which resounds through her body. Other sounds penetrate from the world outside and loud noises can make the fetal heart beat faster, and perhaps make the whole fetus tremble. In due course it learns to recognise certain patterns in the sounds and environment and may grasp the difference between parents' voices.

The baby lives in a shadowy world but some light penetrates through the mother's abdominal wall and the wall of the uterus. The eyelids open for the first time at around twenty-six weeks. The eyes are almost always blue or dark blue and it isn't until some weeks after birth that the eyes become the colour they will stay. Sometimes the baby may get hiccups, which are due to sudden intakes of breath, and you may feel the jerk of each hiccup. The amniotic sac now contains up to 750ml (26fl.oz) of fluid which allows the baby to move quite freely. This fluid increases to about 1 litre (2pts) at thirty-six to thirty-eight weeks of gestation. The baby swallows amniotic fluid during much of the pregnancy but, if it is unable to swallow, then excess amniotic fluid may occur leading to a condition called hydramnios. On the other hand if urination doesn't occur, as in the case of the baby having kidney problems, the amount of amniotic fluid may be very small. This is called oligohydramnios.

By English law, twenty-four weeks is the age of viability. That is to say, it is illegal to terminate a pregnancy after this date unless there are gross abnormalities. Formerly twenty-eight weeks, the time was reduced by Parliament recently, largely because of increased paedi-atric knowledge and the expertise of intensive care units whereby more babies born at twenty-four weeks can now survive, although the risk of handicap is still high.

Changes in You

The uterus is now about 5 to 7.5cms (2 to 3ins) above the navel and the fetal heart can be heard with a simple stethoscope in the antenatal clinic. As the uterus grows it tends to press on certain organs, notably the stomach, and this is when heartburn may occur for the first time (see pages 192–193). The pressure of the uterus also sometimes prevents the diaphragm from expanding and you may therefore feel short of breath on exertion. Other discomforts at this stage may include back pain, pressure in the pelvis, leg cramps and headaches. These are all quite usual and are due to the enlarging uterus and hormone changes in the body.

Your weight will be steadily increasing and you will put on about a pound a week from now on. Your weight reflects a number of features, such as the growing baby, and the increase in the amount of amniotic fluid, partly produced by the baby's urination and partly by the normal hormonal changes that are occurring in your body.

Your visits to the doctor or midwife will still be monthly and you will be weighed at each visit. Try to avoid fatty and spicy foods at this stage and be sparing with fun things to eat such as sugar, chocolates, cakes, etc. Drink plenty of fluids and try and stick to four small, regular meals a day. Nibbling from the fridge, whatever you eat, is bound to make you put on unnecessary weight. An occasional glass of wine will do you no harm whatsoever. It is a good idea not to drink coffee or tea late in the evening, because this will inevitably make you get up in the night to pass water and may prevent you sleeping properly.

Many institutions start planning their antenatal preparation classes around this time and, if you haven't enrolled in a class, now is the time to talk to your midwife or doctor about the antenatal instruction that is available in your area.

Continued Antenatal Care

Every time you go to the clinic or see your doctor, which is usually monthly until the twenty-eighth week, fortnightly until the thirty-sixth week and then weekly until term, you can expect the following to be checked, although there may be variations depending on your particular need:

- weight and blood pressure;
- urine for sugar and protein;
- the heartbeat of the baby;
- the size of the uterus, by feeling;
- the hands and legs for swelling.

By twenty-four weeks the baby is often in the breech position, in other words head up (see pages 307–309). This occurs because it is the simplest way for the baby to adapt to the shape of the uterus. Later in pregnancy most babies turn round so that they are in a head down position.

The size of the uterus can be felt by the doctor or midwife examining you and corresponds with the diagram on page 118. By

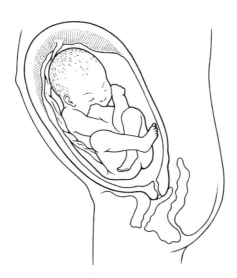

The breech position. Here the baby's legs are flexed.

twenty-four weeks the height of the uterus is just a finger breadth or two above the navel. It is often difficult to actually outline the baby on examination but the heartbeat can be checked quite simply by listening with an electronic stethoscope.

The findings at the antenatal clinic are recorded on your notes and different hospitals have different systems of record keeping. Some will ask you to carry your notes with you, which is the only record that there is, and this seems to be a satisfactory arrangement. The loss rate when women keep their own notes is very small. Other systems include keeping hospital notes, and you will be asked to carry a small co-operation card, which is a miniature copy of all the findings and is small enough to be kept in a handbag. It is a useful guide should a new doctor have to be called in to look after you.

Frequency of Antenatal Visits

The routine pattern of monthly visits to the twenty-eighth week, fortnightly to the thirty-sixth and then weekly to term was laid down by the Ministry of Health in 1929 and this regime is still held as a guide in many obstetric units. However, there is a tendency to regard this as over-doctoring and, provided you are not at any particular risk in your pregnancy, the number and frequency of attendances are diminishing. There are some units where women with a normal pregnancy are seen only four times during the pregnancy, but others conform to the more usual pattern.

Interestingly, the first hospital outpatient clinic in the UK opened in 1915 and the care of women during labour and delivery has a long history, but the idea that pregnancy itself is a condition requiring professional supervision is a relatively recent one. Until the first decades of the twentieth century medical practitioners regarded pregnancy as a state of health, albeit one in which the woman was liable to suffer from a number of unpleasant complications.

In the late 1800s antenatal care was limited to one aspect of the pregnancy, namely history. No one attempted to evaluate the baby, monitor the fetus, nor of course were any routine clinical procedures undertaken. The founding father of antenatal care in Britain is usually thought to be the Scottish physician J.W. Ballantyne, the author of an important article in the *British Medical Journal* in 1901 which led directly to the establishment of the first antenatal inpatient bed in Britain.

The desirability of routine antenatal care was first advocated in relation to poor, unmarried pregnant women, and it is in the institutional provision for such women that one important forerunner of present day antenatal care can be found. The Lauriston Pre-Maternity Home, adjacent to the Royal Maternity Hospital in Edinburgh, gave rise to the prototype of the hospital antenatal care we know today.

Mothercraft or Parentcraft Classes

The idea of these classes, which are variously called antenatal, relaxation or parentcraft classes, are to keep you informed, fit and well during pregnancy so that you are prepared for birth, and for caring for your baby in the first few weeks of life. You will probably find that there are a number of different classes run by different organisations in your area.

The hospital often runs its own classes, but your family doctor or local health centre may also run them so you should be able to find the kind that fits your own needs. The best person to ask is the hospital midwife, community midwife or health visitor, or your family doctor, who will enable you to choose. It is probably worth going to some of these classes as it is useful to know what sort of procedures to expect in the unit where you have your baby, or what the wards and labour suite look like, and to meet others who will be having their babies at about the same time.

The National Childbirth Trust (NCT) runs a separate group of classes for which you have to pay, as it is a private organisation. Instruction is given by trained midwives, health visitors or physiotherapists. The emphasis here is on breathing patterns and relaxation during labour. There will be a local branch of the National Childbirth Trust near your hospital and your family doctor should be able to put you in touch with them.

Most of these classes are aware of the different choices now available to women in terms of their own preference. It is also useful to learn about the different forms of labour that are possible, what the particular hospital unit offers in the way of pain relief and epidural anaesthesia (see pages 269–281), whether bathing pools are available, as well as the mechanisms of labour and how they are managed in different situations. There are usually about eight classes, which start around the twenty-fourth or twenty-fifth week, and partners are welcome to attend. Some are specially organised at times which allow other members of the family to attend if they wish.

Statutory Maternity Pay

A maternity allowance is payable to all women who have been working and making National Insurance contributions at the full rate. The following criteria must be satisfied:

- You have been continuously employed for at least twenty-six weeks continuing into the fifteenth week before the week your baby is due.

- You have average weekly earnings of not less than the lower earnings limit for the payment of National Insurance contributions which apply in the qualifying week.

- You are still pregnant at the eleventh week before the week your baby is due, or have had your baby by that time.

- Medical evidence must be available of the date when your baby is due at least twenty-one days before the maternity absence is due to start.

- You have stopped working.

If you satisfy these conditions, then you qualify for statutory maternity pay even if you do not intend to return to the same place of work after the baby is born. Agency workers, part-time workers, married women and widows paying reduced rate National Insurance contributions can all get statutory maternity pay if they satisfy the qualifying conditions. You are also entitled to statutory maternity pay if you satisfy the qualifying rules with more than one employer.

In addition, there are other benefits including time off for ante-natal care, maternity pay and the right to return to former employment after pregnancy.

There were a number of changes in statutory maternity pay intro-duced in October 1994 which benefit the employee:

- The maternity pay period can now start at any time between the eleventh week before your baby is due and the Sunday following the date your baby is born.

- You no longer have to give up work prior to the sixth week before your expected week of confinement for statutory pay to be payable for eighteen weeks.

- If you are absent from work because of a pregnancy related illness on or after the start of the sixth week before your baby is due, maternity pay will start on the Sunday following the first day of that absence for a reason not connected with pregnancy, or the Sunday of the first week of absence if you have not done any work in that week.

- If you are already sick with a pregnancy related illness in the seventh week before your baby is due and the pregnancy related ill-ness continues into the sixth week, the maternity pay period must start on the Sunday of the sixth week.

- In order to claim maternity pay, you must have been employed continuously for twenty-six weeks into the qualifying week.

How Much is Statutory Maternity Pay?

The following rates are payable:

- 90% of your average weekly earnings for the first six weeks.
- £52.50 for the rest of the maternity pay period.

The other rule that has just been introduced is that you can no longer be dismissed on the grounds of being pregnant and, if there is an attempt to dismiss you on these grounds, this is termed unfair dismissal and can be challenged.

If you would like further information about statutory maternity pay, a pamphlet is available from the Department of Social Security, or can be obtained via your doctor's surgery or antenatal clinic.

Please note that the requirements and benefits for pregnant mothers seem to change constantly and it is important to keep up to date.

Exercise

During pregnancy certain physical and metabolic changes take place which do impose a certain amount of stress on the body. For example, the joints and tissues become softer and slightly more prone to injury; the amount of blood pumping round the body increases dramatically; the lungs are not always able to expand fully; and there is an increased need for nutrition. Most women, however, are accustomed to a certain amount of physical exercise or sport and the basic rule is to continue with what your body is used to in moderation.

Women who don't get any exercise during pregnancy probably become less fit as the months pass, particularly because they are getting increasingly heavier. A good exercise programme which can be built into your daily lifestyle helps to counteract the trend towards decreasing fitness.

Pelvic muscles can be toned in the vaginal and perineal area, and developing a good exercise programme by gradual stages is to be recommended. The degree to which exercise is suitable for you should be discussed with your doctor as strenuous programmes may have to be curtailed if certain complications arise, i.e. bleeding in early pregnancy, heart disease, high blood pressure, etc.

Aerobics

By and large aerobic exercises improve circulation, the transport of oxygen to the baby, and can also reduce the risk of varicose veins and haemorrhoids. They increase muscle tone and strength, possibly relieving backache, and impart a general feeling of well-being and confidence. Aerobics are to be recommended, but too strenuous exercise causing undue tiredness and exhaustion should be avoided.

Relaxation Techniques

Breathing and concentration exercises relax mind and body, help conserve energy for when it is needed, and are valuable in combination with more physical routines which your antenatal attendants will be discussing with you.

Lifting

Obviously you don't want to lift heavy weights during pregnancy because this will almost certainly influence the spine and may cause back problems. Remember when you bend down to keep your legs bent and your back straight, or go down on one knee. This is particularly important when lifting other children.

Are There Any Limits to Exertion during Pregnancy?

There was a time when many doctors believed that even small amounts of exercise could be dangerous to the mother and the baby. Fortunately, today's pregnant woman is no longer regarded as a delicate flower requiring seclusion until her baby is born.

Unbiased research has yet to be conducted into the long-term effects of intense physical activity on a woman's health or her ability to ovulate and bear children, and important questions concerning the safe limits of exertion during pregnancy remain to be answered. While antenatal exercises become a popular and profitable business, many of the old myths about the harmful effects of physical activity on pregnancy still exist. This section helps to provide practical advice about the positive and negative effects of sport and physical activity in pregnancy.

The basic rule is that the appropriate amount of training and physical fitness for a pregnant woman should be determined by her fitness and activity level before pregnancy, her age, and whether there are any associated medical or obstetrical complications.

While a physically fit woman can continue most activities at or slightly below her level prior to pregnancy, it is probably not wise to exceed these levels. Physical fitness achieved through aerobic exercises prior to pregnancy conditions the heart and lungs by increasing the efficiency of the body's intake of oxygen. Rhythmic activities, such as walking, jogging, running, swimming, rowing, biking, aerobic dancing and skipping, all help to increase the pulse rate as the heart works harder to bring oxygen to the body's muscle groups. It would be foolish for extremely sedentary women suddenly to initiate a rigorous aerobics programme during pregnancy.

Many women benefit from mild and gradually increased exercise, such as walking and water exercises. Most physical fitness centres are staffed by experienced professionals who understand the limitations of pregnancy and will advise accordingly.

Do Physically Fit Women Experience Easier Pregnancies and Labour?

The answer is probably yes, and it is logical to assume that aerobically fit women will have more stamina and strength to endure a long labour than unfit women. However, proving this scientifically is not as easy as it may seem. Most experts now believe that regular exercise is associated with less anxiety and stress, greater self-confidence, and a milder perception of pain, though it is probable that there is no relationship between physically fit women and the length of labour.

Is it Safe to Use Weight and Fitness Machines during Pregnancy?

It is possible that the resultant increase in muscle strength eases labour and delivery and makes women less susceptible to the muscular aches and pains that are so common throughout pregnancy.

The degree to which a programme is undertaken should be strictly on the advice of professionals.

Should Hot Baths and Saunas be Avoided during Pregnancy?

There is no scientific evidence to determine safe limits of exposure in a sauna or hot bath but it is probably wise to limit these, and perhaps pregnant women should be advised not to take very hot baths or showers, certainly in the first three months of pregnancy.

Can Exercise Have Any Adverse Effects on the Fetus?

There have never been any scientific studies to show that exercise, or even intense physical activity, early in pregnancy is actually responsible for miscarriage or spontaneous abortion. Following an early miscarriage women are often left with feelings of guilt at having played too much tennis or jogged too many miles, or even having stood or walked for prolonged periods. It is a myth that these activities cause early miscarriage.

A healthy woman, free of obstetric complications, can be reassured that most moderately strenuous activities will not adversely alter fetal health, the incidence of premature birth, or birth weight. Again, if a woman wishes to exercise as close to her exertional limits as possible, she should do so only under careful medical supervision and should probably avoid the first three and the last two months of pregnancy.

There are some general rules which apply to both pregnant and non-pregnant women which are useful guidelines:

- Strengthening exercises and aerobics should not be performed on the same muscles on consecutive days.

- A general warm-up routine should be performed before muscles are made to work against resistance.

- Muscle strengthening exercises should be preceded and followed by stretching exercises that are specific for the muscles that are made to work against resistance.

• Exercises should be performed in a slow and controlled manner. Rapid and jerky movements increase the risk of injury and the most efficient way to improve strength is to allow brief rest periods between exercise sessions.

How Great is the Risk of Trauma?

The implantation of a healthy egg into the uterus in early pregnancy is very strong and the egg cannot easily be dislodged. This fact can be attested to by the millions of women who, prior to the legalisation of abortion, spent hours jumping up and down in attempts to dislodge an unwanted pregnancy.

From the twelfth week of pregnancy the fetus rises enough to be seen and to be felt abdominally. At this point the chance of injury to the uterus by a direct blow increases, although it is still highly unlikely, and injury to the fetus is even more unlikely because the baby swims in its own fluid which acts as a protective cushion. Nevertheless it is probably best to avoid contact sports which might involve a direct blow to the abdomen.

Which Sports Should be Avoided in Pregnancy?

Definite hazards are associated with water skiing, a sport that is best avoided during pregnancy, as accidents involving falling into water at high speeds can force water into the vagina and cervix and may possibly cause miscarriage. Scuba diving is probably not ideal either and certainly pregnancy is not the time to learn.

Horse-riding if you are an experienced rider is probably fine. There are no studies to show that the bouncing movements of the horse are detrimental to the fetus, but pelvic discomfort may be experienced.

If you are an accomplished skier, it is advisable to ski on a slope which is a step below your normal level. In other words, if you are an expert skier, ski at an intermediate level or lower. Many accidents occur on icy slopes so it is best to ski only under optimal conditions.

Ice skating, roller skating and roller blading pose no problems. Golf, tennis and squash are fine within limits and running is also fine providing it is not too strenuous or for too long.

What are the Best Sports and Exercise during Pregnancy?

Aerobic exercises, including walking, jogging, running, cycling, swimming, or any sports that utilise the whole body in a continuous movement, are all fine. Swimming and cycling are particularly good because they are weight independent: in other words, you do not have to support your bodyweight.

Exercise bicycles pose no problems, and of course walking is an excellent way of promoting physical fitness without risking injury.

Muscle Strengthening Exercises

In addition to the obvious physical benefits which they achieve, women who exercise regularly and thoughtfully during pregnancy often note a greater sense of well-being and psychological satisfaction. Properly

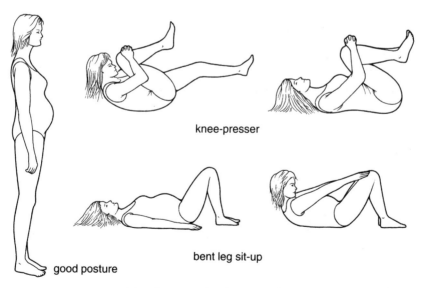

knee-presser

bent leg sit-up

good posture

Muscle strengthening exercises.

performed strength and flexibility exercises decrease the likelihood of injury to the muscles and tendons of the arms, legs and back. As well as preventing pain, these exercises can often relieve pain once it is present.

Physical fitness has its greatest application during labour, especially during a prolonged second, or pushing, stage.

Leg and Thigh Exercises

Strengthening calf muscles: this can be easily achieved by standing about a foot away from a wall, placing the palms on the wall and keeping the heels on the floor, and bending the elbows and moving the upper part of the body towards the wall until the chest presses against it. You should feel a pull in your calf muscles. This position is held for ten seconds and can be repeated ten times.

Sitting on the floor with one leg outstretched and the other at the side, lean forward grasping the foot of the outstretched leg. This helps to strengthen the hamstring muscles.

Another exercise which benefits the quadriceps muscles in the front of the thigh consists of standing with one hand resting on a wall or a table and then grasping the ankle with the other hand. The foot is pulled back until either the heel touches the buttock or you feel a pull in the thigh. This exercise can be repeated five times with each foot, holding for a count of ten, once a day.

Abdominal Exercises

Weak tummy muscles can lead to a higher incidence of back pain during pregnancy, and bent leg sit-ups help to strengthen these muscles. Remember that bent leg sit-ups are never done with the knees straight, and that easier sit-ups can be done with the hands reaching towards the knees.

A good muscle relaxing exercise to perform after sit-ups is the hip twister. Lie on your back with your knees bent and slowly move your knees from side to side while turning the head in the opposite direction. This can be continued for about thirty seconds, gradually increasing to one minute. Lying on the back and getting into a curling position by bringing the knees up to the chest and the head to the knees for a count of six is also good for abdominal muscles.

Back Exercises

Because there is a forward curvature of the spine during pregnancy, there is a particular susceptibility to low back pain and sports-related injuries. Good posture is the most essential part of preventing problems. In addition to the curvature of the spine, the ligaments and muscles that are moved by the back become softened and stretch because of the hormones of pregnancy which makes it even more likely that back problems may start for the first time in pregnancy. Ligament tears, disc problems and sciatica (pressure on the nerves that go down the legs) are all too common in pregnancy and it is vital that you understand how to handle your back and the best way of avoiding problems.

Good posture means walking with the head up straight as if it were pulled by a string, with the shoulders back and the abdomen in as far as possible. This will help to extend the spine in the correct direction and prevent forward slouching.

One of the best exercises to prevent and relieve low back pain is the knee presser. This consists of lying flat on the back and pulling one knee up to the chest, holding it in this position with the hand for a count of five, and working each leg for a total of five times. After this bring both legs up together five times. Gentle push-ups are also useful in extending the spine.

The following suggestions may help in preventing back problems:

- Always remember that the back is susceptible to aches, pains and injuries in pregnancy because of the increased weight of the abdomen curving the spine in the wrong direction.

- Be as upright as you can, both when walking and sitting. Forward bending is not a good idea at all in pregnancy because it increases the likelihood of weakness and disc protrusions.

- If you need to pick things up or lift, go down on the floor with one knee bent or go down with your bottom sticking out sideways, always trying to remember to keep the back straight.

- Never slouch in a chair: always have a cushion behind you and make sure that your bottom is well up against the back of the chair.

- Make sure your bed is comfortable and firm. Ligament problems and stiffness in the back are produced by too soft a mattress. Don't use your hands to push yourself up from the lying position. Roll over on your side and get up sideways so that the back always remains straight. It is surprising how many women after pregnancy maintain this attitude to their back and, far from pregnancy being a problem, it may stimulate thought into the prevention of back problems in the future.

Abdominal Pain

At this stage in pregnancy it is quite common to get abdominal pain for a variety of reasons, most of which are not significant. The commonest type of pain is low down on either side of the groin, just above the symphysis bone, which is usually due to stretching of the ligaments that support the uterus. The woman often complains that the groin starts to ache after walking and this tends to go away after rest.

Don't forget that the uterus actually contracts all through pregnancy (Braxton Hicks contractions) and sometimes it can be quite difficult to differentiate between these contraction-like pains and a threatened premature labour. If you have any worries, consult your doctor or hospital.

Some women describe a 'shooting' sensation in the vagina which is quite sharp and rather like a hot knife. This is a mystery to obstetricians but it certainly occurs sometimes at this stage in pregnancy, usually passing away spontaneously.

Urinary tract infections are common in pregnancy and abdominal pain, especially with urinary symptoms, should be investigated.

Travel

Short trips whether by car, train or plane cause no problems in pregnancy. If planning a longer trip, then ideally this should be undertaken between the sixteenth and twenty-eighth week of pregnancy. This is the safest time because miscarriage or the onset of premature labour are unlikely. Long travel can be fatiguing and uncomfortable, particularly in the car, and it is wise to break the journey every hour or so for a few minutes' walk.

Most airlines do not permit travel for long distances in the last six weeks before the baby is due and, if an urgent journey is necessary, it is best to travel by car or rail. In the past, there was some anxiety concerning lack of oxygen during air travel which, it was thought, might cause problems with the baby's development but there are no grounds for such apprehensions. Modern aircraft are always pressurised.

Again it is important to consult your doctor who may suggest travel is inadvisable if you have had any problems such as bleeding in early pregnancy, or if there is anything in your history or emerging from an examination that suggests instability in the pregnancy, where travel might precipitate problems. If you normally need pills for travel sickness, consult your doctor. Many of them are quite safe and resemble the drugs to help nausea and vomiting which can be taken in the early stages of pregnancy.

Immunisation

As a general principle active immunisation during pregnancy should be avoided and in some cases it is positively contra-indicated. This applies to immunisation with rubella or any other live vaccine. If you are travelling to a country that requires immunisation documents for entry, then your doctor should be consulted. If you are still in doubt, the local office of the Department of Health or one of the major airports will be able to advise.

Primary smallpox vaccination should be avoided at any stage of pregnancy. Vaccination against cholera, yellow fever, typhoid and paratyphoid can be given during pregnancy but are better avoided until sixteen weeks.

Bathing and Douching

Bathe just as much as you would normally, since it has no bad effects on pregnancy. Contrary to former belief, water cannot be forced into the vagina or cause damage to the uterus or to the baby. Don't make a bath too hot because this may cause you to feel faint. Douching is usually unnecessary.

Carpal Tunnel Syndrome

This is the medical term for puffiness and discomfort around the wrist which may occur at this stage of pregnancy, but is often later. Tingling and pain may be experienced in the fingers, especially at night. Picking up objects can be difficult and even writing may cause problems.

The cause of this is simply fluid which is trapped under the normally protective band of tissue lying across the wrist. The fluid presses against the nerves which supply the fingers, hence the discomfort and pain. Mild pain relieving tablets such as Panadol (Paracetamol or Disprin) will help, and occasionally, if the pain is severe, doctors may prescribe a short course of diuretics.

This complaint invariably gets better after the baby is born as the fluid retention disappears. In rare cases a local injection into the tender area or even a minor surgical operation may be necessary to relieve the pressure on the wrist band if the symptoms persist long after the pregnancy is over. It may be helpful to form a splint, holding the arm midway between flexion and extension, which takes the pressure of fluid away from the wrist band.

Bleeding from the Nose and Gums

The lining of the gums and nose responds to hormones in pregnancy as do most other organs and they will become swollen as the amount of blood increases. You may notice bleeding from the gums after brushing your teeth which should cause no alarm and can be ignored. If it persists and becomes a nuisance, your dentist should be consulted in case there is a minor inflammation (gingivitis) which needs to be treated.

Similarly, nosebleeds can occur for the first time in pregnancy. If a nosebleed becomes heavy, there is one simple remedy and that is to pinch the nose firmly between the index finger and the thumb for about thirty seconds. This will almost certainly do the trick. Do not tilt your head back or pack the nose with ice as this will have no effect and you may in fact swallow some blood which is unpleasant. If the bleeding keeps recurring, your doctor should be consulted as occasionally there may be a small polyp inside the nose which is easily treated in the outpatients clinic.

Muscle Cramps

Acutely painful cramp, commonly occurring in the calf and occasionally in the foot, usually in the latter half of pregnancy, may wake you at night as the muscles become rigid and hard. The best thing to do is to get up straight away and massage the affected muscle firmly to increase the blood supply. No one knows why these cramps occur. It was formerly thought that they were due to lack of calcium but this is probably not so. If cramp recurs, your doctor should be consulted as there are effective, safe tablets which can be prescribed to prevent the spasm which causes the cramp.

Headaches

Headaches may occur for the first time in pregnancy, though interestingly migraine sufferers often find that their headaches improve. Headaches are probably due to a combination of change in position and blood flow and to an increase in the hormone oestrogen. Persistent headaches may be associated with raised blood pressure or sinus problems and your doctor should be consulted if treatment with simple pain relievers produces no improvement.

Headaches experienced for the first time in pregnancy can be extremely unpleasant and sometimes even debilitating. No one really knows why headaches occur at this time although it is probably related to blood flow but, if they persist, it is important to talk to your midwife or doctor. Rest assured that if there is no underlying cause they will usually disappear as fast as they arose as your pregnancy progresses.

Fainting Attacks

You may feel faint at any period during pregnancy, especially following a sudden change of position. Sometimes fainting occurs after prolonged standing in buses or a shopping queue, or during warm weather.

A feeling of faintness in later pregnancy is particularly common if you lie flat on your back as the weight of the uterus presses on the main vein of the body which carries blood back to the heart. This causes a rapid drop in blood pressure which is usually short lived. The best thing to do is to turn immediately onto one side or the other, thereby releasing the pressure of the uterus on the main vein.

An epidural anaesthetic (see pages 274–281) increases the likelihood of faintness which is one of the reasons why women are often placed on their side during labour.

Shortness of Breath

Because the diaphragm is raised by pressure from the enlarging uterus, shortness of breath is common in pregnancy. If this interferes with your sleep, the head and shoulders should be propped up by pillows but for safety your doctor should be consulted if this seems anything more than slight, especially if you feel winded by climbing a flight of stairs.

Heartburn

Heartburn is a fiery sensation in the chest which is often associated with vomiting small amounts of bitter, sour fluid. The term 'heartburn' is misleading because it has nothing to do with the heart, but results from regurgitation of the acid stomach juices into the lower part of the gullet. It occurs around mid- or late pregnancy mainly because the uterus enlarges causing a backflow of juices by pressing on the oesophagus and stomach, but it is also due to the relaxation of the small valve at the entrance of the stomach, which is due to the hormone progesterone. When swallowing, the valve closes off, but in pregnancy the valve is a little less active than normal and therefore stomach contents flow up and irritate the oesophagus, causing discomfort and sickness.

Another word for this complaint is indigestion and it can occur at any time for reasons other than pregnancy such as a stomach ulcer or a hernia.

Management of Heartburn

During pregnancy, heartburn is often worse at night when lying flat, and sleeping propped up will reduce the amount of acid regurgitation. Avoid greasy, rich or spicy foods and don't have a heavy meal before retiring. The best treatment, however, is to neutralise the acid contents by taking an antacid such as Milk of Magnesia or Rennie's tablets, or other medication that your doctor will prescribe. These form a film which protects the lower part of the oesophagus from the acid juice and prevents inflammation which partly causes the problem.

Heartburn may start at around the middle of pregnancy and can become more of a problem as the uterus enlarges and pregnancy progresses. It often improves after thirty-six weeks, once the head has begun to descend and the pressure on the stomach is reduced. Sometimes heartburn causes regurgitation of the stomach contents with nausea and sickness, but this is usually self-limiting and can be helped by medicines which your doctor will prescribe.

Backache

Backache, pain in the groin, sometimes in the buttocks, and in the lower part of the abdomen are not uncommon in pregnancy, usually due to stretching of the ligaments and softening of the bones of the spine due to the hormone progesterone. In addition, the normal posture adopted by most women in pregnancy places a considerable strain on the lower part of the spine and the joints of the pelvis. There are of course other causes of backache, for example, a disc in between two vertebrae may occasionally push out, or prolapse, giving rise to acute pain in the back and perhaps down the back of one leg (sciatica).

Pain can also occur at the top of the buttocks, often because of the strain on the joints between the lower part of the backbone and the sacrum and the side walls of the pelvis (sacroiliac joint).

The single most important aspect of treatment for backache is prevention. Women tend to stoop forward during pregnancy because of the weight of the expanding uterus and this increases backache. Walking upright, sleeping on a firm bed, learning how to lift and carry without bending forwards, and sitting back in a chair without slouching will do much to prevent problems with the spine. It cannot be emphasised too greatly that care of the spine and supports in pregnancy is vital in preventing future problems and, indeed, some hospitals run a back clinic where advice is given by doctors and physiotherapists. There is no harm in gentle manipulation by an expert and your doctor should be able to recommend someone in this field.

Occasionally a corset or support may be helpful, though it is far better to educate the muscles to overcome problems by exercise and care with posture.

Insomnia

During the increasing fatigue that most women experience in pregnancy sleep may be seriously disturbed, particularly during the middle and last few weeks of pregnancy, often by the activity of the fetus and the mother's inability to get into a comfortable position.

If you find that you are not sleeping at all at night, then you should consult your doctor because there are a variety of safe and effective sleeping tablets which you can take with no adverse effect on the unborn child. A pregnant woman needs a good night's sleep and it is reassuring to know that your normal sleep pattern will almost certainly return after delivery.

Don't worry if you feel that you really can't sleep at night or you get up a lot and fidget. Your baby will not be affected in any way by your lack of sleep: it is you who will just feel tired. Try to make up any lack of sleep by resting in the afternoon. Some women experience nightmares, particularly in pregnancy and even after a short sleep, but these normally improve as pregnancy advances.

Libido

Sexual desire changes in pregnancy to some extent but reactions are variable and depend on the stage of pregnancy. Mothers carrying their first baby often notice some lessening of sexual desire during the first three months. The middle months of pregnancy are often the most active and fatigue-free so that this stage is frequently the most sexually fulfilling.

Towards the end of pregnancy there may be a definite waning of sexual feelings. Appearance may have something to do with it as some women find it embarrassing to look pregnant, while others feel pride in an enlarging abdomen. Some women get very upset by changes in their partner's attitude towards sex and it is not uncommon for men to find their partners either particularly sexy or the reverse. Both should realise that attitudes to and the desire for sex during and after pregnancy vary considerably and the normal pattern usually returns once the family has settled into a routine.

When is it Safe to Have Sexual Relations?

In general there is no reason why you should not lead a normal sex life in pregnancy. Some doctors advise abstention during the first three months and the last three weeks for fear of either promoting miscarriage or premature labour. In fact there is very little evidence for this and in principle you may enjoy sexual relations as you like unless your doctor prescribes otherwise.

Orgasms are not harmful in pregnancy. Sex cannot introduce infection to the baby because it is safely protected in a bag of fluid surrounding it; neither will sex crush the baby as the bag of fluid is an excellent cushion.

If bleeding occurs at any stage in pregnancy, consult your doctor immediately and refrain from intercourse. It may not be serious but the doctor has to rule out the possibility of certain conditions causing the bleeding that could be aggravated by sex (cervical erosion – see pages 166–167; cervical polyps – see page 167).

Mood Changes

During pregnancy your emotions and behaviour may change as markedly as the shape of your body. The basic tendencies remain the same but variations and exaggerations of previous behaviour can be expected. There are several reasons for this. Firstly, you are under the influence of various reproductive hormones. Many women and their partners know from experience that hormonal variations of the menstrual cycle can also have a marked effect on behaviour. Also, pregnancy places an additional burden on most parts of the body. There is more strain on muscles, more need for blood, oxygen and nourishment; the kidneys, heart and lungs have added burdens.

Along with pregnancy comes change in day-to-day behaviour and these variations may cause stress. As an expectant mother you are learning to play a new social role which involves greatly increased dependency. There may be a new financial need and, since your energies are directed more into growing and carrying the increasingly heavy baby within you, you may become physically less able to take care of yourself. Feelings of fear, worry and anxiety can be heightened in pregnancy and there can be a genuine career/motherhood conflict, perhaps compounded by well-meaning but irritating advice from relatives and friends.

One might expect that the career woman would have a difficult time getting used to the idea of pregnancy. One statistical survey found that among middle-class women the problem is not that simple. True, girls eager to start a family reported delight in pregnancy more often than those immersed in careers and reluctant to give them up for children. On the other hand those who were indifferent to their work were also likely to express happiness at being pregnant and the research suggests that the woman who enjoys work may also enjoy motherhood because this is her characteristic style in dealing with situations.

Pregnancy is notorious for its mood swings. Previously stable women may find themselves going through periods of depression or getting irritable about nothing. Trifles which ordinarily barely ruffle you become momentous and seriously upsetting.

Remember that pregnancy is not an illness or a disease and it is helpful to keep active in the way in which you would normally do. If you are working, don't stop and, if you are not, try to set yourself a task each day either at home or outside so that you are mentally stimulated.

If mood changes become excessive, your doctor can advise a mild sedative and, again, there are plenty that are quite safe in pregnancy. Remember that excessive mood swings are very common and it is helpful if your partner is told this by your doctor so that he understands and is sympathetic to you.

In rare cases, depression may continue in pregnancy, and more specific treatment may be necessary. 'Baby blues' and more acute forms of depression are not that uncommon after the baby is born and this is fully discussed on pages 338–342.

Rest

It is difficult to say precisely how much rest you should have during pregnancy because so many personal factors are involved. However, it is sensible to spend seven or eight hours in bed at night and an hour or two resting in the afternoon. It is very common to feel extremely tired and lethargic in the first three months, as we have seen, because of the complex hormone changes that are occurring in the body. These will be reversed as the pregnancy advances so there is no point in fighting fatigue.

Of course, if you feel tired during this time, then spend more time resting. It is difficult for mothers who are working or who have children to look after but this is the time in pregnancy when as much help as possible should be given by partners and friends to share the load.

CHAPTER 9

The Eighth Month
(28–32 Weeks)

Changes in Your Baby

At about twenty-eight weeks the baby measures 36cms (14ins) long and weighs about 900gms (2lbs). There is now about 750ml (26fl.oz) of amniotic fluid which allows the baby to move freely. By twenty-eight weeks the baby is able to hear much more. In early pregnancy the nerve endings that enable sound to be heard were not connected so sound was experienced like a vibration. The baby is also sensitive to the mother's voice. There is a fine, downy hair covering the body and the skin is damp and shiny. The heartbeat is clearly audible and the normal rate is about 120 to 140 beats a minute which is about double the adult rate.

In a first pregnancy the baby may well have settled into a head down position which is much the commonest. Before this time most babies are in the breech position (see pages 307–309) with the head up and this is because the size and shape of the baby as it grows fits snugly into the pear shaped cavity of the uterus. At about thirty-two to thirty-four weeks the baby usually turns round so that the head comes first (see page 217).

Changes in You

At twenty-eight weeks the uterus is about 7.5cms (3ins) above the umbilicus and sometimes the growth seems rather gradual and at other times it may seem that things are happening quite quickly. By thirty-two weeks the measurement to the top of the uterus from the pubic bone is almost 32cms (12.5ins). Measuring from your navel, the top of the uterus now measures nearly 12cms (5ins).

Your heart is now working about a quarter as much again as before pregnancy and the blood volume has increased by about 2.5 litres (4pts). Because there is added pressure on the blood vessels in the lower half of the body, piles and varicose veins in the legs or the vulva may become more noticeable and, because the stomach empties slowly, a heavy meal may leave you feeling bloated. You may also notice increased vaginal secretions; and pelvic joints soften and stretch ready for birth so that you are usually only comfortable in low-heeled shoes. The uterus sometimes tightens regularly in readiness for the birth and these firm squeezes or contractions are called Braxton Hicks contractions (see page 220).

It may be suggested that you visit the antenatal clinic more frequently at, say, fortnightly intervals rather than monthly. This is because it is important to check that your blood pressure remains normal. If it is going to rise, it usually starts happening about this time (pre-eclampsia, or toxaemia – see pages 203–206).

The more frequent visits also give your doctor or midwife an opportunity to discuss any anxieties that you may have, to make sure that your weight is steadily increasing, and to check that your baby is growing at the right rate. Some doctors routinely suggest another ultrasound scan at thirty-two weeks, although this varies from hospital to hospital. If a scan is suggested, don't be anxious that there is anything wrong. It is often helpful at this stage to be able to measure the size of the baby's head and abdomen accurately and the information from the scan is more precise than just feeling how high the uterus is in the antenatal clinic.

Your iron level may also be checked to make sure that you are not becoming anaemic. There is a progressive slight loss of iron in your body during pregnancy as your iron stores are being used for the continued growth of your baby. If your iron level is a little low, then supplements may be prescribed.

Most pregnant women at this stage feel pretty well, though some begin to feel tired after a full day and it is a good idea to find an hour in the afternoon to put your feet up and close your eyes, even if you don't actually sleep. This is especially important for women who are still working.

Swelling of the legs and ankles increases at about this time, particularly at the end of the day, and this is usually quite normal. It is only significant if the blood pressure is raised which will be detected at your antenatal visits. After a good night's sleep the swelling should have subsided.

You can still play gentle sport and air travel is allowed, although thirty-two weeks is usually the limit for long distance travel. It is wise to enquire of the airlines what their particular regulations are to avoid disappointment. It is normally sufficient to get a letter from your doctor saying how many weeks pregnant you are and confirming that there are no complications.

Incompetent Cervix

An important and quite common problem that can occur at this stage is an incompetent cervix. This condition can cause a painless dilatation of the cervix too early in the pregnancy and can result in the delivery of a very premature infant. Often dilatation or stretching of the cervix occurs and membranes rupture without any warning. The diagnosis of incompetent cervix is usually made after one or more deliveries of a premature infant without any pain before delivery.

The cause of cervical incompetence is usually unknown. Some believe that it occurs because of previous trauma to the cervix such as a previous operation, i.e. a D & C for an abortion, or even a spontaneous miscarriage, when the cervix is surgically stretched. It is also more common after surgical operations on the cervix. Usually this type of dilatation does not occur before the sixteenth week, as until this time the products of conception are not sufficiently large to cause the cervix to dilate and thin out.

Treatment for an incompetent cervix is usually surgical and, if this problem has been suggested by a mid-term delivery in a previous pregnancy, the weak cervix is reinforced with a stitch that sews the cervix shut (Shirodkar stitch). In order to insert the stitch, a quick general anaesthetic in hospital is normally necessary. The procedure is quite simple and the stitch, which is usually a piece of wide thread, remains in place throughout pregnancy. The risk of the anaesthetic and insertion of a stitch causing a miscarriage is absolutely minimal, though there may be a vaginal discharge as pregnancy progresses. Removal of the stitch is much simpler, does not need an anaesthetic and can be done on the labour ward, taking only a few minutes. The best time to insert a stitch is between twelve and fourteen weeks and it is usually removed any time after thirty-eight weeks.

What Happens after the Stitch is Removed?

One might think that the cervix immediately opens as the stitch has now gone and labour ensues straight away. In fact this is unlikely because fibre tissue has formed around the stitch and this usually keeps it closed.

What Happens if You Go into Labour with the Stitch Present?

If contractions start, you should go into hospital immediately as the stitch will need to be removed if labour has been established in order to prevent tearing. Damage does not occur to the cervix in early labour, although the sooner you are in hospital the earlier the stitch can be removed.

Blood Pressure

What is Blood Pressure?

Imagine that the heart muscle pumps blood through the body by rhythmical contractions at a rate determined by the resistance of the walls of the blood vessel through which the blood flows. Each time the heart beats the blood pressure goes up and down within a limited range. It is at its highest when the heart contracts and the lowest between contractions. When the blood pressure is measured there are therefore two readings: the higher, referred to as systolic, and the lower, diastolic. A normal non-pregnant woman might, for example, have a reading around 120 over 80.

If the arteries squeeze too hard on the blood flowing through them, high blood pressure (hypertension) may result and this silent, symptom-free problem is among the most important serious illnesses of modern times.

What is the Normal Range of Blood Pressure in Pregnancy?

Pregnancy brings about enormous changes in the blood volume and pressure, partly because the heart beats much faster and more frequently, and partly because there are hormonal changes in the blood vessels. During the first twenty weeks the blood pressure is fairly static but begins to fall steadily after this time as the placenta pumps blood to the fetus.

High blood pressure problems in pregnancy are medically classified according to whether they begin before or early in pregnancy, or whether they develop for the first time after twenty-eight weeks.

Hypertension in Early Pregnancy

High blood pressure is said to exist if it is raised to 140 over 90 or above, although the lower diastolic level is the important reading. The upper systolic level varies with emotion, anxiety and activity and may be raised, for example, by rushing to get to the clinic on time. The lower level, however, is more constant and does not vary with emotion or worry.

Treatment of High Blood Pressure in Early Pregnancy

Your doctor will probably advise certain precautions such as ample bed rest, sensible nutrition and at least eight hours of rest at night, perhaps spending an extra hour or two lying on one side or the other to improve the blood supply to the baby. Prolonged, vigorous exercise, strenuous housework and stressful work outside the home should be avoided, though it is probably unnecessary to restrict intake of fluids or salt. Frequent checks will be made on your blood pressure and the decision about whether drugs are needed to bring down your blood pressure will depend very much on your doctor's personal opinion.

If your blood pressure really is quite high in early pregnancy for the first time, then it is usual to admit you for further investigations to exclude other causes, for instance kidney disease or diabetes. Women with raised blood pressure may need to attend the surgery or clinic at more frequent intervals than usual to ensure that their doctor can check the level and make sure there is no swelling in the fingers and ankles and no protein in the urine, either of which might indicate the early development of toxaemia.

Careful checks will also be made on the size of your baby to make sure that the growth is not impeded, together with more sophisticated tests of placental function which monitor the baby's well-being.

Mildly raised blood pressure in early pregnancy rarely affects the baby and the important feature is to monitor the situation carefully. Often no medication is recommended for blood pressure that is raised in early pregnancy, though sometimes a mild sedative or diuretic, or in severe cases specific tablets, are prescribed.

What Happens if the Blood Pressure Continues to Rise?

Admission to hospital may be necessary for close observation of both you and your baby and perhaps induction of labour (see pages 314–318) may be indicated as your doctor has to weigh up the risks of allowing your pregnancy to continue against the problems of delivering a premature infant.

Once your baby is born your blood pressure will usually return to normal within a few days.

High Blood Pressure after Twenty-Eight Weeks (Pre-eclampsia or Toxaemia)

Although raised blood pressure on its own does not usually signify problems, the association of high blood pressure in later pregnancy with swelling of the ankles or feet, sharp weight gain and the appearance of protein in the urine indicate that you might be developing pre-eclampsia. This is another reason why these parameters are noted at every antenatal visit.

Why Does Pre-eclampsia Occur?

No one really knows the origins of this condition but it is thought perhaps to be due to abnormalities of hormone secretion by the mother, the mother's kidney secretion, or the abnormal production by the placenta of substances which cause the blood pressure to rise and protein to appear in the urine.

It occurs much more commonly in the first pregnancy, in a twin pregnancy, in association with some conditions such as diabetes, and is also commoner in women who are overweight.

A recent medical trial of low dose aspirin in the management of women who have had a previous history of blood pressure problems in pregnancy, or indeed have these problems now, has shown that this drug can be of some assistance in treating the condition.

The Dangers of Pre-eclampsia or Toxaemia

If left untreated, pre-eclampsia may develop into eclampsia, a term used to describe a convulsion or fit, with its associated dangers to mother and baby (see opposite page). The principal aim is to prevent this complication from occurring.

The management of a woman with raised blood pressure, swelling and protein in the urine is essentially the same as for hypertension. Admission to hospital is usually indicated, observation of the blood pressure, urine and swelling is made frequently, and the fetal growth is monitored by heart rate machines, and repeated ultrasound tests. The woman herself is perfectly well, has no specific complaints, and it is often difficult to understand the need for admission to hospital. However, the blood pressure can change very suddenly and careful observations need to be made four-hourly.

As the pregnancy proceeds a decision will have to be made on final management and a balance has to be struck between whether the baby is still growing in the uterus, or whether its well-being is impaired by the continued rise of blood pressure. Essentially the aim is to deliver the baby before a fit occurs or before the baby starts to suffer in the womb.

The only absolute cure for the condition is delivery and it may be that premature induction of labour will be advised a week or two before term.

Eclampsia

This is one of the most dangerous complications of pregnancy and is happily rare. The word 'eclampsia' literally means a flash of light and is used to describe a fit or convulsion in the mother. The fit is similar to an epileptic attack in a non-pregnant woman and usually follows pre-eclampsia, i.e. progressive high blood pressure, swelling and protein in the urine. In rare cases, a fit may occur out of the blue without any of these preceding signs. Because, however, it almost always follows pre-eclampsia that has become out of control, the fit should be preventable, and in the majority of cases it is.

Why is an Eclamptic Fit Dangerous?

During a convulsion the mother may injure herself, bite her tongue or lose consciousness, just like having an epileptic fit. She may have difficulty in breathing, which would demand immediate and expert medical attention. Also, of course, there is the baby to consider. An eclamptic fit will dramatically reduce the oxygen supply to the unborn child, leading to the baby being distressed or even dying in the uterus.

Women may suffer from one or more of the following symptoms before a fit:

- severe headaches;
- visual disturbances;
- irritability;
- abdominal pain.

If a fit occurs, the woman is immediately sedated with an anti-convulsant drug to stop the fit, followed by delivery of the baby by whichever suitable means, either induction of labour or Caesarean section if there is a need for rapid interference. Once the baby is delivered the blood pressure may stay up for a day or two and there is a small but definite chance that the mother may have further fits which is why the anti-convulsant therapy is continued, although now of course there is no risk to the baby.

Will it Happen Again?

Pre-eclampsia and eclampsia occur commonly in a first pregnancy or in those with certain complications, and severe eclampsia is very unusual in a subsequent pregnancy. However, the blood pressure may take a long time to come down after a baby is born and treatment and further investigations may be necessary. Occasionally the blood pressure remains high in a further pregnancy and the mother will need to be monitored closely in the same way.

The Small Baby (Intrauterine Growth Retardation – IUGR)

Why are Babies Small?

Most small babies are constitutionally small and have no problems in pregnancy or later on. However, the satisfactory growth of the baby in the uterus will depend largely on how well the placenta can supply its requirements. Much interest over the last ten years has centred on a condition in which the placenta fails to function adequately and the baby weighs less than ninety per cent of other babies born at the same stage of pregnancy.

What is the Importance of this Condition?

A baby's birth weight affects its chances of survival, its health in the first few days of life, and its long-term physical and intellectual ability. Generally, the smaller the baby the bigger the problem it may face as a child and possibly as an adult. However, most babies that are born with low birth weight, or are poorly grown, who receive proper care during pregnancy, birth and the first few weeks of life do very well in the long term and they often catch up in size with other children of their age. In addition, their intelligence can be normal and they have no abnormalities in behaviour or movement.

Sometimes, however, a baby that grows poorly in the womb is not only undernourished during pregnancy but also remains so at birth and may always be a little small and on occasions have some intellectual impairment.

What Causes Growth Problems within the Womb?

Unfortunately no one really knows the answer, though there are certain factors associated with a poorly functioning placenta and a small baby. Heredity is one influence, for small women tend to have small babies, and there are also differences among various racial and ethnic groups, so that a normal sized baby for an Asian woman may be smaller than a normal sized baby for a Caucasian woman.

A first baby is usually smaller than his or her siblings, possibly because the blood vessels to the uterus are more developed after one pregnancy and become more efficient in nourishing the next baby. But, in this case, we are talking about a naturally small baby without impairment. Some babies, however, are poorly nourished within the womb and more commonly born to a mother who is under eighteen or over thirty-five. This may be related to a poorly balanced diet and the likelihood that an older woman may have blood pressure or other medical problems which interfere with the placental blood vessels.

A key factor, however, seems to be the nourishment that the baby receives in the uterus and, though it is sensible to eat from the basic food groups, i.e. protein, milk products, vegetables and fresh fruits, the maternal diet may only have a very small part to play in the subsequent development of a growth retarded baby.

Any disease that affects the blood carrying oxygen and food to the baby can impede its growth. The commonest causes are hypertension and certain kidney diseases. A frequent and preventable cause of growth impairment is cigarette smoking (see pages 11–12) and the baby of a mother who smokes heavily throughout pregnancy may weigh 150gms less than it should. The more cigarettes the mother smokes the less oxygen the baby receives and the less it grows.

Some growth problems have more to do with the babies themselves than with their mothers. Twins, for example, are competing for the available supply of food and occasionally one of the babies receives a much larger share which may cause problems for both babies.

Very rarely, certain infections can cause a growth retarded baby, such as German measles and other virus conditions.

How Can Poor Fetal Growth be Detected?

In the first twenty weeks of pregnancy the growth retardation can be suspected if the size of the uterus when examined by the doctor or midwife is consistently smaller than the dates that the pregnancy would suggest. As pregnancy progresses this finding continues, perhaps accompanied by poor weight gain of the mother, or even weight loss. If the baby appears consistently small to the examining hand, this is confirmed by its measurement on the ultrasound machine and serial ultrasound examinations may be necessary to monitor the growth. Doppler ultrasound gives an accurate measurement of the blood flow to the placenta and hence also the growth of the baby.

What Does an Ultrasound Test Measure in a Growth Retarded Baby?

It is not only the head size which fails to increase adequately but also the circumference of the abdomen, and the amount of amniotic fluid in the uterus is also reduced. These three parameters when taken together will indicate to the medical attendant that the baby's nourishment is impaired.

What Can be Done to Prevent Retardation?

You can do the obvious things, like cutting down on smoking and having a balanced diet, and correct management of certain medical complications such as high blood pressure. When there is evidence that the baby is not growing satisfactorily bed rest seems to be of some value because the flow of blood from the placenta to the baby is increased. If it is impossible to rest adequately at home, your doctor may suggest that you go into hospital for a week or two, and it is surprising how well the baby tends to grow with strict bed rest.

Once the diagnosis of a poorly nourished baby has been made the outcome of the pregnancy will depend largely on what happens over the final weeks, because this is the time of most rapid development. Weekly ultrasound monitoring of the baby's well-being is carried out so that the baby's progress can be accurately charted. If the growth rate continues to be slow or the tests confirm that there is a progressive lack of oxygen, then the baby may need to be delivered, as continued and prolonged deprivation of oxygen will increase the problems. Again, the critical timing of delivery will depend on a number of features including the stage of pregnancy, the degree of impaired growth, and the risks in general of allowing the pregnancy to proceed as against early delivery.

What are the Long-term Implications?

Much information has already been gained regarding some of the known causes of poor growth. Conscientious antenatal care to detect and treat high blood pressure and kidney problems, and advice on reducing the consumption of such harmful substances such as nicotine and alcohol, together with timely intervention by induction of labour and accurate monitoring, have helped to focus attention on the problems of the poorly nourished baby.

The prognosis for such pregnancies is getting better every year. Unfortunately, however, there remains a group of women who for no known cause will repeatedly produce babies that grow slowly. Current research is centred around identification of certain proteins and chemicals which may be lacking in the mother's diet in the hope that these substances may be given during pregnancy as supplements to those women at risk.

Finally, recent research has shown that there is a correlation between a poorly grown baby and its future health. It is likely that babies that are born somewhat growth retarded are more likely to suffer from various adult conditions in later life, notably heart problems and raised blood pressure. There are probably other implications too, and much research is at present being carried out in this field.

Prematurity

Approximately ten per cent of all babies each year are born too soon and they are among the most vulnerable of newborns. Delivered into the world before they are ready to survive on their own, they account for seventy-five per cent of deaths not associated with genetic defects, and fifty per cent of neurological handicap in infants. This is one of the reasons why obstetricians and paediatricians alike consider prematurity the biggest clinical problem that they have to face, and in many ways the most perplexing.

A premature birth was arbitrarily defined as any which occurred before the thirty-seventh completed week of pregnancy, or one in which the baby weighed less than 2.5kgs (5.5lbs), regardless of the length of pregnancy. The problem of an accurate definition is compounded by the fact that there is usually a direct relationship between the length of pregnancy and the weight of the baby, but not always. Many babies weighing 2.5kgs or under have been born at term and furthermore some babies born before the dividing line of thirty-seven weeks weigh over 2.5kgs. Therefore, to make a judgement about prematurity on the basis of weight alone seems unwarranted and the chances of a baby's survival are related to the duration of the pregnancy rather than the birth weight.

From the doctor's point of view the most important consideration is how mature developmentally the baby is at birth. In general, babies born prior to thirty-four weeks of gestation, regardless of the birth weight, may be less mature functionally, that is to say their kidneys, lungs and muscles may not work as well as would have been expected of a full-term baby, and it is the immaturity in function of parts of the body that requires special care.

The main point is that premature babies are not simply small but immature. It is quite possible for a baby to weigh 3.2kgs (7lbs) and still be immature and for a baby weighing 2.5kgs (5.5lbs) to be mature. At any particular gestational age there are a range of weights: some babies are abnormally small while some, having acquired a disease such as German measles, fail to grow in the womb (see previous page), and some may have heart malformations or other disorders.

Inadequate nutrition resulting from a defect in the placenta is another cause of failure to grow and, unfortunately, prenatal malnutrition is still a subject that very few doctors understand.

Premature Labour

The Causes of Premature Labour

Despite all the advances in medical knowledge in the last generation, our understanding of the causes of premature labour remain sketchy and consequently the ability to prevent this common occurrence is limited. It is known that several factors seem to be related to prematurity, some of which are preventable and others not. Chronic illness in the mother, complications such as toxaemia, placenta praevia (see pages 221–224), infections of the mother, an incompetent cervix (see pages 200–201), an abnormally shaped uterus, the presence of fibroids and ovarian cysts (see pages 252–253) are just a few of the factors, but together the known causes account for only ten per cent of all women who go into premature labour.

In addition there are other related circumstances such as the age of the mother, with an increased risk if she is under eighteen or over thirty-five, her social situation (prematurity is more common with single parents), and physical, psychological and financial pressures.

How Premature Labour Starts

It often begins without any previous warning at all. There may be a dull, low backache, a feeling of tightness or dragging in the abdomen rather like menstrual cramps, and regular contractions of the uterus which are usually painless. One of the problems is that the uterus does undergo silent contractions during pregnancy (Braxton Hicks contractions – see page 220), and it is often difficult to differentiate between this normal occurrence and premature labour.

Sometimes the first sign is leaking of the fluid from the membranes, often accompanied by a small show of blood, and if this occurs your doctor should be informed soon.

If contractions start without a gush of fluid, it is often difficult for the doctor to know whether they represent premature labour or a false labour and usually what needs to happen is that admission is necessary for a few hours for observation. Electronic measurements record the contractions in the uterus, if any, and an internal examination may be necessary to see whether the neck of the womb is starting to open and labour is definitely going to occur.

The Management of Premature Labour

This largely depends on whether the membranes have ruptured or not and the stage of pregnancy.

Management of Premature Labour with Intact Membranes

The obstetrician here may recommend bed rest in hospital or several extra hours of rest each day at home with restriction of physical activity. If you are allowed home, you may be advised to visit the clinic weekly or twice-weekly to check whether the cervix is dilating. If contractions of the uterus become more frequent and the cervix starts to open, then there are three forms of management:

- an attempt to stop labour;
- allowing labour to continue normally; or
- accelerating labour.

Bed rest is probably more effective than anything and is usually the first treatment. Lately, effective drugs have become available which quieten the uterine contractions and are usually given in the form of a drip in the arm for twenty-four hours followed by tablets. Though obstetricians vary greatly in their attitude to this line of treatment, there is good evidence to show that either the drugs or resting in bed for a few days, or even a week or two can be effective in slowing down or stopping labour. Thus treatment with drugs can provide a short-term advantage.

The majority of premature labours occur between thirty-two and thirty-seven weeks of pregnancy and at this time in an otherwise uncomplicated pregnancy the fetus is large enough to be cared for with the most simple hospital facilities. Most obstetricians agree that there is no need to stop labour if the pregnancy is known to be over thirty-four weeks.

The decision whether or not to inhibit labour depends not only on the size and condition of the baby but also on the presence of any associated complicating factors. It may be pointless or even dangerous to stop premature labour if the mother develops a high fever, in certain cases of bleeding, or medical disorders such as diabetes, or if the baby is known to be abnormal.

Temporary slowing down of established premature labour is particularly useful when there is a need to transfer the mother to a hospital with more intensive care facilities for the newborn when the baby is less than thirty weeks. Most obstetric units have a special care baby unit manned by a paediatrician and staff who are capable of looking after premature babies born at about thirty-two to thirty-four weeks. Some, however, do not have sophisticated intensive care facilities which become necessary for a very small baby and a decision may have to be made as to whether the mother should be transferred to such a unit before birth.

In other instances the obstetrician and paediatrician may decide that it would be safer to deliver the baby on site and transfer it once it has been born. Sometimes an injection of a cortisone-like drug may be given if premature labour is imminent to promote maturity of the baby's lungs and help in preventing difficulties with breathing at birth.

Premature Rupture of the Membranes

The delicate fetal membranes are like a plastic bag attached around the rim of the placenta. The baby is suspended by the amniotic fluid inside. The membrane protects the baby from bacterial infection and allows it free movement. Sometimes this bag bursts, allowing a gush of amniotic fluid which can occur at any stage in pregnancy. If the membranes rupture prematurely, it is likely that labour and contractions of the uterus will follow but this is not necessarily so.

Pregnant women frequently feel damp in the vagina. This may not be due to amniotic fluid as sometimes a watery discharge is present in the vagina, or occasionally leakage of urine can be mistaken for liquor. If it does occur, your doctor's advice should be sought. A diagnosis is easily made by inserting a torch or speculum into the vagina to see whether there is any fluid coming from the cervix. If the membranes have ruptured, you will usually be admitted to hospital for rest and observation.

The main danger from ruptured membranes is the possibility of infection which can affect the uterus and may cause problems for the mother and the unborn baby. For this reason a swab test is usually taken from the vagina on admission to detect any organisms and is repeated after a few days. Occasionally antibiotic therapy is indicated.

The management of a mother with ruptured membranes will depend largely on the stage of pregnancy since the aim is to prolong pregnancy until such time as the baby's immature lungs have the best chance of expanding normally after birth. Sometimes it is possible to collect some of the amniotic fluid and test it in order to establish how mature the baby's lungs are. This is the same test as that performed by amniocentesis when doubt in maturity exists.

Under thirty to thirty-two weeks a conservative policy consisting of bed rest and observation in hospital is usually adopted in the hope that the membranes may seal off, which they often do. Otherwise, if it is thought that the baby's chances of survival are good, or that there is a risk of infection, the doctors may decide to stimulate labour with a drug that starts the womb contracting. Although it is more likely that labour will follow premature rupture of membranes, valuable days or even weeks are occasionally gained by adopting an expectant policy.

It is interesting to note that, far from being a static reservoir, the amniotic fluid is continually recycled every three hours. As fluid drains away more is formed by the baby's urine and the placenta and the umbilical cord so that the size and appearance of the mother's abdomen do not visibly alter despite the loss of fluid.

Delivery of the Premature Baby

The premature baby is small and fragile and therefore more vulnerable to the stresses of labour. Because pain-relieving drugs may diminish the breathing efficiency of the newborn child, epidural anaesthesia (see pages 274–281) is often thought preferable during labour because it can achieve complete pain relief without the risk to the baby that there might be with drugs.

An episiotomy (see pages 263–265) is commonly performed to aid delivery and some doctors prefer to use forceps (see pages 288–292). The episiotomy allows more room for the fragile head and the gentle use of forceps provides a protective cage for the head as it is born, the forceps controlling the rate at which birth occurs so that delivery can be effected with the utmost care.

On occasions, Caesarean section may be preferable, particularly in cases where the premature infant is in the breech position (see pages 307–309). It appears that Caesarean section is of special benefit to those babies below 1.5kgs (3.5lbs) as vaginal delivery, however gentle, can cause damage to the head. Again, there are no hard and fast rules and the obstetricians will have their own personal views on what is best.

Finally where the membranes rupture before the onset of labour, the ensuing labour is sometimes referred to as a 'dry' birth. Such a delivery is popularly believed to be more difficult, but this is not so. Nor is it 'dry' as the amniotic fluid continues to be produced in large amounts even if the membranes have ruptured.

Special Problems of a Premature Baby

Almost all premature babies require some special care. If they are not delivered in hospitals with intensive care facilities, they may be transferred to the nearest centre where they can be nursed in a thermostatically controlled incubator to control body temperature, given oxygen if necessary and fed with a special tube, or given more intensive support with breathing machines.

One of the problems with the premature baby concerns respiration. The immature baby's lungs lack a certain protein called surfactant which is responsible for keeping the tiny air sacs open. Without surfactant the lungs are inelastic and their failure to expand properly causes respiratory difficulties (Hyaline Membrane Disease).

In the 1970s seventy per cent of premature babies with respiratory distress died. Today, however, the mortality rate is less than ten per cent, partly because of a better understanding of prenatal treatment and partly because of advances in intensive therapy after delivery. Mothers are usually encouraged to see their babies at the earliest opportunity and to handle them as soon as possible even though there is inevitably some separation if transfer to an intensive care unit is necessary.

Despite these hazards the prognosis for a premature baby is better than ever. Some perinatal centres quote eighty to eighty-five per cent survival rate in infants weighing 1–1.25kgs (2.25–2.5lbs) at birth and sixty to seventy per cent in those weighing less than 1kg (2.25lbs).

Various follow-up studies seem to confirm that the majority of babies who survive premature birth grow up to be normal and healthy, both intellectually and physically.

What are the Chances of a Subsequent Pregnancy Ending in Premature Delivery?

If there is a known cause for a premature labour such as incompetence of the cervix or a medical disease in the mother which requires treatment, there is a higher incidence of recurrence in a subsequent pregnancy. If there is no known cause, it seems that subsequent premature deliveries are also somewhat more common, although not invariably the case.

CHAPTER 10

The Ninth Month
(32–36 Weeks)

Changes in Your Baby

By now your baby will weigh almost 1 800gms (4lbs) and its total length is about 45cms (19ins). The fingernails now reach the finger-tips. In boys the testicles begin to descend into the scrotum, and the endocrine or glandular system is very active in preparation for birth. The lungs secrete surfactant which is a soapy fluid that keeps them open ready for breathing, and fat is deposited under the skin to provide energy and heat regulation after birth. The majority of babies born at this time survive.

By thirty-six weeks the baby will have taken up its final position, particularly in a primigravid or first pregnancy, when the hitherto unstretched and firm muscles of the uterus and abdomen keep the baby in its birth position. In subsequent pregnancies because the abdominal muscles are weaker, the baby is more liable to keep changing its position and can indeed do this right up to term. The different parts of the baby can be quite easily felt, i.e. which side the back is and, if the baby is in a head down position, how it relates to the opening of the pelvis or the pelvic rim.

Engagement of the Head (Dropping)

The widest part of the baby's head usually descends through the mouth or opening of the pelvis in readiness for birth by about the thirty-sixth week. You may notice when the baby's head becomes engaged because there is a feeling of 'lightening' or less pressure on the diaphragm as the head drops down. Your midwife or doctor will be able to feel whether the head is engaged in the antenatal clinic.

Does Engagement of the Head Always Occur?

The head engages much more commonly in a first pregnancy because the muscle tone of the uterus and abdominal wall gradually encourages the head to descend in the latter weeks of pregnancy. In a second or third pregnancy, however, when the muscles have already been stretched, it is quite common for the head not to engage until labour starts.

Are There Any Other Reasons for Non-engagement of the Head?

Obviously the head will not descend through the pelvis if there is something in the way and, rarely, this can be caused by a placenta lying in a low position (see pages 221–224), or the mouth of the pelvis itself being narrower than usual (see pages 303–304). The commonest reason for the head not engaging is simply that the head is lying back to front (posterior position – see pages 302–303). The baby's head in this position presents a slightly larger width than when it is the right way up but this is usually of no significance as the head engages in the pelvis once contractions have begun and the head starts to turn into its final position. Another cause for a head not engaging is if it is too big, or if the pelvic bones are too tight.

What Happens if the Head Remains Non-engaged at Term?

If it is suspected that there may be a cause for the non-engagement, an ultrasound should exclude a low lying placenta and, occasionally, the pelvis is X-rayed so that the diameters can be accurately measured. If this investigation is requested, don't have any worries about the effect of X-rays because the dose of radiation is minimal and the procedure is absolutely safe at this stage.

Your doctor may do an internal examination to confirm the position of the head and gauge with the fingers the width of the pelvic bones. In rare cases, if the baby's head is too large for a small pelvis, delivery by Caesarean section may be suggested. In the vast majority of cases, however, spontaneous labour is awaited and a careful watch kept on whether the head starts to descend into the pelvis when the contractions of the uterus begin. In a high percentage of cases this does occur and labour proceeds normally. In the event of the head not engaging in advanced labour, an emergency Caesarean section will be carried out (disproportion – see page 295).

Although engagement of the head is a much discussed subject at antenatal preparation classes, please remember that in the great majority of women the head will descend through the pelvis once contractions have started and labour is established.

Changes in You

By now you are feeling pretty heavy. The uterus almost fills the whole abdominal cavity, reaching to just below the ribs. The joints ache a little bit as they stretch ready for the onset of labour and there is a feeling of pressure on the stomach causing heartburn. Sometimes lying flat causes a feeling of nausea and giddiness because the heavy uterus presses on the large blood vessel and slows down the flow of blood to the back of the heart. It is better to lie on your side or well propped up. Sleeping is getting difficult at this stage and you may have short naps rather than a long sleep. If sleep becomes a real problem, there are safe sedatives which your doctor may prescribe.

The dark line down from the navel may show more prominently, and colostrum, a milk precursor especially rich in protein, starts to leak from the breasts. Puffiness of the ankles is quite common and weight gain is continuing at roughly the rate of a pound a week. Abdominal discomfort and even pain is often felt on either side of the abdomen and, if this becomes severe or you have any vaginal bleeding, this of course must be reported to your doctor.

Emotional changes are also pretty common at this stage with mood swings and irritability and this can place a significant strain on a relationship. Concern about insignificant things is quite normal and, as pregnancy advances, anxiety about the health and well-being of the baby also increases.

Practice Contractions (Braxton Hicks Contractions)

The uterus actually contracts very gently from quite early on in pregnancy, although these tightenings are imperceptible to the mother. As pregnancy advances, these contractions are noticed and sometimes can be quite worrying because of their intensity and because they mimic proper labour. These are called Braxton Hicks contractions after the doctor who first wrote about them. They are more common in second and third pregnancies, probably because the uterus has already been primed by the first pregnancy, but they have no other significance. Sometimes they start a number of weeks before the baby is due and last for a number of hours, but usually then die away.

The expectant mother may find it quite difficult to differentiate between these practice contractions and labour itself and sometimes the only way of being sure is to place an electronic monitor on the abdomen (see pages 266–268) which will demonstrate whether the uterus is actually contracting or not. It is often worthwhile taking two Panadol tablets every four hours because the contractions of true labour will not be influenced by mild pain relievers but practice contractions often go away. If Braxton Hicks contractions become a worry, don't hesitate to ring the hospital or your doctor or midwife for advice. A quick visit to the surgery or antenatal clinic should reassure you.

Bleeding in Pregnancy

Bleeding at any stage in pregnancy must be taken seriously and reported to your doctor or midwife. In a large percentage of women either no cause is found or one of the incidental reasons mentioned on pages 166–167, such as cervical erosion or polyps, may be present and they usually need no treatment.

Bleeding occurring for the first time later in pregnancy is defined as APH (antepartum haemorrhage – before birth bleeding) and may be due to one of two important causes. In both instances the bleeding comes from the placenta, either because its position is below the presenting part of the baby and a small part of the placenta gets sheared away (placenta praevia – afterbirth first), or the placenta is situated in its normal correct position above the presenting part of the baby and the cause of bleeding is detachment of an area of placenta from the wall of the uterus (placental abruptio – accidental bleeding).

Placenta Praevia (Afterbirth First)

In about one out of two hundred pregnancies the placenta implants itself in the lower part of the uterus rather than in its usual position higher up and, if it remains low, may cause bleeding. Routine ultrasound in early pregnancy may show the placenta to be lying in a low position. This is usually of no consequence as in most cases the placenta moves upwards as pregnancy advances, though your medical attendant may advise a repeat ultrasound to make sure that the placenta has moved away from the lower part of the cervix. The closer to the cervix the placenta is situated the greater the possibility of bleeding and, if the placenta blocks the cervix completely, then vaginal delivery is usually impossible.

The risk of having placenta praevia is higher in women who have

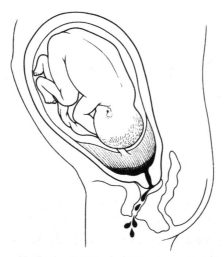

The placenta has developed below the baby's head and becomes partially separated leading to vaginal bleeding.

scarring of the uterus from a previous pregnancy, a Caesarean, uterine surgery or a D & C. The need for greater placental surface area due to an increased demand for oxygen because of smoking, living at high altitude or carrying more than one fetus may also increase the risk of this condition.

How is the Condition Recognised?

Any bleeding from the vagina occurring around mid-pregnancy must be assumed to be due to a placenta praevia unless proved otherwise. Therefore it is extremely important for any blood loss at this stage to be reported to your doctor immediately, even if the bleeding is slight. The bleeding occurs because the placenta pulls away from the stretching lower part of the uterus. The blood is usually bright red, not associated with any pain and is spontaneous in onset. It can be light or heavy and often stops, only to recur later.

Because the placenta is blocking the way, the baby with a low lying placenta does not usually drop into the pelvis in preparation for delivery. Sometimes a placenta praevia is discovered routinely on ultrasound examination without bleeding.

How is the Diagnosis Made?

Ultrasound examination will immediately confirm the position of the placenta as it can be seen quite easily in relation to the baby's head. The placenta normally implants around the middle of the uterus and grows to occupy a position above the baby's head. Occasionally, however, it will grow downwards and either be partially below the baby's head or sometimes completely blocks off the cervix (placenta praevia – see the diagram on page 221).

What is the Treatment?

Because most early cases of a low lying placenta correct themselves long before delivery and do not cause a problem, the condition does not require treatment before the twenty-fourth to twenty-eighth week. After that time the woman with a diagnosed placenta praevia may be put on a modified activity schedule with increased bed rest.

The treatment options depend on:

- the amount of bleeding;
- the exact position of the placenta; and
- the stage of pregnancy at which it occurs.

Remember that bleeding comes from the placenta and is therefore from the *mother's* blood, not the baby's. Many years ago when this fact was not realised, doctors used to think that the only way to save the baby was immediate delivery. This of course resulted in many babies dying from prematurity. Now we realise that the bleeding comes from the mother's side and there is therefore no necessity or urgency to deliver the baby unless the bleeding is serious or the fetus is compromised.

The principal aim, therefore, is to prolong pregnancy until the baby is mature enough to be born. The main body of the placenta may rise above the leading part of the baby as pregnancy progresses but, if the placenta remains so low that it covers the cervix, the baby's head will be prevented from descending into the pelvis during labour, more bleeding may occur and therefore delivery must be by Caesarean section.

If the placenta only partially covers the cervix or is marginally low, then vaginal delivery is feasible. Repeated ultrasound tests may give a guide as to whether the placenta has moved or not and, because the bleeding can be sudden and unannounced, you may be kept in hospital at this stage. Even if bleeding is quite severe, you can receive a blood transfusion which makes up the lost blood and conservative management can still be adopted.

As the time of delivery becomes near, a definitive diagnosis may have to be made by actually feeling the placenta with the examining finger. Because it is dangerous to do this in the antenatal clinic for fear of promoting bleeding, the rule is that vaginal examination is not undertaken unless delivery is proposed: in other words in the maternity unit operating theatre with a Caesarean section trolley available for immediate surgery if examination promotes the bleeding. The advent of transvaginal ultrasound has in many cases obviated the need for a pelvic examination.

If the placenta does not move away from the lowest part of the uterus covering the cervix then the mode of delivery is usually by Caesarean section at about thirty-eight weeks.

Accidental Bleeding (Placental Abruption)

This is the other type of important bleeding that also comes from the placenta but in this case the placenta is situated in its normal position high up in the body of the uterus. What happens is that a small fragment separates from the main body of the placenta causing bleeding within the uterus. This condition is responsible for about one in four cases of late pregnancy bleeding. Bleeding can either be revealed, i.e. external, or within the uterus (concealed). If the latter occurs, the blood collects inside the uterus causing severe abdominal pain and possible asphyxiation of the infant.

What Causes Accidental Bleeding?

We don't really know why the placenta starts to separate, but it seems to occur more commonly in older mothers, those who have had a number of pregnancies, heavy smokers, those with high blood pressure and in women who are recurrently anaemic, lacking iron and folic acid. Very occasionally, separation of the placenta can be caused by trauma, i.e. a fall or a direct blow to the stomach.

What are the Symptoms?

When separation of the placenta from the wall is small, there may be some vaginal bleeding but there is cramping or mild aching in the abdomen and tenderness on feeling the uterus. Very occasionally, particularly where there has been trauma to the abdomen as in an accident, there may be no bleeding at all.

When the amount of separation is moderate, bleeding is heavier but usually internal, giving rise to severe pain in the abdomen caused by a swollen, tender uterus with blood inside. External bleeding is often absent or not heavy. If a lot of bleeding has occurred inside the uterus, the mother may be in a shocked state, feeling weak and dizzy. The diagnosis is again made on ultrasound, mainly by excluding a low lying placenta and also by seeing blood contained within the uterus.

What is the Treatment for Accidental Bleeding?

If an ultrasound shows that the placenta is in its normal place and there is no obvious blood in the uterus with minimal tenderness only when the abdomen is touched, the condition may settle and no treatment is immediately necessary, though continued observation is important in case more severe bleeding occurs.

In moderate cases when the abdomen is tender to the touch all over, the obstetrician may recommend delivery of the baby. This is because, although the baby is used to living in a sea of its own fluid, it cannot tolerate blood and will become distressed or may even die in the uterus. If the pain is severe, there is obviously a lot of blood in the uterus, and the mother is basically not well, then blood transfusion to replace the blood lost is indicated, followed by immediate delivery whatever the stage of pregnancy as there is a great danger that the baby will otherwise die.

How is Delivery Achieved?

Labour is either induced by breaking the membranes (see pages 316–317) which allows the blood to escape and also starts labour – this is the treatment of choice in the mild to moderate cases of bleeding – or immediate Caesarean section is carried out if the condition is thought to be more serious and time is valuable.

DIC (Disseminated Intravascular Coagulation)

One of the complications resulting from this condition concerns the blood clotting system of the mother. Normally, if you cut your finger a clot of blood will form which is part of the healing process and this stops continued bleeding. The pregnant mother's blood, however, has a tendency not to clot under certain circumstances: abruptio placenta is one, and a dead fetus in the uterus another.

Clearly, if blood does not clot it will continue to flow and will only

stop when the blood clotting mechanism is made to recur. The treatment is to give the mother special substances in a drip which replaces
the blood lost and encourages the body to start clotting. Sometimes
the management of patients with a severe clotting disorder can be
quite complicated and needs the attention of not only the obstetrician but a blood and fluid specialist. Intensive care monitoring may
also be necessary.

This rare condition is known as DIC (disseminated intravascular
coagulation), which means widespread non-clotting of blood.

Special Pregnancies

Most women who become pregnant can look forward to nine months
of joyous expectation with slight discomforts and changes in lifestyle.
In about twenty per cent of pregnancies, however, some problems
occur but, thanks to the enormous expansion of medical knowledge,
obstetricians and midwives are often able to anticipate potential difficulties in pregnancy and labour by giving special attention where
required and adapting medical care accordingly.

In this section we will deal with certain mothers in whom the
conduct of antenatal care and delivery may differ somewhat from the
routine, although it must again be emphasised that many of these
women will have a normal pregnancy and labour.

Teenage Pregnancies

While teenagers over seventeen years of age are amongst the most
efficient reproducers in our society, if one looks specifically at schoolgirls aged sixteen and under, there is evidence that these mothers are
particularly at risk in certain ways.

The very young girl is more liable to have raised blood pressure in
pregnancy with the possible consequent development of toxaemia.
Anaemia (see page 160) is also common because young girls tend not
to take their iron tablets regularly. There is often confusion in the
early stages about the diagnosis of pregnancy as many youngsters may
well not realise they are pregnant or will hide the diagnosis from their

family. Periods in the young are often irregular and therefore calculating the EDD (estimated date of delivery) is inaccurate going on the menstrual history alone, although of course ultrasound can help to date the pregnancy precisely.

Teenagers are often poor attenders in antenatal clinics and therefore certain problems associated with the pregnancy cannot be treated early. Young girls are liable to go into premature labour and also the incidence of low birth weight babies (see page 3) is higher in young teenagers.

The psychological problems of young mothers are difficult to assess. Several well-known medical authorities challenge the commonly held view that young mothers are particularly upset by the experience of pregnancy and labour. Others have noted that there may be a relationship between the youth of a mother and behavioural disturbances in childhood. There is remarkably little information about the long-term consequences of a pregnancy in young teenagers – understandably, because it is very difficult for doctors to keep contact over a number of years with these young mothers. The girls usually have no wish, nor have their families, to be reminded of the experience of pregnancy in their early teens.

The concern naturally is to decide whether pregnancy at an early age should be allowed to continue at all as it may have an adverse effect on the girl's subsequent reproductive history and it appears that there might be a slightly increased risk of miscarriage or a low birth weight baby with a subsequent pregnancy.

Finally, of course, in advanced societies schoolgirl pregnancies are undoubtedly socially as well as medically unacceptable. Younger girls often come from families where there may be less control over their behaviour and often from lower socio-economic groups. There is some psychiatric evidence that marriages are more vulnerable when the bride is under twenty and this certainly seems to be the case in Western societies.

In 1979 a report of the Joint Working Party on Pregnant Schoolgirls and Schoolgirl Mothers gave detailed information about the lost educational opportunities likely to be associated with pregnancy in young schoolgirls. Of the young teenage girls twenty-two per cent had left school by the end of the first three months of pregnancy and seventy-four per cent had left by the end of the fifth month. Sixty-one per cent of the girls received no education what-soever between leaving school and the birth of their baby. Once the child was born fifty-three per cent of those girls who were still below the statutory school leaving age at the time of birth failed to return to school.

There is undoubtedly a serious risk of educational deprivation for girls whose pregnancies continue which only aggravates the problems they may face and prejudices their chances in future life.

Pregnancy in the Older Woman

Twenty years ago the term 'elderly primigravida' was used to describe a woman having her first baby over the age of thirty-five, simply because it had been known for some time that a woman's normal fertility was at its maximum at about the age of twenty-three after which there was a gradual decline, so that by the age of forty a woman had greatly reduced chances of conception.

There seems little doubt that the pregnant woman having her first baby in her late thirties and early forties is somewhat more likely to encounter complications which may be the result of the natural process of growing older, but even more important is the fact that her dwindling chances of further pregnancies put more of a premium on the present one. Furthermore her endurance and resistance to disease are not those of a woman in her early twenties and she is therefore likely to require help earlier. There is often a history of infertility which serves only to magnify this point.

Notwithstanding all this, it must be emphasised that the majority of these mothers, properly supervised, are capable of having a safe and successful pregnancy.

The older mother is more likely to miscarry in the first three months of pregnancy and, although there is often no obvious cause, this is probably because of chromosome abnormality of the embryo which is more common with advancing maternal age.

The principal defect in the baby that is related to the mother's age is Down's Syndrome. Whereas the incidence of babies with Down's Syndrome born to women in their twenties is in the region of one in three or four thousand, this incidence increases dramatically with mothers in their late thirties to something like one in six hundred, and by the age of forty a woman has a one in seventy risk of producing a chromosomally abnormal child.

Down's Syndrome can be diagnosed with almost complete certainty by amniocentesis (see pages 141–148) or CVS. Blood screening can also be used (see pages 139–140). Its frequency is not purely dependent on whether this is a first pregnancy as Down's Syndrome may occur in a woman of over thirty-eight who has had previous normal children.

Recurrent chromosome problems in future pregnancies are uncommon unless the mother is a carrier of a particular abnormal gene and blood is usually taken from a Down's Syndrome baby at birth to determine the type of chromosome abnormality. Blood testing should also be carried out on the parents so that an accurate future prognosis and genetic counselling may be given with the risks of a further abnormality fully discussed before embarking on a subsequent pregnancy.

Certain complications of pregnancy are more common in the antenatal period, notably hypertension (see page 202), toxaemia of pregnancy (see pages 203–206), fibroids (see pages 251–252) and premature labour. Moreover the length of labour is increased. Much of this may be due to the greater apprehension of the older woman facing labour for the first time and her stress may influence the way that the uterus contracts.

There is a slightly higher incidence of help being needed in the second stage with forceps, and the chances of Caesarean section for whatever reason are around twenty-five per cent, about four times that of mothers with first pregnancies.

The new mother deserves repeated encouragement and reassurance. Breast-feeding may be less likely to be willingly or successfully undertaken.

The older expectant mother does not require any special treatment on the grounds of age alone but the need for detailed supervision both in pregnancy and labour is obvious. One fact needs stressing: older women are usually more anxious and unsure of their ability to deliver themselves safely. However, careful antenatal supervision and monitoring during labour should minimise complications.

Finally, there is no strict age limit beyond which a pregnancy becomes dangerous. Many women in their late twenties and early thirties ask how late they can wait to become pregnant for the first time and there is no generally satisfactory answer, except to say that ideally the first pregnancy should occur before the age of thirty-five. This will however depend a lot on the woman's previous history, whether there has been a long period of infertility, or whether there are associated medical problems that have developed before and may be aggravated by pregnancy.

Grande Multipara

This is a medical term used for a woman who is having her fifth or subsequent pregnancy and again there are certain complications that occur more commonly with an increasing number of pregnancies. The mother is more likely to be anaemic and poorly nourished and, because of her greater age, hypertension is more common. For these reasons she is also possibly more likely to have placental abruption (see pages 224–225) and more likely to have abnormalities of the blood clotting system (see pages 225–226).

Often the 'minor' disorders of pregnancy, i.e. excessive sickness, urinary infections and varicose veins, are greater with the increasing number of pregnancies.

During labour there may be more difficulty with delivery due to the larger size of the baby, and sometimes very fast labour occurs.

The baby is more likely to adopt an unstable attitude during the antenatal period. In other words instead of lying straight so that the head or the bottom presents, it lies across the abdomen (transverse lie – see page 295). There is therefore an increased incidence of Caesarean section.

Bleeding after the baby is born (postpartum haemorrhage) is common as the uterus is often flabby and does not contract well. There is also of course an increased risk of congenital abnormality, notably Down's Syndrome.

After the birth of the baby, the mother will often not return for examination at the postnatal clinic and it is therefore important to give contraceptive advice before leaving hospital.

Multiple Pregnancies (Twins or Triplets)

Multiple pregnancy is due to fertilisation of one or two eggs shed from the ovary. The reason for this is not well understood, but a fertilised egg may divide into two so that each identical half of the original egg will develop into a twin. Such twins are identical, of the same sex and exactly the same genetic make-up and will develop and look very much alike. Identical twins occur in about one in two hundred and fifty births and their incidence is usually unrelated to hereditary patterns of twinning or to the mother's age or race.

If two eggs are released at the same time and fertilised by two sperm, then two genetically different individuals will develop. Two-thirds of all twins are non-identical.

The incidence of twins in the UK is about one in ninety births though it seems to be more common in the African countries, the highest incidence occurring in Nigeria where twins occur in roughly one in forty pregnancies. The lowest incidence, about four per thousand, occurs in Middle Eastern countries.

Why do Twins Occur?

Heredity plays some part, as there is an increased likelihood of twinning if the woman's mother herself was a twin and the tendency does seem to be passed on by fathers. Usually, however, and certainly with regard to identical twins this is just an accident of nature. Older women between the ages of thirty-five and thirty-nine are more likely to have twins since statistically the chance increases with the number of children already conceived.

The likelihood of twins also increases with some treatments for infertility, particularly drugs used for stimulating ovulation. Here the ovary may be over-stimulated, causing the release of four, five or six eggs which could in theory be fertilised. Because over-stimulation usually occurs only with the complicated, stronger fertility drugs, such treatment is normally undertaken in special centres where facilities for sophisticated monitoring exists. The closer the control of each woman's response to the treatment, the less likely she is to produce more than one egg.

The commonest type of fertility drug called Clomiphene, or Clomid, is mild and does not produce nearly as strong a response from the ovary. Although multiple pregnancies can occur with it, they are uncommon.

How Soon Can Twins be Diagnosed?

Since the advent of ultrasound and its use in early pregnancy twins can be picked up as early as four to six weeks (see the scan on page 62). It is interesting that the actual incidence of twin pregnancies may be much higher than is generally accepted because in some cases only one twin actually goes on to develop normally. This has been brought to light as a chance finding since ultrasound examinations are being done very early, and an initial scan may show two very small pregnancy sacs.

Usually the scan is repeated to confirm twins and sometimes one sac completely disappears and becomes absorbed, but the remaining fetus is unharmed and continues to grow normally.

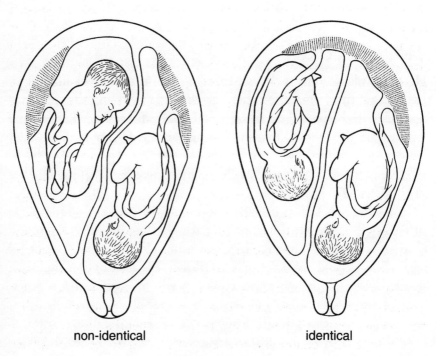

non-identical   identical

Twin pregnancy.

Twins are suspected if there is a family history and if the doctor finds that the uterus is much larger than it should be when calculating the size from the date of the last period. Some women feel excessive movement in the uterus, have a lot of nausea and vomiting in early pregnancy and may feel uncomfortable due to the enlarging size of the uterus at an early stage.

Continuing Care of a Twin Pregnancy

A twin pregnancy does not mean there will be more problems but it obviously increases the potential for complications. The body changes in the same way as in any expectant mother but the changes may be more marked because of the greater needs of the two babies. The uterus therefore becomes larger more quickly and the amount of amniotic fluid is greater and because of these changes the various discomforts of pregnancy may be more obvious.

As the uterus enlarges it presses against other organs in the body: heartburn and indigestion are more common; you may need to urinate more frequently; and your legs and feet may swell after you have been on your feet for only a brief time. Rest is important and you will be advised to try and get at least one or two hours during the day. It is vital that you do not think that you have to eat for two, and intake should be restricted but well-balanced meals with an increased amount of protein, carbohydrate and vitamins are important. Your doctor may prescribe an increased iron intake and advise extra folic acid because two babies drain more of the iron and vitamin reserves and anaemia is common.

More frequent antenatal checks may be advised as blood pressure tends to rise a little earlier in a twin pregnancy and the problems associated with this can be minimised if detected at an early stage. Obstetricians used to advise that mothers come into hospital for a period of rest around thirty to thirty-two weeks, mainly to prevent some of the possible complications and also because it was thought that the babies would grow better in the uterus with prolonged bed rest, thus delaying premature labour. This feature used to be more popular than it is today and many obstetricians now admit women to hospital with a twin pregnancy only if there are any problems other than routine.

It is not uncommon for women with twins to go into labour prematurely and the more babies in the uterus the shorter the pregnancy. An average single baby's gestation lasts forty weeks, a twin pregnancy thirty-seven or thirty-eight, and a triplet pregnancy thirty-four or thirty-five. But remember these are averages only. For reasons that are not fully understood, twins and triplets are less likely to get the time they need to complete their development.

Other than restricting activity in the last six weeks and having as much rest as possible, there is little that you can do to prevent premature labour but, if tightenings or contractions occur, your doctor should be informed immediately as there is an excellent chance that early contractions can be controlled by the administration of drugs to relax the uterus if labour threatens to start too early.

What to Expect in Labour

Generally, the pattern of labour and delivery is the same as for a single pregnancy, especially if both the twins are coming head first which is the usual position. Following delivery of the first twin, the cord is cut and clamped and usually the second baby is delivered within a few minutes. Both placentae are delivered afterwards and you may notice that your medical attendant does not give you the usual injection of Syntometrine (see page 261) following delivery of the first twin as this may impede the second twin's descent.

The second most common way that the babies lie is with the first presenting by the head and the second by the breech. This should be known prior to labour because ultrasound scans are usually done frequently in the antenatal period to assess the correct growth of the babies. If the second baby is coming by the breech, or both babies present by the breech, or unusually if one baby is lying across the abdomen (transverse lie – see page 295), then the delivery becomes more complicated.

During a twin delivery you may notice quite a few people in the labour ward. In addition to the midwife and a member of the medical staff, there will also be an experienced obstetrician who is present in case complications develop. The paediatrician will have been notified and will also be present and there will be two incubators ready to receive the babies.

Twins are best delivered with the mother's legs up in stirrups (the lithotomy position). This may be somewhat embarrassing, but it allows good access for the doctor and speed may be required to deliver the second twin if it is distressed, or help may be needed if it is lying in an abnormal position.

It is common to suggest an epidural anaesthetic for a twin birth, especially if the mother goes into premature labour. This is because the epidural will give complete pain relief during labour and avoid respiratory problems in the babies that may occur if ordinary methods of pain relief such as Pethidine have to be given. In addition, any manipulation or help that has to be performed by the doctor can be done without pain.

By and large there is no indication for a Caesarean if both heads are presenting first. Some doctors feel that a Caesarean may be necessary with the breech presenting if the size of the pelvis is small or if there is excessive delay after delivery of the first twin. Your doctor will base the decision on a number of points, including the size of the babies, the position in labour and any further complications that may occur during labour. Just occasionally it may be necessary to deliver the second twin by Caesarean section if it has taken up an unsuitable position.

Postpartum haemorrhage (see pages 306–307 and 345–347) is more common in a woman who has had twins because of the size of the placental site and the fact that the uterus does not contract after the babies are born as well as it should do. Your attendants will be aware of this and will take steps to ensure that if bleeding does occur you will be given an injection of a substance which firms up the uterus.

If the babies are of a good size and are well following delivery, there is no reason why breast-feeding should not occur, although this is obviously quite tiring, and the same applies after delivery by Caesarean section. If the babies are very small when they are born, then during the first few days or perhaps weeks they will need the special care of the intensive neonatal nursery.

Rare Complications of Twin Pregnancy and Delivery

Twin to Twin Transfusion

One twin can occasionally grow at the expense of the other to such an extent that the weaker twin may die and the remaining baby will often continue to be born in the normal way. This is because one twin literally feeds off the other.

The Diagnosis of Congenital Abnormalities

The triple blood test (see pages 139–140) in twin pregnancy will not give an accurate result and, if amniocentesis is suggested in the older woman, then it is perfectly feasible to withdraw fluid from the two separate sacs. If one twin is found to be abnormal, for instance has Down's Syndrome, and the other is normal, the couple may be faced with the hugely difficult decision of whether to proceed with the pregnancy, or to attempt to destroy the abnormal fetus and yet allow the pregnancy to proceed normally with the other twin.

This is a procedure which is undertaken in certain centres and can happen when superovulation has occurred resulting in six or seven fertilised eggs. The likelihood of that number of fetuses remaining viable is negligible and it is a relatively simple procedure to remove a certain number of the fertilised eggs.

Complications in the Mother

Certain complications occur more commonly in the mother, such as pre-eclampsia (see pages 203–205), hydramnios or excessive amniotic fluid, and placenta praevia (see pages 221–224).

Locked Heads

Very rarely, the head of one baby during delivery can be literally locked against the other which precludes a vaginal birth. Ultrasound or even X-ray will be needed to make the diagnosis and delivery is by Caesarean section.

Induction of Labour

The risk to the babies of having problems due to lack of oxygen because the placentae become less efficient (post-maturity – see pages 309–314) is increased in a multiple pregnancy. For this reason most doctors advocate induction of labour around term rather than allowing spontaneous labour to occur perhaps one or two weeks after the estimated date of delivery.

Rhesus (Rh) Disease

One of the standard blood tests done on a pregnant woman at her first antenatal attendance is her blood group. Every human possesses blood of one of the following groups: O, A, AB or B, and in addition the blood will be Rh-positive or Rh-negative. The discovery of the Rh factor just over thirty-five years ago led to an understanding of why some newborn babies became rapidly yellow and jaundiced or even died shortly after birth while others were stillborn.

It so happens that about eighty-five per cent of European women are Rh-positive and fifteen per cent Rh-negative. If the mother is Rh-positive there are usually no problems, but if she is Rh-negative then there is a potential danger to the unborn child under certain circumstances.

To understand why, imagine an Rh-positive man married to an Rh-negative woman. If the man is strongly positive, his blood group is dominant and the baby will inherit this factor from its father's blood and will be Rh-positive. If the husband is only weakly positive, then the baby will have a fifty per cent chance of being positive or negative.

If a Rh-negative woman carries a Rh-positive baby, the blood of the mother and the baby may mix late in pregnancy and the mother will become sensitised and develop what are called 'antibodies'. These antibodies are stored in the mother's blood and cause absolutely no harm in her first pregnancy but in a second pregnancy they may pass over to the baby and destroy its blood cells by a process of dissolving. To take it to its logical conclusion, the unborn baby will produce more and more red cells but may not be able to maintain an adequate supply of blood and therefore become anaemic, leading to the problems that have already been discussed.

It is vital to realise that, even if the pregnancy ends in a spontaneous miscarriage or is terminated, antibodies may be formed. Once the woman has antibodies she will always keep them and will face possible problems with each successive pregnancy.

Can the Condition be Prevented?

The answer is yes, and one of the most satisfying medical advances in obstetrics has been the gradual elimination of the Rhesus problem. A single protective injection of a substance called Anti-D Immunoglobulin given to a woman shortly after her first pregnancy will destroy the Rh-positive cells, preventing problems in the future, and it is now common practice to give this injection to all Rh-negative women within a few hours of delivery or miscarriage of a first pregnancy. Although an injection of Anti-D given to a woman after her first pregnancy may prevent future problems, there remain a number of women who were sensitised before the advent of this discovery.

Frequent checks are necessary during the antenatal period to make sure that the number of antibodies does not increase because this is directly related to the severity of the baby's condition. Whether the mother has had antibodies or not, at the booking clinic the blood group is checked and the presence of antibodies noted and antibody testing is repeated at about twenty-eight and thirty-six weeks and at term in women who have no antibodies present.

For those who arrive at the booking clinic with antibodies from a previous pregnancy, the procedures are repeated more frequently because it is important to determine more accurately whether there is any increase in levels. If the level of antibodies does increase, then the doctor will need more information from examination of the amniotic fluid (amniocentesis). A sample of fluid is analysed for the presence of a yellow pigment (bilirubin) and its colour and density will reveal the severity of the damage and degree of anaemia developing in the unborn baby.

If amniocentesis shows that the baby is in some danger, then it may be possible to transfuse the baby's blood while it is still in the uterus. This is a complicated procedure done in specialised units where a needle is passed through the abdominal wall into the uterus and into the baby's abdomen. A small tube or catheter is inserted around the needle and a carefully calculated quantity of specially prepared Rh-negative blood is actually injected into the baby's abdomen or into a vein. In other words, the unborn baby's blood is exchanged with fresh blood of the correct group.

These so-called 'intrauterine transfusions' may have to be repeated as frequently as every two or three weeks until the pregnancy reaches a stage where the baby has a reasonable chance of survival. The critical decision, as so often in pregnancy, is to balance the risks of allowing the pregnancy to continue with repeated transfusions against the risks of early delivery when the baby may be too premature to live, and this balance will be decided with your obstetrician. Mothers with Rhesus problems rarely go beyond thirty-eight weeks and in some instances labour may have to be induced much earlier.

As soon as the baby is born its own blood is tested for blood grouping and the degree of anaemia and it may require transfusion of fresh blood. If the blood tests show that it is only mildly affected and is born with slight jaundice or yellowness, then treating the baby in a special light-sensitive medium called phototherapy helps restore the blood picture to normal.

If the mother has an increasing level of antibodies in pregnancy, sometimes despite blood transfusions and all precautions and even early delivery, a baby will succumb, but happily these incidences are now rare.

Future Pregnancies in a Woman Who is Already Sensitised with Antibodies

As we have already seen, Rhesus problems in a first pregnancy are extremely rare today as most women are protected by having the Anti-D injection. There is, however, another way in which a first pregnancy can be affected, and that is if a woman has been given an incorrectly grouped blood transfusion some time in the past. This is pretty unusual but is possible and this is the reason why it is vital to know precisely the blood grouping of any individual before a blood transfusion is given.

The chances of another infant being affected in a similar way will depend largely on the husband's blood group and for this reason it is very important that the husband's blood is tested before embarking on a further pregnancy. As we have seen, if he is only weakly positive then the next baby has a fifty per cent chance of having problems. If the husband is strongly positive, then it is extremely likely that a baby in a subsequent pregnancy will be affected. It is difficult to give an accurate prognosis because the outcome will depend largely on the level of antibodies in the mother when she starts her next pregnancy and how rapidly they rise. It is well worth having an outpatient consultation with the specialist for counselling on the risk of future problems before starting a further pregnancy.

ABO Incompatibility

Although incompatible problems between the blood of mother and baby are almost always confined to women with Rh-negative blood groups, there are a few problems that affect the A, B and O groups.

The best known occurs in mothers with type O group and babies with type A or B. Here again the mother may produce antibodies that destroy the baby's blood cells and release bilirubin pigment into the bloodstream. All pregnant women are screened for these potential problems at the time when their blood is originally tested and, unlike Rh disease, ABO incompatibility rarely threatens the life of the baby before birth. It can occur in a first pregnancy and is likely but not certain to recur in subsequent pregnancies. Often all that is needed is care in monitoring the level of antibodies and possibly timely induction and delivery, but occasionally exchange transfusion of the newborn baby is needed.

Other Red Cell Incompatibilities

Some women possess other, rare antigens called Kell, Anti-C and Anti-E. These can also lead to anaemia of the baby and they are managed in a similar way to Rhesus disease by serial measurements of the blood antibodies and regular checks.

CHAPTER 11

The Tenth Month

(36–40 Weeks)

Changes in Your Baby

The baby is now larger and roll-over movements are less frequent. The body is plump, there is progressive organisation of brain activity, and consciousness is well established. Eye movements are well co-ordinated and vision improves. In the last two weeks, movements may slow down and growth rate declines slightly. The placenta stops enlarging but continues to function. This may be worrying for some women but it is in fact quite normal.

At thirty-six weeks the baby weighs about 2 750gms (6lbs) and its length is 46cms (20ins). By term the average weight is about 3 150gms (7lbs) but there is of course a good deal of individual variation. A 3 400gms (7.5lbs) baby has a crown/rump length of 37cms (15ins) and its total length is 48cms (21.5ins).

The baby actually continues to gain weight a little up to the last week of pregnancy but of course it doesn't have much room to move inside the uterus. The baby is tucked up into a ball and cannot make the big movements that were felt earlier. Its lungs are lined with surfactant, which are the bubbles of foam which keep the lungs partially inflated after each breath out. The baby now practises breathing movements, sucks and swallows, and secretes hormones ready for the life outside, and has a whole range of co-ordinating reflexes that enable it to grasp tightly, lift and turn its head, find milk, make stepping movements, blink, close its eyes, etc.

Changes in You

One month to go and emotions at this stage vary enormously. Some women eagerly anticipate labour starting while for others it is a time of discomfort, inability to sleep, some anxiety about what is going to happen, and insecurity.

Make sure your plans for going into hospital are finalised and arrange with your partner so that he can take you into hospital when the time comes, or make suitable arrangements with family or friends to be 'on call'. Prepare a bag in readiness to take into hospital in case labour starts slightly earlier than expected. In a first pregnancy it is much more common to go overdue but labour can sometimes start earlier and you should be ready for this. You don't have to curtail any of your normal activities such as housework, making short journeys and driving.

It has been suggested by some that you refrain from sexual inter-course in the last month before the baby is due because of the fear of starting off labour. In fact this very rarely occurs and you should not worry about it at all, provided you can find a comfortable position!

For the last month before birth you are not going to be very comfortable much of the time. The ligaments of the pelvis are still softening, allowing the joints to expand and this may give rise to aches. Your energy centres on your body and the baby as you become quieter and meditative. The uterus extends right up to the ribs until the head engages and continues to contract. These contractions are valuable because what they are doing is making the cervix soften or ripen and thin ready for labour to start. The mucus plug which has sealed off the uterus can be dislodged resulting in a 'show' which may be tinged with blood. This doesn't actually mean that you are definitely going into labour.

Your weight will probably stay the same for the last two to three weeks because the amniotic fluid surrounding the baby stops being produced and there is often increased urination. The doctor may examine you at around thirty-six weeks just to see what the cervix feels like, whether it is ripening or not, and to establish the position of the baby's head in relation to the pelvis and if it is nicely engaged or still high. Some hospitals routinely suggest vaginal examination at thirty-six weeks and others don't. This should not be uncomfortable but may be followed by a little bloody discharge which can usually be ignored. Doing a gentle internal examination does not normally promote labour.

Labour can start in one of three ways (see pages 255–257) and some eighty per cent of babies are born within ten days of the due date, although not many on the day! It is useful at this stage to have discussed with your medical attendant what happens when you think you are in labour. Some doctors and midwives like to know early so that they can advise you on the telephone what action needs to be taken, whereas others like to be informed when contractions are coming every seven to eight minutes. Whether you are having your baby with your midwife at home or in hospital, be reassured that your medical attendants will be quite used to lots of telephone calls at this stage, especially if it is your first pregnancy. Never be afraid to ask for advice even if you think you are being a nuisance.

Medical Diseases in Pregnancy

Many women come to their first booking visit early in pregnancy, fit and healthy, and this visit is an opportunity for a full examination which perhaps has not previously been performed. Occasionally certain abnormalities are noticed at this examination of which the mother may not have been aware. For example, a routine check on blood pressure may show it to be above the normal, or sugar may be detected in a urine sample, and so on.

There are also women who arrive at pregnancy with certain medical conditions that have been previously diagnosed. The following section deals with these medical conditions, describing how pregnancy affects the condition and how the condition may affect the pregnancy.

Heart Disease

A woman's heart enlarges during pregnancy and its workload is increased by about thirty to fifty per cent. As the uterus grows it pushes the diaphragm up and the heart is therefore lifted and turned slightly. The speed at which the blood circulates around the body becomes faster and this is why the pulse rate speeds up by about ten beats per minute. Also, the total amount of blood in the body increases by more than a third.

As a result of these changes many pregnant women feel breathless at times or notice that the heart is beating rapidly, often with unpleasant palpitations when lying in bed at night. At other times in life these symptoms might mean something but during pregnancy they are usually merely signs of the normal way that the heart and blood vessels are adapting to the pregnancy.

If, however, an illness that affects the heart or lungs is known to be present before the pregnancy, the changes described and the extra demands of pregnancy require special attention. About one per cent of pregnant women arrive at pregnancy with a known heart complaint, caused by a birth defect or rheumatic fever developed in childhood so that they have a murmur or other problems.

In the course of the last twenty to thirty years there has been a radical change in doctors' attitudes to heart disease and childbearing. Many years ago it was not uncommon to recommend termination of pregnancy where there was heart disease of moderate severity as it was thought that the added strain on the heart was dangerous. Nowadays, however, this is extremely uncommon and is usually unnecessary due to a better understanding of the treatments available.

Like a number of other conditions, heart complaints may be diagnosed for the very first time in pregnancy for the simple reason that this is one of the few times that a healthy young woman may have had a detailed physical examination. If a heart condition is already present before the pregnancy or if it is diagnosed through the presence of a heart murmur early in pregnancy, the heart function needs to be assessed.

When listening to your heart at the first booking clinic the doctor may well hear a murmur and this is almost always due to the pregnancy itself which causes an increased blood flow as we have seen. There may be other signs that alert the doctor to the fact that this is more serious, in which case an expert opinion will be sought.

Management of Heart Disease during the Antenatal Period

In general terms, if heart disease is mild, restriction of excessive activity is the most important factor in preventing future trouble. Anxiety and stress should be avoided, emotional support from family and friends is important, help with housework is advisable, and if you have a lot of stairs to climb at home it may be possible to get alternative accommodation for you. The principle is to avoid factors which will make the condition worse.

You will probably be asked to attend for antenatal visits more often than usual, not to overeat, to reduce salt intake and to report immediately any untoward symptoms such as increased breathlessness particularly at night, swelling of the ankles or pain in the chest. The antenatal visits will frequently be attended not only by your obstetrician but also by a cardiologist, who is a doctor specially trained in the management of heart disease. Many such combined clinics are available for medical conditions that occur before the onset of pregnancy.

If you get very short of breath, hospitalisation may be necessary for rest and treatment. Some obstetricians like to admit mothers with heart problems to hospital routinely around the thirtieth to thirty-second week of the pregnancy whether there are any symptoms or not because the strain on the heart increases particularly from this time.

Heart Disease and Labour

In general a normal vaginal delivery is anticipated in women with heart disease unless there are associated problems which would require a Caesarean birth anyway. Throughout labour oxygen is available through a mask which may help to relieve breathlessness or chest pain. Medication is usually liberal for pain and anxiety, and epidural anaesthesia can be helpful.

The second stage of labour (see pages 260–261) is often shortened as excessive pushing may cause an added strain on the heart and forceps are often used to assist delivery(see pages 288–292). Your doctor may routinely prescribe antibiotics to be given during labour and for a few days after delivery as women with heart disease are more prone to get complications such as infection of the heart valves in the lying-in period.

Breast-feeding is not contra-indicated unless the heart condition is severe. Generally the hospital stay is somewhat longer than usual so that your condition can be assessed before you go home. It is important that a full discussion takes place before leaving hospital concerning contraception as further pregnancies occurring too soon may cause more problems with the heart. Sterilisation may be advised if it is thought that another pregnancy might be dangerous.

In exceptional circumstances heart surgery may be carried out during pregnancy. It is usually only indicated if the heart problem is due to narrowing of one of the valves and continuation of the pregnancy might jeopardise the mother's health. Likewise there may be a very few instances when termination of an early pregnancy is recommended.

Diabetes

Before the introduction of insulin in 1921 few diabetic women became pregnant and, when they did, the results were often catastrophic with the death rate for mother and infant alarmingly high. Since the discovery of insulin as a treatment for diabetes, however, diabetics have become normally fertile and with careful medical control pregnancy no longer threatens the mother's health or life.

However, diabetes even when properly treated still gives cause for concern from the baby's point of view. Before discussing the reasons for this it would seem logical to explain what happens. In order to understand how diabetes affects the body, it is important to know how the body processes or metabolises food. Compare the food you eat with petrol that goes in your car. If this fuel is not stored and utilised properly, neither the body nor the car can run smoothly. In humans the main fuel for energy production is glucose or sugar and the substance which is responsible for regulating the storage and metabolism of the body is insulin, a hormone secreted by the pancreas, a gland in the abdomen. The level of sugar in the blood normally rises every time you eat, triggering the release of insulin. By converting the sugar into energy or storing it for future use, insulin brings down the level of sugar in the blood, usually within two hours after eating.

Diabetes interferes with the way in which insulin is released after a meal and in severe cases the pancreas may produce virtually no insulin at all. Because there is not enough insulin to metabolise food the level of sugar in the blood remains high, the kidneys are unable to process all of it and therefore sugar is spilled into the urine. This is one of the reasons for testing for the presence of sugar in the urine at each antenatal visit.

No matter how much food is eaten, because the body's fuel is not being used properly, a condition similar to starvation develops. Deprived of fuel, the body begins to break down the fat that it has stored up for energy and this produces another substance that is tested for in urine, commonly called ketones. If the ketones build up to a high level, they produce an upheaval in the body's chemical balance which brings on nausea, vomiting, abdominal pain, drowsiness and even coma.

The Detection and Management of Sugar in the Urine in Pregnancy

If it is known that you are a diabetic before contemplating pregnancy, your doctor will advise you on how the pregnancy should be managed. Sometimes, however, sugar may be picked up for the first time in pregnancy when testing the urine. It does not necessarily mean that you have diabetes, for pregnancy itself sometimes causes an overload of sugar in the body. If the sugar persists in the urine for two or three visits, a confirmatory test to see whether you are developing diabetes is done by testing the blood. Normally, you will be given a glucose drink and then blood is taken at regular intervals throughout the day to see how your body copes with this added load of sugar.

A persistent finding of sugar in the urine and a confirmatory blood test indicate one of two conditions. In rare cases, this may indicate true diabetes, but commonly this finding is due to gestational or temporary diabetes, which is a condition similar to diabetes proper except that it starts in pregnancy, affects the pregnancy in a similar way as diabetes proper, but disappears once the pregnancy is over only to recur if you get pregnant again. The other significant point is that about fifty per cent of women who have temporary diabetes in pregnancy will develop diabetes proper within seven to ten years.

Gestational diabetes is normally screened by a blood test of the sugar level at the first visit or booking clinic and again at twenty-eight weeks.

Management of Diabetes in Pregnancy

Many diabetics or temporary diabetics require daily injections of insulin which they are taught to give themselves, the dose being regulated depending on the amount of sugar in the urine or blood. Nowadays simple blood testing kits are available to enable women themselves to monitor the dosage of insulin required.

Pregnancy causes alterations in the sugar metabolism so that accurate control becomes increasingly difficult. Because the dosage of insulin needed to control the blood sugar changes rapidly in pregnancy, readjustments must be made constantly in early pregnancy, often meaning a short stay in hospital until the condition is stabilised.

Strict control of sugar levels before and during pregnancy is particularly important in preventing certain complications in the mother and baby. Also, the survival of the baby and the diabetic mother will depend largely on the degree of control of the diabetes. For some poorly understood reason, babies of diabetic mothers on insulin are at risk of death in the uterus in the last six weeks and the risk is directly related to how bad the condition or how imperfect the control is. Treatment during pregnancy is therefore monitored closely and some diabetic mothers will need to spend a part of their pregnancy in hospital.

Certain pregnancy complications are known to occur more commonly in the diabetic, such as blood pressure problems and toxaemia of pregnancy. The amount of amniotic fluid may become excessive which can cause a condition called hydramnios.

Because the risk to the mother's survival increases as term approaches, many diabetic mothers are delivered before forty weeks and the exact timing depends on a number of factors, including the severity of the disease, associated complications and the maturity of the unborn child. Twenty years ago the majority of pregnant diabetic women were delivered by Caesarean section three or four weeks before the due date. Sophisticated monitoring techniques and recent advances in the control of sugar metabolism during labour have improved the outlook to such an extent that delivery may often be safely postponed to thirty-nine weeks or term, and vaginal delivery is frequently permissible. The incidence of Caesarean section is increased in the diabetic and is indicated if the controlled amount of sugar is still too high, if there are associated complications, or if the baby is thought to be too large for a safe delivery.

Once delivered the newborn baby of a diabetic mother needs careful nursing and supervision. The babies are often large because of an excess of fat under the skin and behave like premature ones, needing special feeding, attention to warmth and strict control of their own sugar needs.

It must be emphasised that good control of diabetes with blood sugars in an acceptable range before and during pregnancy reduces the risk of miscarriage, fetal abnormalities, excessively large babies and stillbirths.

Inheritance of Diabetes

Diabetic mothers will often enquire what the chances are of their children developing the disease. No clear-cut answer can be given as the genetic mode of inheritance has not been determined with certainty. If the mother alone is diabetic, there is approximately a twenty per cent risk: if both parents are diabetic, the risk is considerably higher.

It is therefore vital that postnatal advice regarding family planning is given and that counselling occurs before a further pregnancy. While some physicians are chary at prescribing oral contraception for diabetics, it is not specifically contra-indicated provided diabetic control remains good and the woman is seen regularly for check-ups.

Epilepsy

Epilepsy is a condition suffered by about one per cent of the population where recurrent, sudden attacks of muscle contractions and/or coma may occur. The term 'epilepsy' is derived from the Greek word for seizure and is used to refer to a number of seizure disorders which can be minor or major.

Epilepsy occurring for the first time in pregnancy is unusual and during the later stages of pregnancy may be confused with the fit of eclampsia (see pages 205–206). If a woman arrives at pregnancy with a known history of epilepsy and is having anti-convulsant treatment, then her doctor will advise on the safety of continuing or changing medication. Many anti-convulsants are safe in pregnancy and the level of medication can be monitored by blood testing. Again, the principle here is to balance the risk of no treatment and problems that seizures or fits can produce against the possible implications of drug therapy on the fetus. Because many of the anti-convulsant drugs remove folic acid from the blood, supplements of this vitamin are usually prescribed (see page 110).

With careful control of drug treatment, epileptic women do not have a higher rate of complications, miscarriages or malformations during pregnancy. In about a third of cases the rate and severity of the fits increase.

Mental Illness

There is no specific psychiatric disorder peculiar to pregnancy, though mental illness occurs in about one in a thousand pregnancies, either as pregnancy complicating a known disorder where the woman is already under psychiatric supervision, or where the stresses of pregnancy and labour and particularly the lying-in period precipitate a mental breakdown in a patient who has often had previous reactions to stress.

Because postnatal depression is such an important condition, a complete section is devoted to this problem (see pages 338–342).

During pregnancy depression or anxiety are common and quite considerable uncontrolled mood swings can sometimes occur from the very first weeks of pregnancy. These are generally induced by the circulating level of hormones and you may, for no apparent reason, find decisions difficult to make, feel tetchy and moody, and be prone to bouts of crying and insomnia. The line between simple anxiety in pregnancy and a proper depression is a difficult one, especially as many women will tend to hide their feelings, and it may well be that your partner is unsympathetic simply because he does not understand what is actually happening.

The fewer stresses, social, domestic, financial and obstetric, you have to face the less likely you are to suffer depression, and here much can be done by multidisciplinary treatment involving the doctors, midwives, social workers and health visitors.

Sometimes excessive mood changes are really precipitated by inability to sleep, in which case a mild sedative can be given, which your doctor will prescribe, without any effects on the fetus.

Serious mental depression can be treated perfectly satisfactorily with a number of drugs and your doctor will know which are safe and how to give them. If you are already taking anti-depressant drugs or others associated with a mental illness, it is important that you tell your doctor at the booking clinic so that the dosage can be adjusted or the tablets changed to give the minimum risk to you and your baby.

Fibroids

The wall of the uterus is made up of muscle tissue which allows it to expand in pregnancy and contract in labour and fibre tissue woven closely together to give it its strength. Sometimes the muscle tissue forms itself into knots which are at first no bigger than a pea but can grow and multiply, occasionally becoming so large that they cause a swelling which becomes obvious to the woman or to her doctor.

Fibroids are so common that they exist in twenty-five per cent of all women, though they are more common in women who have not conceived, or are infertile. They are also more frequent in the Afro-Caribbean population.

A woman may arrive at pregnancy knowing that she has fibroids, or these can be diagnosed for the first time when she has an internal examination or an ultrasound. Fibroids are frequently symptomless and are discovered quite routinely. In many instances they give no problems during the pregnancy or delivery but this depends largely on exactly where they are in the uterus. Fibroids are commonly in the muscle wall of the uterus in which case they rise out of the pelvis with the uterus and usually cause no problems. Occasionally they can project into the lining canal of the uterus and as a little polyp in the vagina and this can be a cause of vaginal bleeding.

Women with fibroids sometimes find it more difficult to conceive and occasionally also miscarry. Depending on the position of the fibroid, sometimes they may obstruct labour preventing the head from pushing down into the pelvis, in which case a Caesarean section may be necessary.

Fibroids sometimes undergo certain changes during pregnancy called degenerative changes which give rise to quite acute abdominal pain and tenderness. Normally no treatment is necessary for this and the symptoms usually settle by themselves.

The great majority of pregnant women with fibroids are able to have their babies normally and it is only rarely that fibroids interfere or cause problems with the pregnancy. After pregnancy the fibroids often shrink to their original size although they may not disappear completely.

If a woman has repeated problems thought to be due to fibroids, such as recurrent miscarriages and prolonged infertility, or if they cause problems in labour and pregnancy, then surgical removal of the fibroids may be indicated some months after the baby is born.

Cysts on the Ovary

The ovary is a complex structure consisting of many different kinds of cells, all of which can cause enlargement and the formation of cysts. Cysts occur in the ovaries because the outer lining of the cells are

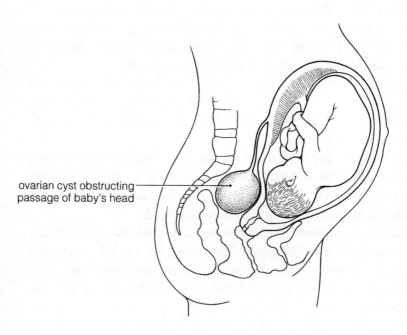

ovarian cyst obstructing passage of baby's head

Side view of ovarian cyst in pregnancy.

continually forming fluid and the whole ovary is contained within a bag or capsule, so that when the ovary enlarges or distends a small cyst or bag of fluid is formed. Usually the cyst remains small and will go unnoticed but sometimes they grow to the size of a hen's egg or larger and can be felt by the doctor during an internal examination. They may cause pain if the fluid inside the cyst increases and other complications occasionally occur such as twisting of the cyst or leakage of the fluid into the abdominal cavity.

Cysts of the ovary are usually benign but can occasionally become malignant and it is for this reason that an exploratory operation may be advised for cysts over a certain size that do not disappear.

If a cyst is discovered on routine examination at the first antenatal visit, its size and position is noted and an ultrasound can give further information. A small cyst is usually re-examined in two or three weeks' time to note any change in its appearance or size. If the cyst is quite large, say the size of an orange, then it is unlikely that it will disperse spontaneously and, as it can cause problems with advancing pregnancy, an operation may be advised. The best time for surgery in a pregnancy is after the twelfth week because a spontaneous miscarriage is less likely after this time. The exact timing of the procedure and what the surgeon will do depends on the nature of the cyst and its type although usually the cyst is shelled out leaving the ovary tissue behind to fulfil its normal function.

Just occasionally the surgeon may feel that it is in the patient's best interests for the cyst and the ovary to be removed together. It is important to realise that the remaining single ovary will take over completely all the functions of two.

Just as fibroids may be noticed for the first time late in pregnancy and occasionally cause difficulties with delivery, so an ovarian cyst may be noticed for the first time even after the baby is born and may need surgical treatment during the lying-in period.

It must be emphasised that, if surgery is needed during pregnancy for an ovarian cyst and this is done after the twelfth week, the chances of disturbing the pregnancy are remote. The scar heals well and should not give problems even as the uterus and abdomen enlarge.

CHAPTER 12

40 Weeks and Beyond

Changes in Your Baby

As already mentioned, the baby does put on a little weight beyond forty weeks, but the rate of growth is now pretty small. The placenta, which is vital for feeding the baby, becomes less efficient after forty-one to forty-two weeks and this is why many doctors will suggest that labour is induced if nothing has happened by then (see pages 314–318).

A baby born over forty-two weeks is called 'post-mature' (see pages 309–314) and at birth it has rather dry, cracked, peeling skin, long fingernails and abundant hair. It also has much less vernix covering the body and less fat.

Changes in You

In the few weeks leading up to term and even beyond there is no need to curtail your normal activities. Sitting at home waiting for something to happen will only cause anxiety. Although you will be quite heavy and uncomfortable, normal day-to-day activities are fine but a rest in the afternoon is advisable. You can still drive your car and enjoy a normal life, and in fact it is much better to keep busy at this time.

Remember that the date you have been given when the baby is due is only approximate. Very few women actually go into labour on that day, but most will go into labour within a few days either side of it. If it is not your first pregnancy, then don't assume that you will necessarily go into labour in the same way as before.

Don't be worried if you feel that the baby is moving less than before. As has already been discussed, this is quite common as pregnancy advances but, if you do have concerns or really don't think that your baby is moving very much, then give the hospital or your doctor a ring, and a quick visit and a listen to the baby's heartbeat will be reassuring.

Most women inevitably feel pretty uncomfortable as the days tick by before labour starts. While some are full of energy and feel raring to go, others find the last few days before labour irritating because of the weight of the baby, swelling of the legs, general aches and pains and backache that are common at this stage, together with difficulty in finding a comfortable position in which to sleep.

If you have not gone into labour by forty weeks, then you will be seen weekly over the next week or two to check your blood pressure, urine and, more importantly, the state of health of the baby. There are some obstetricians and midwives who like to monitor the baby's well-being by doing a heart record once or twice a week as you go beyond term. This may give an idea of how well the placenta is still functioning. You may also be asked to count the number of movements over a twelve-hour period – there should be at least ten lots of movements in this time.

Ultrasound may be used to predict how much amniotic fluid is present. If the amniotic fluid becomes too scarce, this is one of the important factors that show whether the placenta is in fact starting to fail and the baby should be delivered. The actual decision on how and when to induce labour if nothing has happened is an individual choice and each hospital and obstetrician will have somewhat differing views. There is a tendency now for lack of interference but it is common to suggest induction of labour by the end of the forty-second week (postmaturity – see pages 309–314).

Labour and Birth: Why, When and How?

Despite enormous advances in the scientific understanding of child-birth and its problems, the exact cause of the onset of labour is still a mystery. It is probably the result of a combination of factors, some chemical, some hormonal and some mechanical. Occasionally labour can be stimulated by trauma, though this is uncommon, and it can be artificially promoted by deliberate breaking of the bag of membranes or by initiating contractions of the uterus with drugs.

Labour starts approximately 280 days after the first date of the last period, although many women have episodes of mild contractions which occur throughout pregnancy, called Braxton Hicks contractions (see page 220). Suddenly for no explicable reason these painless contractions become quite regular and painful, denoting that labour has begun. Forty weeks or 280 days is of course an average as the baby usually reaches maturity between the thirty-sixth and the forty-second weeks, and in ninety per cent of all women labour will occur during this time.

Many women have episodes of 'false' labour in the last few weeks of pregnancy when the uterus contracts and tightenings can be felt. There are several clues that can help to distinguish a false alarm from real labour:

- False labour often starts at night. A good test is to get up and walk about as false labour pains usually fade away after a few minutes, while with true labour nothing stops it until the baby is born.

- At the onset of real labour there is often a slight vaginal blood staining (the so-called 'show'), although it is true to say that a show can occur several days before true labour begins. If the show occurs together with contractions, labour has almost certainly started.

- A mild sedative will make false labour go away and there is no harm in taking a sleeping tablet or pain reliever just to see what happens if regular pains occur during the night.

Despite all this, it is sometimes difficult to tell false from true labour and, if in any doubt, you should consult your doctor or midwife. Even they may not always be sure and occasionally if you start contractions your doctor will admit you to hospital and watch you carefully in order to determine what exactly is going on.

Many people believe that most babies arrive at night but in fact this is not true. There is, however, a slight variation in the birth rate throughout the year, with the greatest number of births usually occurring in the summer and autumn months.

Once you begin to have contractions, keep track of the intervals between them. In real labour the intervals between contractions become shorter and shorter while the contractions last longer and longer, while false labour pains are more erratic. A good rule of thumb is wait until the contractions are coming every ten minutes before calling your doctor. If you wait this long you can be quite sure that they are the real thing and that you can still get to the hospital in plenty of time.

What has been described is the average onset of labour but not all labours start this way. Sometimes the pains are further apart, sometimes closer together right from the start and again, if you are not sure what is going on, call your doctor or midwife. Sometimes the membranes rupture before labour begins. Often there is not the gush of water that many women anticipate: there may be no more than several tablespoonfuls. Once the membranes have ruptured there is a dribbling that cannot be controlled and, while the dribble may not amount to much at any time, it is often enough to saturate two or three sanitary towels in the course of the morning or to make a change of underclothing necessary four or five times in the same interval. Labour usually begins within a few hours.

If your membranes should rupture, let your doctor or midwife know because it is probably best for one of your medical attendants to monitor whether the labour has started properly. Also, very rarely, if the membranes rupture with the baby not sitting tucked into the pelvis, or with the baby in an abnormal position, the umbilical cord could prolapse (see pages 305–306). This is a medical emergency and the baby needs to be delivered straight away.

Most women dread rupturing their membranes in the middle of a shopping centre, in the cinema or even in bed, and it is worthwhile having sanitary towels available and to place a plastic sheet over the mattress as the expected time approaches.

The Stages of Labour

The expulsion of your child into the world by labour is divided into three stages. The purpose of labour of course is to dilate and stretch the cervix completely, push the presenting part (usually the head) through the pelvis and deliver the baby out to the world, probably the shortest and most dangerous trip your child will ever take.

The First Stage of Labour

This is the longest and the hardest and is the dilating stage. The length of the first stage varies hugely from woman to woman and also

The first stage of labour

This begins when the uterus starts to contract at regular intervals and continues until the cervix opens or dilates to about four inches or ten centimetres, wide enough for the baby's head to pass through. This first stage is the longest part of labour.

The second stage of labour

This lasts from when the cervix is fully dilated until the birth of the baby.

The third stage of labour

This follows immediately after the birth, when the baby takes its first breath and you experience your first contact together, and lasts until the placenta has separated from the uterus and is expelled.

depends on whether this is a first or subsequent pregnancy. As a rough average, the first stage may take up to twelve hours in a first pregnancy and considerably less in a subsequent one. This stage of labour may be greatly drawn out, especially with the first baby, as the cervix does not dilate at a constant rate: early in labour dilatation is slow and at the end of the first stage it usually speeds up.

Early in the first stage the contractions come every 10–15 minutes and last 20–30 seconds. They usually do not hurt much – many women experience menstrual cramps that are far worse. As labour progresses, however, the contractions do become closer together, last longer and are more severe. At the end of the first stage the contractions are coming every 2–3 minutes and last for 40–50 seconds.

Dilatation of the cervix is accomplished by reducing the volume inside the uterine cavity. Imagine the contractions of the uterus that you felt throughout most of your pregnancy are like flexing your arm, tightening the muscles and then letting the arm straighten again, thus relaxing the whole muscle. Now that labour has begun the contractions change in a very significant way. Each time the muscles tighten they grow a little shorter. Comparing it with your arm again, each time you flex the muscle your elbow will bend a little more until finally your hand is touching your shoulder. This is where labour contractions differ from any other muscle contractions. In the cavity of the uterus, as the muscle fibres get shorter, the capacity of the uterus to contain your baby gets less and therefore it pushes against the cervix to find a way out. The cervix, being properly prepared, slowly stretches to provide that way out.

During the first stage of labour there is no advantage in voluntary pushing or bearing down and you probably won't feel any desire to do so. It is also important to remember that the first few hours of labour are usually concerned with ripening of the cervix. Imagine the cervix to be a longish cylinder. When the uterus starts to contract and before the cervix actually opens it becomes shorter and shorter until it is rather like a flat disc with a little hole in the middle. It is only when it is flat that it can actually open. This is why in labour, despite good contractions for a few hours, the midwife or attendant may say to you that the cervix has not actually opened very much, but it has effaced. Effacement means flattening and this is a good sign because once it is effaced then it can open and you are really on your way.

As the cervix nears full dilatation, or ten centimetres (four inches), the baby's head will descend further into the pelvis and the cervix will usually have disappeared completely so that it can no longer be felt on vaginal examination. The baby's head presses down and helps the cervix dilate and gravity here clearly assists the process. As long as the amniotic sac is intact it will even out the pressure on the baby's head. When the waters break, however, contractions often intensify following the direct pressure of the baby's head on the cervix.

During the first stage you will inevitably need some help in the way of pain relief, and this topic will be discussed later in this chapter.

Transition Stage

The phase of labour between the first and second stages is not recognised by every midwife or doctor, or by every woman in labour. This is the stage from the end of the first to the beginning of the second stage and it is the shortest one, averaging about one hour. Coming to the end of several hours in the first stage, many women may become discouraged and feel that they cannot go on without some pain relief. From the physiological point of view it is the time when the hormones are preparing the woman's uterus to change its contractions from those which dilate the cervix to those which push the baby out. These changes in hormones can cause changes in the mother before she reaches the second stage.

Some women feel an irresistible urge to push during this stage, although the cervix may not be fully dilated. Sometimes the contractions just stop completely for a while and, if they do, take this opportunity to rest. You feel a little shaky or hot and a little confused and discouraged. This is the time when great support is necessary, and all these symptoms and signs indicate that your baby will soon be born.

The Second Stage of Labour

This is the expulsive stage, defined as the time from full dilatation of the cervix to the delivery of the baby. In first labours this stage lasts maybe an hour or two. Subsequently, it is much shorter and may take only half an hour. When the baby's head reaches the floor of the pelvis and starts to distend the vaginal opening you will feel an urge to bear down and push. With this urge comes some relief from the discomfort, although the contractions are often still hard and frequent at this stage.

Complete dilatation of the cervix is the signal for the start of the second stage, and the baby's head will gradually descend to the floor of the pelvis as you push down with each contraction. When the head begins to separate the vaginal opening, preparations are made for delivery.

Pushing is instinctive. It does not hurt the baby but it is hard work, much harder if you are lying on your back because you actually have to push the baby up hill. Your medical attendant will help to show you how to push, which you should do during a contraction.

Babies are born most easily with the occiput, or the back of the head, in an upward position so that the baby is looking down when born. As the head emerges the skin of the vulva may become stretched and, because it is very thin, may tear a little. It is at this stage that the attendant may deliberately cut the skin to prevent tearing (episiotomy – see pages 263–265).

The head, when fully born, turns by itself to the left or right depending on which side of the mother the baby's shoulders are, and is grasped by the doctor or midwife who places one hand beneath the jaw and guides the head downwards. The front shoulder slips out and then a pull upwards brings out the rear shoulder. With gentle, continued traction the remainder of the baby follows easily.

At about the time that the shoulders are delivered, or when the head comes, the midwife will give you an injection of a drug called Syntometrine which keeps the uterus firm and helps the placenta to start to detach from the uterine wall. This injection can also prevent heavy bleeding which can occur between the second and third stages.

Some mothers like to feel the baby being born and actually even assist the last part with the arms of the baby so that it can be born on the mother's abdomen. Other women may prefer to hold the baby once delivery has been completed by the attendant. Make sure that you have discussed with your deliverer what your preference is at this stage.

Finally, if you have had an epidural, you may not feel the pain, although you probably will feel contractions, and the insatiable desire to bear down may not be that obvious, but essentially pushing is exactly the same though you may take a little longer to get the hang of things.

The Final or Third Stage of Labour

This is concerned with delivery of the placenta. In the past, the practice was to wait for the placenta to detach itself from the wall of the uterus and the mother was encouraged to expel it herself. This 'natural' expulsion of the placenta, however, often caused problems. The placenta sometimes failed to detach itself from the uterus or only started to come away in part, thus causing bleeding.

Nowadays a policy usually is adopted of pulling on the cord soon after the baby is born, following the injection of a drug just as the head and shoulders are being born. This hastens detachment of the placenta and causes the uterus to tighten up, reducing the likelihood of haemorrhage. There is nothing wrong with waiting until after the baby has been born for a short while to see if the placenta will detach itself spontaneously and the midwife or doctor will be explaining what is happening at the time so that this can be discussed.

Once the baby is born the cord is cut and clamped and separated from the placenta. Here again, there are some who claim that the umbilical cord should not be divided immediately after the birth but that the baby should remain attached to the placenta until the cord ceases to pulsate. They say that the newborn baby gains extra oxygen from the blood as it is pumped along the cord in the first few minutes of life. Although it is usual practice to sever the cord immediately, there is no danger in waiting and if you feel strongly about this you should convey your feelings early in labour.

Some Controversial Issues in Labour

Enemas

Enemas used to be a standard part of obstetrical admitting procedures and were supposed to clean out the mother's bowel so that she would not worry about passing motions as she bore down in giving birth. Typically, the mother may have loose bowel movements in any case the day or so before labour begins, which is Nature's method of achieving the same objective. It is true that a full bowel can impede progress in labour by creating an obstruction to the descent of the head, but a mother who has been eating correctly and taking regular mild exercise is unlikely to suffer from constipation late in pregnancy.

Many hospital units have changed their policies and the old established tradition of 'enemas for all' is gradually being replaced by a question concerning the woman's recent bowel habits, followed by the less dramatic effects of suppositories if she is uncomfortable or wishes to feel 'cleansed'. No harm will be done if some faecal material is passed during a push.

Shaving

Shaving of the pubic hair is a practice that was introduced when routines used in preparing a patient for surgery were adopted in obstetrics, since it was supposed to reduce the chances of infection to mother and baby by eliminating a site where bacteria might thrive. Few hospitals now advocate shaving in labour as a routine and many units adopt a policy of no shaving at all, or perhaps clipping of pubic hair in response to the mother's request. Moreover, some authorities believe that shaving can actually create infection in the mother as the inevitable nicks in the skin make an open passage for organisms. Don't be afraid to discuss the question of shaving with your midwife or doctor before you go into labour.

Episiotomy

Episiotomy is the name given to the procedure of deliberately cutting the skin behind the vaginal opening (the perineum) to help delivery of the baby's head, either because the skin is too rigid or because the vaginal entrance is too tight to allow the head to pass through without tearing.

Opinions have long been divided about whether an episiotomy should be carried out routinely in an uncomplicated delivery and even about which type of episiotomy should be done. Its liberal use has been questioned both by the medical profession and the public. Before discussing the relative merits and problems of routine episiotomy, we should acknowledge that there are certain times when an episiotomy is medically indicated:

- If delivery is complicated by manipulative procedure, for instance forceps, because the forceps tend to stretch the skin and may cause tearing.

- During the delivery of twins.

- With a premature infant when the head is small and softer and more prone to injury if delivery is rapid.

- If there is evidence that the fetus is distressed and the delivery of the head needs to be performed urgently.

- If an episiotomy was done in a previous pregnancy, the skin becomes more fibrous and non-stretchable and severe tearing may sometimes occur unless delivery of the head is very controlled.

If a normal delivery is anticipated in a woman having her first child, no definite decision about an episiotomy is usually made until the head starts to distend and stretch the skin. At this stage the attendant assesses whether the skin seems sufficiently pliable to allow delivery to occur without tearing a little. Repairing a deliberate cut is simpler than stitching a ragged tear: it will in general heal better and is less likely to cause problems at a later stage.

The more contentious argument in favour of episiotomy concerns long-term effects. There are those who believe that the muscles of the pelvic floor may be irreparably weakened by the expulsive efforts of the mother if the second stage is too long and this may lead to slackness and prolapse of the uterus.

The main disadvantage of an episiotomy, or indeed a tear, is the discomfort afterwards and there is no doubt that the first few days of the lying-in period are much more comfortable if there has been no cut or tear. It is also argued that, even if the skin is cut, the incision might extend further, producing a tear as well so that the disadvantage of allowing the skin to tear slightly is exaggerated.

A small skin tear is often inevitable and usually of little consequence. A tear extending down into the anal canal can be disastrous, however, as an opening that occurs between the vagina and the rectum may lead to the passage of faeces through the vagina, months of discomfort and future surgery. The anti-episiotomy lobby say that it has never been demonstrated that routine episiotomies reduce damage to the pelvic floor structures and in fact incision and repair may lead to poor anatomical results. They also maintain that sexual response can be marred because the vagina may become tight and the scar may cause difficulty with intercourse – complications that are not unknown but rare.

An episiotomy is performed by making a single cut with scissors in the skin between the vagina and anus, directed slightly outwards from the midline, so that any extension of the cut does not tear downwards into or near the anal canal. Many women are afraid of an episiotomy because of the pain of the cut. However, if the timing is right and the incision is made just as the head distends the skin of the vagina, there should be little discomfort. Unless an epidural is present when there will be no feeling, the skin is usually anaesthetised with a local solution rendering the area insensitive.

Many women ask how long the cut will be and how many stitches will be used for repair. The answer is that episiotomies tend to be the same for all and are usually the length of an average surgical scissor blade (1.5ins) and the stitches used to close the cut vary from three to six in number. Most attendants favour thread that dissolves in a few days, avoiding the need for subsequent removal. Some women are frightened that their first bowel action will be painful and might disrupt the stitches. While the first bowel movement may be a little uncomfortable, straining does not damage the cut. Once the bowels are opened there are usually no subsequent problems with defecation.

Finally, it must be stressed that the midwives and doctors responsible for supervising delivery are well aware of the indications for and arguments against episiotomy. There are usually no hard and fast rules before a normal uncomplicated delivery and the decision to perform an episiotomy will be made in the best interests of mother and baby.

Positions in Labour

Confinement to bed used to be considered a necessity when everyone was heavily sedated for labour and all labouring women were clustered together in a large ward under the supervision of one or two nurses. It is probably true to say that uterine contractions are less frequent but stronger when the mother is upright and some say that labour is more efficient. Also, many mothers are more comfortable when standing up or moving about, especially in the early stages of labour. Those advocating natural childbirth also maintain that women should be free to choose their own position during labour and delivery.

Provided that labour progresses smoothly and the head of the baby fits snugly into the mouth of the pelvis, mobility is permitted until late in the first stage. If problems arise that call for stricter supervision, or the mother is considered to be 'at risk' for other reasons, she will be advised to remain in bed so that electronic monitoring of the baby's heartbeat is possible. Some units possess remote-controlled equipment, consisting of a small portable radio receiver carried by the mother which can relay the activity of the baby's heart rate to a central console in the labour suite, thus allowing freedom of movement and continual assessment of the baby's condition. It is, however, important to realise that modern obstetric care, which has done so much to improve the safety of mother and baby, demands restrictive supervision in the form of fetal monitoring (see the next section).

Mothers are mostly encouraged to walk about in early labour but, as the contractions become stronger, you may prefer to rest in bed, though not necessarily on your back. Indeed lying on the side encourages the uterus to contract efficiently and is more comfortable for the mother, since it avoids the feeling of faintness which can arise when the weight of the uterus presses directly on the main veins which run along the backbone. Delivery is usually conducted with the mother lying on her side or her back and it may be necessary for the legs to be supported in stirrups if forceps are used, or delivery is other than normal, as this gives the doctor a better view. If you have strong feelings about positions in labour and want to sit, crouch or adopt any other position, tell your doctor or midwife early so that your request can be noted. Again, if you have strong views of how you would like your labour conducted, convey them at an early stage to your medical attendants.

Finally, please remember that everyone concerned with your care wants a safe and happy outcome for you and your baby but labour and delivery, especially for the first time, are an unknown quantity. Perfectly straightforward labour can suddenly change so that the best laid plans need to be altered and this might cause disappointment. Discussion of specific views and anxieties with the antenatal sister and doctor who see you in the clinic and an understanding of the policies of the hospital unit or opinions of your medical attendants, together with the knowledge that obstetric care needs to be adaptable, will do much to avoid dissatisfaction and promote confidence.

Monitoring the Well-being of the Baby

Being born is a stressful and complex process. Every time the uterus contracts the blood vessels that supply the baby with oxygen are narrowed and therefore the baby is forced in effect to hold its breath. Healthy babies are able to do this without any problem in the same way as adults, but other babies are more vulnerable during labour. Again like adults with lung problems, they cannot hold their breath for an extended period. If deprived of oxygen for too long, they could suffer permanent damage or die, and to avoid these dangers continuous recording of the baby's heart rate is maintained throughout labour and delivery.

In the past doctors, and nurses, monitored the baby's heart by listening through a small stethoscope pressed against the mother's abdomen at regular intervals during labour, just like the stethoscope used in the antenatal clinic. When electronic fetal monitoring was introduced this provided a continuous surveillance of the baby's heart rate and of the contractions, rather like an electrocardiogram (ECG) is used in an adult.

The introduction of fetal monitoring has had an enormous impact on the approach of obstetricians to complications during labour, but the widespread reliance on fetal monitors and the necessity for the mother to be restricted in her movements have caused some controversy. Yet there is little disagreement about the value of close supervision in complicated or high risk labour, e.g. when the baby is distressed, when there has been vaginal bleeding, or in a twin pregnancy. In some hospitals all women in labour are monitored, at least initially, and at regular intervals during labour. If there are any signs that the baby may be distressed, monitoring continues throughout labour and delivery. Low risk pregnancies are often managed by a forty-minute fetal heart recording and, if normal, the baby's heart can be listened to with a hand-held stethoscope every fifteen minutes during and after a contraction.

If you have very strong views on this subject, then make them known early to your medical attendants when the whole question can be discussed and your feelings noted.

There are basically two types of electronic fetal monitoring – external and internal. In external monitoring the pads are placed outside the mother's body and two belts around the abdomen. One belt holds the small instrument which records the tightness and stretch of the abdomen during contractions and tells how long and far apart the contractions are, and the other holds an instrument

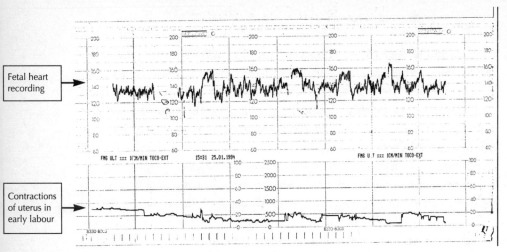

Fetal heart recording →

Contractions of uterus in early labour →

Examples of continuous monitoring of the baby's heart rate, together with amplitude of uterus contractions.

called a transducer which actually records the baby's heart rate. These belts are reasonably comfortable and do not interfere with labour. Once the amniotic membranes have ruptured and the cervix is open, one or both of these external monitors may be replaced by a more sensitive and accurate internal device placed directly into the uterus.

A small electrode is attached to the baby's scalp that can produce a very accurate record of the baby's heartbeat. Occasionally a fluid-filled plastic tube may be placed in the uterus to record the internal pressure during contractions. These tracings are frequently checked during labour and give the doctor an accurate, continuous and visual picture of how the baby is withstanding the stresses of labour.

If the baby's heart rate is abnormal or there is any other sign of distress, a tiny specimen of blood can be obtained through a prick in the baby's scalp and the acidity of the blood sample can be measured. This procedure can give an accurate assessment of whether the baby is severely distressed or not and is known as fetal scalp sampling.

As with most sophisticated tests, its true value is best seen in units where blood sampling is done as a routine by experienced operators, and the technique is limited by its availability in the individual hospital unit.

Pain Relief in Labour

For thousands of years women gave birth without drugs for pain relief and in many parts of the world they still do. If it were not for the risk of complications of one sort or another, any healthy normal woman carrying a normal baby could in theory go through labour and delivery without medical intervention. That is not to say that any woman would want to be alone in her labour, or that every woman should count on a childbirth free from all discomfort.

Effective, safe drugs exist today which can alleviate and sometimes even abolish the pain of labour, either when given by mouth or by an injection such as a local anaesthetic. Yet more and more women are today expressing dissatisfaction with accepted medical pain relieving methods and want a different sort of help in which the use of drugs can be kept to a minimum, so that they can expect to achieve a greater emotional fulfilment. Most of all, of course, women want to be conscious and aware of what is happening when their baby is born.

Several systems aimed at achieving these goals have been developed in the last few decades and, although they may differ considerably in their methods, it is customary to group them in the category of 'natural childbirth'. Before discussing these methods in more detail, it might be interesting to dwell a little on the history of pain relief during labour.

Before the early nineteenth century there was little reference to the use of any help for pain in labour, although pain relieving drugs were known and employed in other branches of surgery and medicine. Indeed, there were pages devoted to the instruction of medical personnel in the proper conduct of births but little was included about mitigating drugs. Not only were labour pains unrelieved, but nothing was done to reduce the horror of certain obstetrical operations.

The first accurate account of an anaesthetic drug delivered to a woman in labour described the use of ether by Sir James Young Simpson in 1847 to help the delivery of a poor woman in the slums of Edinburgh. On the same day, by chance, he was appointed as one of Queen Victoria's physicians and wrote, 'Flattery from the Queen is perhaps not common flattery but I am far less interested in it than having delivered a woman this week without any pain.'

In the early 1900s a German doctor called Gauss was the first to advocate pain relief in labour. He introduced a combination of two drugs, morphine and scopolamine, the first of which dulled pain and the second dimmed memory, calling his technique 'twilight sleep'. While under its influence, the patient remained in a kind of mid-state between consciousness and unconsciousness and, although these drugs have been largely replaced by more effective and safer methods of pain relief, morphine and scopolamine are still in use in other branches of surgery and constitute the main components of a pre-medication (pre-med), the sedative injection often given an hour before surgery.

Nowadays there are two different methods of diminishing or controlling the pain of labour: pain relieving drugs (analgesics) and anaesthetics. These obliterate all sensation, either through the production of transitory unconsciousness which is a full general anaesthetic, or by temporarily interrupting the pain pathways by an injection of local anaesthetic.

Pain Controlling Drugs

There are many different drugs used for the relief of pain in labour and each hospital unit will have its preference, but the ones commonly used are derivatives of morphine given by injection, often together with a mild tranquillizer, which has the double effect of inducing a sort of drowsiness and preventing nausea. This regime is usually successful in producing reasonable pain relief when given at intervals of 3–4 hours during the first stage of labour.

An ideal drug for relieving pain in labour would be one which acted on the mother alone without crossing the placenta to affect the baby, but unfortunately no such drug exists at the present time. Most pain relievers cross the placenta and enter the baby's circulation so that the administration during labour is very carefully controlled, not only in amount but also in timing.

The relief of pain in labour is a tricky business. Each time a drug is given the doctor must ask three questions:

- Is this drug in the dose prescribed safe for the mother?

- Is it likely to lengthen the labour by slowing down the force of the contractions?

- May it harm the baby?

There is a correct dose for every particular drug for each individual patient at different stages of labour. This dose can be judged only when the labour itself is viewed as a whole and when the condition of both mother and baby is taken into consideration. It is therefore critical to judge the optimum time and dosage of a drug to be effective and yet prevent depression of the baby's respiration, so that the baby will be born in a good condition. Here it must be stated that most of the strong pain relievers have antidotes which can be given to the baby as soon as it is born if its breathing is a bit sluggish.

Inhalational Analgesia

Safe pain-relieving gases can be administered by inhaling through a mask under instruction from the midwife. These are particularly useful for the strong contractions of a rapid labour, or for the transition from the first to the second stage. The gases are a mixture of gas and air and many women find satisfactory relief from the acute pain of a strong contraction once they are used to breathing correctly.

TENS (Transcutaneous Electrical Nerve Stimulation)

This is a method of pain relief in which electrode pads discharging an electrical stimulus are placed on the back. The patient controls the amount of electrical input with a hand-held control, varying its strength by using the booster and choosing whether the stimulus is constant or pulsating. The principle here is to interfere with the passage of pain signals to the brain by sending tingling sensations across the skin, which release the body's own pain-killing hormones (endorphins). Many mothers find it extremely useful and a good distraction technique, something to rely on and hold their concentration in the early stages of labour. Other women find it of no value, certainly once the contractions have become fairly strong. Obviously there are no effects whatsoever on the baby.

If this principle appeals to you, then discuss it with your midwife as not all labour wards possess TENS machines. They can, however, be hired and can be used for backache in pregnancy as well as early labour.

Anaesthetics

Anaesthetics are available to eliminate birth pain and can be divided into two main categories: general and local.

A general anaesthetic implies an effect on the whole body, creating temporary but complete unconsciousness, whereas a local anaesthetic is an injection which simply interrupts the pathway to the brain cells from the area where the pain stimulus is received, so that the pain is removed and yet the patient is conscious. Imagine an electric light with the wall switch as the stimulus, the connecting wires as the pathways, and the electric bulb as the brain which receives stimulation. If the conducting wires are cut, the bulb will not light no matter how many times the switch is operated.

General Anaesthesia

A general anaesthetic can be given for any purpose associated with pregnancy or childbirth and is administered by a specialised doctor. There is no reason why you should not be given a general anaesthetic during your pregnancy if an operation not concerned with your pregnancy is required. Nowadays anaesthetics will not harm you or your baby, but all drugs including anaesthetics are best avoided in the first three and the last three months of pregnancy.

Putting a woman to sleep completely for delivery of the baby is now an uncommon procedure because it has been largely replaced by local anaesthetics (epidural – see page 274). Before epidurals were used so frequently it was often necessary to use a general anaesthetic to achieve complete relaxation of the mother for certain manoeuvres during pregnancy, such as turning a baby round or even sometimes in induction of labour if the stretching of a very tight cervix caused a lot of discomfort. Similarly, some forceps deliveries could not be satisfactorily performed without general anaesthesia because of the discomfort produced.

Why is General Anaesthesia Rarely Used Today?

The main disadvantage of a general anaesthetic is that serious accidents can occasionally occur. Years ago it was thought that anybody could put a woman to sleep to have a baby and, when deliveries were conducted at home, it used to be common practice to involve even the husband or a relative as some sort of temporary anaesthetist. In hospitals, novice anaesthetists were frequently used for delivery anaesthesia.

We now know that obstetric anaesthesia can be difficult and dangerous in inexperienced hands, firstly because there is the interest of two patients, mother and baby, to consider, and secondly the labouring mother is often poorly prepared for anaesthesia. Remember that, if you have a general anaesthetic for any surgical procedure when you are not pregnant, it is usual to demand admission to hospital for rest and pre-operative starvation before the scheduled operation. A mother in labour, however, may enter the hospital after a hectic day at home, possibly having just eaten a full meal, in which case she runs the risk of being sick during anaesthesia and that could lead to serious complications.

Nowadays general anaesthesia, when required, is administered by a senior doctor skilled in the art of anaesthesia in maternity work and fully aware of the hazards so that, if a situation arises where a general anaesthetic is necessary, for instance Caesarean section, modern techniques and the drugs available make it a very safe procedure.

Local Anaesthesia

The simplest form of local anaesthesia involves an injection into a tissue with a solution which deadens the area temporarily, for example before episiotomy, so that the cut is not felt and suturing of the wound can be performed without pain.

Another type of local anaesthesia is called pudendal nerve block and this is sometimes used before some sort of manipulative delivery, such as with forceps. The pudendal nerve supplies sensation to most of the area of the pelvis, the vagina and the muscles of the pelvic floor. The block is performed by injecting these nerves in the side wall of the pelvis with a local anaesthetic solution. The injection itself is virtually painless and provides a loss of sensation in the vagina and the vulva so that a complicated delivery can be achieved without undue discomfort.

A third type of local analgesia is not very much used in the UK but is popular in the USA. It is called the paracervical block and here the cervix itself is injected in three places to deaden its nerve supply if the contractions are extremely strong in the later stages of labour. Also, of course, delivery will be made much easier if the dilated cervix has very little sensation.

The Epidural

This technique more than any other has revolutionised the modern management of pain relief during labour and delivery, because it provides a near ideal situation of abolition of pain coupled with minimum side effects to the baby and the mother.

What is an Epidural?

There is a fine space in the spinal column (the extradural space) which is continuous from the base of the skull to the tip of the spine. This space contains spinal nerves as they enter and leave the spinal cord. The nerves that carry pain stimuli from the uterus to the brain arrive at the spine in the upper lumbar region, i.e. about the middle of the back.

An epidural anaesthetic is simply a local anaesthetic which is injected into this space and flows down causing numbness of the spinal nerves. The extent of the pain relief will vary according to the amount of local anaesthetic injected. Ideally you will be able to sense a feeling of the uterus tightening and relaxing during contractions but the pain will be abolished, and likewise during delivery there may be very little sensation of pain during the actual birth. If a forceps delivery or episiotomy is necessary, this will cause no pain whatsoever, nor will the stitches that are needed to repair the cut.

How is an Epidural Done?

The technique of epidural anaesthesia is highly specialised and is carried out by an obstetric anaesthetist trained in the procedure. You will usually be placed on your side with head bent and knees up

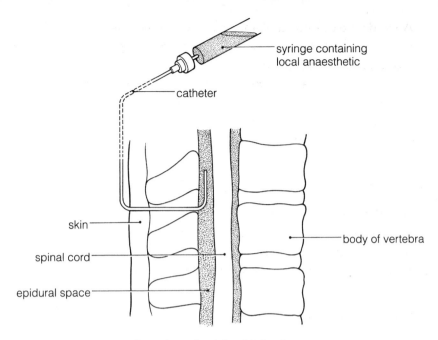

Location of epidural injection.

towards the chest, so that the spine is stretched to allow the vertebral bones to be opened out. A local anaesthetic is injected to numb the skin and deeper tissues of the back before the introduction of the needle between two of the vertebrae. The anaesthetist will sense when the needle has arrived in the epidural space and insert over the needle a tiny plastic tube (catheter) through which the anaesthetic solution can be injected. This tube can be left in place for hours without discomfort or risk and is usually strapped to your back where it should not cause any discomfort. It is usual to continue labour on the side to avoid dizziness caused by pressure of the uterus on the main blood vessels. Repeated injections through the catheter can be given at 2–4 hourly intervals and these 'top-ups' are totally painless.

When can an Epidural be Given?

An epidural can in fact be given at any stage in labour, but of course it is much easier before the onset of severe contractions as you will be able to relax and allow the procedure to be done when you are not distressed. An experienced anaesthetist can introduce an epidural very late in the first stage of labour, and even in the second stage if conventional forms of pain relief have not worked.

What are the Indications for Epidural Anaesthesia?

These can be divided into medical reasons, when the doctor may suggest that an epidural would be in the mother's and baby's interests, or social reasons where the mother may elect to have a painless labour and delivery. Most obstetric units in the UK provide epidural anaesthesia though the extent to which the procedure is available varies widely. Some hospitals offer an 'epidural service'. In other words any patient may choose to have an epidural from when labour starts, but this will depend largely on the availability of the service at the particular hospital. Epidurals are often discussed early in pregnancy or at one of the antenatal classes but, if the subject has not been brought up, it is as well to ask whether and when this is available.

In other hospitals epidural anaesthesia is available only on a limited basis and only if there are medical indications. This does not stem from any bias but usually from the nature of the procedure which is time-consuming, involving expertise, nursing care and special anaesthetic skills, all factors which vary greatly in different hospital units.

Medical Indications for an Epidural

There are a number of instances when the medical attendants may suggest an epidural during labour. The commonest reason is inadequate help from other forms of pain relief. If you have high blood pressure or pre-eclampsia, an epidural provides the double advantage of giving excellent pain relief and lowering the blood pressure during labour, thereby reducing possible complications. Premature labour is another medical indication, because with a small baby one does not want to cause difficulty with respiration as conventional drugs pass via the placenta to the baby.

There are other indications including a very long labour, persistent posterior position of the baby's head (see pages 302–303) and a delivery that will probably demand some special manipulation, such as a breech birth or twins.

Is the Procedure Painful?

Having an epidural does cause a little discomfort and, like any injection to relieve pain, the result is not always the same. An epidural given in labour takes ten to fifteen minutes to take effect and the more advanced the mother is in labour the more difficult it is for her to turn on her side and keep reasonably still.

An ideal epidural should abolish the pain and yet the mother should be aware of contractions. Sometimes the effect is one-sided, in other words some pain is felt on one side of the abdomen and leg while the other side is numb. This is due to the way in which the anaesthetic fluid tracks down the very narrow space and can be managed by withdrawing the little catheter slightly or turning the mother from side to side.

Rarely there is difficulty inserting the needle through the skin and the procedure may have to be repeated.

Epidural Anaesthesia and Caesar`ean Section

Because of the disadvantages of a general anaesthetic, most Caesarean sections are now performed under epidural so that you may remain awake during the operation, can see your baby being born and can even handle it once it has been removed from the uterus. If you have been in labour for some time already and have an epidural present, then the obstetrician will surely advise that the operation be done with the same epidural rather than employ a full general anaesthetic.

In units where epidural anaesthesia is common, elective Caesarean section, i.e. the operation being done before labour (see pages 293–294), may be done with epidural, although the decision on whether this is suitable or acceptable to you will be taken only after considerable counselling. Although epidural anaesthesia may remove or abolish much of the pain in labour, it is often difficult for a mother to be confident that an operation involving a cut into the abdomen will be painless. You can, however, be reassured that this is in fact so.

If requested, your partner can be present during the operation if it is done under epidural, and neither of you need worry about seeing anything you don't want to because the operative area is covered by a screen.

What is it Like Having a Caesarean Section under Epidural?

The first point to make is that you are lying on your back and will see nothing until the baby is actually delivered from the uterus, as a screen or a drape is placed between you and the operative site. You may see the surgeon's face, but none of the actual operation. The anaesthetist usually sits at your head explaining the various procedures and is always ready to give a full anaesthetic should the procedure not be quite as painless as it should be, or for other operative reasons.

Being wheeled into an operating theatre under arc lights may be rather daunting when you are awake, but the medical and nursing personnel are fully aware of the situation and you usually get quite accustomed to the atmosphere after a few minutes. During surgery you will not feel anything sharp, though you may hear snipping noises as scissors cut various tissues. It takes only a few minutes from the first incision into the skin to actually deliver the baby but, because extreme gentleness is required, the procedure usually takes a little longer than it does when a full anaesthetic is used.

Just before the baby is delivered, the assistant may press quite firmly on your abdomen to help delivery of the head through the uterus. This may cause a little discomfort, but only until the head is out. Once the baby is delivered the surgeon will need to repair the cut in the uterus and it can be another half hour or so before the operation is over. Some manipulation of the uterus is unavoidable during the sewing procedure and there is a little aching sometimes, particularly when the blood and fluid are cleaned out prior to the finish of the operation. Within an hour or so of going into the operating theatre you will be back in bed, fully awake, with your baby at your side.

The anaesthetist may give an extra dose of anaesthetic after the operation to deaden any pain in the scar area as the tissues come to life again, but the epidural cannot remain indefinitely and is usually withdrawn within a few hours of the operation.

Post-operative recovery without full anaesthesia has many advantages. You are mobile, you do not feel nausea, there is little bloating of the abdomen, the bowel does not distend with often unpleasant, painful wind, and you can be sitting up the same evening having a light meal and holding your baby.

Are There Any Complications from Epidural Anaesthesia?

As in any procedure that demands skill, the effect is not always full in terms of pain relief. The injected fluid sometimes works better on one side than the other and, although the pain from contractions may be abolished, a persistent backache may remain, particularly if the baby is in the posterior position (see pages 302–303).

A fall in blood pressure is the commonest complaint of an epidural anaesthetic and occurs in approximately five per cent of women. This is why the blood pressure is taken at frequent intervals after an epidural anaesthetic has been set up, and this is also the reason why it is mandatory to have a drip or intravenous fluid running into the body during the epidural which will bring the blood pressure up again. A drop in blood pressure may induce feelings of faintness and is usually immediately corrected by turning onto the side.

Very rarely, the needle may impinge on the dura (the membrane immediately surrounding the spinal cord). This may cause a small leak of the fluid in the spinal canal, and a headache. Should it occur, the anaesthetist will not go on to inject the local anaesthetic but will simply try at a different level. Instances are recorded, although they are extremely rare, of an injection of the local anaesthetic given after the dura has been pierced with resultant temporary loss of power and sensation to the legs.

Epidural anaesthesia is sometimes blamed if weakness or loss of sensation in the legs, or lack of bladder control, follow labour. These complications are usually not due to the epidural itself. Weakness of the bladder or inability to pass urine shortly after delivery, or even inability to control the bladder for a few weeks, do sometimes follow a normal labour and are more frequent after a difficult vaginal delivery.

The most common complaint that mothers have is persistent backache around the area where the needle was originally introduced. Sometimes this persists for a few days or even a week or two and is usually due to stiffness of the muscles around the site of the needle. It clears quite spontaneously and there are no long-term effects from this.

Finally, headaches may occur. The incidence of headache is difficult to calculate and usually presents a problem only if a leak of fluid has occurred from the spinal cord. In this instance, the headache may persist for a few days and the mother is nursed flat on her back. It is very rare for headaches to last longer than a few days.

Does an Epidural Increase the Likelihood of a Forceps Delivery?

It is true to say that some help with delivery is not unusual in mothers using an epidural for pain relief and there are a number of reasons for this. The urge to bear down may be less obvious and make 'pushing' more difficult to appreciate. This in turn may prevent rotation of the baby's head as it meets the pelvic floor and there may be a need for assistance with the forceps.

However, in units where epidurals are used frequently, the instance of forceps delivery is only very marginally increased. This is because, although the sensation of bearing down may be altered, it is not necessarily abolished. When an epidural is 'topped-up' at the right time in the right dose, the mother should be able to feel the descent of the head and, although her legs may need support as they may be heavy and floppy and the sensation or feeling is not quite the same, there is no reason why she should not be able to expel her baby normally if she has had training before. In a unit that is used to performing epidurals, the complication rate is extremely small, the efficiency rate very high and in over ninety per cent of women the relief of pain during labour and delivery is complete.

Finally, the success or otherwise of epidural anaesthesia depends as much upon the skill of the anaesthetist as on correct counselling given earlier in the antenatal period, so that the mother understands the procedure, knows why it may be used and a little bit about what to expect.

Mobile Epidural

When a conventional epidural is set up you will be confined to the labour bed. This is mainly because the strength and amount of the local anaesthetic not only takes the pain away but makes the legs very heavy so that it is not possible to walk around. A mobile epidural involves exactly the same procedure as a normal epidural but uses a much more dilute solution of anaesthetic, so that the pain is minimised and yet mobility is not reduced and you can walk around. As labour progresses and the contractions become stronger, the more conventional type is often added.

The other advantage of a mobile epidural is that you can actually control the amount of anaesthetic entering the system with a little pump which is hand-held and connected to the catheter or tube where the epidural is inserted into the back. You therefore feel much more in control of events.

Not every hospital unit favours mobile epidurals but, if this appeals to you, then ask the antenatal sister or labour ward superintendent or doctor whether the procedure is available.

Spinal Anaesthesia

Here a similar principle is adopted but on a single shot basis. The fluid that is injected doesn't actually go into the area called the 'epidural space' as previously described. It goes into another fine space just adjacent called the 'subarachnoid space'. The advantage is that very small concentrations are necessary, somewhere around a tenth of the amount needed for an epidural, but of course it is short lived.

The principal use of spinal anaesthetic is for a Caesarean section rather than in labour when continuous anaesthesia is needed for the pain. Spinal anaesthesia is common in the USA and a number of anaesthetists in this country favour this method for a Caesarean section.

Caudal Anaesthesia

This means a single injection in an area at the base of the spine below the end of the spinal cord, and it is not generally practised in this country. The indication for a single shot caudal might be in a woman who has gone through labour without much help and without anaesthetic of any sort in whom the second stage of labour is particularly difficult or painful. A single injection into the caudal area will abolish the pain for an hour or two to enable delivery to be more comfortable.

Natural Childbirth

Drug relief of pain in labour has become established practice over the years. However, not all women are equally enthusiastic about pain relief. Some women, though grateful for help, feel cheated by not being consciously aware during their child's birth. They feel that they are not able to take an active part in the expulsive stage.

Over the last decade, a counter-reaction has set in against extensive medication during childbirth and it is customary to group all expressions of it in the category of 'natural childbirth'. Whether under the name of 'preparation for childbirth', 'psychoprophylaxis', or 'natural', all the schools of thought have the same underlying principle that, since childbirth is a natural healthy process, there must be some method of preparation that will reduce and sometimes eliminate pain, and certainly the fear of pain.

The founder of natural childbirth in the 1950s was an English obstetrician, Grantly Dick Read. Like everyone else, he knew that people accumulated myths and misinformation about the pain of childbirth and handed down tales from generation to generation. He was interested in the fact that none of the other healthy, natural processes was accompanied by much pain – so why childbirth? He asked himself two questions: is labour easy because a woman is calm, or is she calm because her labour is easy? And, conversely, is a woman frightened and in pain because her labour is difficult, or is her labour difficult because she is frightened?

Dick Read came to the conclusion that fear was in some way the main agent for producing pain in a labour that was in every other respect a perfectly natural process. He surmised that fear stimulated the particular nerves that caused muscles to go into spasm, with consequent cramp-like pains. A vicious circle was then set up: fear caused pain, pain increased fear. Eliminate the fear, he proposed, and the pain, if not entirely absent, would at least be reduced.

Drawing on the work of their great physiologist, Ivan Pavlov, the Russians went into training for childbirth on a big scale. Pavlov was the discoverer of the conditioned reflex, the body's automatic response to some stimulus, like the leg kicking out when the doctor taps with a rubber hammer just below the kneecap. Pavlov proved that a programme of training to set up a competing or distracting stimulus could alter the natural response to pain like that of labour. A woman might be conditioned to the new stimulus, which would lessen the painful one. Thus experts developed a system of breathing in quick pants to offset the discomfort of the contractions and a system of exercise to promote relaxation. The Russian ideas were picked up in France and developed by Dr Lamaze, and his technique spread throughout Europe and the USA.

The basic principles of natural chidbirth are:

- that a thorough understanding of the process of labour and childbirth goes a long way to help relieve unnecessary tension and apprehension; and

- muscular relaxation helps the body's efficiency and increases comfort during labour and delivery.

That there is pain and discomfort during pregnancy is undeniable, but this can be displaced or altered by concentrating on special breathing processes after conditioning. Women are taught how to change their breathing deliberately during labour, adjusting to the changing characteristics of the uterine contractions. Synchronising the breathing with the signals that are received from the uterus demands great concentration on the woman's part. This strenuous activity creates a new centre of concentration in the brain and thereby causes the painful sensations during labour to be perceived in a different way and at a lower intensity. Many antenatal classes for natural childbirth include the baby's father who becomes an assistant teacher and gives moral and physical support in labour.

Many antenatal preparation classes incorporate a certain amount of this 'Lamaze' technique but there are other centres specialising in it, notably the National Childbirth Trust.

About ten years ago, two French doctors proposed a revolutionary change in the management of labour, with the emphasis placed on freedom of choice for the mother concerning the manner in which she would like her labour conducted and the position she would like to adopt for the birth, enabling her to play a much more active part. Both doctors maintained that medical attendants interfered too much in the labour suite, and they questioned the value of 'high-technology' heart monitors and more conventional forms of pain relief.

Le Boyer felt strongly that not enough emphasis was placed on the way the child was actually born and advocated a serene environment with low lights, and in some instances delivering the baby under water. He maintained that this method of delivery had a profoundly advantageous effect on the psychology of the child and that delivery under water allowed the baby to express itself in active movements from the moment of birth.

Michel Odent had similar views but also proposed that the mother be free to adopt any attitude that she liked during delivery, preferably squatting, in as natural an atmosphere as possible.

The publicity given to these two doctors and their 'active birth' methods promoted the British Active Birth movement, culminating in the First International Conference on Active Birth in 1982. The idea was to explain to women the choice between being positive birth-givers and passive patients. The methods have also inspired a critical examination of the standard of obstetric practices which induce passivity, such as fetal monitoring, epidural anaesthesia and induction, as well as the doctors who promote them.

Despite the differences which still exist between the advocates of natural childbirth and high-tech delivery, many hospitals are becoming much more flexible about birth methods and no doubt this trend will increase with demand. The Association for Improvements in Maternity Services believe that the central issue concerns control. At home, they say, the midwife is a guest but in the hospital the territory is controlled by professionals.

The whole question of maternity care has been under scrutiny in the last few years, culminating in a report by the Select Committee of the House of Commons which endorsed the principles of freedom of choice for the mother in terms of where she has her baby and how, and who her medical attendants should be. Coupled with this, those responsible for antenatal care are conscious of the fact that antenatal visits to hospitals are time-consuming for the mother and, in a woman with an absolutely normal pregnancy, the nine or ten visits that have been a customary part of care for so long are probably unnecessary.

There is a move to provide more community care so that midwives and family doctors can see women in their own surgeries or even at home. In this way expectant mothers will be able to see the same or at least a small group of midwives, who will be known to them and who will take the responsibility of care and make decisions, with hospital doctors used perhaps more as a back-up should problems arise.

For women who do not wish to come to the hospital for their antenatal care and delivery, and yet do not want to have their babies at home, midwifery led units are another option. The principle of these units is that midwives are entirely responsible for the care of pregnancy, look after and deliver the expectant mothers in a free-standing unit close to a major hospital so that if complications arise all the back-up facilities are close at hand. There is some argument in the profession as to whether this principle should be taken further but it is likely that this sort of service will increasingly become an option.

So what is the answer: natural childbirth or high-tech delivery? As in so many controversial issues, there must be a middle ground. Supporters of monitoring and machines in labour would argue that there are women who have lost babies through inefficient births. On the other hand, there are stories of inhuman insensitivity among the medical team, and such stories would support interference of the right kind and attack interference of the wrong kind. Everyone is for good medicine and happy patients but everyone is also for saving babies.

There is no doubt that those responsible for looking after pregnant women are conscious of the feelings of their patients and adapt their own policies to provide more freedom of choice within the limits of putting safety first. At present it is time that is so often in short supply and many hospital departments are issuing birth plan guides to each pregnant woman so that the medical attendants, and particularly those responsible for the actual delivery, are aware of the woman's requests and anxieties.

It is not really a question of high-tech versus natural birth, or even home versus hospital delivery. The problem lies in adequate communication. It has been pointed out that it may not be the technology that is the trouble but the attitude that goes with it. Listening to patients, giving adequate explanations of why certain procedures may be necessary, how they are to be done and what the effects may be, will surely go a long way towards taking the bitterness out of the debate. With the system as it is, a compromise must be sought on both sides. It is the only way in which to develop further scientific improvements which would in turn give mothers more freedom of choice.

Water Births

Within the last few years there has been a vogue for delivering the baby under water which has caused a few ripples throughout the medical profession. It basically stemmed from the fact that many women find lying in a warm bath in early or even advanced labour soothing and it may also help the pain of contractions. The logical extension of this was to complete the birth under water in a purpose-built bath with a controlled temperature.

The medical profession, whose prime concern is the safety of the mother and the baby, feared at first that babies born under water might experience problems in breathing, that the water might be a cause of infection, that it was difficult to monitor the fetal heart, and there may be some difficulty in observing the skin of the vagina and perineum if it was about to tear. This method of birth became quite popular in the early 1990s despite the anxiety of clinicians, and a number of hospitals in the country do have birthing pools installed in their units.

When the House of Commons Health Committee was reviewing the Maternity Services in 1992 their report recommended that all hospitals should provide women with the option of a birthing pool where this was practicable, but there was a lack of relevant research on labour and birth in water and a clear need for a properly controlled study to assess the risks and benefits. One such study was recently reported in the *British Medical Journal*, consisting of question-naires sent to the Heads of Midwifery Units in 219 hospitals in England and Wales. There are now records for 1992/93 of 8255 women who had laboured in a birthing pool but got out for birth and 4494 women who gave birth in water. Women who laboured but did not give birth in conventional baths were not included in the figures for labour only, though births in conventional baths were included.

Twelve babies who died after their mothers laboured or gave birth in water or both in 1992/93 were reported, but none of these cases was thought to be directly related to labour or birth in water. There were, however, fifty-one reports of some complications in babies, including breathing problems and infection. Thirty-three women had quite serious problems including excessive bleeding and tearing of the lower genital tissues.

The report found that, although labour and birth in water was becoming widely available throughout the NHS, the number of births in water in each hospital was generally low, so the experience of most health professionals providing this form of care is likely to be limited.

The authors of the report (Allardyce, Renfrew, Marchant, *et al.*) are collaborating with other researchers to monitor adverse outcomes in babies and suggest that information about labour and birth in water should be collected routinely as part of local audits.

The conclusions of the study were that there was no evidence so far to suggest that labour and birth in water should not continue to be offered as an option to women in England and Wales. However, questions remain about the possible benefits and hazards, and the conditions of clinical practice and the use of resources. Further scientific trials could address some of these issues.

Assisted Delivery

During the second stage of labour attendants helping the mother are keeping a careful eye on two things: firstly, whether the baby's head is advancing with every push and contraction and, secondly, how the mother and baby are withstanding the pressures of labour.

There is a rough limit on the second stage of labour because, after a certain time and under certain circumstances, the baby may become distressed, the mother exhausted, and help may be necessary to deliver the baby.

Timing of the Second Stage of Labour

The second stage begins when the cervix is fully dilated and ends with the delivery of the baby. In a first pregnancy the second stage can last up to three hours but in subsequent pregnancies, because the tissues have already been stretched and the head descends rapidly on pushing, delivery of the baby is often complete within half an hour to an hour.

Does the Length of the Second Stage Matter?

During this expulsive stage of labour there are many pressures on the baby's head and there is a general guide as to how long this stage should last. The reason that a limit is set is because after a certain time in the second stage the baby may become distressed. This could lead to a lack of oxygen via the cord, with the result that when the baby is born it may need resuscitation or special help from the paediatricians to encourage it to breathe normally. Most hospitals have guidelines for the length of the second stage so that the midwife supervising the labour can call the doctor if it is unduly long so that delivery can be hastened.

The important feature is not necessarily the length of the second stage but whether there is continued advance of the baby's head with each contraction and push, and the heart rate recordings on the baby show it to be withstanding these forces satisfactorily. Occasionally the baby's head gets stuck in the pelvis and presses on one of the nerves called the perineal nerve, which causes some pain down the leg and sometimes urinary problems. This normally resolves spontaneously.

Provided that the baby is far enough down the birth canal and is in good condition, delivery can be effected by applying the forceps or the vacuum extractor. If the baby is too large to be safely delivered vaginally, or becomes acutely distressed, delivery may have to be by Caesarean section.

Let us now examine these three methods of assisting birth in some more detail.

Forceps Delivery

Historical Details

The origin of obstetric forceps is shrouded in mystery but they were probably invented by a member of the Chamberlen family in the late 1500s. Most of the Chamberlens were Royal Surgeons or Physicians and attended several English queens. This obstetrical dynasty extended from the admission of Peter Chamberlen the Elder to the Guild of Barber Surgeons in 1596 to the death of Hugh Chamberlen Junior in 1728.

The forceps were probably invented in about 1600 by Peter the Elder and kept as a hereditary secret to be buried with Hugh Junior. According to contemporary standards, delivery with forceps was wholly unethical and members of the family who used the forceps would do so only after all bystanders had been sent out of the room and the patient had been heavily draped so that she could not see what was being done. The steel blades and handles were wrapped in leather so that no metallic sounds could betray their presence.

The existence of the forceps was hinted at as early as 1616 at a scientific meeting when a disparaging reference was made to the boast of Peter Chamberlen the Younger that he and his brother and no others excelled in the management of difficult labours. Gradually the secret of forceps deliveries leaked out and the physician, William Giffard, who used the forceps openly on 6th April 1726 in London, is regarded as having introduced forceps into general use in England.

By 1733 when Edmond Chapman published the very first account of the forceps, there were already several models in existence and their use was well known to all the principal men of the profession. This retention of an important medical secret transmitted from generation to generation for a century and a quarter is unique in history.

The Modern Forceps

Forceps are essentially tongs, and in their modern obstetric use are an instrument capable of helping in delivery without injury to the child or to the mother. They are simply made so that the two blades fit accurately over the baby's head and the handles of the forceps come neatly together when they are properly applied so that the blades cannot damage or harm it. On the contrary, they form a cage around the baby's head which protects it from any injury that may occur through pressure from the bones of the mother's pelvis. So protective can a forceps delivery be that many obstetricians advocate it for avoiding injury to the soft and easily damaged skulls of small premature babies.

Indications for the Use of Forceps

There are four main reasons for forceps delivery:

- Distress or exhaustion which prevents the mother from pushing satisfactorily. Although she may have worked extremely hard to deliver the baby, the final bit may be just too much.

• Fetal distress. In other words, evidence that the baby is suffering general pressure on its head from the stresses of labour or has a continued irregular or slow heartbeat because the placenta is supplying less oxygen to the child. Any number of accidents may interfere with the baby's oxygen supply towards the end of labour – the cord may slip down or prolapse into the vagina, there may be bleeding caused by premature separation of the placenta, or a protracted labour may simply have exhausted the unborn baby.

• Delay in the second stage of labour. We have already mentioned that there is a rough time limit in the expulsive stage and, if after a certain length of time there is little advance of the baby's head with each push, the doctor examines the mother to see what is holding things up. It may be that the head is bigger than was thought, or that it is tilted in such a way as to present a larger diameter than is usual for passage through the pelvis, in which case the position has to be rectified by turning the head with the forceps.

• Some obstetricians advise the routine use of forceps in certain conditions to protect the mother or the baby from undue stress in the second stage of labour. As already mentioned, some doctors prefer to deliver the small premature head using forceps if the woman goes into labour a few weeks before term because this head is particularly vulnerable. During a breech birth it is common to deliver the head of the baby with the forceps for the same reason. There are certain instances when it is inadvisable or even dangerous for the mother to push too hard, for instance if she has high blood pressure or has a heart complaint, when effort should be kept to a minimum.

The Technique of Forceps Delivery

Before the forceps are actually applied the doctor will need to ensure that certain conditions are met. There must obviously be complete dilatation of the cervix so that the blades can be introduced without damaging the soft tissues, the membranes must have ruptured, and the head must be low enough and in a suitable position.

There are two main types of forceps: those that are applied straight to the baby's head when its position will allow easy delivery with a straight pull in time with the mother's contractions, and others that are specifically designed to turn the baby's head and its body inside the uterus if, for example, the head is in a posterior position (see pages 302–303).

Obviously any forceps manipulation can be uncomfortable without adequate pain relief and numbing of the local tissues. This is provided either by a local injection used to numb the nerve supply, or an epidural anaesthetic which may already be in place. Years ago it was common to use a full or general anaesthetic for forceps deliveries but this is rarely done now since there are good alternatives and it is best to avoid a general anaesthetic where possible (see pages 272–273).

Forceps deliveries are never done in a hurry. The operator first examines the baby's head to define its exact position in relation to various bony landmarks, to see whether it is low enough to be safely delivered, and whether the baby needs to be turned or just helped straight out. Similarly force is never used although the amount of traction or pulling that is required will vary in every case, depending on the size of the baby and its position. The head descends lower in the pelvis with each gentle pull until the skin is stretched, and delivery from then on is as normal, though episiotomy is generally needed as the blades of the forceps stretch the skin and there is a danger of tearing. In some women who have had babies before, the tissues stretch nicely during the technique and forceps delivery may be carried out without an episiotomy.

Complications during Forceps Delivery

As in any specialised technique, problems may occur, but forceps delivery for the correct indication, done in the right way, is a totally safe procedure. Occasionally there are small tears in the vaginal skin which require a few stitches, and the baby may have forceps marks over its head which can be quite frightening to the mother but invariably disappear completely within twenty-four hours and usually cause no damage.

Of course it is possible that excessive traction with a difficult delivery may cause some bruising of the scalp and very occasionally even more permanent neurological effects. No one can deny that difficulties have occurred, even in the most experienced hands, but it is important to realise that these complications are extremely rare. The mother must be guided by her attending doctor and midwife who

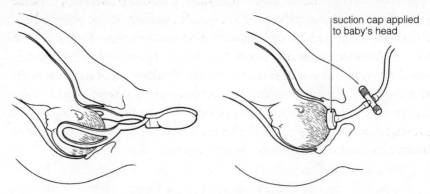

Above left: Forceps applied to baby's head.
Above right: Ventouse (vacuum) delivery.

will have assessed the need for forceps delivery, and in the vast majority of cases delivery with the forceps will turn out to be the safest and most expedient way of delivering that particular baby.

Vacuum Delivery (Ventouse)

This method of delivery is used as an alternative to forceps and used to be far more common in parts of Europe than in the UK. The technique makes use of a suction cup that is closely applied to the baby's scalp, where it is held by a pump, rather similar to a suction cap placed over a sink when the outlet becomes blocked. Gentle pulling on the cup causes the baby's head to descend into the pelvis for delivery. It is a good alternative to the forceps, especially when there is uncertainty over the exact position of the baby's head caused by the normal swelling over the scalp that occurs as the head passes through the pelvis. Gentle traction exerted after application of the cup will cause the baby to turn round spontaneously, following the line of least resistance, and this method is often now used in labour wards.

Perhaps the most frequent indication for use is when there is a need for delivery before the cervix is fully dilated because the baby is distressed. As we have seen if the forceps are applied in this situation, the remaining rim of cervix may be damaged, but the cup can be inserted through the undilated cervix and the head brought down slowly so that the cervix gradually eases away with no damage.

Babies, after ventouse deliveries, have a rather strange appearance when born, as the suction produces a soft swelling at the point where the cup was applied but this usually disappears within twenty-four to forty-eight hours with no effects. Unlike the forceps which do stretch the skin and can be unpleasant without adequate numbing of pain in the pelvis, the ventouse can be applied to the head of the baby without specific pain relief, although of course if an epidural is present it is much easier for the mother and the operator. Episiotomy is not always necessary for the same reasons.

Caesarean Section

A Caesarean birth is an operation performed under general or epidural anaesthesia in which a cut is made through the walls of the abdomen and the uterus, and the baby is lifted out of the womb. Until the twentieth century the risks of operating were so great that such deliveries were extremely rare. As recently as the early 1960s, Caesareans were performed only when there was clear danger to the mother's survival. They then accounted for between two and five per cent of all births. Now, more than ten per cent of all births are Caesareans.

Many obstetricians feel that this method of delivery is safer than labour and vaginal delivery for particularly vulnerable babies, including those that are especially small for their age, premature, some types of multiple pregnancy, babies in an abnormal position, such as a breech birth, or cases in which the placenta is lying in front of the baby and delivery is impossible without excessive bleeding. But perhaps the most important reason for a Caesarean birth is a disproportion in size between a large baby and small pelvic bones.

Historical Details

One of the earliest reports of Caesarean section occurs in AD 23 when Pliny the Elder mentions the operation as the source of the surname given to the Roman emperors and relates the name 'Caesar' to a Latin word meaning 'cut'. It was imaginatively assumed for years that Julius Caesar was cut from his mother's womb. In fact it seems highly improbable that he was born in this way, primarily because his mother survived his birth for many years and Caesareans at that time were almost certainly never done on living women. Also, the Romans favoured a very different origin for the name of their emperors. In the Punic language *caesar* meant 'elephant' and, since Julius once slew an elephant, he probably earned this heroic name which passed on to his successors.

The early history of the operation is equally vague. It was reported in 1500 that Jacob Nufer, a swine gelder, wiped his butcher's knife on his lederhosen and delivered his own wife by Caesarean section in front of a group of thirteen 'midwives'. Frau Nufer is said to have survived the operation and subsequently presented Jacob with two more children who were born normally.

In January 1794, in an American frontier settlement, a Mrs Bennett was confined in her first pregnancy. Labour was difficult because she had a small pelvis and neither her husband nor the consulting doctor was successful in the attempt at delivery by forceps. There was therefore no alternative but to attempt a Caesarean and, since the local doctor firmly refused to have anything to do with so dangerous a procedure, the task fell to the husband. Assisted by two women, Bennett laid open the abdomen and uterus with a single reckless stroke of the knife and rapidly delivered his daughter. The wound was closed with stout linen thread and mother and child confounded expectation by recovering well. The first Caesarean section baby in the USA lived to be seventy-three years old.

Before 1870 few women survived for many days after Caesarean birth, partly because of the crude surgery and partly because the operation was reserved for desperately ill women.

The results of Caesarean section today are a far cry from those of eighty or even thirty years ago. The procedure has now become extremely simple, adding little if any extra time to hospital stay, and is as free from danger as any other uncomplicated operation. Among the reasons for this improvement are advances in general surgical technique, antibiotics to prevent infection, the availability of blood transfusion, and expert anaesthesia.

Why is a Caesarean Section Performed?

A planned, or elective, Caesarean section is performed when the reason for its necessity is apparent before labour. This is usually done a week or two before the due date to prevent the possibility of going into labour at an odd time and having to rush to the hospital for the operation to be done as an emergency. If the Caesarean has been planned and you do go into labour, do not be anxious about this but you should go to the hospital as soon as possible.

Caesarean section is done as an emergency when a reason becomes apparent once labour has begun.

There are number of reasons for Caesarean section, both planned and emergency, but the following are the commonest indications:

- Cephalo-pelvic disproportion. This term means that the size of the baby is disproportionate to the size of the pelvis and that delivery, although possible, might cause problems. This can be either because the baby is too large for the pelvis, the pelvis is too small for the baby, or the baby is presenting in an unfavourable position with a large diameter.

- Inefficient contractions. Occasionally labour does not ensue despite stimulation and, if the cervix just doesn't dilate, then a Caesarean section will need to be performed.

- Placenta praevia (see pages 221–223). A Caesarean section may be performed if the placenta is very low lying causing bleeding. If the placenta is only partially low lying, then usually vaginal delivery is feasible (see page 223).

- Associated medical conditions. There are certain diseases where the stress of labour may cause problems to the oxygenation of the fetus by the placenta and it is therefore advisable to avoid this stress. Examples include diabetes, high blood pressure and pre-eclampsia.

- Abnormal presentations. When there is a breech birth sometimes the baby's head remains in an abnormal position, such as a transverse lie or brow.

- Prolapsed cord. This is an unusual but acute emergency where the cord presents outside the vagina and, if the head was allowed to

YOUR PREGNANCY: MONTH-BY-MONTH

descend, it would compress the cord and cause problems with the baby (see page 305).

- Genital herpes. If the mother has an active ulcer which is weeping at the time when the baby is due, then it is usually considered safer to avoid vaginal delivery (see pages 88–90).

- Fetal distress (see pages 304–305).

Some of the indications for a Caesarean can be seen to be absolute; in other words it is the only safe way of delivering the baby. Others are relative, when the decision depends on a number of factors, including the woman's age and past history of problems, or events during the present pregnancy. In each individual case the obstetrician will weigh up with the mother the relative risks of vaginal against abdominal delivery.

Some women find a Caesarean section a great disappointment after looking forward to a vaginal delivery, and it is important to see your obstetrician so that you and your partner can have a relaxed discussion about what the procedure entails, what it will be like in the operating theatre, whether you can have epidural anaesthesia and be awake, and whether your partner can be with you. There are films of Caesarean sections that you can see so that you know what is going to happen, and talking to mothers who have had Caesarean sections or subsequent pregnancies after a Caesarean section may be useful.

The Technique of Caesarean Section

The operation lasts about forty-five minutes but the baby is usually delivered within the first five to ten minutes. The remaining time is for stitching the uterus and the abdomen. Like other operations, a Caesarean delivery requires certain surgical preparations, including shaving of the abdomen and upper pubic hair. However, the premedication injection given an hour before surgery in most other operations is usually avoided as it contains sedatives that cross the placenta and may affect the baby. You may be given a milky drink which is an antacid and neutralises the acidity of the stomach.

A catheter will be inserted to keep the bladder emptied. This may be left in place after the operation for a day or two to avoid you having to get out of bed to go to the toilet, and also if you are having an epidural the bladder takes a day or two to start functioning again after the procedure. You will have an intravenous drip inserted into your arm so that fluids can be fed directly into the bloodstream.

The commonest position for the cut is crosswise below the pubic hairline so that the scar will be hidden. It may, however, be necessary to employ a vertical cut from below the navel towards the pubic hairline and this is something that the doctor will talk to you about beforehand.

A fuller description of Caesarean section under epidural is given on pages 277–278.

Recovery after a Caesarean

The wound of a Caesarean is quite uncomfortable for the first few days and the most important part of aftercare is adequate pain relief. If you have an epidural, this may be left in place for a few hours or even a day or two. If you have had a general anaesthetic, pain relieving drugs are administered, either by injection or by mouth depending on your needs.

There is no need for you to worry about whether these drugs will affect your baby through the breast milk. If you have had an epidural, you should be having something to drink, or possibly eat, the same day and you will be completely aware and be able to hold your baby and start breast-feeding. By the second or third day the scar will be becoming less painful, but cramp-like wind pains can occur as the bowel is starting to work again. This is particularly so with a general anaesthetic because the bowel is temporarily paralysed and it takes a few days for it to re-establish its normal motion. The first sign of bowel activity is the passage of wind from the top or lower end, usually followed by a bowel action by the third or fourth day. If the bowels have not opened by this time, an aperient is usually given or suppositories inserted into the back passage.

By the fourth or fifth day the skin of the incision has healed and the stitches or clips are removed. All surgeons have their preference in closing the skin of a scar: some use small staples or clips, others use silk stitches which have to be removed, and others use dissolvable sutures. The removal of clips or stitches is a procedure that many dread but most women are equally surprised to note how painless it really is. If you have had a general anaesthetic, activity is encouraged as it is important to move the legs and ankles to restore the blood circulation. Nowadays most women remain in hospital for only four to five days.

Once a Caesarean Always a Caesarean?

In the past, it was unusual to allow a woman who had previously had a Caesarean birth to have her next baby normally, but nowadays it is often reasonable to have a vaginal delivery following a Caesarean. This change in attitude has been largely brought about by improved techniques in surgery and more accurate methods of monitoring subsequent pregnancies and labour so that problems resulting from a previous Caesarean can be detected early.

The decision about whether to advise a patient to have a baby normally after Caesarean section depends on a number of factors. Firstly, could the reason for the Caesarean recur in a subsequent pregnancy? If the operation was performed because the pelvic bones were too small, for example, then the situation will remain the same in a subsequent pregnancy. If, on the other hand, the Caesarean was done for an emergency which would not necessarily recur the next time, i.e. for acute distress of the baby during labour, then it may be possible to allow a normal labour.

Understandably this decision is a critical one and it demands full assessment of all the facts involved and a frank discussion with the mother. Even if it is considered that labour should be permitted, there is always the chance that a Caesarean may eventually be needed and the mother must be made aware that this possibility exists. Moreover, and very importantly, she may have very definite views herself and the decision will certainly be influenced by her wishes. Some mothers may not want to undergo a prolonged labour that might end in a Caesarean and may opt for a planned Caesarean this time.

Rupture of the Scar

The main worry with a woman in subsequent labour after a Caesarean is that the contractions may put a strain on the scar in the uterus and very occasionally this scar gives way. Rupture of the scar in the uterus may have serious consequences, both for the mother and the baby, as there may be heavy bleeding and abdominal pain. In extreme cases the baby may die and the mother may need surgery to repair the tear, or perhaps even removal of the uterus if the tear is so large that it cannot be sewn together. Happily, rupture of the Caesarean scar is a rare event, although obviously if there is a previous scar in the uterus the force of labour during vaginal delivery may weaken it.

How Can Rupture of the Scar be Recognised?

There are two types of rupture: one is slow and silent and occurs during pregnancy when the mother may experience pain in the scar area; but much more commonly the scar will give way during labour. Scar rupture will be suspected if the mother has constant abdominal pain between contractions and the baby's heart rate on the monitor shows it to be in distress.

Particular care with the scar has to be taken when an epidural is being used for pain relief because the mother will not feel pain and the diagnosis may be more difficult to make. Happily, scar rupture is a rare condition and many women have satisfactory births by vaginal delivery after a Caesarean.

Pregnancy after Caesarean Section

A time interval of around nine months is usually suggested following a Caesarean section before trying to conceive again but, if a pregnancy does occur within a few months, it doesn't normally constitute a problem. The uterus heals remarkably quickly and the scar is usually completely sound within two months of surgery.

Nevertheless, some time is usually required to adjust after pregnancy and delivery and this takes a little longer after a surgical operation. Caesarean section has no effect on fertility and a woman should be able to become pregnant again just as easily after the operation as she did before.

There is no place whatsoever for a home confinement following Caesarean section because of the risk problems with the scar. Fetal monitoring of the contractions of the uterus throughout labour is usually advisable for the same reasons.

How Many Caesareans Can a Woman Have?

Each time that a cut is made into the uterus the scar, which is more or less in the same place, becomes somewhat weaker and it is customary to suggest to most patients that three Caesareans is the ideal number to have. This is not to say that more than three are absolutely contra-indicated, especially if one baby fails to survive or if the woman declines a permanent form of contraception. Some doctors may bring up the question of sterilisation at the time of a third Caesarean which is simple to do and may be convenient for some women (see page 433).

Can I Choose to Have my First Baby by Caesarean Section?

Some women who feel that they don't want to go through the stress of labour may choose a planned delivery by Caesarean – perhaps through fear of labour, perhaps a friend has had a bad experience, or maybe even the convenience of knowing the day the baby will be born.

If you feel strongly about this, then ask to see the consultant early on in the antenatal clinic and express your views. The final decision on whether to have a Caesarean for a non-medical reason will depend on a full comprehension of the pros and cons outlined by the consultant. During the discussion perhaps some of your fears of vaginal delivery may be allayed and you may change your mind. Remember that the obstetrician's main concern is the safety of the baby and the mother during the birth process and that subjecting a woman to an operation, however safe, which could be thought of as unnecessary will be uppermost in their mind.

If you remain adamant that Caesarean section is the choice for you and the surgeon is convinced that you fully understand the implications and risks, then agreement will have to be reached between you and your partner and the consultant.

Some Complications in Labour

Difficult labour is uncommon in modern childbirth because of the detection and prevention of probable causes before labour starts.

Such measures include the strengthening of contractions by drugs, adequate rest, good methods of pain relief, intravenous glucose solution to overcome dehydration and the prevention of infection by antibiotics. More than ninety per cent of women will not have a difficult labour. To the remaining few, comfort can be given with the assurance that modern obstetrics accepts the challenge of the abnormal with total confidence, and obstetric care during pregnancy and labour should ensure a happy outcome.

However even if the chance of having a long and difficult labour is slim, no discussion on giving birth would be complete without its inclusion.

Prolonged Labour

Twenty years ago or so prolonged labour was defined as one which lasted for twenty-four hours or more. Modern antenatal care and the management of labour have virtually eliminated labours lasting this length of time. During your visits to the antenatal clinic a careful note is made of any factors which may predispose you to complications so that they can be corrected. Together with an increased use of Caesarean section for the distressed baby or the mother with a small pelvis, many of the reasons for prolonged labour can be eliminated.

There are, however, several circumstances in which labour does last longer than usual and a delay in labour is normally stated to exist when progress, as assessed by descent of the head and dilatation of the cervix, is slow.

There are three main causes for delay in labour, known as the three P's. There may be:

- faults with the 'Powers';
- faults with the 'Passenger';
- faults with the 'Passages'.

Faults with the Powers

Sometimes the uterine contractions do not follow a normal rhythmical pattern. They may be too short, too feeble, too infrequent, or a combination of the three. Sometimes the contractions are too strong, too frequent and therefore equally ineffective.

If the contractions are too weak and infrequent and labour is established, then the uterus can be stimulated by giving controlled amounts of a drug called Syntocinon intravenously (see page 316). Conversely, if the uterus contracts too strongly and fiercely with only a few seconds in between each contraction, treatment is directed towards adequate sedation with sufficient doses of pain relieving drugs or by epidural anaesthesia.

There are many reasons why a uterus does not perform in a regular fashion but often there is some discrepancy between the size of the head and the width of the mother's pelvis (disproportion). This can be because the baby is large, it can be lying in an awkward position or, rarely, something is obstructing the passage of the head such as a fibroid or ovarian cyst (see pages 252–253).

Faults with the Passenger

Delay in labour may be caused by an enlarged size or position of the baby's head. The normal position of the fetus in labour is with its head down and bottom up, so that the spinal column is parallel with the long axis of the mother's body and the back of the baby is towards the mother's abdominal wall. In this position the head is bent forwards or flexed so that the baby's chin practically rests on its breastbone. The head, therefore, presents its narrowest diameter to the mouth of the pelvis and the baby is born with the back of its head coming first. This is known as an occipito anterior position. (*Occipito* means the back of the head and *anterior* means pointing to the front.)

If, however, the head is not well flexed, the diameter of the head that is presenting is increased and, although the baby's head may be quite normal in size and shape, its position artificially increases the size that has to pass through the pelvis, causing a certain amount of delay. Here the position is occipito posterior: in other words the back of the head is pointing to the back of the pelvis. Conveniently called 'posterior positions', in reality ninety per cent turn round spontaneously during the second stage of labour so that the head is actually born in the normal way. Many babies adopt a posterior position at the start of labour. This is one of the reasons why the head may not engage during pregnancy and labour is more likely to start with ruptured membranes rather than contractions of the uterus.

Occasionally, rotation from the posterior to the normal does not occur and, if there is no progress during the expulsive stage of labour even if the mother is pushing well, it is usually easy to turn the baby's head round with the forceps or the vacuum extractor (see pages 288–293). Sometimes, if this position persists and the baby is quite large, then vaginal delivery may not be feasible and a Caesarean section will be advised.

Occasionally the baby's head lies on its side, so-called 'deep transverse arrest', or sometimes the face of the baby, or even its brow, may be presenting. This can normally be felt on vaginal examination. These abnormal positions are not common and usually result from a combination of the baby's size with some asymmetry or narrowing of the pelvic bones. There are certain instances when abnormal positions are deliverable vaginally, but this will depend on a number of features. Occasionally an attempt to deliver the baby will be made in the operating theatre so that if, after gentle manipulation, delivery is deemed to be unlikely, then Caesarean section can be done straight away.

Faults with the Passages

By this we mean that the birth corridor, which includes the bones of the pelvis as well as the soft tissues of the cervix and vagina, may be swollen or tighter than normal. The bony pelvis is roughly funnel-shaped and the child enters the circular mouth of the funnel, which we call the inlet, and comes out through the outlet. If any diameter of the pelvis is diminished below the limit of ordinary variations, there may be delay in labour and vaginal delivery may not be advisable.

How is a Small Pelvis Diagnosed?

One can often gauge the size of the pelvis by the mother's obstetric history, by her height (taller women have a larger pelvis), by internal examination or, rarely, by X-rays. One of the reasons why a vaginal examination is performed at the first visit, and sometimes repeated about a month before the baby is due, is so that the doctor can estimate the pelvic size and get an idea as to whether the shape and size of the bones are adequate for that particular baby.

In a first pregnancy the widest diameter of the presenting part of the head should be engaged by the thirty-sixth week, that is it should have descended well into the pelvic mouth. If any doubt exists about the adequacy of the bones, sometimes an X-ray is taken and various measurements of the important diameters can be made. If the pelvic bones are too small, labour will not be permitted to start and Caesarean section will be the chosen method of delivery. If the bones are just slightly smaller than usual, then the mother is usually allowed to go into spontaneous labour. This is often called a 'trial' labour and a careful watch is made of progress so that Caesarean section may be done if it seems unlikely that the baby can be delivered safely through the vagina.

Finally, the bones of the pelvis may be wide enough but there may be a delay due to other structures in the birth canal, such as fibroids, ovarian cysts (see pages 251–253), or resistant tissues including the perineum or muscles. It has to be said that genuine disproportion between the baby's head and the bones of the pelvis is unusual and most forms of measurement of the size of the pelvis are pretty inaccurate. In effect every first labour is a 'trial' and nowadays it is most unusual to suggest delivery by elective Caesarean section without allowing the mother a certain amount of time in labour to see if the head descends and how well the cervix dilates.

Fetal Distress

This term denotes a shortage of oxygen to the baby. Any number of occurrences or accidents may cause interference with the oxygen supply: for example, the cord may prolapse (see opposite page), or become shortened from looping itself round the baby's neck or body so that it is made taut. Another reason is that bleeding may occur from the placenta which separates prematurely, or there may be excessive pressure on the head from a short, stormy labour or a very long one.

The baby will indicate distress in a number of ways. Commonly, its heart rate will be affected and this can be detected either by listening with a stethoscope or it can more readily be picked up on the electronic monitor. A baby's normal heartbeat is around 120 per minute, and a persistently abnormal beat, (above 160 or below 100) or an irregular rhythm may indicate all is not well. Normally when the membranes rupture the fluid is clear and colourless. Sometimes the colour is yellow or brown. This is called meconium and simply means that the baby is emptying its bowel contents in response to a stressful stimulus. What happens is that the valve around the baby's anus relaxes and its intestines go into spasm, expelling faeces while it is still in the uterus. This is not necessarily a cause of fetal distress and can occur under certain normal circumstances but, if taken together with an abnormality with the baby's heart rate, then the signs may indicate that all is not well.

If any of these signs of distress are noticed, they are closely monitored by electronic machines, or a small sample of blood is taken from the unborn baby's scalp and the level of acidity directly measured on a machine which can tell to what degree the fetus is distressed (see page 268). If there is evidence of distress, continuous close monitoring of the baby's condition will indicate whether labour can be allowed to proceed or immediate delivery is indicated. The method of birth depends on how far the labour has proceeded. If the cervix is nearly open and the baby is ready for delivery, forceps can usually be applied but, if the cervix is only a few centimetres dilated, then the baby will have to be born by Caesarean section.

Prolapse of the Umbilical Cord

This is one of the few acute emergency situations in maternity care which calls for immediate delivery of the child. What happens is that a loop of cord protrudes below the head of the baby and appears in the vagina, either inside the intact bag of membranes or, if the membranes have ruptured, it may actually be seen outside the vagina.

Prolapse of the cord is happily rare and can occur when there is room for a loop of cord to pass by the presenting part, whether it is a head or a breech, often at the time that the membranes rupture. To give the cord room enough to pass by the head, obviously the presenting part will not be snugly fitting into the pelvis, so it is much more common in situations where the presenting part is not engaged (see page 320). This is why the midwife or medical attendant will always perform a vaginal examination when the presenting part is high and the membranes rupture.

What is the Treatment for Prolapse of the Umbilical Cord?

Essentially the baby needs to be delivered immediately because, if a loop of cord is below the head, it will be compressed by the head as it passes through the pelvis during delivery and could cause sudden death of the baby by cutting off the blood supply of oxygen as the cord is pressed against the side of the pelvis. If the cervix is fully or nearly fully dilated, then delivery can usually be assisted by immediate application of the forceps but, if this complication occurs earlier in labour, then emergency Caesarean section will be necessary.

Bleeding after Birth (Post-partum Haemorrhage)

This term is used to denote bleeding after delivery of the baby. A certain amount of blood loss inevitably occurs both during and immediately after a birth but it may occasionally be quite heavy. There are several causes for this.

Bleeding may come from the episiotomy cut or, rarely, from a tear of the cervix or skin. These wounds are usually recognised quite easily at the time and dealt with accordingly by stitching. It may occasionally be necessary to give the mother a general anaesthetic so that a more thorough examination higher up the birth canal can be made. If no tear is visible, then bleeding is usually due to one of two other causes: either a relaxed uterus or a fragment of placenta which has broken off and remains in the uterus.

The uterus obeys a very simple rule: if it is completely empty, it will contract and, when it has contracted, it will neither bleed nor will it become infected. In certain instances, however, it fails to contract properly and therefore haemorrhage may occur. Sometimes a fragment becomes detached from the placenta as it is being expelled and remains in the uterus. The uterus can only partially contract and will bleed until the fragment either comes away by itself or has been removed. This is why careful examination of the placenta is always carried out after birth to ensure that it has come away in one piece. If the placenta is complete, the uterus can be gently massaged, which encourages it to harden and then the bleeding usually ceases as the uterus becomes firm. If bleeding occurs before delivery of the placenta, the treatment is to remove the placenta quickly. This is usually done by pulling on the cord or by inserting two fingers in the cervix and teasing the placenta out.

Occasionally the placenta gets trapped in the uterus. This is a potentially serious situation because, as long as the placenta is contained in the uterus, bleeding can occur at any time. If the usual methods for delivery of the placenta fail, it may have to be removed by inserting a hand into the uterus. As this procedure can be painful, a general anaesthetic is necessary unless the pelvic tissues are already numbed by an epidural.

In rare cases, bleeding may occur at any time during the lying-in period or even three to four weeks after delivery when the mother is back at home. The usual cause for this late bleeding is a hormonal change prompted by the pregnancy, or infection due to some retained part of the placenta, and conservative treatment with tablets is usually all that is necessary.

If bleeding continues, referral back to the hospital may be necessary for further assessment and sometimes a D & C or scraping operation is necessary to ensure that the uterus is empty.

Breech Birth

Because of the shape of the uterus, most babies start off with the bottom or breech coming first and remain like this until about the thirty-fourth week of pregnancy. Following this the baby usually turns round by itself so that the head comes first, but in about four per cent of pregnancies the bottom remains the presenting part.

Sometimes the baby is prevented from turning round if the pelvic bones of the mother are small or if the placenta is in the way, and breech presentations are more common with a premature infant and in the second twin.

As previously stated, breech presentations are common up to the thirty-fourth week but the majority of babies would have turned round by then. If the baby is found to be presenting by the breech at thirty-four weeks, some obstetricians favour gentle manipulation of the baby in an attempt to turn it round so that the head presents. This procedure, which is done in the clinic, is quite simple and often successful. Other obstetricians favour non-interference arguing that, even if the baby can be turned quite easily, it will almost certainly revert back to its original position and there may be good reasons why it does not rotate. Although it is possible for the baby to turn round quite late on in pregnancy (particularly in a woman who has had previous pregnancies, because the uterus is lax and the baby swivels around much more while swimming in its fluid), breech presentation by thirty-six weeks almost invariably means that it will not now turn.

Management of Breech Labour

Like many features associated with pregnancy, medical opinions have varied throughout the years as to the best and safest method of delivering a mother with a breech presentation. Formerly there was more active management, consisting of attempting to turn the baby in the antenatal clinic. This was done more often than it is today, and vaginal delivery was also practised more frequently.

Even if vaginal delivery of a breech presentation is performed by an experienced doctor, and incidentally it is always the case that a doctor of at least registrar standing (see page 100) is present at breech delivery, there are certain complications that may occur, making breech vaginal delivery somewhat more hazardous than the baby presenting by the head. Essentially this is because during labour it is the buttocks of the baby that do all the work during the passage of the baby through the birth canal and the head of the baby has not had time to protect itself and get used to the pressures of passing through the pelvic bones by moulding (see pages 371–372) and adapting its shape. The head, therefore, is relatively unprotected and extreme care has to be exercised during delivery.

Currently, many obstetricians favour elective or chosen Caesarean section when the baby is presenting by the breech. The rationale here is that even the slightest risk of a problem may not be worth taking and it is known that there is an increased complication rate in breech delivery compared with deliveries where the head comes first. These remarks apply principally to mothers in their first pregnancies. If in a subsequent pregnancy the baby presents by the breech and the mother has had a baby of a reasonable size before and the pelvic size and shape is confirmed, then a breech delivery may be permitted.

There is a vogue for trying to turn the baby round from the breech position and this can be attempted at around thirty-seven weeks, by External Cephalic Version (ECV). The mother is often admitted for a day, given a drug which prevents contractions, and then slowly the doctor attempts to move the baby around. This is usually not a painful procedure and is successful in fifty per cent of cases.

If you and your doctor decide that a breech delivery is safe and feasible, an ultrasound scan late in pregnancy can assess the size of the baby and accurate measurements of the pelvic width and length are performed by X-rays. You need have no worry about the X-ray at this stage causing any problems whatsoever to the fetus.

With a breech delivery, labour is not very different from normal although inevitably there will be more interference so that delivery is slow and controlled. Many doctors favour an epidural anaesthetic during breech delivery as any manipulation required is painless for the mother. Again, your legs will probably be put up in stirrups so that there is enough room for the medical attendants to help. An episiotomy (see pages 263–265) is mandatory to allow sufficient room for the head to come through at the end of delivery.

Finally, it must be emphasised that vaginal breech delivery will only be suggested by the doctor in a woman with a first pregnancy who is of normal height and weight with an average size baby, where room through the pelvic bones has been confirmed as being ample, and provided there are no associated complications in pregnancy such as high blood pressure, medical conditions or any other situation that may prejudice delivery.

Going Overdue
(Prolonged Pregnancy, Postmaturity)

Very few mothers deliver their babies exactly on the calculated due date, although the great majority will deliver within two weeks either side. The length of pregnancy in the human is on average 266 days from the date of conception. The duration of pregnancy, however, is usually calculated as 280 days from the first day of the last normal, regular period, which is the same as ten lunar months or forty weeks. For many women the magic date is circled in red on the calendar and every day of the forty weeks that precede it is crossed off with great anticipation. Then at long last the big day arrives and, as in about half of all pregnancies, the baby doesn't, and anticipation dissolves into discouragement. The baby carriage and crib sit empty for yet another day or week, and in ten per cent of pregnancies sometimes two weeks.

Though women who have reached the forty-second week might find it hard to believe, no pregnancy on record ever went on for ever, even before the advent of labour induction. Studies show that about seventy per cent of apparent overdue pregnancies aren't overdue at all. They are only believed to be late because of a miscalculation of the time of conception, usually thanks to faulty recollection of the exact date of the last period. Nowadays, as ultrasound examination is used to confirm the due date, diagnoses of prolonged pregnancy have dropped dramatically from the long-held estimate of ten per cent to about two per cent.

The expressions 'post-term pregnancy', 'prolonged pregnancy', 'post-date pregnancy' are used synonymously. From the medical point of view the definition of an overdue pregnancy is one which lasts forty-two completed weeks or more (294 days).

The Incidence of Prolonged Pregnancy

The rough incidence for post-term pregnancy ranges from four to fourteen per cent, with an average of about ten per cent. Pregnancies going beyond forty-three weeks average five per cent.

Many reports in the medical literature suggest that a prolonged pregnancy occurs more commonly in a first pregnancy, although probably there is no statistical evidence for this. Similarly, the influence of the mother's age is conflicting. Some authorities say that prolongation of pregnancy is higher with increasing maternal age but others dispute this.

It appears that there is a considerable drop in the risk of post-term birth between the first and later pregnancies but this is not always so. If the first birth was not prolonged, the risk of the second birth being so is about twelve per cent. If, however, the first birth was post-term, then this increases to nearly thirty per cent. So if a woman has had two prolonged pregnancies, then the risk of the next birth being prolonged increases to about forty per cent.

The Causes of Prolonged Pregnancy

As long as the mechanism of the start of labour remains an enigma, the reason for some pregnancies to go beyond the due date is just as obscure.

Determining the Duration of Pregnancy

One of the problems constantly faced in antenatal clinics used to be that of dating a pregnancy in that women are not always certain of the exact duration of the pregnancy, and even the two people involved are not always certain when the fruitful union took place.

The information that helps doctors to assess the correct estimated date of delivery include: the date contraception ceased; the date of the last period; the determination of pregnancy duration on the first internal examination; the first appearance of an audible heartbeat; and the rate of growth of the uterus as pregnancy advances.

Nowadays, an accurate estimated date of delivery to within a few days can be determined by ultrasound scanning by measuring the size of the baby in early pregnancy and the diameter of the baby's head later.

Does Going Overdue Matter?

The main concern is that the supply of oxygen from the placenta to the baby lessens during the last few weeks of pregnancy and in some women becomes critically low if the pregnancy is prolonged beyond the forty-second week. If the placenta does not supply oxygen in adequate amounts to the baby, then in theory the baby can suffer and, very occasionally, can die from lack of oxygen. Happily, this is rare.

The dangers are accentuated in the older mother with a previous history of problems with the placenta, or with the mother who has suffered some bleeding during pregnancy.

The precise time beyond forty weeks at which the baby may be endangered by lack of oxygen is uncertain and this is why each hospital has its own policy for suggesting the best time for delivery, which can become quite confusing for the mother. Some specialists suggest that pregnancy should not be allowed to continue beyond the forty-second week, whereas others suggest induction only if there is evidence that the placenta is not working well.

What Methods are Available for Assessing the Baby's Well-being?

There are a number of features which suggest to the doctor that perhaps the baby is not growing as well as it should do. These include a lessening in the number and frequency of the baby's movements (although the rate of activity of the baby is slower even in normal pregnancies as term approaches); a persistent weight loss by the mother over two or three weeks; poor growth of the baby as shown by ultrasound measurements; and possible abnormal heart patterns seen when the baby's heart is monitored electronically.

Measurement of the amount of amniotic fluid (liquor volume) is also helpful in assessing the well-being of the fetus. There are pools of amniotic fluid easily visible by the ultrasound which can measure their depth and give an indication of whether the amount of fluid is normal or not.

How is Prolonged Pregnancy Managed?

When a pregnancy appears to be overdue, the practitioner will have to evaluate the situation and consider two main factors:

• Is the estimate of the due date accurate?
• Is the baby continuing to thrive while remaining in the uterus?

Most babies continue to grow well into the tenth month, though occasionally this can be a problem if the baby becomes too large.

Occasionally, however, the once ideal environment in the uterus begins to deteriorate. The ageing placenta fails to supply adequate nutrition and oxygen and, under these conditions, it becomes difficult for the baby to do well. Babies born after spending time in such an environment are called 'postmature'. They are thin, with skin that is dry, cracked and peeling, and have lost the cheesy coat common in the newborn. Being older than other new arrivals, they have longer nails, more abundant hair and are generally open-eyed and alert. Those with longer days in a deteriorating uterus may have a greenish colour (meconium staining of the skin and cord).

Both because they are usually larger than forty-week babies and have wider head measurements, and may be somewhat compromised by lack of oxygen and nutrition, postmature babies are at increased risk of having a difficult labour and are more likely to be delivered by Caesarean. They may also need some special care in the neonatal intensive care nursery for a short time after birth. Still, those born at forty-two weeks after uncomplicated pregnancies are at no greater risk of permanent problems than babies born at forty weeks.

When it has been determined with certainty that a pregnancy is past forty-one plus weeks, the practitioner may examine the cervix to see if it is ripe and may choose to suggest induction of labour. Delivery by induction or Caesarean will be suggested whether the cervix is ripe or not if there are certain added complications, such as high blood pressure, diabetes, or if there is a suspicion that the baby is not doing well for other reasons.

If the cervix is not ripe, the practitioner may choose to try to ripen it by giving a drug such as Prostin, either by vaginal pessaries or as a jelly before inducing labour, or the decision may be to wait a little longer before performing more tests to see whether the baby is still thriving in the uterus, and these tests may be repeated frequently until labour begins.

Some doctors will wait beyond forty-two weeks before deciding to intervene assuming the baby continues to pass its tests and the mother is doing well. If at any point test results indicate that the placenta is not working adequately, or there are any other signs that the baby is in trouble, then action will be taken and, depending on the situation, labour will either be induced or a Caesarean section performed.

Future Developments in the Management of Prolonged Pregnancy

It should be stressed that the ultimate fear, i.e. death of the baby due to lack of oxygen in week forty-two, is only slightly higher than in weeks forty and forty-one. Even in week forty-three, the death rate of babies is quite modest, yet the question must be asked: Can these deaths be prevented?

One suggestion that all pregnant women should be delivered by a certain set date, say during week forty-two, is hardly feasible and has to be weighed against some of the hazards of induction. The only sensible answer lies in continued medical trials to establish a set of rules based on the history, examination of the mother, measurement by ultrasound, electronic and biochemical tests, etc., in order to select the small percentage of pregnancies in immediate need of delivery. Then, perhaps, one could let Nature run its course with the rest, which would presumably be to the benefit of mothers and their offspring.

Induction of Labour

Induction of labour means the artificial stimulation of labour before it starts of its own accord. In general terms it is recommended for medical reasons associated with the safety of the mother and baby. Induction, however, has been the subject of much criticism by sections of the public and press who believe there are occasions when it is carried out for the convenience of the medical staff and might be regarded as meddlesome interference.

Before discussing some of the medical reasons why the doctor suggests induction of labour, let us just consider this last argument in more detail. There is no doubt that from time to time in modern society there is pressure to deliver a baby for social reasons: discomfort, difficulties in sleeping, partner's activities – if for instance he is going to be away at the time the baby is due – or even to coincide a birthday with a particular star sign! Also, in fairness, there may be situations when it is safer and more practical for the hospital to recommend induction, particularly in units with limited staff, so that

MEDICAL INDICATIONS
FOR INDUCTION OF LABOUR

- **Going overdue (Postmaturity)**
  As we have seen, only about five per cent of babies actually arrive on the due date and it is hard for some doctors and quite a lot of mothers to remain philosophical when the magic date passes. Both are concerned in case the baby is postmature, or late, and fear that the placenta may be becoming inadequate to support the baby, and the baby may therefore be outgrowing its food supply. Very few babies are truly overdue, as eighty per cent of all babies who are born from spontaneous labour without induction arrive after their due date.

  Hospitals vary in the time they will allow a woman to go overdue before they advise induction but most women, provided they and the baby are well, will be left until at least forty-two weeks.

- **Raised blood pressure**

- **Pre-eclampsia (see pages 203–206)**

- **Rhesus incompatibility (see pages 237–240)**

- **Bleeding in late pregnancy**

- **Diabetes**

- **Intrauterine growth retardation (see pages 206–208)**

delivery can be planned to take place during daylight hours when there are more professional attendants available.

In reality, few obstetricians recommend induction of labour purely on social grounds despite the fact that the methods evolved to start labour going are much safer now than ever before. Even when there is an apparently strong reason for induction, the final decision will only be made if the medical attendant is sure that the patient's estimated date of delivery is correct, so that the baby will not be born prematurely, and if it is probable that the outcome will be as successful as if labour had started on its own.

How is Labour Induced?

Methods of induction depend on an understanding of the way that labour works. Until the beginning of the seventeenth century, it was generally believed that the fetus made its exit from the uterus in much the same way as the chick pecks its way out of an egg, by its own efforts, pushing with its feet and opening the uterus by direct pressure. It was not until the end of the eighteenth century that the first scientific method of inducing labour by breaking the bag of waters (artificial rupture of membranes) was suggested. The efficiency of this method depends on the fact that breaking the membranes causes the amniotic fluid to drain away, which in turn alters the pressure within the uterus and starts contractions. This method is still the most efficient.

In 1909 an English gynaecologist called Blair Bell found that an extract from the pituitary gland, which lies between the brain and the roof of the mouth, caused the uterus to contract when injected into the mother. The active substance was isolated and first used to induce labour two years later. A purified form of this drug, Syntocinon, can stimulate contractions when given by a drip into a vein in the arm, and this method is generally used nowadays in conjunction with others.

New drugs which are capable of stimulating labour have been discovered within the last ten years. These are substances called prostaglandins (so named from their original source, the prostate glands of animals) which are present in high quantities in the amniotic fluid. Formerly given in the form of a solution to drink, or injected into a vein in the arm, these drugs can now be given as a gel or pessary simply placed in the vagina which softens the cervix and encourages dilatation.

Once inserted into the vagina the gel or pessary dissolves slowly, initiating mild contractions of the uterus. If no contractions have started within four hours, a further pessary or gel is inserted and this process can be repeated safely four-hourly. The great advantage is that this method of induction causes gradual contractions which are not suddenly painful, makes the cervix stretch which encourages proper labour to ensue and, on the rare occasions when repeat pessaries or gel do not induce labour, no harm will be done by leaving things overnight and starting again the next day.

Can Induction Cause Problems?

It is commonly thought that induction of labour causes the contractions of the uterus to be stronger sooner and to remain so for longer, and the contractions are therefore more painful for the mother, and indeed this may be so with the Syntocinon drip method. An induced labour does not generally last longer than normal, and the likelihood of a normal delivery is the same. In other words, induction of labour does not necessarily increase the risks of interference with forceps.

Does Induction Increase the Risk of Caesarean Section?

In general the answer is no, although it must be said that occasionally, if the cervix is very unripe and tight and yet there is a good reason to get the baby delivered, then this small risk will be discussed with your obstetrician. What occasionally may happen is that, despite all the methods of induction, the cervix just does not dilate, or the uterus does not contract properly and, once the membranes have leaked, then there is a certain time beyond which the baby should be delivered or infection may occur. It has to be emphasised, however, that this is rare and in the great majority of instances the outcome is entirely successful for the mother and her baby.

Induction of labour has a very real place in modern obstetric practice when there is anxiety about the prolongation of pregnancy, though the timing of induction and the methods used do vary between hospital units. If induction is proposed, make sure you ask what it entails, which method is going to be used, and what the indications are. So often dissatisfaction and anxiety can be prevented by a few minutes of discussion so that you understand the reasons, know what to expect and are aware of how induction will be carried out and what it means in terms of restriction and mobility of position.

Acceleration or Augmentation of Labour

This means that labour has started but is not progressing well. If the waters have broken spontaneously but contractions do not follow or are ineffective, then a pessary or a Syntocinon drip may be suggested. Alternatively, if contractions keep coming and going and labour does not really start, then the waters may be broken followed by a drip. If labour is progressing slowly and you feel comfortable and all is well with the baby, then you may prefer to let things proceed at their own pace without any intervention and discuss this further with your medical attendants.

Encouraging Your Own Labour

Although there are no absolute methods of hastening labour, there are a few ways and means that may help in starting things off. Sexual intercourse may stimulate the cervix and make the uterus contract, but usually this only works if you are about to go into labour anyway. The principle here is the same as having an internal examination by the doctor or midwife, as this increases the production of the hormone prostaglandin which is partly responsible for initiating labour. Also, this hormone is present in the sperm which then will have the same effect.

Keeping active by walking and taking warm baths may be helpful, but it is unlikely that some of the old wives' tales such as going for car rides along a bumpy road or eating spicy food will do much other than make you uncomfortable and give you heartburn!

Stillbirth

The death of a baby, whether in the early few months of pregnancy or later, must be one of the most difficult situations for any woman to come to terms with. Miscarriage, which we define as the loss of a pregnancy up to twenty-four weeks, is hard enough but to lose a baby when it is fully formed, either in the uterus during or after labour, is indescribably sad and it may be that readers will find this chapter difficult to contemplate. To have gone through a pregnancy and yet have nothing to show for it seems unbearably cruel and yet many women who have experienced a stillbirth often express regret that they were not as well prepared as they were for other aspects of pregnancy.

What is a Stillbirth?

Stillbirth refers to a death at or before the birth of the baby after twenty-four weeks' gestation. The term perinatal death which doctors often use includes stillbirth and the death of a baby in the first week of life. This definition excludes the loss of a baby in the second, third or fourth week of life which is considered less attributable to causes in pregnancy and labour.

The perinatal death rate is used as a measure of obstetrical events but it also investigates the biological background of the mother, her past diseases and her educational attainments, as well as the management in pregnancy and in labour. In order to assess the causes and thereby prevent unsuccessful pregnancies after the twenty-fourth week, doctors express the perinatal mortality per thousand total births and the present rate in England and Wales is approximately nine per thousand.

You can see from the diagram on page 4 how perinatal mortality has dropped over the last forty years and much of this is due to improved health in the population, but some of the later decline can be attributed to improved obstetric care.

There are three major factors that can affect a woman's obstetrical performance: her age, the number of children she has, and her social class. With increase in age goes increase in the number of children, but the very old or young mothers are at the highest risk. The lowest risk occurs with second and third babies whatever the mother's age. These trends are not fully understood but may be associated with the lack of antenatal care in the younger mother and the increasing chance of incidental disease or complications in pregnancy that befall the older woman.

A woman's previous pregnancy may give some warning of events to come and a certain reproductive pattern undoubtedly exists. Some of the high risk factors are recurrent and so could affect further pregnancies. This pattern might be genetically determined, familial or acquired. There is a slightly higher risk if there has been a previous miscarriage, or ectopic pregnancy, or if a former pregnancy resulted in a premature or stillbirth.

All these factors can be recognised at the first booking visit in early pregnancy, and this is why the background pattern is recorded so that your practitioner is able to plan the management.

Why do Stillbirths Occur?

There are many theories for the unexplained death of a baby. Often no single reason is apparent and several factors may be involved. The three major causes are: congenital abnormalities; prematurity (see pages 210–211); and asphyxia due to lack of oxygen as a result of a failing placenta. Occasionally something may go very wrong during labour causing the baby's death. Sometimes there are known causes such as the premature separation of the placenta (abruptio placenta – see pages 224–226), Rhesus disease (see pages 237–240), or accidents to the umbilical cord.

Unfortunately, there remain instances where there is no obvious cause whatsoever for the baby dying, either before or during labour, and this so-called unexplained stillbirth is one of the hardest facts for the mother and her medical attendants to understand.

Intrauterine Death, or Death of the Baby before Labour Starts

When a baby dies, most of the feelings of being pregnant fade pretty quickly. One of the first things that the mother may notice is that the baby isn't moving. The problem of course is that frequently babies stop moving, or apparently do so, for several hours and sometimes even for as long as a day.

If the baby has been moving well and strongly in later pregnancy and there is a sudden change, then the doctor or hospital should be alerted. They will probably suggest that the baby's heartbeat is checked, either with the ordinary stethoscope or with an electronic monitor or ultrasound. The mother may also notice that her breasts decrease in size quite quickly as the uterus shrinks and the hormones that maintain the pregnancy are withdrawn.

If death of the baby has been confirmed, no harm will come to the mother. The doctor or midwife must decide how to tell her if she is unaware of the situation and how to treat her. Usually the natural reaction of the parents is to ask for the dead baby to be removed as soon as possible, but there is no need to rush into induction if the parents prefer to wait a while for the situation to sink in.

As soon as the parents have decided that they wish the dead baby to be induced, the mother is admitted to a side ward of the hospital and labour started by the insertion of a vaginal pessary of prostaglandin (see page 314). Sometimes several pessaries at four-hourly intervals are needed to initiate labour because the uterus before term is unwilling to start contracting and must be made to do so. Usually and thankfully labour starts within a few hours. Contractions start, or possibly the membranes rupture, and sometimes help is needed with an intravenous drip of a substance which keeps the uterus contracting (Syntocinon – page 313). Once the uterus contracts strongly, normally labour is over quite quickly and although the mother will be encouraged to push the baby out she will not have to do this for long.

Sometimes, unfortunately, the baby may have died during a perfectly normal labour, usually because something has gone wrong with the oxygen supply from the placenta, or possibly because there has been an accident with the umbilical cord. It may either have been constricted or wound tightly round the baby's head. One of the problems here of course is that it is impossible for the doctors and midwives to know just to what extent these kinds of problems are the actual cause of death and often it can only be suggested that that is what might have happened.

In labour the uterus contracts regularly and as it does so it temporarily cuts off the blood supply to the placenta at the height of the contraction. A healthy baby can accept this as it lasts for only a few seconds every few minutes but, if the exchange of blood through the placenta is already compromised by another factor, then the baby is less able to endure the trauma and may become distressed. Sometimes a lack of oxygen in labour occurs because the uterus has been contracting strongly and rapidly with too short an interval between; or there has been sudden bleeding of the uterus because a little bit of placenta has come away from its main trunk; or because the cord has prolapsed (see pages 305–306); or, rarely, because of difficulties with delivery.

Can a Baby Die Because of Difficulties with the Birth Process Itself?

It must be said that this is an extremely rare cause of death. If the baby was delivered with forceps and more difficulty than usual was encountered, the baby might suffer some internal bleeding which could lead to problems.

In fact this is extremely unlikely because babies withstand a huge amount of pressure and, if a delivery is thought to be difficult, then an experienced doctor used to manipulative techniques will be called to help out. This is one of the most difficult facts to appreciate because it is very reasonable for parents to be well aware that something has gone wrong during the birth, and it is also very understandable for them to be angry with the doctors or midwives if they suspect there may have been an error of judgement.

Congenital Abnormalities and Defects

There is of course a natural dread in all parents that their child may not be normal. Such fears cannot be helped, yet the worrying prospective parent can gain reassurance from the fact that 97 per cent of human progeny are perfect at birth and that of the 2.5 per cent who are imperfect half have only minor defects, such as extra digits, small appendages to the ear, birthmarks, etc. Congenital abnormalities sufficiently serious to cause the child to be stillborn occur once in about two hundred deliveries.

The second source of solace is that many abnormalities which were very serious a few decades ago can be wholly eradicated by modern medicine.

And thirdly, of course, medicine has advanced to such an extent that a great many abnormalities can be detected before birth by ultra-sound and appropriate measures adopted, either by termination of the pregnancy if the parents wish, or delivery of the child in a unit capable of dealing with a suspected abnormality that might be treat-able with surgery.

After the Stillbirth

Whether the baby is stillborn, dies shortly after delivery, or lives for several weeks before dying, the parents need to say goodbye, and this is not an easy process.

In the blur of unanticipated events and shocking news, parents often feel confused and overwhelmed. How did it happen? Why did it happen? Was there any hope? Could death have been prevented? The past and present seem so complicated that it is hard even to think of what to do next.

Many parents wish to see the baby or have a photograph, or even preserve a lock of hair. Quite often the anguished mother simply does not know what to do. If born with severe birth defects, the medical team may hesitate to show the baby to the parents. On the other hand, the parents may want to see the baby as the malformations may prove that the death was a blessing in disguise.

If a baby's appearance is normal, parents often take comfort in the fact they have produced an attractive child. Some mothers want to hold their baby after delivery or prefer to wait a little. The midwife will usually wrap the baby in a little nest on the bed and it can be reassuring to see how perfectly formed the baby is. To have seen the child and taken pleasure in those parts which are perfect is comforting both in this experience and for a future pregnancy.

Some hospitals routinely photograph all the babies who die and, if months or even years later parents want some way of remembering their child, these photographs can be a comfort. If parents want to take photos, then of course they will be encouraged to do so.

Difficult as it may be to face such a decision at a time of deep grief, parents will be told that an autopsy could provide important informa-tion that could influence a future pregnancy and, because mothers so often feel they are to blame, a post-mortem may lift the burden of guilt.

Even if it doesn't reveal one conclusive cause of death, very often it can confirm that nothing the parents did was at fault and information from the post-mortem may help other babies facing the same danger.

The baby will need to be registered, often a painful and poignant reminder of what has happened, and hospital chaplains will be pleased to arrange a service of blessing. There is no hurry for the parents to make the difficult decision on whether or not they want a funeral and the form it should take.

Physical Changes after the Birth

There is not much difference between having a live or a stillbirth in that much the same things happen as the body gets back to normal (see pages 331–335). The breasts may become uncomfortable as they produce milk and this can be stopped with a course of tablets.

The family doctor will have been informed immediately either by the hospital or midwife and a visit to the practice may be helpful at this time. Before the mother is discharged from hospital, and obviously this will be done as soon as is convenient from her point of view, an appointment is usually given to come back and see the consultant. This is an important step and, although it may be an extremely painful experience, much can be done at that interview to provide comfort for the parents. If a post-mortem was carried out, the results should be available for discussion. It is often helpful to repeat the interview process a few weeks later in case there are unanswered questions or difficulties that may not yet be resolved and consultants will be only too happy to see the couple again.

Two important features which need to be addressed at that interview involve the mother's apprehension that there was something that perhaps she did to influence the death of the baby; and, if the parents have decided that they would like another pregnancy, when they can start to try for another baby and what the likelihood would be of a similar occurrence.

It is fair to say that there is no way in which the mother can cause this sort of a misfortune. Women often feel they didn't rest enough before labour, or that they took too much exercise, or didn't pay enough attention to their diet. They can be reassured that these are natural questions that will be asked but have no bearing whatsoever on what has happened.

There may be certain tests that the hospital staff would like to do in cases of unexplained stillbirth in order to check for rare viral conditions such as toxoplasmosis, or cytomegalovirus (see pages 84–85). If the baby was born with a congenital malformation, genetic counselling by experts can give an accurate prediction of the likelihood of a similar occurrence in a future pregnancy, and consultation and any blood testing can be arranged by the hospital staff in experienced centres.

From the physical point of view, there is no reason whatsoever why the couple should not try for another pregnancy within a couple of months of the tragedy. It used to be thought that three to four months was the ideal time so that the cycle could get back to normal but in fact this is really not the case. If the couple decide they want to go ahead, there is no contra-indication once all the investigations have been done. Even if there was a complicated vaginal delivery or Caesarean section, the couple need not wait for more than a few months before embarking on another pregnancy.

How Does the Bereaved Mother Come to Terms with the Tragedy?

Several factors push her reactions to stillbirth under ground and some of the most severe effects are insidious and delayed. Commonly, the mother gets over it surprisingly well. The stillbirth seems like a bewildering non-event and shame may be the prime emotion. The feeling of inferiority and failure makes people want to hide away and this is sometimes made even worse by kindly offers of a side room in the ward. There are feelings of guilt with nothing to feel guilty about; feelings of disease with no illness present; and above all feelings of emptiness and loss with only the most precarious knowledge of what has been lost. There has been a dead baby when there has been no knowledge of a live one.

The work of mourning is to cherish memory and imagination and that is where doctors and nurses try to help. It is always hard to find words of comfort after a death. When a baby dies friends and relatives have no fond memories to recall, no words of praise and affection for the person who once was. With the best of intentions, they may make comments such as 'It was just a baby', or 'There'll be other children'. Such comments meant to help can hurt deeply for they minimise the parents' experience and dismiss the infant as a non-person. It is far better to communicate a simple, shared sense of sorrow and loss.

As well as help from friends and family, there are ways in which support can be found from others who have had a similar experience and are ready to contact bereaved parents. The Stillbirth and Neonatal Death Society (SANDS) has many branches nationwide (address on page 456). SANDS befrienders will sometimes visit bereaved patients in hospital or there may be self-help groups where other parents who have been in the same situation can meet each other.

Finally, the next pregnancy is actually a period of psychological risk which is multiplied by the intense pressure of optimism. Everybody hopes that, if only the new baby is normal, everything will be all right. Fortunately, recurrent stillbirths of unknown origin are extremely rare and most women may be reassured that a subsequent pregnancy will end happily.

Cot Death (SIDS – Sudden Infant Death Syndrome)

In the face of all the progress in medical research and infant care, the sad fact remains that several thousand babies die each year without having exhibited any recognised symptoms of illness, and the term 'sudden infant death syndrome', or 'cot death' as it is more commonly known, affects about fifteen hundred babies up to eight months of age each year in the United Kingdom.

In a typical case the infant is put to bed at night, seemingly in good health, and is found dead the next morning. The age range for this condition is between five weeks and five months, with the peak coming between two and four months. Rarely, if ever, does this occur prior to three weeks of age or after six months. This particular span would tend to lend some credence to the old explanation of cot death – that the mother somehow 'overlay her infant in sleep' or that the infant suffocated in his pillow of blankets. A younger baby would not

---

WAYS IN WHICH PARENTS CAN REDUCE
THE RISK OF COT DEATH

Sleeping position
Recent research has shown that cot death is more common in babies who sleep on their stomachs. By making sure that your baby goes to sleep in the right position the risk can be reduced. Babies should be laid down to sleep on their backs or on their sides with the lower arm forward to stop them rolling over.

Don't be too worried that babies might be sick and choke if laid on their backs. There is no evidence that this happens.

The right sleeping position seems only to be important until babies are able to roll themselves over in their sleep. Once they can do this it is safe to let them take whichever position they prefer.

Temperature
Babies should be kept warm but they must not be allowed to get too warm. Use lightweight blankets which can be added or taken away. Duvets or baby-nests can be too warm.

Tobacco smoke
Create a smoke-free zone for your baby.

---

be exposed to those hazards and an older one should be able to defend itself, but in point of fact suffocation is extremely rare. The infant whose breathing is interfered with thrashes about and kicks up a considerable fuss.

There is no cause for parents to blame themselves for such a calamity, nor is there any evidence of a genetic influence. The chances of a repeat occurrence in an infant born later is not increased.

So, what do we know about the causes of cot death? Various explanations have been offered but none of them as yet is conclusive. Some authorities believe that these infants are the victims of sudden massive infection. Others, that it is an allergic response within the body, but almost certainly there are a number of causes. More recently a theory has been put forward that there is an enzyme deficiency in the liver that makes the baby unable to convert fat into sugar for energy, but this is unlikely to account for many deaths. One modern theory is that the incidence of cot death can be reduced remarkably by the position of the baby: if he sleeps on his back or side, then this may have a protective influence.

Unfortunately, cot death can strike the rich and the poor, the conscientious and the careless. This is one situation where the educated parent is no better equipped than the uneducated to protect the child. Nevertheless the parents who have to bear this tragedy understandably tend to blame themselves and may overwhelm subsequent children with exaggerated protectiveness.

The important question is whether cot death can be prevented. It is thought that inherent breathing difficulties may be responsible for the death of the baby and all babies will stop breathing before they die. It is also further suggested that, if an attack of difficulty with breathing can be detected as soon as it occurs, there may be a chance of recovery. Current interest surrounds the use of breathing monitors called 'Apnoea Alarms' for newborn babies. Sensitive to the child's normal respiration, they can trigger off warnings if the child is having breathing difficulties. It is difficult to organise a controlled trial and it may never be possible to produce absolute proof that the alarm actually reduces the incidence of cot deaths, though it is not unreasonable to suppose this may be so.

If your baby seems unwell, seek medical advice as soon as possible; and in a future pregnancy ask to see the paediatrician early on so that you may discuss the implications of what happened previously and find out what positive steps can be taken to avoid a repetition.

Finally, there are a number of self-help groups that may be of huge assistance in comforting and explaining the condition to the parents (addresses on pages 455–456). The Department of Health has also issued a leaflet entitled 'Reducing the Risk of Cot Death', which contains a number of helpful recommendations.

PART 2

CHAPTER 13

After the Birth

Doctors use the word *puerperium* (meaning 'having brought forth a child') to cover the period of several weeks which starts immediately after delivery of the baby and is completed when the reproductive organs have fully returned to their non-pregnant state. The return to normal after the baby is born involves extensive physical changes in the uterus, the vagina, the breasts and the body, together with huge emotional changes. Some of these changes occur rapidly but many last several months.

Although it may be quite a relief not to be pregnant any longer, the discomforts of late pregnancy are sometimes merely exchanged for others experienced after the birth.

Changes in the Uterus and Vagina

Almost immediately after delivery the abdomen loses its big swelling and at first looks pretty flat, although the uterus which can be felt by the midwife or doctor, is usually still much bigger than in the non-pregnant state. The uterus does not actually return to its normal size for about two months, although most of the changes occur within the first few weeks.

Similarly the neck of the womb or cervix which has had to open in order to let the baby's head through gradually contracts down so that within a few days it will have re-formed and become small and narrow.

Afterpains

Surprisingly, throughout a fertile lifespan, the uterus never really stops contracting. These contractions are usually felt as menstrual cramps at period times, or as Braxton Hicks (see page 220) contractions throughout pregnancy, and after delivery as afterpains.

After birth the contractions can be quite strong and painful because they are the means by which the uterus reduces its size over the first few days. The faster and harder it contracts down, the less likelihood there is of any bleeding. The contractions are usually not severe with the first baby, but women become more conscious of them after subsequent pregnancies. They are more severe in breast-feeding women because the suckling infant makes the pituitary gland in the brain release a hormone into the bloodstream that causes contractions of the uterus. In other words suckling is Nature's way of making the uterus come down in size. The discomfort of the afterpains which may last for a few days can usually be controlled by simple pain relieving drugs such as Panadol or aspirin. These afterpains are a perfectly normal occurrence.

Blood-stained Discharge (Lochia)

A certain amount of bloody vaginal discharge is inevitable no matter how delivery occurs. It may be heavier than a period at first but usually lessens over the next few days. Sanitary pads should be worn as tampons are not really advisable.

This lochia comes from the uterus, mainly from where the placenta was attached, and as the uterus becomes smaller over the first few weeks the bleeding usually gets less, although it may not stop completely until many weeks have gone by. The amount of bleeding at first may be quite frightening, especially if you were used to having light periods, and sometimes a few small blood clots are passed as well. All this is normal. The lochia, which remains red for the first few days, usually changes to a reddish brown, turns brown by about the fifth day and then finally you will notice a little pinkish loss until it ceases altogether.

Just like afterpains, the lochia is often heavier if you are breast-feeding, and the amount and the colour helps the doctor and midwife to see how quickly the uterus is becoming smaller again. The more rapidly the uterus contracts, the sooner the lochia becomes brown and stops altogether.

Sometimes this discharge has an offensive smell and this is usually of no significance but, if it persists, the midwife may take a swab from the vagina to ensure that there has been no infection.

The Bladder

Many women will have emptied their bladder during labour or may have been catheterised, so that immediately after delivery the bladder is empty. Because of this and the stress that is put on the bladder during labour, it is not uncommon to have some discomfort on voiding. There may be difficulty in passing urine at first as everything feels numb and bruised. Occasionally the bladder becomes temporarily paralysed, particularly after a long and difficult labour or a forceps delivery, because of bruising, or following an epidural anaesthetic when the bladder takes a little time to start working again because of the anaesthetic. When this happens a small catheter is usually passed into the bladder and is left draining for one or two days. After removal voiding usually is quite normal.

It is not uncommon in the few weeks after delivery for you to notice the rather distressing complaint of leakage of urine on laughing, coughing or sneezing and this is termed 'stress incontinence'. It is usually due to hormonal changes affecting the bladder wall and very often disappears as the weeks go by. It can be helped enormously by muscle exercises which the physiotherapist will teach you. If stress incontinence persists for some months after delivery, consult your gynaecologist because there may be other causes, such as a mild prolapse of the bladder, which can easily be treated.

The Bowels

It is quite common not to open your bowels for a day or two after the birth, partly because the bowels will have been well cleared out at some point before or during labour, and you also may have gone a day or two with very little to eat. Drinking plenty of water and getting up and walking about will usually help to get the bowels working. Constipation is not uncommon for a day or two and any stitches may lead to a natural reluctance to exert any pressure in this area. Your midwife or health attendant will usually ask about bowel action and will encourage you to drink plenty of water, or prescribe a laxative.

The worry that a bowel action when it does come may burst any stitches is unfounded and you can be reassured that this hardly ever occurs. If you have had any stitches or an episiotomy (see pages 263–265), the cut is quite tender for a day or two because it is in a very sensitive area between the vagina and the back passage. There may also be some bruising and soreness.

Generally, this discomfort rapidly improves over a day or two, and creams and other medications will give relief. Although the discomfort does get better, sometimes even for a few months the site of the little cut may throb uncomfortably during the first few days of each period.

Most stitches are rapidly absorbed and do not need to be removed. Sitting on an inflatable rubber ring, drying the area with a hair-dryer after bathing and using salt in the bath to encourage healing are useful hints for coping with stitches. If discomfort from the stitches continues for a week or two after the baby is born, tell your doctor or midwife in case there is an obvious local cause.

Haemorrhoids (Piles)

Piles do not occur as a result of the bearing down required in the second stage or of the stretching of the back passage or rectum, but they may become more pronounced if the pushing stage goes on for too long. As in earlier instructions regarding the care of haemorrhoids (see pages 126–127), avoid straining when you move your bowels, be sure that there is enough bulk and stool softener in your diet, and if necessary ask for local medication for pain relief. An ice pack applied to the area will soothe sharp pains and help the swelling go down and, if you are at home, a pack of frozen peas does the trick splendidly.

If you have suffered from piles during your pregnancy, you may be reassured that they will get smaller, the pain will lessen and may even disappear over the next few weeks. If they remain troublesome, then your doctor should be consulted and further treatment may be indicated.

Weight and Fluid Loss

During delivery and for the first few days afterwards you will lose a certain amount of weight – possibly as much as 7kg or 8kg – due mainly to the absence of the baby, the placenta and the amniotic fluid, and also extra circulating blood volume. Often there is an irresistible urge to empty the bladder very frequently for the first couple of days as the body gets rid of the excess fluid in pregnancy.

Sweating, particularly at night, is a common complaint for the same reason and is quite normal. It is one way in which the body actually loses weight. This sweating is usually due to circulating hormones and settles spontaneously after a few days, but occasionally lasts a couple of weeks.

Emotions

In the first few days after delivery many mothers feel quite low and, although basically they may be happy, there may be an uncontrollable urge to cry – the so-called 'baby blues' (see pages 338–340). The important thing to remember is that this is a very common finding, and really not surprising when one thinks of the huge emotional changes prompted by any fears or anxieties that may have been present during pregnancy, the type of labour, and the enormous relief that all is over. A lot of publicity is given to these feelings of depression and therefore many mothers expect them automatically but this is certainly not the case. If they do occur, then they are usually mild and of short duration and no treatment is necessary. Such feelings are not surprising given the stresses of the next few days, i.e. the baby becoming more demanding, especially if sharing the parents' bedroom.

Diet

As a new mother you should eat a normal diet as soon as you feel like it. It is particularly important to keep fluid intake high because this encourages milk production. Vegetables, fruit and protein, i.e. meat, fish, cheese and eggs, are important rather than nibbling the things containing carbohydrates and fats, i.e. chocolates, biscuits, cakes, etc.

Rest

Rest is important after the baby is born and an adequate amount of sleep is essential to promote breast-feeding. Most women don't sleep very well for the first few days after birth, partly because of the excitement and relief, and maybe because there is the baby to feed and, if in hospital, the daily routine starts pretty early. Try and pick a time during the afternoon which is sacred to you and your baby and, even if you don't sleep, close your eyes and rest and exclude visitors. Not everyone wants to be surrounded by visitors and friends for the first day or two and you can make this known to the ward sister if you are in hospital and perhaps limit the first few days of visiting to close family only.

The position that you take up when you are in bed should be the one that is most comfortable for you. You may lie on your side or back or front as you please. Lying on the abdomen for an hour or two a day used to be advocated but this has no influence on the position of the uterus and is not necessary. You will be allowed out of bed as soon as you wish after delivery, providing there are no complications such as excessive bleeding.

Coping with Hospital

Some women enjoy being in hospital away from the anxieties of home, confident that there are experts to help, and friendly nurses or other patients to support them. For others the constant interruptions day and night from staff and other patients, average food, lack of sleep, and the absence of family and friends may be frustrating. If ward life doesn't suit, then there may be a single room which you can move to if you are in a multi-patient ward, or vice versa.

One of the problems with hospital stay is conflicting advice by your attendants. Everyone looking after you is trying to do their best, but doctors and midwives are not on the ward the whole time and advice can be muddling if it comes from different sources. This is particularly apparent with breast-feeding. If you feel unhappy about this, do talk to the senior midwife or sister on the ward, or the doctor, so that the problem can be ironed out.

Going Home

To many women, leaving for home with their new baby is a joyous though sensitive occasion and they look forward with anticipation to returning to their family. The chocolates are gone, the roses have wilted, your elbows are raw from hospital sheets, you are tired of being awakened to see if you are asleep, and of having lunch at breakfast time. However, it may feel strange and unreal to leave the protective atmosphere of hospital, and some mothers feel rather concerned about how they will cope, how other children will react, or whether they know what they have to do. Also, the baby responds to another environment in a different way and may begin to behave differently from the way they did in hospital.

Examination on Discharge

The doctor or midwife will check you before discharge to make sure that the uterus is shrinking satisfactorily, the lochia is not too heavy and is turning from red to brown, and that any stitches are healing well. A blood test is often done to check the iron level because many women lose a little bit more blood than average, and you may be prescribed iron tablets to take for the first few weeks at home, particularly if you are breast-feeding.

If you weren't immune to Rubella (German measles – see pages 80–82) during your pregnancy, the hospital staff will know this and may be able to give you an injection before you leave hospital. This vaccination will not affect the baby even if you are breast-feeding.

This is a good time to discuss contraception for the future and the midwife or doctor will be pleased to advise you (see pages 410–433). You will have been shown by the midwife how to clean the baby's umbilical cord if it has not already dropped off and the baby will be checked by a paediatrician.

Advice on Leaving Hospital

When you leave hospital the doctor or midwife usually answers any questions you have and tells you a number of things to do and not to do. The following opinions may or may not differ from the guidelines you get from your own doctor, and by all means follow that advice. These instructions are meant only as a simple guide.

The most important thing is to get plenty of rest. It is especially relevant with mothers leaving hospital so soon after delivery. For the first couple of weeks get off your feet for a while in the morning and again in the afternoon if you can, and go to bed early. You may be up in the small hours feeding the baby for the first few weeks. In the beginning try to limit the number of friends and relatives who come to see you. They can sometimes be exhausting and friends, however close, should not visit if they are likely to pass on infection.

There is no reason why you should not go outdoors, even in cold weather, and the same goes for your baby. Babies are a good deal tougher than you think. Nor is there any reason not to climb stairs but, if you go up and down stairs a few dozen times a day, you are not getting enough rest.

Postpartum Depression or 'Baby Blues'

For the majority of women, the euphoria which they experience at the moment of birth continues throughout the postpartum period. However, for many the emotional high of childbirth is often followed by varying degrees of postpartum depression, or 'blues', usually manifested by one or two crying episodes without apparent cause during the first three to seven days after delivery. Often the mother feels very much better by the fifth or sixth day and there is a rapid recovery with no further difficulties.

Why do 'Baby Blues' occur?

The answer really is that no one knows, although there are a number of theories commonly discussed. The baby is usually becoming more awake and demanding by about the third or fourth day; the woman herself may be feeling stronger but the demands of being a mother and dealing with everything at once just seem too much; there is difficulty with sleeping and relaxation; and anxiety about whether the baby is coping with the first few days of life satisfactorily. Some women feel rather lonely in hospital without their partners; and breast-feeding may be taking a little bit more time than usual to be established. Some believe that early mild depression is caused by the dramatic change in concentration of the female hormone oestrogen, combined with reduction in the amount of blood in the body following childbirth.

These factors, in addition to a variety of physical discomforts such as pain from the episiotomy site, piles that are becoming a nuisance, and afterpains when the uterus is contracting, all contribute to the problem.

Mothers who for a variety of medical reasons are separated from their infants during the first two days of life are believed to be more susceptible to postpartum depression or 'blues' because they have lost the opportunity to bond during this critical time.

Interviews with women suffering from postpartum depression reveal a wide range of concerns. A commonly reported problem is arguing with parents or partners and the strong conviction that their partner is not as supportive as he could be. For some, the reality of caring for a demanding and irritable baby for twenty-four hours a day is far more difficult than they had anticipated, while for others the concern is the change that their bodies have undergone. Some women express feelings of isolation because the baby suddenly becomes the focus of everyone's attention.

While postpartum 'blues' usually start in hospital, they may intensify when you arrive home and are confronted with the added burden of household chores, unannounced visitors, a demanding partner and too little sleep. During the early weeks of motherhood you may well find yourself tired and listless, and quite easily upset or irritated. You may even feel somewhat guilty that other women in the same situation are coping better, and all these feelings are not unusual.

What Happens if the 'Baby Blues' Don't Get Better after a Few Weeks?

The first thing to do is to talk to someone and find a shoulder to cry on. For some women their partner is the best person to talk to, while others get more help from talking to friends, other mothers, or professionals like a health visitor or doctor. It's important to see people: make the effort to contact your friends and get to know other women in the same situation. Your Child Health Clinic is one place to start. It isn't difficult to get together a group of mothers to meet and chat, say once a week or a fortnight. Put up a notice on the clinic notice-board. If you talk to your health visitor, she may know of groups like this that already exist. The National Childbirth Trust runs groups and events in your area. Contact your local branch or write to the Meet a Mum Association.

Find things to do that are for yourself rather than your baby. You can spend so much time and energy caring for your baby that you forget about yourself. Do whatever you enjoy: even a long, lazy bath can help. Ask your partner or a friend or relative to babysit so that you can have some time that is really your own and don't feel guilty about taking it. Go out for an evening: go to a film or for a meal, or whatever you enjoy most. Find out if there is a local babysitting circle by talking to other mothers who live nearby.

Above all, don't try to keep up appearances. Let everybody but your baby and your partner fend for themselves. Be as open as your personality allows you to be and try and get enough rest and sleep for the first few weeks. Childbirth is a pretty tiring situation and, if you feel tired, lie down with your feet raised slightly above your head. Find time to do this: you don't have to go to sleep as resting will give your heart, lungs and body time to recover.

Severe Depression

Unfortunately sometimes the mild depression characterised by 'baby blues' starts to take on a slightly different form and becomes a much stronger version of what has been described above.

The classic complaints are tiredness, difficulty in concentrating, inability to sleep, weight loss, gloomy thoughts, tearfulness, lack of interest in sex, a sort of social withdrawal, change in eating habits, and so on. This is quite an alarming situation to the mother and at times the emotions run very high and some women are frightened that they will actually neglect or harm their babies.

Often there are no specific reasons why mothers become quite severely depressed. Those who have had a history of depression or treatment before are certainly more liable to have problems in the lying-in period. Hormonal changes that occur in the first few weeks in the body can be contributory causes but no one really knows why this occurs.

What Can be Done about Severe Depression?

Again, the first thing to do is to get help from friends, relatives, your medical advisers, and lay groups such as the National Childbirth Trust Postnatal Support Group. If your feelings continue to worry you, talk to your family doctor who will be able to help, either by directing you towards counselling or psychotherapy, or under certain circumstances suggesting medication.

Your doctor may prescribe anti-depressant tablets, which usually take a week or two to have any significant effect. Most of the anti-depressants that are now used do not interfere with breast-feeding, but this is something you should talk to your doctor about. Your doctor may suggest that help in the form of a psychiatric consultation is necessary and, if that is advised, then take the advice. There are specialists in psychiatry who are trained to understand the emotional difficulties that occur after birth and very often a consultation with an expert will do much to put your mind at rest.

Above all, talk about your feelings: don't keep them to yourself, even though this may make you feel somewhat inadequate.

Postpartum Psychosis

Very rarely, and sometimes quite suddenly, mothers may develop a very serious mental illness which may require medical treatment and hospitalisation. The complaints are very variable, but you must seek help from medical attendants if:

- You feel you cannot do anything on behalf of your own recovery.

- Your depressive feelings lead you to become dependent on alcohol or drugs, or cause you to feel completely helpless with thoughts of abusing your own child.

- You are afraid you may harm yourself or others.

- You and your partner need help in coping with the problems that parenthood and your depression have made in your relationship.

- You feel a sense of complete withdrawal from everyday life into a world of your own, perhaps with delusions or hallucinations or feelings of persecution. You may feel impelled to do bizarre or dangerous things to yourself and/or your baby.

- You are able to express your fears but cannot recognise or explain what is happening to you.

Urgent help from your family doctor and health workers is essential as there are good treatments and cures which are often gradual and take time to be effective. The help of a psychiatrist is usually needed. Sometimes treatment with medication is required, which may have to be continued for some months with close monitoring. Some mothers need to be admitted to hospital for treatment, at least during the initial acute phase.

One of the problems with severe mental depression leading to psychosis is that it takes quite a long time for the problem to be resolved. If hospitalisation is needed, there will be a time of adaptation once you get home and it is very important that your partner and the rest of your family understand everything that has happened, and provide support.

Finally, remember that severe mental illness after childbirth is extremely rare, whereas the 'baby blues' and mild depression are common. Don't be afraid to discuss your feelings with your partner and anyone who you think might help. You can also contact an organisation called the Association for Postnatal Illness (address on page 455) and there are leaflets published by the Health Education Council that may help you to understand postnatal depression and which can be obtained from your local doctor's surgery.

Complications in the Lying-in Period

It is of course possible for a woman soon after the baby has been born to develop any particular illness coincidental to the pregnancy. There are, however, certain known complications that can occur and no discussion of the lying-in period would be complete without their mention.

Infection

Up to nearly forty years ago infection in the mother, or puerperal fever as it was termed, was a killer. Until that time if an infection gained access into the uterus, and this was in the days before antibiotics, this would lead to generalised infection in the body with disastrous consequences. Nowadays, of course, the whole management of labour, the appreciation of how infection can arise and be prevented, and the correction of many other minor abnormalities or deficiencies during pregnancy, all help to avoid puerperal infection.

In addition, the measures taken during labour and delivery are done under strict antiseptic control. The cleaning of the vulva, the use of antiseptic creams and sterile instruments, all make serious infection at this stage unusual, and, most importantly, if an infection does occur, it can be located and treated with an appropriate antibiotic before any further damage is done.

Infection in the Uterus

This was of course the classic cause of the old puerperal fever, but this is now very rare indeed and easily treated.

It is not difficult to see why the uterus can become infected during labour and vaginal delivery when it is easy for organisms to gain access via the vagina into the uterus. Often the first sign of an infection is that the discharge normally occurring for a few days after the birth called lochia (see page 332) becomes rather offensive, quite profuse and even resembles pus. When the doctor feels the uterus it may feel tender and there may be some abdominal pain. The temperature and pulse rate are often raised.

If this occurs a swab test is normally taken from the vagina and sent to the laboratory for bacteriological culture and isolation of the organism. Antibiotics will then probably be prescribed.

One of the commonest causes of an infection in the uterus is the presence within the uterus of small fragments of placenta which sometimes fail to be delivered with the majority of the placenta. In some instances this may need to be dealt with surgically and the small pieces of offending placenta removed.

Infection in the Vagina

Many women, certainly those having their first baby, will have either had an episiotomy (see pages 263–265) or a small tear which requires stitching, and this area can become infected. The discomfort around the lower genital area gets worse, there may be an unpleasant discharge, and sometimes if the infection is deeper a small abscess may form. Again, a swab test will be taken and with correct antibiotics this is usually not a problem and the whole area heals nicely.

Occasionally the stitch line of the episiotomy or tear breaks down and gapes quite widely. This can be quite worrying as it appears that the wound has completely separated leaving quite a large hole. In fact this is Nature's response to the infection and, once under control, the gaping wound heals by itself and usually no stitches are necessary or even indicated. The whole process may take a few weeks, but the healing will always occur in time.

Healing by what is termed 'secondary intention' – in other words, the gaping wound heals by itself from below upwards – may lead to some scarring and tenderness during intercourse, at least in the first few weeks or months. As the whole area heals, however, and stretches the problem sorts itself out. It may be helpful when first resuming intercourse to use some lubricating cream or anaesthetic jelly. This sort of occurrence usually causes no problems in a subsequent pregnancy.

Urinary Tract Infection

As we have seen, urinary infection is very common in pregnancy, largely because the short urinary channel is close to the vagina and organisms frequently gain access. In pregnancy this is slightly more common than in the non-pregnant state because there is an alteration in the bladder lining which is usually hormonally induced during labour. It may be necessary to catheterise the bladder on more than one occasion during labour, or before Caesarean section and, although catheterisation is performed in a strict aseptic manner, this sometimes may contribute to infection. It is easy to see how, during the whole process of delivery, organisms may gain access into the urinary channel.

The symptoms of urinary infection are usually frequent urination and pain or stinging when passing urine. A urine culture will be taken to identify the organism and the appropriate antibiotic will be given. In rare cases infection may spread upwards from the bladder along the tubes called the ureters into the kidneys. This is know as pyelitis (see pages 129–130). This is not common after the baby is born but does occur occasionally and aggressive treatment with antibiotics and increasing fluid intake usually cures this once and for all.

Infection of the Breast Tissue (Mastitis)

Mastitis occasionally occurs during pregnancy before delivery but unfortunately is much more frequent after the birth and during breast-feeding. The causes and management of mastitis are discussed on page 360.

Bleeding after Birth (Postpartum Haemorrhage)

A certain amount of bleeding inevitably occurs during and immediately after delivery of the baby, but it may occasionally become excessive. There are several sources of bleeding after delivery: the blood may come from the episiotomy wound or from a tear of the cervix or skin. These wounds are usually recognised quite easily at the time and are dealt with accordingly by stitching. It may occasionally be necessary to give a general anaesthetic so that a thorough examination higher up the birth canal can be made.

If no tear is visible, then bleeding is generally due to a relaxed uterus or a fragment of placenta which has broken off and remains in the uterus.

The Relaxed Uterus

During the delivery of the baby's head the midwife usually gives an injection of a drug called Syntometrine, which makes the uterus contract and clamp down on itself, preventing bleeding from the raw area where the placenta was formerly attached. Sometimes the uterus fails to harden and contract and, if it continues to be lax, it doesn't act as its own haemostat and prevent bleeding, which may occur very soon after the delivery of the baby and the placenta. This is usually managed by massaging the uterus with the hand, which responds to pressure by hardening, or sometimes an intravenous drip is set up which contains more of the drug Syntocinon which also has a hardening and tightening effect on the uterus causing it to contract and firm up. In most cases this simple treatment does the trick.

Retained Placenta

The placenta (see pages 261–262) usually follows delivery of the baby within a few minutes and is helped out by the attendant pulling on the cord, but occasionally the placenta may remain in the uterus and be reluctant to be delivered. There is a danger that as long as the placenta remains in the uterus bleeding may occur, as part of the placenta may start to come away leaving perhaps the main section inside. If part of the placenta fails to be delivered within ten minutes or so, the doctor will do a gentle examination to see whether the placenta is actually coming through the cervix. If no placenta is felt in the vagina or if the cord snaps, which is not an uncommon occurrence, then it may be necessary to retrieve the placenta. This is called 'manual removal'. Essentially what happens is that the operator has to put a gloved hand through the cervix inside the uterus and release the placenta. This procedure can be done under epidural anaesthesia but, if an epidural is not being used, then you will usually be put to sleep with a general anaesthetic for a short time.

Retained Products

Sometimes a fragment becomes detached from the placenta as it is being expelled and remains in the uterus. The uterus can only partially contract and will bleed until the fragment has been removed. This is why careful examination of the placenta is always carried out to ensure that it has come away in one piece. The same rules apply here and bleeding will only stop when the whole of the placenta is delivered.

Occasionally there is no bleeding for the first few days and it only starts on the eighth or ninth day. This may also be due to a small piece of placenta which is retained. Bleeding may be quite heavy and it may be necessary to readmit you into hospital and for you to have a gentle cleaning operation called a D & C in order to make sure that there is no placental tissue remaining. If much blood has been lost, it may be necessary to have a blood transfusion.

Late Bleeding

Bleeding may occur at any time during the lying-in period, even three or four weeks after delivery when you are back at home. The usual cause for this late bleeding is a hormonal change prompted by the pregnancy and conservative treatment with tablets is normally all that is necessary.

Again, it is possible that a few pieces of the placenta have remained trapped inside the uterus and this will often manifest itself by brisk, bright bleeding with perhaps an offensive discharge. This must be reported to your doctor and it may be necessary to admit you to hospital for a scraping operation together with antibiotics.

Blood Clots in the Legs (Thrombosis)

A complication of pregnancy that can be a serious problem is a blood clot in the legs or groin. The blood clot itself develops in a vein and women are more susceptible to clots during pregnancy, delivery and particularly in the lying-in period. The reason for this is that there are changes that occur naturally during pregnancy, and particularly after childbirth, which tend to increase the blood's clotting ability, sometimes too much, and the enlarged uterus makes it difficult for the blood in the lower part of the body to return to the heart.

The probable cause of blood clots in the legs in pregnancy is that the blood flows round the body in a much slower fashion than usual (called 'stasis'). The problem has many names including 'venous thrombosis', 'deep venous thrombosis', 'thrombo-embolic disease' and 'thrombo-phlebitis'. It is not limited to pregnancy, but pregnancy is certainly a time when this condition is more likely to occur with more serious consequences.

There are two types of veins in the body which are connected to each other: the superficial veins near the surface which can easily be seen, and deeper veins which are not visible. It is the deeper veins which give a more serious problem.

Superficial Thrombo-phlebitis

This term is applied to the veins that are very close to the surface of the skin which become inflamed. You may notice a tender, reddened area that runs in a line over a vein that is near the surface in the thigh or calf. This type of thrombosis does not usually require hospitalisation and is treated with a mild pain reliever, elevation of the leg, and support of the leg with bandages or support stockings. It occurs commonly with pre-existing varicose veins. The vein often feels firm, hard and tender, rather like a cord, and sometimes the redness or inflammation may extend along the vein for several inches and may be extremely painful on standing or walking.

However, it's important to emphasise that this sort of thrombosis does not generally have unpleasant consequences and does not affect the mother or the baby.

Deep Vein Thrombosis (Clot Formation in the Deep Veins)

This is a more serious problem which is more difficult to diagnose and, fortunately, much less common. Women who are at a somewhat increased risk of developing clots are those who have had previous thromboses, are in the older age group, have had two or three previous deliveries, have been confined to bed for long periods, or are overweight or anaemic, and it is also somewhat more common after Caesarean section.

Here there are no obvious, cord-like, red areas in the leg but the whole leg may feel heavy and painful, particularly in the calf or thigh region, with swelling. Deep vein thrombosis is unusual during pregnancy but can occur after delivery, most commonly on day six, seven or eight.

Complaints of acute pain in the leg with swelling should be reported to your doctor. It is important to make an accurate diagnosis of thrombosis because, if untreated, some of the clot may break away and pass into the circulation of the veins and move to the lungs when it is called a 'pulmonary embolus', which can be more threatening.

The diagnosis of a deep vein thrombosis is made by examination of the leg, ultrasound tests and special X-rays. Treatment consists of hospitalisation and the administration of a specific blood thinning drug, of which the commonest is Heparin. This is given in a drip into a vein and thins the blood, allowing the clot to be dissolved. While the Heparin is administered, bed rest is necessary, the leg may be elevated and mild pain relief prescribed. Treatment may continue for a varying period of time after birth depending on the control of the blood clotting mechanism as confirmed by blood tests. In most hospitals the advice of a consultant pathologist with expertise in blood problems is usually sought, and treatment is monitored jointly. It is important to remind those in charge of a subsequent pregnancy if thrombosis has occurred.

Pulmonary Embolus

This means that the blood clot has moved from one of the veins in the leg or pelvis, travelled along the veins of the heart and ended up in the lungs where it lodges and cuts off the blood supply. The part of the lung that is blocked by the clot cannot obtain any blood supply and collapses. You may experience sudden and severe pain, usually in the lower part of the chest, accompanied by shortness of breath and a feeling of faintness. Again, the treatment is by complete bed rest, sedation and anti-coagulants.

It has to be said that, although it is a very uncommon problem during pregnancy, it is a very serious one but happily only occurs in about one in every three to four thousand pregnancies. Treatment with anti-coagulants is often satisfactory but occasionally the blood clot blocking off the lung may have to be removed surgically.

Treatment may be continued for six to eight weeks, but the injection treatment is only required for the first two days and then a blood thinning tablet can be given which acts in the same way.

Inversion of the Uterus

This is an extremely rare condition where the uterus turns itself inside out when the placenta is being delivered. What happens is that, as the cord is being pulled down, if the placenta is reluctant to come away the whole of the uterus may descend and literally be pulled down outside the vagina. Immediate treatment is necessary, usually by administering an anaesthetic and pushing the uterus up again. This can cause severe shock to the patient and the situation needs to be dealt with as an emergency, but as soon as the uterus is replaced in its normal position all is well.

Infant Feeding

Breast versus Bottle

Until this century the majority of mothers had little choice but to follow Nature's method of nourishing babies, but the woman of today has a choice between breast-feeding, bottle-feeding or a combination of both. Breast-feeding is a wonderful experience for both mother and baby but it is not by any means the only wonderful experience and just as good a relationship can be established with a bottle-fed baby. Certainly, though, breast milk is the ideal food for the baby in the first few months and breast-feeding should be easy and pleasurable to the mother and her child.

Studies have shown that the percentage of women who breast-feed varies from region to region and country to country. It depends a lot on socio-economic class. Over the last few decades there has been one consistent trend which has overridden the local variations, and that is a drastic reduction in breast-feeding everywhere. From as far back as we have records, at least from the time of the Ancient Greeks, there has been a search for an adequate substitute for mothers' own milk. To avoid breast-feeding, women in favoured social positions used to hire wet-nurses to feed their babies and the wet-nurse, a lactating woman with milk to spare, was a familiar figure in Ancient Athens and Rome, in London and Paris of the seventeenth and eighteenth centuries, and in Colonial America.

Her frequent appearances in the novels of Charles Dickens are a reflection of how numerous her kind must have been a hundred years ago.

Fashionable women were not the only employers of wet-nurses. Mothers without milk and the guardians of infants whose mothers died in childbirth also turned to the wet-nurse for help.

Other studies discussing breast- and bottle-feeding found that a mother's performance in breast-feeding bears a close relationship to her attitude towards breast-feeding. There was a study made in the postpartum period of mothers who had a positive attitude towards breast-feeding which found that they gave much more milk than those whose attitude was negative.

Breast-feeding has been linked with sex in ensuring the survival of the human race. There is a close connection between the response of intercourse and lactation. In both suckling and sexual excitement uterine contractions occur and so does erection of the nipples, and women have sometimes been known to eject milk during sexual excitement. Nursing women show a higher level of interest in sex in the lying-in period than do mothers who are not nursing.

Since breast-feeding obviously requires the co-operation of your baby as well as you, its success or failure will partly depend on the efficiency of the baby's sucking and your responsiveness to this stimulus. Only a very small percentage of women (less than one per cent) are physically incapable of nursing. You may want to breast-feed but temporarily can't because of illness or separation from your baby, for example if it is very small and premature. However in most circumstances, and with the right support from professionals you can maintain milk production, either by manual or mechanical expression, until full nursing becomes possible. Most hospitals encourage contact between mothers and their premature babies far earlier than was once the practice.

Finally, mothers do need a lot of care and attention. You should not be pressurised into doing anything other than looking after your baby and yourself. Breast-feeding is actually quite hard work and it is important that you eat well and particularly that you have an adequate fluid intake and get enough rest. It often takes several weeks to get breast-feeding going fully.

So What Makes a Woman Decide to Breast-feed?

Class and Culture

A woman's attitude towards breast-feeding is unquestionably linked to her role in society as determined by geography, education, socio-economic class and culture.

Class differences count heavily in rates of breast-feeding in the United States, England, Switzerland and Sweden, but not for instance in France. In the United States there is a higher rate of breast-feeding among women with a college education than among those with a high-school education. A study in California showed that, while well-educated mothers were more inclined to start breast-feeding, they were not as likely as less well-educated mothers to keep it up.

There is of course a strong association between breast-feeding and the attitudes of partners, families and friends. There is good evidence to show that the peer group has an influence on whether a mother elects to breast-feed and it seems likely that the prevailing attitude among doctors in a given community will also have an effect.

Social and Psychological Factors

If you decide to breast-feed just because 'it's the thing to do' but deep inside you would rather not, the chances are that you are heading for trouble. You should respect your own feelings and try not to fight against them. Friends, neighbours and relatives may discourage you directly by asking suggestive questions, such as 'Are you sure he's getting enough?' or 'Why don't you just give him a bottle?' or, more frantically, 'Do something so that I can get some sleep'.

Many young couples lack helping hands to relieve them of some of the downright hard work of baby care. The new mother, home, sore from the hospital, perhaps feeling a bit blue and unsure of her new role, over-sensitive to the mildest negative remark, tired from a seemingly endless number of feedings and with little chance to sleep herself, zealously committed to the ideal of nursing and feeling that she is less of a woman if she cannot make the grade, may have problems. If we add to this financial insecurity, a move, and some marital misunderstanding, breast-feeding may be an uphill struggle. It is important to understand

THE BENEFITS OF BREAST-FEEDING

Availability
One of the most important advantages for you and your baby is that it is always there. Unlike a bottle of artificial milk, there is always some milk in the breast: there may be times in the day when your milk supply will be more plentiful than others, but there will always be some there for your baby.

The Perfect Food
Breast milk, unlike cows' milk which needs to be modified before it is suitable for feeding to your baby, is perfect. It is made by the breasts as your baby feeds.

Relationship
There is little doubt that breast-feeding causes a very happy relationship between you and your child. For you, the mother, there is a special closeness with your baby and for your baby there is the closeness that breast-feeding brings, i.e. warmth, comfort, security, love, food and drink, all rolled into one.

Protection against Infection
Breast milk lines your baby's stomach, providing a means by which your baby is not alone in fighting any infection. All your antibodies, past and present, are there ready to stop any unwanted bacteria, setting up protection over long periods. Gastro-enteritis, an inflammation of the bowel leading to diarrhoea and vomiting, is much less frequent in breast-fed babies.

Some Other Advantages
Breast-feeding helps involution, or the gradual contraction of the uterus so that it gets back to the non-pregnant position and size, and this is why afterpains are felt for a few weeks rather like the pain experienced during a period, but these soon disappear.

Breast-feeding often gives you time to be available to play and talk with your baby; it can be cheaper in that there is no need to buy all the bottle-feeding equipment; and there is little risk of contamination of the milk or of infection during feeding.

There is also some evidence to show that breast-feeding may protect your baby against allergies which are quite common in the newborn, such as eczema or asthma.

that these pressures affect many new parents and you should plan accordingly with your partner to try and avoid unnecessary stress.

Preparation for Breast-feeding

Preparation for breast-feeding should start in early pregnancy and one of the nursing staff or midwives will usually discuss with you the whole question of whether you wish to breast-feed and what the advantages and problems may be. There is absolutely no need to make up your mind at this stage, but it is very helpful to consider whether you wish to breast-feed or not at a convenient time during pregnancy. Some breasts are obviously suitable for feeding, have a rounded contour and a protuberant nipple, while others may be flattish with the nipple inverted. Nipple-shields were often used to bring out the nipple but this practice is not common nowadays and it is surprising how often breasts which are seemingly not suitable for breast-feeding work well once lactation has commenced.

The First Few Days

After delivery of the baby, whether or not nursing is planned, the breasts will secrete a milky fluid called colostrum. This appears usually after about the sixteenth week of pregnancy and it is quite common therefore to notice a milky discharge during pregnancy which is absolutely normal. This fluid is a precursor of milk: it is thicker and yellower than later milk and somewhat different in its make-up. It has a particularly high protein level which helps to protect the baby against the bacteria which causes gastro-enteritis. Some say that these are sound reasons for giving the baby a few days of breast milk, even if breast-feeding is not planned.

True Milk

This usually appears from about twenty-four to ninety-six hours after delivery and the milk sometimes comes so suddenly that many women can tell the exact moment. Others who have been breast-feeding their baby from birth are not so sure however and it may be that the sensation of 'coming in' is no more than a feeling that the breasts are too full.

The Let-down Reflex

This term was coined to explain the mechanism whereby the milk is expelled, having first been made available in the breasts. This reflex is a complicated chain of reactions of which the mother is quite unaware until there is a tingling in the breasts and the milk suddenly surges into the nipple area.

To understand this, picture the milk stored in little sacs in the breast which are called alveoli. When the baby sucks, nerves in the breasts are stimulated and impulses are carried to the main pituitary gland at the base of the brain. The pituitary gland is stimulated to release a hormone called oxytocin which reaches the breasts by way of the bloodstream and causes the cells of the breasts to squeeze out of the little sacs into the larger channels leading to the nipples. The baby's suckling of course then empties the ducts, and this let-down phase refers to the expulsion of the milk from the little sacs or alveoli. Other signs of this let-down reflex are strong contractions in the uterus which have already been described. This reflex is quite easily stopped. When a mother is frightened or upset she doesn't let her milk down: the milk is in the breast but the baby can't get it easily.

The four symptoms of the let-down reflex are:

- The mother may feel cramps or lower abdominal pain while nursing.
- Milk drips from the breasts while not being sucked.
- The breasts drip at expectation or sight of the baby.
- The nipple pain stops after the baby sucks for a few seconds.

Getting Started

For the first few days the nipples are very delicate and they need time to toughen up, so there is quite a lot of tenderness while nursing. It is often wise just to allow two minutes on each breast to start with, which will give your baby enough colostrum at first.

Although there are many rules about the length of sucking, the best guide is your baby's behaviour. When your baby slows down and seems full and your breasts feel deflated, it is probably time to stop. Most mothers get the feeling of this and become their own experts. It is better to do it this way than actually watching the clock but, if you are better with figures, then about five minutes of sucking per breast is right. Try two to five minutes for the first two days, building up to about ten minutes at the end of a week.

Ten minutes of sucking usually empties a breast and additional nursing is icing on the cake. Most babies of about 3–4kgs (6.5–9lbs) will be content on feeds at about four-hourly intervals, i.e. five to six feeds a day. Smaller babies are often happier on three-hourly feeds, six or seven feeds daily. There is nothing wrong with night feeds: if a baby will not settle after being made comfortable and given a little water, they are probably hungry. Water doesn't really pacify a hungry baby and they will not learn to sleep at night by screaming for hours. There is no danger of the baby forming a habit of waking up to be fed in the night. When the baby gets enough food during the day they will sleep for longer periods, eventually from about 10.30 p.m. until about 5 a.m.

Special Tips

Get comfortable. If you have had stitches and you prefer to use a rubber ring or a pillow when sitting down, do so, or you may be happier lying down. Some mothers find it helps to change positions. If the baby is being fed in a sitting position, it is probably more comfortable to lift the baby up to the breast, but using a pillow or cushions. This also has the advantage of the baby resting on the pillow so your arm doesn't get tired.

Holding the Baby

Hold your baby with the whole of its body facing you. To begin with it might be easier to support the head which should be just underneath the breast rather than the crook of the arm. If the baby is too far over, they will find it hard to get both the nipple and the areola in the mouth.

Experimenting with Positions

Let the baby smell and touch your skin and breasts, so that the baby becomes excited by the taste and will often open the mouth wide, searching for the breast. Then the baby can be drawn closer and breast milk offered. *Remember to bring the baby to the breast and not the breast to the baby.*

Supporting the Breasts

It is probably easier to support the breast when offering it to the baby either by putting the hand flat against your own ribcage underneath the breast or by cupping your breast in your hand, making certain that the fingers are not near the areola or nipple. This will lift the breast to make it easier to offer to the baby and for the baby to take. Don't press the breast because this may sometimes cause blockage in the channels along which the milk runs.

Coming off the Breast

The important thing is not to suddenly drag the baby off the breast as it might hurt and will make the nipple rather sore. It's often helpful to wait until the baby has stopped to take a breath, or put your little finger in the corner of the baby's mouth, breaking the suction, and then remove the breast.

Caring for the Breasts

Breasts need to be bathed every day with water, not necessarily with soap. They should never be rubbed dry but always patted, and good support is also helpful. After feeding, the nipples should be left open to the air for a little time and pads inside the bra may soak up any milk that may leak. The wet pad should not be left in contact with the breasts for any length of time as this may cause cracked nipples.

Burping

On breast or bottle, babies tend to swallow air while feeding and a large enough air bubble in the stomach will cause discomfort. To relieve this the baby often has to bring up the bubble: sometimes it comes up by itself if the baby is sat up on the lap facing forwards and the back is gently rubbed, or the baby can be supported face down on the shoulder. Success in either position is usually signalled by a belch which can be startlingly loud.

Most mothers like to burp their babies after a feed but if nothing happens in five minutes it does no harm at all to put them down again unless they feel uncomfortable. Some babies burp and others don't. There is no need to sit for hours waiting for the burp to come up if the baby is quite comfortable.

Spitting up Milk

Some babies spit up small quantities of milk while burping. There is no special significance in this and a little milk will always come up with the burp. Spitting up may occur at a pause in the feeding or at almost any time after feeding: even as long as half an hour afterwards. Milk on the crib bedding near the baby's face can be found by chance. Spitting up never bothers babies and they often sleep through it. If it occurs while the baby is being held, then gently turn the baby face down to let the regurgitated milk run out of the mouth.

If the baby does spit up, it is rarely more than a teaspoonful but, if it seems that the amount coming back is consistently greater than this over several feeds and if the baby still seems hungry, it is as well to let your doctor know.

Hiccuping

Hiccuping often follows feeding, especially in very young infants. This isn't abnormal and nothing needs to be done about it. Sometimes burping may stop it, but many babies actually hiccup on their way to sleep.

Common Breast-feeding Problems

Engorgement of Breasts

This term really means heavy and hard breasts and it often occurs on the third and fourth day following delivery. This can be quite painful and if the breasts become too swollen the baby may find it difficult to feed, grabbing at the nipple and making it sore. It may be helpful to bathe the breasts in warm water before feeds and to gently stroke the breasts towards the nipples for a few moments. Expressing milk in a basin of warm water may help (see pages 360–361). Usually with perseverance the engorgement gradually settles.

Blocked Ducts

The ducts are the tubes along which the milk flows from the sacs of the breasts to the outside. If the milk blocks these ducts, then obviously the breasts may not be drained sufficiently, and you may experience tender, lumpy areas in the breasts which feel painful and bruised. Again, applying a warm compress at the start of the feed may help, feeding the baby from the affected side first, or perhaps expressing the milk first if the baby isn't keen to suck.

Blocked ducts usually settle by themselves but occasionally they may lead to mastitis (see page 360).

Cracked Nipples

Occasionally a crack can develop in the skin of a sore nipple causing quite a sudden sharp piercing pain in the nipple. If the pain is extreme, the breast may have to be rested for a feed or two, feeding the baby from the other breast and usually expressing the milk from the painful one. After a feed it is important to allow the nipples to dry thoroughly and then apply a little cream sparingly. Again, before feeding, dusting cornflour on the nipples using a piece of cottonwool often helps seal the cracks and protects them when the baby starts to feed.

It may be better not to use a bra, but to wear loose-fitting tops so that the breasts can breathe and the skin is exposed to the air as much as possible. The final point is to make sure the baby latches onto the nipple properly. Cracked nipples usually heal themselves.

Mastitis

The word 'mastitis' means an infection of the breast and it can be of two types. One is a localised infection, or abscess, and the other is a more general infection of the breasts. Both are part of the same process which is caused by a little organism which may be picked up. Both problems tend to occur more frequently when the breasts are overfull. One or both breasts may become inflamed and red and you may feel feverish. Your midwife, health visitor or doctor ought to have a look at the breasts and will probably advise you to stop breast-feeding temporarily and express the milk until the infection has cleared up. There is no problem at all resuming breast-feeding. Your doctor may take a swab from the breasts and treat you with antibiotics.

Very occasionally an abscess occurs that is a localised swelling which is red, hot and tender and forms itself into a single lump. It may be necessary to make a little nick in the skin and let out some of the old milk which may have become infected. Often this can be done very simply with a little local freezing injection, but occasionally if the abscess is large and deep it may require general anaesthesia and a day or two in hospital.

Expressing the Breasts

There are a number of reasons why expression might be necessary, including storage of milk if the baby is too ill to be able to suck; if the baby is being nursed in a special care situation; if you will not be around at the time that the next breast-feed is called for; and even at night. There are also a number of ways of expressing:

Hand Expression

Following a feed, the breasts should be stroked with the flat of the hand, beginning at the ribs and working towards the nipple, gradually going over the whole breast. This encourages the milk to flow down the little tubes or ducts. This can be done either by breast-feeding the baby first and expressing the second breast immediately afterwards, or with the help of a warm flannel or warm hot-water bottle applied to the breast.

Breast Pumps

There are a number of manual and electric pumps which can be applied to the breasts to help expression. These should only be used on your doctor's or midwife's advice as, more often than not, expressing can be quite satisfactorily done with the hand.

Special Situations and Breast-feeding

Caesarean Section

There is no reason whatsoever why Caesarean section should prevent breast-feeding. Moreover, as most Caesareans are done under epidural rather than full anaesthetic, breast-feeding can be established very soon after the baby is born. If an anaesthetic is given, this will not in any way influence the amount of breast milk, and breast-feeding can be attempted in the normal way.

Drugs

Many women worry about the effect on breast milk of certain drugs they may be taking or that may have been administered during labour. There are in fact very few drugs that affect breast milk and very few contra-indications to breast-feeding. If you are taking drugs for any particular disorder such as diabetes or epilepsy or high blood pressure, then discuss the question of breast-feeding with your doctor before you go into labour.

Twin Pregnancy

The thought of actually having to feed more than one baby may fill women with horror and some may even have been told they will be unable to produce enough milk for two. In fact most mothers find it perfectly feasible to breast-feed twins, or even triplets, as the body will produce enough nourishment for the babies. It is also quite important that breast-feeding of twins or triplets is encouraged as the antibodies in breast milk will be particularly valuable if the babies are very small and therefore more vulnerable to illness.

It may be more difficult just to get breast-feeding going with two or three babies if they are particularly small and if the second baby is crying while you are feeding the first. If you feed them simultaneously, you just don't have enough hands, and if the babies are very different sizes this may create different feeding patterns. You must find out the right way of feeding with medical help: perhaps feeding the babies separately, attending first to the one who wakes first and then waking the second baby once the first has finished.

There is nothing wrong with feeding the twins at the same time, though it is important that you make yourself comfortable. One baby of course may be a far stronger sucker than the other and may tend to grow more quickly. The smaller baby may need shorter and more frequent feeds initially, but this usually levels off after a couple of months.

Medical Conditions

Occasionally the mother's or baby's health might be affected by certain conditions that preclude breast-feeding, such as severe heart disease, which may pose too much of a strain on the mother's health, but this is most unusual.

In general, breast-feeding may confidently be undertaken in the presence of a number of medical conditions providing this is discussed first with your doctor. There are very few reasons why breast-feeding is completely contra-indicated.

Artificial or Bottle-feeding

If you have decided to bottle-feed, or change from breast to bottle, there are several items that need to be looked at:

- Choosing a formula;
- Equipment and supplies;
- Sterilising;
- Preparing the formula; and
- The management of the breasts if milk persists.

Choosing a Formula

Cows' milk differs from human milk in having a higher concentration of protein and salts. The kinds of protein and salts are somewhat different as well. The calorie content, in other words the number of calories per ounce, is about the same. If the newborn were given undiluted cows' milk, the higher concentration of these salts and protein would put a heavier load on the kidneys than they would get from normal milk. In order to prepare the correct formula, the cows' milk is modified so that the concentration of protein and salts in early infancy is reduced.

Bottle-feeding usually means using modified cows' milk, although special soya products are occasionally prescribed if a baby is allergic to cows' milk. In fact soya milk formula is at the moment the first choice of many mothers.

If you begin to bottle-feed in hospital, the hospital may have its own specially prepared small bottles of formula that are not necessarily available in shops, but if this popular brand seems to suit your baby then the formula powder can be bought to be made up at home. Your health visitor, doctor or paediatrician will be able to advise you.

Not all brands of formula suit all babies and it is quite common to try out a few before you find the one your baby thrives on.

Equipment and Supplies

You will need teats, bottles and sterilising equipment. There are many different types of teats, some designed specifically to be as close as possible in shape and texture to the feed at the breast, but the simple rule is to use a teat that when the bottle is inverted allows a steady stream of droplets to emerge. If the hole is too small, there will be too few droplets and the baby will have to struggle to feed. If the hole is too large the milk will flow too quickly and the baby will be uncomfortable.

The bottles themselves can be glass or plastic. Glass is easier to see through to check that the bottles have been cleaned properly but they are heavier and can break and for this reason plastic ones are often preferable. Whichever the type, it is important that they come with caps that will allow the teats to be inverted and covered for storage.

Sterilising

Everything you use should be sterilised very thoroughly, either by sterilising tablets in cold water, in which case a large plastic container with a lid is necessary, or by boiling water, when a large saucepan with a lid is used. Whichever way, everything will need to be washed carefully first. After washing the bottles and teats in hot soapy water with a bottle brush, rinse everything in cold water before sterilising. If you decide to use the chemical means of sterilisation, then full instructions will be on the packet and bottle. If using the boiling water method, everything needs to be submerged in boiling water for ten minutes, then left in the saucepan until ready for use. It is probably sensible to sterilise all equipment until the baby is about six months old.

You can either make up each feed just before your baby needs it or several bottles can be prepared and stored in the fridge. Any bottles left over at the end of the day should be thrown away, as should any amounts left in a bottle after a feed.

Some babies quite enjoy cold formula straight from a fridge but the normal process is to heat it up in a bottle warmer first, or in a bowl of hot water, and check the temperature by shaking a few drops of formula onto the back of the wrist. It should neither feel too hot nor too cold.

Preparing the Formula

Babies up to five months old require about 120 calories a day for each kilogram they weigh, or 55 calories per pound. This usually means about 200gms of made up formula per kilogram. The number of bottles given to the baby can vary: an average is about six bottles of 100gms (4oz) a day, but different babies have different requirements and it doesn't matter if the baby is offered larger or smaller amounts. Bottle-fed babies often like water between feeds and may well become rather thirsty especially in hot weather.

Management of the Breasts if Milk Persists

If you have decided not to breast-feed or if for some reason breast-feeding becomes unsatisfactory and there is a need to change to the bottle, nature will automatically switch off the hormonal mechanisms for the production of milk in the breasts but this may take a few days. Often no specific treatment is needed and a well-fitting bra will support the breasts if they become uncomfortable.

Milk production can be satisfactorily stopped by a drug called Parlodel (Bromocriptine) in a dose of 2.5mgs three times a day. This is quite safe to use, has no real side effects in the dose prescribed and usually milk production will have diminished and disappeared in five days.

If you have decided that you do not wish to breast-feed immediately the baby is born, then you should discuss the question of suppression of milk with your midwife or doctor.

Breast and Bottle

Many mothers who decide to bottle-feed don't realise that it is perfectly feasible to breast-feed as well, as long as the baby thrives on a combination. As long as the baby sucks the breast regularly, even if it is only once a day, say in the evening, milk will continue to be produced in a quantity that corresponds to the amount of sucking.

After feeding, especially in early infancy, the baby is likely to fall asleep. Many young infants will pass a stool while feeding and you can hear and feel the intestines rumbling. It is quite a good idea to change a wet or soiled nappy before putting the baby down.

Finally, one of the best things about bottle-feeding is that the new father can be involved right from the beginning with feeding and feeding time activities. It is a good idea for the father to feed the baby for the first time within the first twenty-four hours so that he can take the plunge and gain confidence.

Weaning

There is no set limit to the time nursing should continue: it depends on how much the nursing couple enjoy it. If nursing has gone well, with abundant milk and with evidence of special feeling between mother and baby, there is no harm in continuing to nurse for many months, or even up to a year. When the time comes to stop it is as well to do it gradually so that the breasts don't become uncomfortable, dropping one or two feeds per day is a good rule of thumb to follow.

Vitamins

Vitamins are organic chemicals contained in minute amounts in the foods we eat and needed by our bodies to remain healthy. Deficiencies of certain vitamins are associated with specific disorders. Most people are aware that every child from birth onwards requires vitamins in their diet but not everyone realises that in the consumption of vitamins it is possible to overdo a good thing.

The vitamins to consider are A, B, C and D. The B vitamins are usually well represented in the foods given to babies, including human and cows' milk, and they are therefore only mentioned in passing. A child's diet, however, may be short on vitamins A, C

Vitamin A
Found in milk, butter, cheese, egg yolks, carrots, squashes, sweet potatoes, animal fats and fish liver. Human milk contains vitamin A, usually in adequate quantities; cows' milk varies with the season, depending on the available forage, but in general contains adequate amounts for infants.

Vitamin A is important to vision and a deficiency can cause night blindness and other disorders of the eye. It is also, as is Vitamin D, essential to the growth of bones.

Vitamin C
Found in almost all fruits and vegetables, especially citrus fruits, tomatoes, berries and leafy green vegetables. Cows' milk is an unreliable source of vitamin C and supplementation is required. Human milk contains adequate amounts if the mother receives 60mg daily in her diet.

Vitamin D
Found in fish oils and eggs. It is manufactured by chemicals in human and animal skin under the action of sunlight. This vitamin is passed poorly into human or cows' milk and therefore the general principle in the UK is to add it both to cows' milk and commercially prepared milk.

and D and parents should have a little information on these.

A baby's daily needs of vitamins are 1500mgs of vitamin A, 30–60mgs of vitamin C and 400mgs of vitamin D. How the infant receives these makes little difference. If the diet contains all of them, there is no need to give supplements but, if the diet is inadequate, supplements of the deficient vitamins only are needed. By the time a child is on the full range of solid foods and juices and consumes vitamin D-fortified whole milk – usually no later than one year – they should receive all the necessary vitamins from their diet and supplements are uncalled for. In summary:

- Breast-fed infants whose mothers consume adequate amounts of vitamin C per day need a vitamin D supplement of 400mgs per day until this is supplied by fortified milk.

- Bottle-fed infants taking vitamin D fortified or homogenised milk need 30–60mgs per day of vitamin C until their diet supplies adequate amounts, i.e. 50gms (2oz) of fresh, frozen or bottled orange juice.

- Bottle-fed infants on commercial formulas, i.e. SMA, etc. containing adequate vitamins, need no supplements.

Beginning Solids

There is a modern trend to introduce solids at earlier and earlier ages until many babies now begin within one or two weeks of birth. There is no really compelling justification for this but no doubt manufacturers of baby foods who stand to profit by extended use play a part in this trend. Also, there is some competitiveness between mothers. It is true that some minerals that are contained in solids are important, one of which is iron, as human breast milk and the usual formulas are deficient in iron. Iron should really be in the diet no later than the three-month mark and is found in fortified cereals, meat and eggs, which were traditionally advocated on these grounds.

Another factor entering into the decision to begin solids, whether or not with the spoon, is the contention that milk alone doesn't satisfy. Parents often give solids in the hope that feeds will be stretched out and sleeping through the night will occur earlier, but it has to be said that there is no connection between the age of introduction of solid foods and the daily number of feedings or the age of consistently sleeping through. Most experts seem to say that if a baby seems hungry, giving the baby more milk is just as effective as giving solids.

If solids are started, one routine which is quite satisfactory is to offer a little cereal at the 10 a.m. and 6 p.m. feeds at somewhere between two and a half and three months, perhaps starting with a few small spoons of rice cereal diluted with formula or, if breast-feeding, with ordinary whole milk. Gradually the mix can be strengthened and the volume increased and, if the baby continues to take it well, then oatmeal or barley can be introduced and at two- to four-week intervals fruits, vegetables and meat in that order. It is usually a good idea to introduce new foods one at a time, separating them by at least two or three days.

One philosophy is in general to encourage parents to go slowly and keep things simple during the first few months. A number of quite normal events such as colic or heat rash are likely to be a little disturbing to the new mother and, if you proceed slowly, you will be less inclined mistakenly to attribute these minor problems to new foods as opposed to things that occur naturally to most babies.

Feeding Programme

It would be a great mistake to regard any schedule for introducing new foods as ideal or sacrosant. Every mother knows her baby best. Developing a menu or a programme that is convenient and logical, however, is quite sensible and the following is a suggested routine:

Two-and-a-half to Three-and-a-half Months (or Earlier)

Give the baby a milk feed at four-hourly intervals. You will find that the 2 a.m. feed can usually be discontinued between four to eight weeks of age. Juice between feeds can be given and rice cereal may be offered before the 10 a.m. and 6 p.m. bottle.

The average baby gradually takes between one and three table-spoonfuls of a progressively thickened feeding, and eventually works up to at least ten tablespoonfuls per day.

About Three to Four Months

By now you may have experimented with barley and oatmeal cereal. Fruits are also often introduced about this time – you might try apple sauce or banana. If the baby tolerates these, all well and good but if the baby seems fussy or has loose stools, they can be discontinued temporarily.

If bottle-feeding, the milk will probably have been changed to whole milk, although of course evaporated milk or a commercial formula can be used indefinitely. Sterilising becomes unnecessary, merely using a clean bottle and nipple, taking the milk out of the fridge and warming the bottle and discarding whatever the baby does not drink.

Four to Five Months

Over the next few weeks it is usually possible gradually to reduce the milk intake of the baby to about four bottles per day: at about 7–8 a.m., 11 a.m. to noon; 4–6 p.m.; and a bedtime bottle. Each family of course will work out the best schedule for themselves. It is possible that the bedtime bottle is becoming less necessary, particularly if the baby has to be wakened. If the baby is hungry during the 2–4 a.m. period, then convenience would suggest waking the baby between 10 and 11 p.m.

For breast-feeding mothers who want to delay solids until after five months there are no particular objections. However, a source of iron should be included by about three months in the form of iron drops or fortified cereal.

The Newborn Baby

Newborn babies don't always look like those in advertisements. In fact they often look quite strange for the first few hours of life, although within a few days their appearance changes dramatically.

'How is my baby?' This is always the new parents' first question and for the majority of babies the answer is an unqualified 'fine', but how does the doctor arrive at this judgement so early, what does the doctor look for, and how can we tell that the baby really is in normal good health?

The medical assessment of a newborn is usually done by the paediatrician, a doctor who has specialised in looking after children, particularly newborn babies. It has to be said that doctors and midwives are also trained to take care of newborn babies but the paediatrician has made this their speciality. In some hospitals the obstetric doctors examine the babies and in others the paediatric doctors in training. The senior paediatrician (see page 100) is usually brought in if an abnormality is found or if a decision needs to be made.

Features of Newborn Babies and how they Function

The Head

After birth the baby's head is not perfectly rounded because it is more flexible than an adult's and is capable of changing its shape or 'moulding' as it travels down the birth canal. Because the bones of the baby's skull are not tightly knit together as they are in adults, the head can adapt without injury to the squeezing of the birth process. The separation of the bone, or sutures, can be felt by running the finger over the head and a distinct impression of a small groove separating one bone from the other can be easily felt.

In the middle of the head towards the front is one major 'soft spot' known as the fontanelle. The covering is very tough and you can press on it without fear of damage. As the baby grows older the bone structure comes together to cover the space completely. For most infants the closure is accomplished somewhere between six months and one and a half years. In the quiet baby, particularly when it is held in a sitting position, the soft spot appears slightly depressed. When a baby cries the soft spot tends to tense up and if you look carefully you can see the fontanelle pulsate in rhythm with the pulse. This is all quite normal.

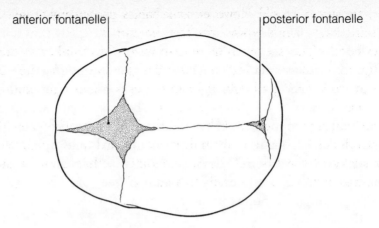

anterior fontanelle

posterior fontanelle

Side view of baby's head showing suture lines and fontanelles.

There is also another soft spot towards the back of the head called the posterior fontanelle. This is a much smaller one, closes rapidly after the birth and in many infants is barely detectable. It is not unusual for the baby's head to be slightly pointed. Occasionally the pressure exerted during birth will cause the skin to swell, forming what is called a caput. If the pressure is more extensive, then the underlying tissue can bruise and this is what we call a cephal-haematoma which occurs on one side of the skull. This is a localised collection of blood that forms at the time of birth between the skull and the scalp and is quite harmless. The blood often lingers for a couple of months before disappearing but does always go away. As it does so, the swelling may harden or calcify, producing a bony lump which stands out prominently against the natural contour of the skull, but in three to four months this has also gone.

The Eyes

The eyes of the newborn are fully formed at birth. The colour of the eyes, more specifically of the iris, is always blue due to the absence of melanin, the body's natural pigment, in the iris. If your child is destined to have any eye colour other than blue, melanin will be produced as the baby grows and the permanent eye colour will be fixed by the time the baby is three months' old. However, some babies, particularly those with dark skins, have slightly brown eyes from the start.

Newborn infants see much more than we used to think. An infant can fix on a red or soft yellow object dangled before the eyes and follow it, and shining a bright light in the eyes causes tight shutting of the lids.

One final point: when the baby cries there are no tears because the tear glands don't function at birth. It is not unusual for the eyes to get a bit sticky in the first few days, sometimes with a crust or mild inflammation which can be easily treated.

The Skin

At birth the skin is covered with a greasy coating known as vernix. Most of this comes off in the first bath given to the baby in the delivery room or nursery, but occasionally bits of vernix remain behind the ears and in the folds of the buttocks. The skin of the normal newborn is coated with long hair, known as lanugo, which characteristically disappears over the first few weeks. If some interference with the normal way the placenta works has occurred, the baby may be slightly undernourished and show some of the hallmarks of placental insufficiency. In other words there might be less body fat, the lanugo may not be there, and the skin may be much more cracked.

Forceps deliveries may leave marks on the skin of the face and head, but these fade within a few days. Small faint red spots or blotches are often seen on the upper eyelids, at the nape of the neck, or over the bridge of the nose and the forehead. Clusters of little blood vessels present in the newborn period and early infancy account for these markings. Why they occur is a bit of a mystery. In the old days marks at the bottom of the neck were often called stork bites.

The common strawberry birthmark (see pages 384–385) is often not present in the newborn and doesn't show up until after the baby is at home. Sometimes in hospital one can detect small bright red spots on the baby's skin that we can predict will blossom into a strawberry birthmark.

A very common rash seen after the first day or two and for the next few weeks is called erythematoxicum. The characteristic spot of this rash is a red blotch with a small white raised centre. It usually appears more on the face, neck and trunk than on the arms and legs and may come and go right before your eyes. The condition is transient and harmless but can cause anxiety if not understood. It somewhat resembles heat rash or prickly heat. Prickly heat is caused by trapped sweat that accumulates deep in the skin and sets up an inflammation. Heat rash can afflict all ages but is more common in babies. It manifests itself in small, pinpoint red blotches with slightly raised white centres which usually come and go very quickly, present in the morning and gone by noon. It is one of the conditions best left alone as powders and cream on the affected skin usually only aggravate the plugging of the sweat glands.

Genital Organs

The genitals of both sexes are normally disproportionately large. The vagina of a baby girl may appear a little red or inflamed and there may even be some discharge or a few drops of blood. This is usually a response to maternal hormones. In boys the penis and foreskin may be partly fused at birth and it is not always possible to retract the foreskin. However there is no need for any special cleaning of the penis in a young baby and no need to pull back the foreskin.

Perhaps this is a good time to discuss circumcision. A question which parents have to settle is whether or not to have a baby boy circumcised, as it is often customary to perform this simple operation on the second or third day while the mother is still in hospital.

Circumcision

This is a small surgical procedure consisting of removal of the foreskin from the penis, and there are religious indications for the operation as well as social ones. The Jews circumcise their boys on the eighth day of life to fulfil Abraham's Covenant with God; the Muslims perform circumcision at puberty as a symbol of reaching manhood; and aboriginal tribes in the Australian desert circumcise their boys partly ceremonially as an initiation to manhood and partly for hygiene as the desert sand can irritate the foreskin.

Male circumcision has a long religious tradition but in modern times it has become a routine procedure, largely because it is the custom. It is said that mothers demand it, doctors profit by it and babies cannot complain about it! Apart from religious indications, however, there can be certain advantages in circumcision.

It is true that the penis may be somewhat cleaner, and it may prevent phimosis, a condition in which the foreskin adheres to the penis and cannot be retracted. It is said that the smegma or secretion in the inner lining of the foreskin makes a good culture medium for infection and this in turn predisposes uncircumcised men to infections of the urinary tract. Uncircumcised males are somewhat more likely to develop cancer of the penis, although this condition is pretty rare. Previous claims of higher incidence of cancer of the cervix among wives of uncircumcised men have not been proven. In general, paediatricians tend not to be in favour of circumcision because they rightly regard the baby as their patient and are reluctant to inflict any invasive procedure on him.

Sometimes paediatricians perform the operation and sometimes the obstetricians. The actual procedure is simple enough: the foreskin, or skin covering the mushroom-shaped tip of the penis, is removed by applying a specially designed clamp. In ritual circumcision no anaesthesia is used, the foreskin being cut and the penis being wrapped in tight dressing to prevent bleeding and the dressing changed every twenty-four hours. The modern technique involves inserting a plastic shell and ring around the foreskin which, deprived of blood, drops off in a day or two.

If circumcision is requested for social rather than religious reasons, discuss this carefully between yourselves, and your doctor should be able to advise you on the pros and cons.

The Umbilical Cord

Within a few minutes of birth the cord stops pulsating, becomes limp and white, and is usually clamped or tied and then cut. The clamp will be left in place for forty-eight hours before it is removed. The cord stump then dries and shrivels and the action of the skin bacteria softens the tissue at the base so that within three to seven days it usually drops off. The stump should be kept clean by washing it twice a day with warm water.

Reflexes

The newborn is endowed with certain co-ordinated patterns of behaviour, known as reflexes, which operate from circuits within the lower centres of the brain. Appropriate stimulation will automatically elicit these reflex responses, for instance the baby's automatic response to bright light and loud noise. If the cheek of a newborn is stroked, the baby will turn the mouth towards the stroking object, be it a finger or, as Nature intended, the nipple of the mother's breast. This reflex is known as the rooting response. It is completely automatic and serves to zero the baby in on the source of nutrition before the baby knows where the food comes from. Sucking occurs by reflex if something touches the lips, the inside lining of the mouth, or the soft palate.

There are other quite well-known reflexes that the baby exhibits. If the newborn baby is startled by a shout or sudden noise or change of position, the arms and legs move in a characteristic way. First of all they go outwards, then upwards and then inwards. The hands open and then clench tightly into a fist as though the baby was trying to grasp a branch of a tree to prevent falling, and the legs go through a similar sequence of movements. In addition, the baby's head bends down and forward. This reflex is known as the 'scare response', or Moro reflex, after the neurologist who first wrote about it.

Another reflex is the grasp reflex. If pressure is applied by a finger to the palm of the baby's hands or to the balls of the feet, the fingers and toes will curl in as though trying to grasp the pressing object. This hand grasp is often so strong that the infant can be lifted off the crib. If the soles of the feet are stroked, the foot will pull up and the toes fan out and the large toe elevate. This is called the Babinski reflex, again after the doctor who first described it.

In addition to these reflexes, most of which will disappear within three months as the child grows and increasingly develops voluntary movements, there are others which remain to perform vital functions needed for survival. The breathing reflex is fully functional seconds after birth, the child will blink or close eyes if the light is too bright, will react to smells and withdraw from painful sensations. The newborn also has an instinctive hunger reflex and a need to expel urine and to defecate, all of which become increasingly voluntary with time.

Breathing

The noisy breathing of small babies frequently alarms parents. Infants' respiration in sleep may be loud enough to awaken a person in the same room. Parents frightened by these noises overlook the fact that the nasal passages of a small baby are very narrow and a tiny speck of dust can trigger a sneeze. Babies breathe about twice as rapidly as adults because of their relatively small lungs. They also breathe rather shallowly, particularly when they lie on their stomachs, and they may seem to be hardly breathing at all.

There are also a number of snuffly noises which babies make. Hiccups are actually quite common and they are caused by sudden contractions of the diaphragm muscle.

Bowel and Urine Functions

The first stool a baby passes is called meconium which is collected in the rectum while the baby is in the uterus. Meconium is a sticky, tarry substance and you may need quite a lot of soap and water and patience to clean it off the baby. As the meconium is passed the baby's stools change to green, brown and then after a few days to a rather yellow, curdy and loose-looking motion. The stools are bright yellow if breast-fed and usually darker and more solid if bottle-fed. Babies normally begin life by passing several bowel motions a day for the first few weeks but this gradually changes.

Once urine flow is established after birth, sometimes up to thirty-six hours later, babies urinate very frequently. Occasionally the first urine may be a reddish colour resembling blood. This is usually caused by the presence of urate crystals and is harmless but it is a good idea to keep the nappy to show the midwife or a nurse.

All babies commonly urinate or empty their bowels while feeding and this is perfectly normal and healthy behaviour.

Routine Tests on the Baby

The Guthrie Test

This is a test carried out on every baby on the eighth or tenth day and involves taking a tiny drop of blood from the baby's heel which is then tested to find out if a condition known as phenylketonuria is present. This is a rare condition to do with a disorder of metabolism which can cause severe mental retardation, but can be controlled by a special diet if diagnosed early.

Hypoglycaemia

Your baby may be tested to determine the blood sugar level but this is usually reserved for babies who have some sort of a problem, such as being rather small for the dates when born, possibly due to some inefficiency of the placenta. These babies when breast-fed benefit from colostrum, but they often need to be given complementary bottle feeds of formula milk until the breast milk comes in. It is therefore useful to know the baby's blood sugar level.

Blood Group

In certain cases when the mother is Rhesus negative and the father is Rhesus positive (see page 237), it is important to ascertain the baby's blood group. The blood is usually collected from a vein in the umbilical cord at delivery, or from a simple prick in the heel of the newborn baby.

Bilirubin

Some babies develop jaundice in the first few days of life which may be quite normal, or may have other causes (see pages 399–401). Serial blood tests on the baby may be necessary to monitor the level of this jaundice.

Is my Baby Sick?

Before discussing some of the diseases and disorders of the newborn, one question often asked by parents is how can they know whether their baby is all right or ill. Babies don't talk; they can't tell you if their stomachs hurt or if they don't feel well. This is particularly worrying for the young parents in the first few weeks of their new experience at home. Help and support from family and friends and professionals is obviously of considerable use, but the following explanations of the baby's behaviour may be helpful.

Poor Feeding

Over the first four to six weeks of life most bottle-fed infants will take somewhere between two and four ounces at a time, increasing the intake as they grow. When a marked change in your baby's appetite occurs, you should take some notice. The significance is not so much in the number of ounces at any one feed but a change from, say, three to four ounces every four hours to only one ounce or one and a half ounces on a regular or irregular schedule. Though this change may merely reflect a transient decrease in appetite, it does call for an explanation and it might just be worth a phone call to your doctor.

Not only is change in volume important, but there is also the vigour of feeding, especially if you are breast-feeding and cannot be sure of the baby's intake. One clue would be continued fullness of the breasts after feeding and, if you observe that the baby has become poky all of a sudden and if you have to force the baby to eat, or if the baby spits up half of what has just been swallowed, or takes an inordinate length of time to feed, these just might be mentioned to your doctor or health visitor.

Lethargy or Listlessness

The usefulness of the infant's general vigour as a clue to well-being will of course depend on the baby's temperament. As we have seen, some babies from the start seem very active while others appear quite passive. Here again it is a change in behaviour that is important. If your previously active infant with a loud or piercing cry suddenly or gradually seems less eager to move or thrash about, or if the cry sounds weak, or if you have to prod the baby to stimulate any response, take note. You may only be intruding upon the quiet time or the baby may only be settling down to sleep, but you will have to go through a number of these occasions before you are entirely comfortable that there is nothing amiss.

Irritability

There is another clue, however, that parents can look for. Sickness doesn't always manifest itself in decreased activity. Sometimes a sick baby may become overactive or irritable and this is rather like a change in personality. The baby starts to scream and arch the back, may reject a feed almost as if being jabbed with something sharp, and you may look at this colicky baby with consternation and think that the baby is ill. It will take time, experience and help from midwives, health visitors and doctors before mothers can recognise how the irritability of colic differs from genuine sickness.

If the baby is not well, the irritability tends to be persistent and the cry is different. It may take the mother of a colicky baby several telephone calls or visits to the doctor before she understands the significance of this change in behaviour.

Spitting up and Vomiting

As we have previously seen, spitting up is worrying but very common in the first few months. The infant may drink four ounces with vigour and then a few minutes or even hours later bring up what seems to be an equally large amount. What distinguishes this regurgitation from the vomiting of a baby who is sick or who has some other problem? As a first step the parents might ask themselves the following four questions:

- Is the baby sucking and feeding with vigour?

- Does the baby take in a good volume of fluid and only really spit out the last ounce?

- Does the baby vomit at every feed or just once or twice a day?

- How is the baby functioning otherwise? Is the baby alert, moving about, with normal bowel movements, etc., or does the baby look pale, lethargic and excessively irritable?

With factual answers to these questions, the parent is in a good position to decide whether they need a doctor's advice, and also this will be quite useful information for the doctor.

Bowel Movements

If bowel movements change suddenly, either in colour or consistency, i.e. becoming very watery and explosive, this may be significant of some bowel infection. Some babies, breast- and bottle-fed, may have seven or eight loose stools a day but, as long as the movements remain yellow in colour and don't have much water content, then the frequency doesn't really matter very much. At the other extreme, many infants only have one bowel movement every other day and some perfectly normal babies can skip two or three days between movements.

It is worth adding that the same illness that affects an older child or an adult with a cold may produce diarrhoea in the infant. Again, irritability and diarrhoea may be the only manifestation of earache or sore throat in an infant, because the intestinal tract represents the main pathway for a variety of stresses, infection or otherwise.

Diarrhoea is relatively common in infancy but usually it doesn't matter very much and responds to normal dietary management. However, excessive diarrhoea can lead to dehydration and, because of the baby's smaller reserve of fluids, dehydration occurs much more quickly. If there is constant diarrhoea, call your doctor.

The following tips might be helpful to differentiate a normal from an abnormal situation. Illness is more likely if:

- Unexplained vomiting occurs – persistent and projectile.

- The stomach keeps distending. There is failure to gain weight. The baby becomes pale, weak, listless and irritable.

- There is excessive difficulty in passing a stool, or excessive diarrhoea.

Pallor

Parents should not really wait for or rely on a dramatic change in the infant's colour to alert them to deterioration in health. Instead of being only an early warning, a significant degree of paleness, or duskiness, could be a sign of disease and, if there is a marked change in the colour of the skin, your doctor should be notified.

Sneezing and Coughing

Sneezing is very common in well babies. Tiny particles of dust or lint can bring it on in a reflex action and it happens all the time.

A cough, however, is something else. A cough too can be a minor occurrence, no more than a clearing of a little drip of fluid from the back of the throat, but a cough, especially if it persists and is associated with other signs of ill-health, like a discharge from the nose or high fever and so forth, can mean some infection. Parents may find it reassuring to know that coughing to a certain extent serves a defensive purpose and keeps the mucus out of the baby's chest. Your doctor will probably want to know how often the baby coughs, whether the coughing keeps the baby from sleeping or interferes with feeding, whether you have noticed any increase in the baby's rate of breathing, whether the baby seems lethargic or irritable, warm, feverish, and so on. These questions will all help to tell the doctor whether the cough is significant or not.

Fever

An elevated temperature can signify the presence of infection but in infants it is again unreliable: a new baby could be quite ill without fever. In short, any fever in a young infant probably warrants a discussion with your doctor, although it may not be indicative of a serious problem. On the other hand, if a new baby seems ill in other respects, the absence of fever should not be reassuring.

Normal temperature, taken by mouth in older children and adults, is 98.6 degrees Fahrenheit. Rectal temperature is normally 99.6. There is a common misconception that temperatures below normal are dangerous. Except for the patient actually at death's door, this is not so and a temperature of 97 or 97.6 is quite consistent with good health. Too often a child's high fever frightens parents needlessly. It really makes little difference whether a child shows 103 or 104 degrees: children quite commonly run quite high temperatures with minor infections.

We have to differentiate here, however, between early infancy and the whole of childhood. The early infant's fever has more significance because they have so few means of communicating that something is wrong. In later childhood, however, parents have more cause to be anxious about the child whose temperature is only 101 degrees, but who shows excessive irritability or lethargy with marked general discomfort or localised pain, rather than about the child with a temperature of 104 degrees who is happily colouring pictures in a book and voicing no complaint.

The Chronic Problem

It would be consoling if we could be sure that problems like spitting up, coughing and diarrhoea would disappear within a few days. Such symptoms, even of brief duration, are worrying in infancy. What happens when they persist week after week? Well, it goes without saying that that is the time to discuss things with your doctor or health visitor. Nevertheless the average mother does find it hard to accept that her infant is not seriously ill when loose stools continue to appear day after day, or when the nose keeps right on running despite the doctor's apparently thorough examination and confident prescription.

Two points can be made regarding persistence of problems of this kind. Infants like older people take time to improve after contending with seemingly minor problems. Just as a parent will feel run-down after a cold, so a baby may take a week to return to normal good health. More importantly, perhaps, as long as a baby is sucking and feeding well, appears alert, smiles, coos and in particular gains weight, we can endure the chronic problems in expectation that ultimately all will go well. While a healthy baby may sometimes gain weight at a slow rate, and even a sick baby may show some gain, it is very unusual that a sick baby will gain weight regularly.

Diseases and Disorders of the Newborn

There are a huge number of abnormalities that exist in the newborn, some congenital and some acquired, and then there are mild abnormalities, moderate and severe ones. It would be beyond the scope of this book to cover all the diseases and disorders, but some of the more common ones that occur in the newborn will now be outlined in alphabetical order.

Airway Obstruction (Difficulty with Breathing)

Noisy breathing, known as stridor, is not an uncommon symptom in young infants. It is usually caused by resistance to the passage of air, which sets up vibrations resulting in noise, and occasionally this can obstruct breathing. There are a number of minor causes of these complaints, as well as more serious ones like croup. Severe stridor can be recognised shortly after birth or, in milder forms, may go undetected until the baby has been taken home from hospital. The principle here is to inform your doctor straight away if it seems as if the noise and obstruction are causing breathing problems, as the cause will have to be found.

Birthmarks

Many babies are born with birthmarks. The cause of haemangioma, which is the medical name for this sort of appearance, is not known. Essentially there is a cluster or growth of small blood vessels on or under the skin. They are not cancerous and usually no more than an inconvenience and they rarely require treatment. They tend to disappear on their own but the process may take many months, even years.

The most common birthmark is a salmon patch which is a cluster of small red spots on the nape of the neck, across the bridge of the nose, or on the upper eyelid – and these are the ones said to be left by 'the stork's beak'. They never require treatment and usually disappear over the first year.

Another common one is the strawberry mark which may occur in as many as ten per cent of all babies. Bright red, this mark looks as if a strawberry has been cut in half and stuck to the baby's skin. Often it appears on the face or neck: it can be tiny and often enlarges rapidly, getting quite big by about six months. At the age of three a third of all strawberry marks have disappeared; sixty per cent disappear by the age of four, and seventy per cent by the age of seven. The remainder can be removed, or may be treated with X-ray, but most paediatricians rather tend to wait and see. Occasionally a strawberry birthmark may extend deeper into the skin and form more of a lump, but again conservative treatment is advised.

The third common haemangioma is the port-wine stain. This is an area of skin that appears to be normal except for the red covering. The commonest variety is a patch shaped like a diamond on the forehead, extending to the bridge of the nose, and when the infant cries the diamond flushes. Even in adults the colouring of the patch gives a clue to the emotions. The port-wine stain, which can occur elsewhere on the head or body, is usually prominent in blondes. There is no treatment for it and it usually fades in time.

Cleft Palate and Harelip

These are two often related birth defects which appear frequently enough for most people to have seen them or know of them. Harelip is almost always a defect of the upper lip, varying from a small notch in the lip itself to a sizeable gap, extending from the edge of the lip to the nose. Cleft palate can vary from a small slit in the soft palate, which is at the back of the mouth at the opening to the throat, to a half-inch gap stretching from the soft palate across the roof of the mouth, the hard palate or the upper gums.

The gums may also be involved in these defects, and the teeth as well. There are rare cases of babies with chromosome abnormalities who have had both harelip and cleft palate in association with much more serious congenital defects.

The soft palate, which has a conical body known as the uvula projecting downwards in the back of the mouth, is composed mainly of muscle and moves when you talk or swallow. It acts as a valve, closing off alternately the upper and lower parts of the throat. The soft palate keeps air from entering the throat in the act of swallowing and food from entering the nose in the act of breathing. The sealing action of the soft palate makes it possible to whistle, gargle, blow up balloons and utter a number of sounds, including those for the letters 't', 'b', 'd', 'p', 'h', 'v' and 'f'. Obviously a cleft impairs or destroys the sealing action of the soft palate. There will be problems in feeding and later of speech. Children with cleft palates are more liable than others to middle ear infections and there is certainly an aesthetic problem that can be psychologically disturbing.

About a third of children with harelip or cleft palate will have one or more known relatives with the same defects. The hereditary influence seems stronger for harelip, but prediction on the evidence of a known family tree is not yet a precise art. On the other hand, we have no evidence to suggest that these defects arise from anything mothers may have done in pregnancy.

The treatment of harelip and cleft palate is surgical repair. It is customary to repair the lip in the first few weeks of life, but the palate is a more individual matter and is usually done when the child is one or two years old. The surgery may sometimes have to be done in several stages, the idea being to correct the defect early so that development of speech will be interfered with as little as possible. For the majority of these children the results of the programme of surgery are excellent, but speech therapy may have to be continued into the school years.

On a few occasions recently a diagnosis of harelip and cleft palate has been made by ultrasound in the antenatal period and attempts have been made to perform some sort of reconstructive surgery with the baby still in the womb. These procedures are obviously at a very early stage but it is an exciting development which may enable a diagnosis to be made sooner and appropriate treatment instituted.

Club-foot

In club-foot, which is a congenital deformity of unknown cause, the entire foot is bent downwards and twisted inwards and the foot is in a fixed position. The child cannot move the foot, nor can the doctor manipulate it, and this may affect one foot or both. The club-foot doesn't usually improve on its own and, left untreated, the deformity will seriously impair the child's walking.

A child with club-foot should be taken as early as possible to an orthopaedic specialist, as the earlier treatment can be started the better the prospects. Usually a series of plaster-casts is applied, beginning in infancy and extending over a period of months, and the foot is stretched into the normal position. Casting alone will not correct the most rigid forms of club-foot and surgery may be required.

Colic

According to reliable studies, a large percentage of small babies, some say as high as eighty per cent, cry from three to four hours every day for no obvious cause. In its most extreme form this regular crying every day is known as colic, and statistics show that it is an unfortunately common disturbance of the first three months of life. It can begin at any time between the second and sixth weeks and gradually fades away by three months. The regularity of the pattern is so marked that the disturbance is commonly called 'three months colic'.

Some babies have their colic in the daytime and are peaceful in the evenings, but theirs is not the most familiar pattern. Classically, the baby begins to stir uncomfortably soon after the evening feed or even before the feed has finished. The thighs are drawn up onto the abdomen as if in intense pain and the baby shrieks and wails for three or four hours with hardly a respite. The belly may be distended and the baby may pass gas, and neither rocking the baby nor burping has any effect. Finally, at about 10 or 11 p.m. when the mother's and father's nerves are raw and screaming too, the baby falls into a limp sleep. The baby may or may not gulp down the 10 p.m. bottle before dropping off and the next morning is completely happy and feeding well, only to repeat the performance at 6 p.m that evening.

Babies with colic are usually well throughout the day by all the usual signs, thrive normally and suffer no permanent impairment. No one really knows why colic occurs; even Dr Spock couldn't differentiate between true colic and periodic irritable crying.

The best advice for the parents of a colicky baby is to arrange somehow to get away for a few hours from time to time and get a sympathetic relative or reliable sitter to watch the baby. A change of scenery will do you good and, even if you take the baby with you, fresh air and the motions of a car trip may even quieten the baby.

When it comes to colic, the temptation for the doctor is to prescribe for the parents rather than the baby. To be confronted night after night with a frantically screaming baby who rejects and ignores every effort to be soothed is a trial for even the most saintly mother and father. Young parents encountering colic for the first time are bound to feel frustrated and angry at their inability to control the situation. The fact that the doctor can't offer any remedy doesn't actually help matters. Extremely conscientious parents also ask themselves whether they are causing the colic and the answer is no.

Dislocated Hips

In the language of the mechanical engineer, the hip is an example of a ball and socket joint. The ball of the hip joint is the upper end of the thigh bone, and the socket is formed by the three major bones of the pelvis. The head of the femur fits snugly into the socket and is held in place by ligaments and muscles. If the head of the femur comes out of the acetabulum (or the ball out of the socket), this is a displaced hip.

Sometimes in early embryonic growth the two parts of this joint do not fit together accurately so that the hip joint partially dislocates. Careful testing of hip movements is an important part of a physical examination of the newborn and infant that every doctor is taught to do. With the infant on the back on the table, the examining doctor abducts the thighs; that is, the doctor rotates the legs and pushes on them as if trying to make the knees touch the table. A dislocated hip offers resistance to the movement, but obviously diagnosis must be confirmed by X-rays.

To some extent the stage of the condition will determine the treatment. The guiding principle is to hold the head of the femur in normal relationship with the socket. In early dislocation a heavy wadding of napkins is put on the baby to hold the thighs apart, in 'frog-leg' position. For complete dislocation, some form of mechanical traction is required and the child wears a sort of body-cast for a few weeks. Surgery may be necessary in the older age group.

Down's Syndrome

This is a common cause of children with learning difficulties and results from a genetic abnormality in the chromosomes whereby an extra chromosome is present in the cells of the baby (see page 140).

Down's Syndrome occurs in about three births per two thousand and accounts for approximately ten per cent of children with learning difficulties in institutions. Physical as well as intellectual growth is impaired and characteristic physical findings include a small head, flattened in the front and back, a lateral upward slope of the eyes, small ears, small jaw and mouth, protruding tongue, short, flat nose, delayed eruption of teeth and a short, broad neck. Looseness and laxity of the muscles and a pot-belly are also notable in the infant and young child. The hands and feet tend to be flat, broad and square.

The diagnosis is confirmed by direct analysis of the chromosomes and it is now possible to make this diagnosis during pregnancy (see pages 139–142). There are several different types of Down's Syndrome depending on the number and type of chromosome aberrations, some being a one-off situation and others having an increased risk of a similar problem recurring. Blood tests on the mother and father, together with expert advice from a genetic counsellor, may be helpful.

Down's Syndrome babies may be quite fit and well or may have a number of other associated abnormalities. It is not uncommon for heart problems to exist, there may be kidney complications, and the occurrence of leukaemia is ten to twenty times greater than usual.

The baby with Down's Syndrome who is in good health may survive into the early twenties or beyond, though the question of institutionalisation may arise as the child reaches school age. There are a number of self-help groups which may be of value and these are listed at the end of the book.

Hernias in the Groin (or Inguinal Hernias)

The word 'hernia' means the protrusion or displacement of an organ of the body beyond or outside its normal position. For example, Nature intends the intestine to reside in the abdomen and when a segment or loop of intestine escapes its normal limits by protruding from the stomach cavity into the groin we say that the wayward loop has 'herniated'.

There are a number of other areas where hernias can occur apart from the common one in the groin, i.e. in the diaphragm or chest, or around the navel or tummy-button. In diaphragmatic hernia, a congenital failure occurs where an opening is left through the diaphragm because of the failure of the muscle to grow together in intrauterine life. The contents of the abdominal cavity, the stomach, the intestines and so forth, can actually intrude into the chest and this may cause difficulty in breathing or kinking of the bowel and so on. Diaphragmatic hernia is extremely rare in the newborn and is curable surgically.

The inguinal hernia is very common in young boys and particularly premature babies. It can also of course occur in adult life. Most cases of hernia in children are detected within the first year of life. Often the parents will notice a little bulge in the groin which may come and go depending on whether the baby is relaxing or straining and may disappear under pressure from the doctor's or parent's hand. If the hernia persists under all conditions it may be blocking off some of the bowel, though it is unusual that hernias in young children need surgery and they often right themselves spontaneously.

Hydrocephalus

During the past twenty years new treatment has been developed for hydrocephalus, which used to be known as 'water on the brain' or 'water of the brain'. The other important fact is that the diagnosis can be made with reasonable certainty in the antenatal period, certainly after sixteen weeks, by ultrasound scanning so that a decision on management of the pregnancy can be made with the parents long before term.

Essentially, the head of the child with hydrocephalus grows at a faster rate than normal. It occurs because there is excessive pressure from the spinal fluid, which is the clear fluid surrounding and supporting the brain and the spinal cord. In hydrocephalus the brain doesn't increase in substance but it expands in form under pressure from excessive accumulation of fluid, just as the skin of a balloon expands from the pressure of the air you blow into it. The skin of the balloon doesn't weigh any more than it did but, having been thinned out, it appears much bigger. A similar process occurs in hydrocephalus, where there is a thinning out and enlargement of the geometry of the brain structure. The bones of the skull, because they are not solidly joined, spread apart and the fontanelles (see pages 371–372) stretch out as well. In theory the stretching can damage the brain to the point of death. This condition occurs just as a one-off situation in about one in a thousand babies, and there is no specific reason for it.

As mentioned earlier, the diagnosis can be suggested by ultrasound scanning. It is now commonplace for most hospitals to ask for a routine scan at about seventeen to eighteen weeks, when the size of the head compared with the remainder of the body may seem obviously asymmetrical. Sometimes there are other features of the skull which the X-ray staff are aware of and which might suggest the diagnosis of hydrocephalus at an even earlier stage.

Management of Hydrocephalus

The problem of course if the diagnosis is made in the antenatal period is what to do about it. There are treatments which are available when the baby is born, but the hydrocephalus can be associated with other abnormalities, which makes the parents' decision as to whether or not to continue with the pregnancy even more difficult.

Essentially, the parents will be faced with a situation where there is either the unlikely outcome of a healthy, living child, or hydrocephalus in its mildest form. The latter can be treated at birth by reducing the fluid by means of a fine plastic cannula and, provided there are no abnormalities, the baby can live a pretty normal life.

At the time of writing, there have already been huge advances made into the management of hydrocephalus but it is really beyond the scope of this book to go into them in detail.

Hypospadias

This relatively common birth defect appears in the external genitalia of both sexes, but more often in boys than girls. In the male there are three main features, all to do with the opening in the penis through which the urine comes out. Instead of being at the tip, this little opening is sometimes on the underside of the penis; the shaft of the penis may be bent down; or the foreskin may be defective or completely absent on the underside, lending the penis a sort of hooded appearance.

In the most common form, which requires no treatment, the urethral opening is just below the normal site but in severe cases it may occur anywhere along the shaft as far as the junction of the penis and the scrotal bag. In very rare instances the scrotum is divided into two, with the urethral opening between the sections. Occasionally hypospadias is accompanied by other disorders of the urinary tract and, if it is found, it is advisable to do further X-ray examinations of the child.

Hypospadias in girls (displacement of the urethra) isn't so noticeable for obvious reasons, and can sometimes only be discovered at a routine gynaecological examination. In the most severe cases the opening can be in the vagina and make itself known by causing difficulties with urination. But for all practical purposes the nature of hypospadias makes it a problem primarily for the male.

This condition does not constitute an emergency but, if the more severe forms are not corrected, they may interfere with sexual activity in adult life and there are certain definite psychological implications. The treatment of course is surgical; the incompletely formed foreskin can be removed, and the misplaced opening corrected. The results on the whole are very good, but often more than one operation may be required. The best time for surgery depends on the individual condition and the personality of the patient.

Incompatibility of Blood Type

We have already talked about the Rhesus factor difficulty (see pages 237–240) but the subject of blood differences goes beyond this and deserves a mention.

All human beings have distinguishing characteristics, such as the colour of their hair or eyes. They allow certain groupings to be made so that we may belong to the group of blonds as distinct to brunettes, or to the group of the blue-eyed as distinct from the brown-eyed and so forth.

The same is true of human blood cells. They are all blood but they fall into distinguishing groups or types, determined by minute variations in chemical structure. The four major blood groups, as we have previously discussed, are O, A, B and AB, and O and A are by far the most common. As we have seen, there is a further distinction which some people have but others lack, i.e. the blood molecule known as the Rhesus (Rh) factor, with the Western population usually divided into eighty-five per cent who are Rh positive and fifteen per cent Rh negative. When we describe a person's blood we give the type first and then say whether it is positive or negative with respect to the Rh factor. For instance, to say a person is A positive means that their blood group is A and they have the Rhesus factor. If they are O negative, their blood type is O and lacks the Rhesus factor.

As mentioned previously, when an antibody against a baby's red blood cells crosses the placenta from the mother to the baby, a haemolytic disease of the newborn occurs, in other words destruction of the baby's red cells. This leads to fewer and fewer red cells being formed and the baby becomes anaemic, which has other consequences, i.e. jaundice and illness and possibly death. The treatment and management is outlined on pages 237–239.

The public hears much about the problems in relation to the Rh factor, but there is also a more common condition involving the A, B and O groups which again causes similar problems in the newborn, though not so severe. One of the ways in which to tell whether this sort of a problem exists is to do blood tests on the mother in the antenatal clinic, rather as with Rhesus disease, and look for the presence of antibodies. Treatment for the condition is similar.

Infections in the Newborn

It isn't that long since death from infection in the first year of life was lamentably common and in the underdeveloped regions of the world of course it still is. Happily, modern medicine has changed that picture completely in Western societies. Antibiotics, which came into general use in the 1940s, have revolutionised the care of children with infections, and knowledge of how to manage infection generally has made notable advances.

Infant mortality, that is the rate of death of babies under a year old, is a tenth of what it used to be and infection, which was once the leading cause of infant death, is now way down the list.

Widespread immunisation is required by law in the UK and this has all but eliminated some of the worst scourges. Since the introduction of the vaccine in 1950 the once dreaded poliomyelitis, which crippled or killed thousands of children every year, has become a disease of the past. Measles, which almost any mother could diagnose on sight only a few years ago, is so rare that today's medical students cannot recognise it. Obstetric care, sterilisation of artificial milk, formulas, and technological improvements in treatment have all checked the spread and seriousness of infections among the newborn.

There is a group of children, however, for whom infections hold special risks. Some cannot manufacture antibodies properly, some have chronic diseases such as cystic fibrosis (see pages 138–139), and premature babies are particularly susceptible to infections during the first weeks.

Shortly after birth the baby begins to accumulate the host of micro-organisms, the normal flora, which will establish peaceful germ colonies on the baby's skin, mouth, throat and intestines. If healthy, the baby is in good shape to live with this multitude of quite ordinary germs, unless they multiply too rapidly or get into parts of the body where they do not belong. We all live with our normal flora. These germs of course are to be distinguished from the less common and much more dangerous ones which we classify as virulent because they are associated with disease, and we try to shield the baby against these germs by stimulating the baby's immunity.

Cystic fibrosis is an inherited condition for which no cause is known, with an incidence of about one in two thousand babies. It is a generalised disorder affecting glands which secrete abnormal cells, resulting in excessive sweating, blockage of the bowel and chest complications. The pancreas, which is a gland sitting next to the liver, is affected in eighty per cent of cases, preventing proper digestion and absorption of fats and leading to malnutrition and failure to thrive in the young child. Often lethal, the average life expectancy is between twelve and sixteen years with a risk of recurrence in either sex of one in four.

The baby's endowment of antibodies is somewhat higher at birth than the mother's own supply. The baby gets relatively more antibodies that combat viral illnesses, but fewer of those dealing with some kinds of bacterial illness. When some germ does gain a foothold we usually find it to be one for which the baby has not received enough antibodies. If you like, Nature's book-keeping seems to have been at fault. Of course, if the mother herself is lacking in antibodies, she cannot pass those types to her offspring. For example, the infant whose mother has had measles, or been immunised against it, is born with a supply of antibodies which will protect the baby for the first four to six months. On the other hand, the infant whose mother never had the disease, or immunisation, is susceptible to measles from birth.

The newborn's supply of antibodies gradually reduces until at the end of four to six months only a certain small quantity remain, which will stay for another four to five months. At about three months the baby will have stimulated and started the manufacture of the same kinds of antibodies that were received from the mother, and by the time the baby is three to four years old the production of antibodies will be up to the normal levels. So as infants come into contact with the common and uncommon germs of their environment they make their own antibodies.

Some of these infections are mild so that no symptoms are produced even though antibodies are manufactured. For those dangerous germs against which the baby has received little or no protection from the mother, treatment is needed with techniques of immunisation. Whooping cough, or pertussis, is one good example. The diphtheria/pertussis/tetanus injection, which the baby receives at an early visit to the paediatrician, stimulates the manufacture of antibodies against those organisms. Were we not to immunise the baby, then it would be susceptible to infection by micro-organisms and would be poorly equipped to cope. Some antibodies, such as the measles antibody, linger in the body for as long as nine or ten months and provide immunity during this period. For this reason measles inoculation is often delayed until the supply of maternal antibodies has dropped to a certain level.

So, when can a baby become infected? Firstly, it can happen during the antenatal period while still in the mother's uterus, and secondly, during or after delivery. We have known for a long time about the possibilities of infection in the womb prior to rupture of the mother's amniotic sac. In these cases, infection is passed from the mother's bloodstream through the placenta to the baby's bloodstream. A classic example of this sort of infection transmitted from mother to infant is of course syphilis (see pages 86–87). Although this is pretty rare, there is a suggestion that this condition is somewhat on the increase. Another disease transmissable from mother to unborn baby is typhoid fever. Most of the transmissible bacterial diseases have, however, been brought under good control.

Infections acquired in the uterus became the focus of attention at the end of World War II when it was learned that the German measles virus (see pages 80–82) could affect the fetus in the first few months of pregnancy. A significant number of the fetuses whose mothers contract German measles in the first three months of pregnancy may develop infection. The mothers may or may not show symptoms themselves.

The fetus is also subject to attack by cytomegalovirus (see page 85) which appears in the latter part of pregnancy. It can be transmitted through the placenta and probably also from infections of the cervix as the baby passes through the birth canal. As in rubella (German measles) the affected infant may secrete the virus for many months after delivery and may be a reservoir for infection of others. The unborn baby is also susceptible to transmitted micro-organisms, one such being toxoplasmosis (see pages 84–85).

Once the baby is born, infection of the amniotic fluid and membranes can spread to the infant directly. This may occur when the membranes have ruptured and delivery has not ensued (see page 317). This is why it is important that the hospital knows if the membranes have ruptured so that they can advise you how soon to come into hospital. Many units have different ideas about how long a woman can be left with her membranes ruptured if she doesn't go into labour. Normally within a few hours of the waters breaking contractions start and labour will ensue.

Occasionally, however, nothing happens. It is generally agreed that, if the contractions have not followed spontaneous rupture of the membranes within six hours, then it is probably best to stimulate labour with Syntocinon (see page 316) given in an intravenous drip. The reason is that the longer the period since the membranes ruptured, the higher the chance of organisms getting into the uterus through the gap. Usually a swab is taken and sometimes antibiotics are prescribed, certainly if labour has not started twelve hours after the membranes have ruptured.

Again, it must be emphasised that each hospital, each clinic, and each doctor and midwife has their own guidelines. However, nowadays there are labour ward protocols for each unit which have been drawn up by the doctors, midwives and managers in order to give levels of care in certain circumstances. These protocols must be followed and they allow the decision-making process to evolve from the most senior level downwards.

Infections at delivery were once very common, but the precautions of modern obstetrics have greatly reduced the probability. Most babies are born in hospital delivery rooms under clean conditions, they are transferred to nurseries where scrupulous cleanliness is the watchword, they are bathed in antiseptic solutions, and their umbilical cords are treated with chemicals to reduce the growth of harmful bacteria.

Once home from hospital, the infant is in a different situation of course. All families are subject to illness which can be passed on to the newborn, but fortunately most of these illnesses are not likely to pose problems of major concern. A cold due to a virus, sore throats, diarrhoea, and so on are common and the infant just out of hospital is susceptible, but for reasons that are still not clear they tend to produce very much milder symptoms during the first few months.

Newborns can have infections of the urinary tract or of the chest, or meningitis of the skin, or skin infections. In other words they are prone to the same kinds of infection as older people. The difference lies in the speed in which infections of the newborn can spread from where they start. Consequently, illness that can be handled readily in older children and adults does tend to cause more concern when the patient is an infant. The doctor is more liable to hospitalise the very young baby who has a urinary tract infection, or bad diarrhoea, or who is running a fever without any particular symptoms. Many infections of the newborn, even quite serious ones, may produce non-specific symptoms.

On occasions infection will be found in the bloodstream, a condition known as sepsis, but this is pretty rare. Another possible site of infection is the stump of the umbilical cord, which is normally cut off from the blood supply and is poorly equipped to resist heavy invasion of bacteria. This infection, which is of major concern in underdeveloped countries, is known as omphalitis. Proper care of the cord is routinely practised in hospitals and sanitary surroundings have drastically reduced the incidence of this infection.

Intestinal Obstruction

The causes of intestinal blockage, even in young children, are numerous and varied. A foreign body, an area of inflammation or a tumour may block passage through the intestine. If detected early, most causes of intestinal obstruction can be relieved with confidence and complete recovery.

Although intestinal obstruction is not common, certain symptoms should be recognised, i.e. crampy abdominal pains which will cause a lot of crying in the infant, vomiting and bloating, and gradual dehydration, showing the usual signs of lack of fluid such as a dry tongue, pasty skin, sunken eyeballs, and so on. Whatever the cause of the obstruction, it needs to be treated surgically.

One common cause of obstruction is called meconium ileus, which is a rare manifestation of cystic fibrosis (see pages 138–139). In this condition something happens to the pancreas in the womb, preventing proper digestion of the contents of the baby's intestine. The material becomes so gluey it can't be propelled through the bowel and it becomes blocked at several points.

Another cause is twisting of the intestine upon itself, or the kinking sometimes seen with a hernia. In young children one section of bowel may telescope into itself (intussusception – see opposite page). It must be emphasised that these conditions are rare, are all amenable to surgery and there is usually no long-term problem.

Intussusception

This is an unusual bowel condition that occurs mainly in infants and young children. It requires medical attention and usually surgery. What happens is that the child cries in severe pain and passes stools that look like blobs of currant jelly. It is blood-tinged mucus which gives the stools this unmistakable appearance. A section of intestine spontaneously telescopes itself into another. Think of a heavy, flexible hose or tube that you are holding with both hands and imagine bringing the hands together to force the tube into itself. In intussusception this is more or less what happens: a section of small bowel swallows itself and by continuous contractions sucks in more and more of the bowel. The blood vessels get sucked in as well, the blood flow is shut off, and there is swelling and gangrene of the small area of bowel that is telescoped.

As might be expected, the pain is very severe. It might come in short bursts with intervening periods of lethargy and is usually signal enough for the parents to get in touch with the doctor. The appearance of the currant jelly stools is the clincher if one is needed. Essentially, the treatment consists of either an enema, which might push the telescoped section of bowel out again or, if this approach fails, then surgery is the only recourse when either the little segment of bowel is pushed back or removed. Thereafter there should be no problem.

Jaundice

This is not a disease but a symptom and can represent a variety of ailments and appear at any age. Someone who is jaundiced will show the characteristic yellowing of the skin and eyes, and a mild degree of jaundice is common enough among the newborn to be regarded as normal. Well over fifty per cent of all normal newborns will become jaundiced for a few days, the yellowness usually appearing on the second or third day and gradually disappearing by the end of the first week. This so-called normal (or physiological) jaundice doesn't bother the baby in the least and may not even attract the mother's attention, but the doctors and nurses in the hospital will be keeping a sharp eye on it.

Jaundice can, however, be due to other conditions which are more important. The actual physical cause of jaundice is a yellow chemical called bilirubin which is normally present in small quantities in the blood of everyone. This chemical is actually a breakdown product of haemoglobin, which is the oxygen-carrying red pigment in the blood cells. The red cells are constantly being formed and removed from the bloodstream. They are produced in the marrow of the bones and have a lifespan of about 120 days. In old age or any time after 100 days they deteriorate and are then removed from the circulation. These old red cells are destroyed and the haemoglobin is altered chemically, a product of this chemical breakdown being the bilirubin which causes jaundice. The bilirubin is then carried in the blood to the liver to be further processed and here all but a small amount of the bilirubin is excreted into what is called the bile or the liver secretion. This goes through the bowel channels to the bowel, into the stools and out of the body.

The remaining bilirubin in the body re-enters the bloodstream from the liver. The amount of bilirubin normally present in the body is small but measurable. A chemical analysis or blood test can distinguish the bilirubin on its way to the liver from the bilirubin that is being processed and returned to the bloodstream, and it is this measurable amount of bilirubin that is critical in jaundice.

Hepatitis is the disorder most people associate with jaundice in the adult. Here the liver is inflamed and cannot properly perform its work of dealing with the bilirubin produced in the normal destruction of old cells. The bilirubin therefore accumulates in the bloodstream and the patient becomes yellow. Another cause is gallstones which block the bile system; and in certain anaemias red blood cells are destroyed so fast that the liver cannot deal with the bilirubin.

The kind of jaundice so often seen in a baby during the first week of life is due to the baby's liver having only a limited ability to process bilirubin because it is not yet sufficiently mature. Doctors and nurses become expert at judging by skin colour alone just how much jaundice a baby has. If, however, there is any question at all, a laboratory test which measures the amount of bilirubin will be ordered, and this may be repeated several times to monitor the curve over the next few days.

Premature babies, again because the liver is immature, develop increased bilirubin and become jaundiced. Breast-fed babies are more likely to get jaundice than those who are bottle-fed, though this is because nursing mothers produce a larger than normal amount of hormone and pass it along to the baby in the milk. The baby's liver removes this hormone but more has to be done by the same enzyme that is involved in the bilirubin processing.

Another cause of jaundice in the newborn, often a severe kind, results from the differences in the blood types of the mother and baby (Rhesus disease – see pages 237–240).

Finally, the illness resulting from very high bilirubin levels, or to put it another way excessive jaundice, is called kernicterus. Not all babies with high levels of bilirubin will develop kernicterus but there is a strong association between the two. If the jaundice becomes too high, there can be severe symptoms, serious damage to parts of the brain, and cerebral palsy and deafness can occur. This, needless to say, is extremely rare and the jaundice is hardly ever allowed to reach critical levels. It is obviously important that the doctor not only finds the underlying cause, but also manages to keep the jaundice within safe bounds.

Lung Collapse

Sometimes air leaks into the chest cavity and is trapped between the lungs and the ribcage and the diaphragm, a condition which is called pneumothorax. In the newborn, a pneumothorax can complicate a number of respiratory difficulties associated with obstruction of the airways.

Air in the chest cavity can also compress the lungs and thus decrease the volume available to the baby for breathing. Shortness of breath and blue coloration can result. The doctor can identify pneumothorax by listening to the chest and with X-rays whenever an infant exhibits difficulty with breathing. Treatment is directed at the underlying cause: for example, antibiotics if there is infection, or sometimes the air can be relieved by inserting a small tube between the ribs and the pocket of air.

Monilia (Thrush)

This common fungus occurs very often in the vagina of women, and particularly when pregnant. It can occur in the baby as well, often in the mouth, and the baby can pick it up 'in transit'. Treatment is quite easy and there is no significant problem with this condition.

PKU (Phenylketonuria)

One in ten thousand babies is affected by this comparatively rare condition, but it is quite commonly talked about. In the first place the practice of testing the infant for PKU is widespread; secondly, the disease is a textbook example of how defects can be transmitted by genes; and thirdly, the condition demonstrates dramatically the interdependence of mind and body.

PKU is a disorder of the metabolism, or bodily processing, of one of the essential proteins called aminoacids, and the particular one is phenylalanine. Think of aminoacids as the basic building blocks of all the proteins, and the process of digestion as splitting the proteins into these little constituents. Each aminoacid is crucial to the accomplishment of some particular step in the normal process of growth and development.

In PKU the body fails to process phenylalanine because there is a deficiency or derangement of a certain enzyme. This can be simply diagnosed by a routine blood test taken from the baby's heel on about the third or fourth day. If this substance, phenylalanine, is not metabolised properly, it remains in the body in high amounts and its byproducts can damage the brain, causing retardation and fits. Furthermore, it can interfere with the overall growth and well-being of the baby. Severely affected infants may eat poorly, vomit and fail to thrive.

The treatment of this condition is quite simple. The idea is to provide a diet which contains the exact requirement of this aminoacid and no more. For example, fruits and vegetables are low in phenylalanine, and a synthetic milk with all the essential aminoacids but a reduced amount of phenylalanine has been developed. Since the total regime of care is complicated, however, communities have found it worthwhile to establish treatment centres. The present indications are that the treatment for PKU can safely be concluded for most children by the time they go to school.

Pyloric Stenosis

This means that the muscular valve controlling the flow of food and gastric juices from the stomach to the beginning of the small intestine (duodenum) thickens enough to block off the tract partially or completely. Since milk or other food then has no way to get out of the stomach except by the mouth, the baby vomits. Vomiting in the course of a feed or soon afterwards is the first symptom the parent will see, but many babies are a little sick while they feed anyway.

The vomiting tends to be projectile: in other words it comes out with force and travels some distance. This is in contrast to normal spitting up which is more of a drool. If this projectile vomiting continues, then the baby will become dry and develop malnutrition. Very often the vomiting begins several weeks after the baby has left hospital and is much more common among first-born children and boys. The diagnosis is made by examination and X-ray tests. The treatment, which is quite simple, is a small surgical operation, well tolerated by babies, under general anaesthesia when a little cut is made into the muscle of the stomach to relieve the obstruction. The child is usually up within a matter of hours.

Finally, there is no strong hereditary influence and therefore, if one child in a family has the condition, the chances for later siblings are only slighter greater than for any other child.

Spinal Defects

Think of the spinal column as a stack of bony rings, bound together with ropes or ligaments, and fitted so that the whole structure can bend forwards, backwards or sideways. Up the tube or canal formed by the column of stacked rings runs the spinal cord, which is attached to the brain and the base of the skull. This cord is a kind of biological cable of nerve endings, connecting the control centres of the brain to a network of nerves that spread all round the body. Messages in the form of coded impulses travel along this cable in both directions.

At every level, from the neck to the lower back, nerves branch out from the cord through the spaces between the bony rings, called vertebrae, and the cord and the brain float in fluid called CSF (or cerebro-spinal fluid) contained in a membranous sac called the meninges. So the fluid and sac together compose a shock absorber to cushion the delicate brain and spinal cord.

Occasionally, and we don't really know why, the bony circle of a vertebra fails to fuse, the ring doesn't close and this leaves a defect known as spina bifida (literally, two-part spine). Here there is an opening in the vertebral structure and this can involve one to five or even six of the vertebral units.

Spina bifida can be very mild and only detected by a small dimple in the skin of the lower back at the site of the defect, which is sometimes a normal occurrence. In less simple cases, however, there is a defect of the skin, the membranes actually protrude quite visibly through it and you can even see the spinal fluid through the transparent sac. This is known as a meningocoele. Some of these conditions are operable and some unfortunately can cause degrees of impairment from mild disability to complete interference with bowel and urinary function.

Until thirty years ago the diagnosis was not made until the baby was born, but this condition can now be detected with reasonable certainty in two ways. First of all by a blood test, which is often performed at about sixteen weeks together with the Down's blood screen (see pages 139–140), where a substance called alphafetaprotein is measured. It is this substance which is raised to a high level in cases of spina bifida and also in some cases of hydrocephalus (see pages 390–392). This test is not absolutely diagnostic but, if this fails to pick up the condition, most women in the country now have a routine scan at sixteen to nineteen weeks when it should be possible for such defects to be identified and a decision made with the parents as to how to proceed.

In severe cases, where there is for instance a spina bifida and a hydrocephalus at the same time and the outlook for the child is very poor, then it may be that termination of pregnancy is requested. If this is not the case, then pre-term diagnosis can assist in ensuring that either the baby is delivered in a special care unit with all facilities for surgery, or that the various experts are present at birth so that the situation can be fully assessed as soon as possible.

Unfortunately, we still don't know why the condition occurs and, having occurred once, it is somewhat more common in a future pregnancy.

Tracheoesophageal Fistula

Some babies are born with an abnormal condition between the windpipe (trachea) and the oesophagus (gullet) which is the tube conveying food and drink from the back of the throat to the stomach. This uncommon birth defect is known medically as tracheoesophageal fistula and it can take various forms, but always requires surgery.

If you press at the base of your throat just below the Adam's apple, you can feel the trachea. It extends from the pharynx, or voice box, into the chest several inches below the notch of the collarbone. At its lower end it divides into two major branches called bronchi which carry the air you breathe into the right and left lungs. Just behind the trachea is the oesophagus and under normal conditions the two tubes are of course separate. If, due to some abnormal developmental problem, there is a connection between the two tubes, or if the oesophagus ends, which it can sometimes do, in a blind pouch, then nothing swallowed from the mouth – food, drink or saliva – can reach the stomach.

The baby with this condition is in serious trouble and to make matters worse gastric juices are regurgitated up through the oesophagus into the trachea and the lungs, setting up an intense reaction with pneumonia. Babies with this condition are unable to feed and are likely to develop lung infections; they drool, choke and gag, and become extremely ill. This condition obviously needs surgery during the first few days of life, the effects of which are usually very satisfactory.

Undescended Testes

The testes in the male form early in developmental life but to start with they remain high in the baby's abdominal cavity and remain there until quite late in pregnancy. In most baby boys the testes descend into the scrotum, or sac, at the time of delivery, but occasionally one or both testes remain outside the scrotum so that when the doctor routinely examines the newborn baby no testes are felt in the sac.

We don't really know why this happens. It may be related to a maldevelopment of the testes and it is commoner in the premature infant. The important thing is that testes that remain in the abdominal cavity after puberty will almost certainly not be able to produce spermatozoa, even if surgery brings them down to their normal position in the sac. The treatment is therefore relatively simple surgery which requires hospitalisation for a few days, and the outlook is excellent. The timing of surgery will depend on a number of factors. If one testis only is affected, it should be operated on no later than the onset of puberty but usually between the ages of five and nine. If both testes are undescended, normally one is repaired in infancy and the other at the age of five or six.

Urinary Tract Defects

Birth defects involving the urinary tract are relatively common and, since interference at any point with the tract may have important consequences for the whole system, and since urine is the principal vehicle for removing the body's waste products, the importance of this subject is obvious.

What do We Mean by the Urinary Tract?

There are two kidneys, the ureters, the bladder and the urethra. Urine is manufactured in the kidneys, or to be precise in the nephrons of the kidneys, and is accumulated in the cavities of the kidneys which are called pelves. These are drained by a long tube which carries the urine down to the bladder where it is stored until it is passed from the body through the urethra. The urethra in the female is very short but in the male of course it traverses the length of the penis.

It is easy to picture how any blockage in the urinary system would pose strain on the other parts. Suppose, for example, a blockage existed between the bladder and the urethra. Accumulating urine would stretch the bladder, the bladder would contract to get rid of the urine and would thicken its muscular wall, the ureters would have to pump harder in an effort to get urine into the already full bladder, urine would go back up the bladder and eventually into the kidneys. The increasing pressure of retained urine would stretch the kidneys and this chain of damaging developments might end in kidney failure. The same sort of picture would occur if a blockage were located anywhere else.

How Can Blockages in the Urinary Tract be Diagnosed?

Sometimes they can be detected by feel: a kidney that is much bigger than it should be in the newborn can be felt in the flank. But in some cases problems appear only after infection has set in – difficulties in voiding, dribbling and complete failure to toilet train are signs requiring attention. Abnormal frequency of urination, fever, abdominal pain, nausea, vomiting, cloudy or blood-stained urine are all symptoms of a possible urinary infection.

There are a number of tests to see whether and where there is an obstruction. In fact nowadays the fetal urinary tract is very well demonstrated antenatally on an ultrasound scan of the mother's abdomen, and not infrequently some abnormality is brought to light in this way. Most of the abnormalities we are talking about are surgically correctable in the first few years of life.

Postnatal Check

Some of the functions of the body return to normal within a few days following childbirth while others take a few months. Six weeks after delivery is chosen as the standard time for the postnatal visit, which takes place either in the hospital or at your doctor's surgery. Bleeding from the uterus and discharge should be ceasing by this time and yet your first period will probably not have arrived. In some cases the check-up is arranged on the same day as the baby clinic so that mother and baby can both be seen and examined. This is also a convenient time for you to discuss contraception.

There are three important reasons why you should be encouraged to attend for a postnatal visit. Firstly, it gives you an opportunity to ask about any particular problem that persists and to discuss any aspect of your labour and delivery, especially if the delivery was complicated, and it is helpful to discuss it with those who were involved with the decision at the time.

Secondly, you are examined to make sure that your body has returned to the pre-pregnant state and that any problems existing while you were in hospital, such as high blood pressure, have disappeared.

And thirdly, and perhaps most importantly, it allows discussion about contraception and how a future pregnancy might be managed. If, for example, genetic counselling is indicated, this can be arranged at an early date.

In this country all recently delivered women are visited by a midwife or health visitor for the first ten days.

Postnatal Examination

Questions and Answers

You will be asked whether there is any bright bleeding from the vagina, or whether the dark-stained discharge called lochia (see page 332) still persists or is getting less. Women often notice a discharge for a number of weeks after delivery and usually it is replaced by a white or yellow discharge which may persist for longer.

Your doctor will want to know whether there is any discomfort in the pelvic region, particularly if an episiotomy or tear needed any stitching and, if you suffered from piles or haemorrhoids at any time during pregnancy, whether these are improving. Some women complain of intense pain at the time of opening their bowels after delivery which passes off after a few minutes and then causes no problem until the bowels are opened again. This is often due to a small crack in the skin just inside the anus called an anal fissure. The crack usually heals by itself but, if things become uncomfortable, then a local anaesthetic ointment can be used temporarily.

Bladder function is often altered after pregnancy and women may find that they are passing urine more frequently, or sometimes they have difficulty in starting, or experience leakage of urine while coughing or sneezing. All these complaints are not uncommon at six weeks and usually return to normal soon afterwards. It takes a little time for the muscles in the pelvic floor to redevelop their strength and a course of postnatal exercises if consistently performed can improve this complaint.

If you are breast-feeding, it is unlikely you will menstruate until lactation ceases but, if not breast-feeding, you may have had a period by the time you come to the clinic. There is no set time for menstruation to begin again after childbirth in the mother who is not breast-feeding.

The first few periods may be slightly heavier than normal and the pattern may change. Many women who have had a regular twenty-eight-day cycle notice that their periods become more frequent after childbirth but this is not invariably the rule. There is no reason why internal tampons may not be used three to four weeks after delivery.

There is no reason why intercourse should not occur within three to four weeks of delivery, even if there has been an episiotomy, provided that care is taken, although it is customary to advise the couple to refrain from sex until the postnatal check. This does not, however, apply if the woman has had a Caesarean section when intercourse can occur earlier as long as it is comfortable.

Examination by the Doctor

You will usually be weighed on your arrival at the postnatal clinic, your urine is tested and your blood pressure taken to ensure that any rise has returned to normal.

The breasts are examined to ensure that lactation is satisfactory and that there are no swellings or cysts, or that the breasts have returned to normal if you are not breast-feeding.

The abdomen is felt to make sure there is no abnormality and that the muscles have regained their strength.

An internal examination ensures that the external and internal stitches have healed, that the cervix is healthy and that the uterus has returned to its normal size. A cervical smear may be taken if not performed earlier in your pregnancy.

The postnatal clinic may be an ideal time to fit a coil (see pages 424–429) or a diaphragm, and this can usually be arranged at your request.

Advice for the Future

The postnatal visit is also a good time at which to discuss the spacing of pregnancies, particularly if there was an abnormal delivery, say a Caesarean section, in which case you may want to know how soon you can become pregnant again.

In general terms menstruation, and therefore ovulation, returns within a few weeks if you are not breast-feeding, though it may take two or three months before your periods become regular. If you are breast-feeding, as we have seen, menstruation does not usually occur and pregnancy is therefore extremely unlikely, though possible.

If a Caesarean section was necessary, you will want to know what the chances of having a repeat Caesarean (see page 298), and it is usually wise not to become pregnant again for about six months so that the scar in the uterus may heal soundly. If, however, pregnancy does occur, it is unlikely that it will give rise to any problems.

Many doctors advise that iron and vitamin supplements should be continued for at least six weeks, especially if you are breast-feeding, to make up any deficit that may have occurred during the birth.

If the baby was born with a congenital abnormality, the postnatal visit is a time to arrange a consultation with an expert in genetic counselling.

The Baby

It is usual for your baby to be weighed and to have the eyes, cord, genitalia and skin checked, and for you to have a general discussion with the midwife or doctor about how feeding is going.

This would be a time to raise any queries you may have about the daily care of your baby, what one might expect to happen over the next few weeks and months, and to find out the timetable for immunisation against the infectious childhood illnesses, such as diphtheria, tetanus, polio and whooping cough. Usually the first visit for immunisation is at three months, then at six months and again at nine months.

Family Planning

Although contraception may not be high on the agenda in the recently delivered mother's mind, unplanned pregnancies in the first few months after childbirth are not that rare. Advice is available from the midwife or doctor before leaving hospital, or from the family doctor, health visitor, midwives, or family planning clinics and of course it costs nothing. Most of the currently available methods of contraception are suitable for the recently delivered mother, with certain reservations, and in this section we will describe each method so that an informed choice can be made.

Please remember that it may take some time before the periods return to a regular pattern and, if breast-feeding, the periods are unlikely to occur at all. It is, however, possible to conceive even when the periods are not coming and therefore thought should be given to other contraceptive methods in the early weeks or months after childbirth.

Pregnancy will occur if healthy semen enters the woman's vagina and finds suitable conditions in the vaginal passage to survive; if the sperm travels into the womb and down the Fallopian tube; if fertilisation takes place; and if the womb provides a satisfactory bed for the fertilised egg to implant and grow. The deliberate prevention of a pregnancy can therefore be achieved if any of these conditions are altered or interrupted.

METHODS OF CONTRACEPTION

* Natural methods

* Barrier methods – male and female

* Hormonal methods

* The intrauterine device (IUCD)

* Sterilisation

Natural Methods

Withdrawal (Interrupted Intercourse)

This is one of the oldest and simplest methods of birth control whereby the penis is withdrawn from the vagina just before the ejaculation of sperm. Although practised by many couples, this method of contraception is often thought to be unsatisfactory because of the frustration of both partners and the fact that occasionally sperm deposited on the outer lips of the vulva can get into the vagina and cervix.

The Rhythm Method (Safe Period)

This method of contraception is particularly practised by couples who for religious reasons are unable to rely upon mechanical or other methods. Intercourse is planned to take place in the phase of the menstrual cycle which is least fertile and depends on three facts:

- Ovulation only occurs once every cycle and the egg will survive for only about thirty-six hours.

- Ovulation usually occurs twelve to fourteen days before the first day of the next period.

- Sperm can only survive for about seventy-two hours after ejaculation from the penis.

The rhythm method is only about seventy per cent effective and the main reason for the high failure rate is that ovulation does not necessarily occur exactly at the same time in the middle of each cycle, even if the periods are regular.

The only way to ensure that the rhythm method is pretty safe is to keep a strict record of the menstrual cycle for at least a few months. The cycle is from the first day of one period to the first day of the next. The timing of ovulation, i.e. the few days around which you are likely to become pregnant, can be predicted by a rise in temperature which occurs after the egg has been shed. This can be charted by taking one's own temperature every day on waking. It is important to do this before getting up or having anything to eat or drink because the temperature of the body at rest is the important fact (see pages 16–17).

The accurate detection of ovulation can also be assisted by understanding that the fluid that is produced at the cervix or entrance of the womb changes in appearance and gets much heavier about five days before ovulation. At first it is thick and sticky, then becoming much clearer and wetter and this is so that the sperm can travel through easily. The more discharge there is and the wetter the vagina feels the more fertile you are, and therefore intercourse should be avoided for the few days when there is quite a lot of damp discharge.

After Childbirth

Clearly the temperature and rhythm methods are less effective soon after childbirth because the periods take some time to start back again. Even when they do they can be irregular for a while and therefore it is very hard to predict the 'safe' phase. It is important that you obtain sound advice from your doctor, midwife or family planning people before risking this method of contraception until the menstrual cycle becomes regular again.

Male Barrier Methods

The Sheath (Condom/French Letter/Durex)

This is the oldest and the commonest contraceptive in use today and was originally used by Roman soldiers in order to prevent infection from venereal disease. The principle is that the sheath is placed over the erect penis before intercourse so that during ejaculation the sperm remain inside the sheath and do not enter the vaginal passage. Modern sheaths cause no allergic reactions and should only be used once. Care should be taken to ensure that the condom does not come off the penis after ejaculation before withdrawing from the partner.

The chief disadvantage is interruption of lovemaking as the sheath has to be put on the erect penis. Sheaths can burst but this is uncommon and, if pregnancy results from this method, it is usually due to incorrect use rather than a hole in the sheath. For complete safety against pregnancy it is probably better to combine the sheath with a special cream (spermicidal jelly) which is placed in the vagina and will kill off any sperm that do happen to remain after the sheath has been removed.

After Childbirth

Family planning with the sheath can be used as soon as the woman is ready for sex.

Female Barrier Methods (The Diaphragm Cap and Sponge)

The Diaphragm Cap

Invented in 1882, the diaphragm was first marketed by a Dutch firm – hence the name 'Dutch cap'. This is the commonest type of mechanical contraception used by women and consists of a soft rubber diaphragm with a coiled spring around the rim. Available in different sizes, an internal examination by your doctor will assess the size that is right for you. The cap fits snugly into the vagina so that the cervix is completely covered with the membrane, preventing sperm deposited in the vagina from getting into the cervix.

It is first necessary to teach you how to feel your own cervix. You must be certain that when the diaphragm is correctly positioned the cervix is completely covered. This takes a little time and patience but the skill is easily acquired and after a week or so you will be confident enough to fit and remove the cap. Spermicidal jelly is usually smeared in the dome of the diaphragm and around the rim of the cap to give further protection.

It is usual to leave the diaphragm in place for about six hours following intercourse, after which it is removed and washed. It can be left in the vagina for a longer period of time, when further spermicidal jelly should be used.

Apart from failure to protect completely against pregnancy, and the failure rate is very low, the method has virtually no complications although some women find the procedure of inserting, removing and washing the diaphragm irksome.

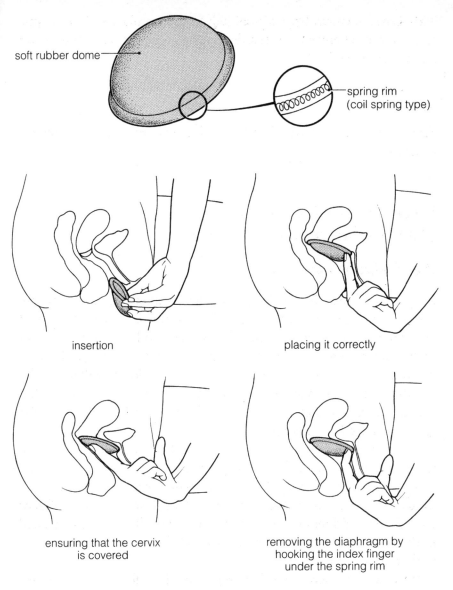

soft rubber dome

spring rim
(coil spring type)

insertion

placing it correctly

ensuring that the cervix
is covered

removing the diaphragm by
hooking the index finger
under the spring rim

The diaphragm or cap.

After Childbirth

The diaphragm really only becomes effective six to eight weeks after birth. The reason for this is that the cervix and the vagina change their shape during pregnancy and birth and it takes about this amount of time for the pelvic organs to return to normal. The postnatal clinic is therefore a good time for the correct size to be assessed by your doctor.

The Cervical Cap

This is another form of barrier method which is kept in place by suction. Again it is important that the instructions are understood and that you are taught how to use this correctly.

The Sponge

This is round and soft and contains a spermicide. This is put into the vagina before sex to cover the cervix and should stay in for about six hours. It works for about twenty-four hours after insertion. The sponges are a little more expensive and not quite as reliable as the cap and not all family planning clinics have them.

To insert, the sponge is moistened with a little water so that it feels foamy and is then bent in half with the dimple up and the loop down. It is inserted as high as possible in the vagina so that the dimple fits over the cervix.

After Childbirth

The sponge can be used when the bleeding has stopped, but is probably the least reliable form of contraception and its use should therefore ideally be limited to the times at which fertility is low, i.e. during breast-feeding.

Hormonal Methods (Chemical Contraception)

The Contraceptive Combined Pill

In the early 1950s an American scientist, Gregory Pincus, first suggested that it might be possible to prevent a pregnancy with hormone tablets which stopped the egg being released by the ovary each month (ovulation). It had been known for some time that small doses of the female sex hormone oestrogen normally produced by the ovary could inhibit ovulation successfully, but in the process almost always caused bleeding and irregular periods. It was also known that progesterone, which is a hormone produced in the second half of the menstrual cycle, was primarily concerned with keeping the menstrual cycle regular.

For the next few years scientists concentrated on isolating a progesterone drug so that a suitable mixture of the two hormones could be taken together to prevent ovulation and to maintain a normal pattern. The first contraceptive pills were marketed in the early 1960s.

How Does the Pill Work?

Although there are a host of different brands of contraceptive pill available, their mode of action is similar. In order for an egg to be formed and shed the ovary is stimulated by the pituitary gland in the brain which sends out special ripening messages, or hormones. The pill simply prevents the pituitary gland from putting out these ripening hormones and therefore ovulation will be suppressed.

How is the Pill Taken?

Every packet of contraceptive pills has its own instruction leaflet and this should be followed precisely. Most pills come in packets of twenty-one and the first tablet should be taken on the first or fifth day of the period depending on instructions. One tablet a day is taken, preferably at the same time, until the pack is finished. A gap of seven pill-free days follows, during which the period occurs. The new pack should be started after the seven pill-free days regardless of whether a period has occurred or not. In this way a regular pattern will be established that is easy to remember and the schedule will be three weeks on the pill and one week off.

For those women who have difficulty in following this pattern a different brand of tablet is available which comes in a pack of twenty-eight. The first twenty-one pills contain hormone and the last seven are dummies, and one tablet is taken every day without a break.

Because the body takes a little time to react to these hormones, the pill may not be entirely successful in preventing ovulation during the first cycle and therefore it is safer to use additional forms of contraception during the first two weeks. If it becomes necessary to change the pill, similar precautions should be taken. Thereafter, if the pill is taken as directed, the success rate in preventing a pregnancy is virtually one hundred per cent.

Most women find that they are less likely to forget the pill if it is taken first thing in the morning rather than at night. If the morning pill is forgotten, the pill can be taken the same evening and this will not alter effectiveness in preventing conception. If the pill is forgotten for two or more days, bleeding may occur, which can be ignored but additional methods of contraception should be used for the remainder of that cycle.

Side Effects of the Pill

Some side effects are common during the first few weeks. Nausea, sickness, swollen and tender breasts, headaches, an increase in vaginal discharge, some weight gain, or irregular spotting are not uncommon. These are usually temporary and disappear after two or three cycles. If they do not, then your doctor should be consulted.

Apart from these minor effects, there are certain long-term complications of the pill that should be considered. Mood changes and bouts of depression may occur and libido can be temporarily reduced. Sometimes an increase in sexual desire occurs but rather than being directly due to the female hormone oestrogen, this often occurs because the fear of pregnancy is removed and sex can take place without any worries or inhibitions.

Adverse Effects of the Pill

Risks to health from taking the combined pill, and in rare instances risks to life, are now well recognised but these risks are generally kept to a minimum by careful prescribing. The most serious are associated with thrombosis (clotting) of the leg veins and the risk of a clot breaking off and travelling to the lungs preventing the passage of air, known as pulmonary embolism.

The more minor risks include high blood pressure, and some researchers have recently indicated a link between pill use and later development of certain cancers such as cancer of the breast, neck of the womb and liver. Other research, however, has not borne this out and work is continually being carried out to provide a clearer picture, but it may be some time before the answers are available. Doctors are well aware that the risks may be dose related so in general the dosage of the hormone in the combined pill is kept as low as possible.

There are also other risk factors such as age, cigarette smoking, obesity, and various diseases which themselves predispose to complications, such as diabetes.

Varicose veins are not in themselves a contra-indication to the pill and there is no proof that the pill causes cancer of the breasts. The breasts, however, are sensitive to female sex hormones and during the premenstrual phase of the cycle the breasts may feel lumpy and tender. If an unsuspected cancer of the breasts already exists, the oestrogen content of the pill could cause the growth to increase but in no way would it have caused the cancer to arise in the first place.

The Pill and Future Fertility

If you wish to become pregnant, the pill should be stopped at the end of that packet. Your periods may take a month or two to return, although this should cause no concern. It is ideal to wait for two or three periods before trying to get pregnant because your doctor will then be able to tell more accurately when the baby is due. This is because ovulation often occurs irregularly for a while after stopping the pill and, if your periods are also irregular, calculations of the estimated date of delivery may be inaccurate.

Sometimes the periods take longer than two to three months to return and this may worry you if you are trying to conceive. Though only one per cent of women who take the pill do not menstruate after finishing the pill, this complication can seldom be predicted. It seems that those who have an irregular menstrual cycle and who missed periods frequently before being on the pill are more prone to have trouble in this respect. Many doctors, therefore, don't recommend the pill for women with very irregular menstrual cycles. Most women on the pill find that their periods are very scanty. If no period occurs at the end of each cycle for three successive months, your doctor should be informed but, provided your periods return after coming off the pill, there is no significance in absence of menstruation while taking it. Your doctor may therefore advise giving the pill a break for a month or two to see whether your periods return.

If your periods do not restart and you want to start a pregnancy, no specific treatment is usually needed as the periods usually come back within six months. If you wish to conceive, then menstruation and therefore ovulation can be stimulated with special tablets taken for five days every month. Occasionally periods do not return despite treatment with these tablets and, should this occur, tests may be needed to exclude other causes of lack of periods before sophisticated treatment with fertility drugs is tried. Though it is usually possible to get the periods started with treatment, a small number of women whose periods stop following the pill remain resistant to fertility drugs and because menstruation and ovulation do not return there may be some impairment of fertility.

Medical research into the effects that the pill has on the body, both immediate and long-term, should eventually result in reducing the complications to a minimum. For the present there are still a number of questions about the pill for which there are no definite answers.

Does the Pill Have to be Prescribed?

It has recently been suggested that the pill should be available over the counter but there are good reasons why it is best to see your doctor first. The pill could be inadvisable under certain circumstances, for example if you have had a previous thrombosis, if there is active disease which could interfere with pill taking, and so on. Examination by your doctor should ensure that no such conditions exist and that the genital organs are normal. Although each packet of pills contains a well-prepared leaflet outlining the way in which the pill should be taken and what to do if there are problems, it is helpful if these matters are explained by your doctor first.

For How Long is it Safe to Take the Pill?

Most doctors believe that, although the pill is not contra-indicated absolutely in the late thirties and early forties, it is probably more sensible to seek alternative forms of birth control at this age. Birth control pills are potent hormones that affect many systems of the body and with advancing age natural changes do occur and it may be prudent to keep outside influences that may accelerate these changes to a minimum.

Having said that, there are many instances where the pill is suitable for the forty plus age group provided that a correct preparation can be chosen which suits the individual woman, and that there are no at risk problems such as high blood pressure, heavy smoking or being overweight.

Is it Necessary to Come off the Pill to Give the Body a Break?

Again, advice may vary but there is no scientific evidence to suggest that coming off the pill for a few months makes any difference whatsoever to the frequency of complications or subsequent fertility. If there are no contra-indications and no side effects develop, you may safely continue with the pill without a break for as long as your doctor advises.

What are the Risks of Unplanned Pregnancy While Taking the Pill?

This question has been recently highlighted because it was found that certain tablets containing the same hormone as the pill, but in a higher dose, were used as a form of pregnancy test. These tablets were given for two or three days after a missed period and produced a small bleed if the woman was not pregnant. It had been suggested that there was an increased instance of abnormalities in the unborn children of women who had been given two or three of these tablets in the early weeks of pregnancy, but this has not been substantiated.

Moreover, there is no evidence to suggest that, if a woman becomes pregnant inadvertently while taking the pill, similar effects occur, although there may be a slightly higher risk of miscarriage.

Can a Period Safely be Postponed with the Pill?

If a period is going to coincide with an important event, say a holiday or a crucial examination, bleeding can be prevented simply by continuing to take one pill a day after the pack is finished without a break. As soon as is convenient the pill can then be stopped and the next period should come within a few days. Changing the pattern of the periods in this way will cause no harm whatsoever but it is best to check with your doctor first.

After Childbirth

It is normal practice to wait for your first period after your baby is born before starting the pill. If you are not breast-feeding, periods usually return within a few weeks of the birth. Breast-feeding mothers, however, do not start their periods until lactation has finished and, although it is extremely unlikely that a pregnancy will result during this time, it is possible, and that is why alternative methods of contraception are advised while breast-feeding continues.

The pill can reduce the amount of milk produced by the breasts and, although some of the pill contents are transferred through the milk to the baby, no harm will come to the infant. If you are particularly anxious to start the pill straight away, there is no reason why you should not, providing breast-feeding is not occurring.

The Progesterone-only Pill (the 'mini-pill')

This contains no oestrogen and works in a different way from the combined pill. The progesterone-only tablets change the consistency of the fluid that comes out of the cervix which normally attracts the sperm deposited during intercourse. The sperms are repelled from gaining entrance to the womb – in other words the discharge from the cervix becomes hostile. If some sperm do get through the cervix, the progesterone also makes it difficult for the egg to travel along the Fallopian tube, partially preventing sperm from penetrating the egg. It also changes the consistency of the lining of the womb, making it less receptive to the fertilised egg.

How is the Progesterone-only Pill Taken?

The progesterone-only pill is taken every day, preferably at the same time, without a break and it is usually started on the first day of the period. It is slightly less effective than the pill proper but the success rate is in the region of ninety-five per cent.

Are There Any Complications?

Although the progesterone-only pill was developed mainly to avoid oestrogen-associated complications, some minor side effects are seen, such as weight changes and vaginal discharge, and occasionally breast changes. The principal problem, however, concerns the periods themselves. Whereas the combination pill characteristically produces a short but very regular period, the progesterone-only pill can sometimes cause irregular bleeding and sometimes absence of periods as well.

After Childbirth

This is probably the most widely used contraceptive for the recently delivered mother and particularly if she is breast-feeding as it can be started almost straight away after the birth, does not affect the breast milk and causes no harm whatsoever to the baby. If you decide to take the progesterone-only pill, this method of contraception can safely be continued once breast-feeding has finished for as long as you wish.

Injectable Hormones

This method uses a similar hormone to that contained in the 'mini-pill', i.e. progesterone, but can be given by injection which lasts for about two to three months depending on the type used. The periods and fertility may take up to a year or more to return after stopping the injections, and this is therefore a disadvantage.

There is also a suggested link between the use of injectable contra-ceptives and a woman later developing a thinning of the bones (osteoporosis), rather like the bone loss seen in post-menopausal women. Injectable hormones certainly do not increase the chances of getting cancer of the breast, uterus or cervix.

This form of contraception is probably the least used and is often reserved for the woman who finds it difficult to remember to take pills and for whom other methods of contraception are unsuitable.

After Childbirth

The injections can be given at any time after birth, although it may cause some irregular heavy bleeding if given early on. It is often prudent to wait until after the postnatal check but it does not affect breast-feeding and, although a small amount of hormone enters the milk, the baby is not harmed in any way.

Contraceptive Implants

These are small soft tubes which are inserted under the skin so that the hormone is released over a number of years. This is a newer method of contraception but the principle is the same as for the injectable contraceptive. They are often inserted into the skin of the upper arm and it is said that the contraceptive effect lasts for about five years. If you are interested in this method, then talk to your doctor, midwife or Family Planning Clinic.

The Intrauterine Device (IUCD/Coil)

Centuries ago camel drivers in the Middle East recognised that pebbles placed in the uterus of the animal prevented pregnancies during long trips in the desert. This principle led to the knowledge that any foreign body inside the uterus would act in the same way. Materials originally used were metals (gold, platinum or silver) but because these produced unpleasant reactions in the womb they have now been entirely replaced by special forms of plastic causing little or no reaction.

Modern IUCDs come in different shapes and sizes (see the diagram on page 425). They easily regain their shape after insertion in the uterus and end in a thread or tail which hangs for about 2cm outside the cervix so that their presence can be confirmed.

How Does the IUCD Work?

The precise way in which it works is uncertain but it is believed that the presence of a foreign body in the womb sets up a minor degree

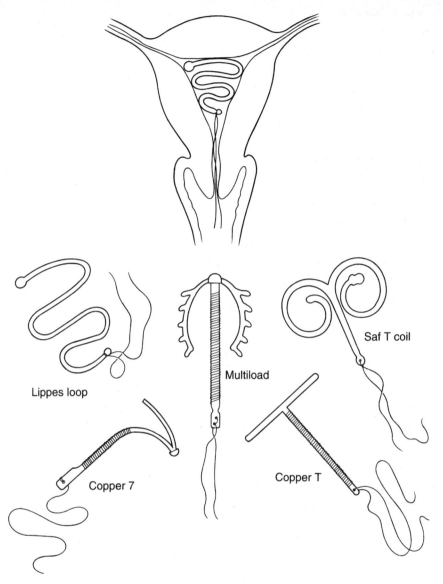

Intrauterine devices past and present.

of inflammation in the walls preventing the fertilised egg from implanting. There is little evidence to support the belief that the IUCD causes the uterus to expel the fertilised egg as in a very early miscarriage.

425

Some of the latest IUCDs have certain metals or hormones incorporated in them which increase the effectiveness of preventing a pregnancy by altering the chemical composition of the lining cells of the womb and making the environment unsuitable for the fertilised egg.

The effectiveness of an IUCD in preventing a pregnancy is second only to the combined oral contraceptive pill and has the great advantage of convenience. Once inserted contraceptive worries are over and there is no need to use additional creams or jellies. As the device is inserted by a doctor, there is no need for either partner to take an active role in contraception and this method has proved extremely effective in underdeveloped countries.

Before the newer, smaller types of IUCD were produced, intrauterine contraception was limited to those who had already had children as it was easier to insert a coil through a cervix which had already been stretched by childbirth. This limitation is no longer valid.

It is common practice for a coil to be inserted in a doctor's surgery or in a hospital clinic without any form of anaesthetic. The neck of the womb is grasped with a blunt instrument and a fine probe is passed through the external opening of the cervix to assess the ease of insertion and also to measure the depth of the womb. This is important because for success the device must be placed against the top of the womb and not just partially inside. Occasionally if it is impossible to pass the probe through the neck of the womb or if the procedure is too painful, it may be advised that insertion should be undertaken under general anaesthetic.

Having measured the size of the womb, the doctor will choose the correct size of coil which will then be inserted through the neck of the womb. The whole procedure takes a few minutes and, although it is common for minor colicky pains to occur for a few moments after insertion, these usually pass off.

The best time to insert an IUCD is during a period or immediately afterwards because the cervix is soft and stretchable and there should be no possibility of the woman being pregnant at the time.

Suitability

Many women like the coil because it doesn't interrupt intercourse and it works as soon as it is in place. It is most suitable for women who have had children because the cervix will already have been stretched and the insertion is easier. Formerly it was believed that the insertion of an IUCD caused more problems in a woman who had not conceived, but the smaller types of coil are perfectly satisfactory if other forms of contraception do not suit.

What about Side Effects of the IUCD?

Pain and bleeding may continue for a few days after insertion and the bleeding pattern of menstruation may be altered. It is not unusual for periods to become heavier and perhaps irregular but usually these symptoms settle after the first two or three months and the modern IUCD can be safely left in place for three to five years.

Women are often taught how to locate the thread of an IUCD with a finger so that a check can be made at regular intervals to ensure that the IUCD has not come out. Expulsion of a coil does not necessarily imply complete failure of that method and sometimes the uterus just rejects the coil. It is possible for a further insertion to be attempted, perhaps with a different type of coil.

Sometimes the thread which sticks out of the cervix is not identified and yet the coil is in its correct position. An X-ray or ultrasound will confirm the presence of the coil in the uterus which can be removed with a special instrument in the clinic, or occasionally a general anaesthetic is needed.

The principal contra-indication for an IUCD is infection of the womb and Fallopian tubes and this is the main reason why it is not always recommended as the first form of contraception for the young girl who has not conceived. The incidence of infection has been greatly reduced by modern sterile techniques as well as the less irritant forms of IUCD.

Failure Rate

The failure rate of an IUCD is about three per cent. If pregnancy occurs with an IUCD in place, which does happen occasionally, there is a small chance of a miscarriage in the first weeks but there is no evidence to suggest that the developing baby is affected in any way should the pregnancy proceed. Some doctors like to remove the coil gently and others leave it in place until after delivery of the baby.

Sometimes the thread that lies outside the cervix irritates the partner's penis and intercourse may become painful for him. This is usually because the thread is too short rather than too long and the doctor may be able to adjust things accordingly.

The presence of an IUCD has been linked with tubal pregnancy (see pages 110–113). There is an association between the two conditions and it is wise not to use this form of contraception if you have already had an ectopic pregnancy. An IUCD is also inadvisable if you suffer heavy and painful periods, have had infection in the pelvis, or if certain conditions exist in the uterus such as large fibroids.

After Childbirth

The usual time to insert an IUCD is six weeks after childbirth, although occasionally it can be inserted before you leave hospital if you are most anxious for this method of contraception and do not wish to use any other. Insertion soon after birth increases the risk of infection and there is a higher incidence of expulsion of the coil.

Caesarean section does not preclude the use of an IUCD, but again you will probably be advised to wait for six to eight weeks before insertion is undertaken.

About ninety thousand women in this country are pregnant before marriage and a hundred and twenty thousand women undergo legal termination of pregnancy every year. Despite the increased availability of free contraception, there remains a great need to publicise this fact and to educate couples in the principles of family planning.

It is also important for those who seek advice to understand one basic principle. Most of the side effects and complications of any form of contraception are relative and not absolute and the correct contraception must be tailored to the individual's needs. For example, a woman in the 'at risk' age group for oral contraception, i.e. late thirties/early forties who smokes heavily, may still want to take the small risk of problems with the pill if no other method of contraception is suitable and one hundred per cent protection is required. Similarly, the woman who has heavy periods may still prefer to run the risk of increasing this problem with the IUCD rather than be forced to change her method of family planning. Each couple, guided by their doctor, must make a choice of the method that suits them best at any particular time.

Sterilisation

Sterilisation is an unfortunate word because, although it is taken to mean a procedure for rendering a man or woman incapable of producing offspring, the implication of the word may wrongfully be assumed to imply an alteration in sexual feelings and performance. It is the most effective and the most final form of birth control and should to all intents and purposes be considered irreversible.

Sterilisation procedures involve the surgical interruption of the Fallopian tubes in the female and the vas deferens, the tube leading from the testes or sperm sac to the penis, in the male.

Female Sterilisation

There are many different techniques for blocking off the Fallopian tubes. They can be divided, tied, cauterised or removed and each surgeon will have their preferred method. There are also two methods of approach. A special torch (a laparoscope) may be inserted into the abdomen just beneath the navel and, by means of an instrument which can be passed down the sheath of the torch, the Fallopian tube can be grasped and burnt or closed with a ring or clip. The other method, which is less commonly performed nowadays, involves a full cut into the abdomen and a stay in hospital of two to three days.

The Torch or Laparoscope Method

This method has the great advantage of speed and economy. Occasionally it is performed under local anaesthetic but usually admission to hospital and a full anaesthetic is involved, although the whole procedure can be performed as a day case.

The success rate of this procedure is about ninety-nine per cent. The occasional pregnancy that occurs is due either to an unsuspected pregnancy already present before the operation, although this can be avoided by choosing the correct time in the cycle to operate, or in rare cases because the two ends of the tube that have been destroyed by burning, or occluded by a ring, join up again. The only other disadvantage of the procedure is that in some instances menstrual flow may tend to become heavier.

Tying or Removal of the Tubes

By no means major surgery, this procedure does involve a formal cut into the abdomen so that the tubes can actually be tied or removed, and this inevitably will involve the patient in a two- to three-day stay in hospital with a little discomfort from the abdominal scar.

This method is preferred by some surgeons because the success rate is literally one hundred per cent. It is also carried out when laparoscopy is unsuitable.

Are There Any Side Effects after Sterilisation?

With the laparoscope method no special aftercare is needed. There may be one stitch in the navel which either dissolves or needs to be removed within a week. Some discomfort and swelling in the abdomen may be experienced, and it is not uncommon for pain under both shoulder blades to be noticed which is due to air in the abdominal cavity.

Female sterilisation techniques should not alter hormone production and therefore have no effect on attitudes to sex or performance, though sometimes the periods can become a little heavier than usual.

There is a small but definite failure rate of about half a per cent in female sterilisation and, if the woman does get pregnant, fertilisation and growth could occur in the tube, leading to an ectopic pregnancy (see pages 110–113).

Newer Methods of Sterilisation

Operations on the Fallopian tubes can be performed through the vagina, although this is not commonly done. The advantages include no post-operative discomfort, no visible scar and an early discharge from hospital. Because the operation is done through the vagina the operating space is more limited and the technique is not always easy.

Another technique involves the passing of a telescope-like instrument through the vagina into the neck of the womb so that the internal openings of the Fallopian tubes into the womb can be identified and these can be blocked, either by a hot current or certain chemicals. This technique is not commonly performed.

Hysterectomy

Finally, sterilisation by removal of the womb (hysterectomy) has a small but definite indication. It is usually reserved for the woman who is over forty with an existing problem in her womb such as heavy periods or fibroids. In this instance it would seem illogical to perform a short, quick operation with a laparoscope only to find hysterectomy might become necessary in a year or two's time. Some surgeons may advise hysterectomy in the older woman in the absence of disease in the womb as it can be argued that, if no further children are desired, the uterus becomes a useless organ, and with advancing age is more prone to be the seat of menstrual problems and cancer. Against this argument, hysterectomy has more risks, is a major procedure, and may have psychological repercussions without full consultation.

Male Sterilisation

This is the male equivalent of tubal tying. What happens is that the tube along which the sperm are transported from the testes to the penis (vas deferens) is divided. Because each vas is situated just under the skin on either side of the scrotal sac, locating and dividing these channels is much easier than female sterilisation. Moreover, it is often done under local anaesthetic in the Outpatient Department. A small cut is made into the top end of the scrotal sac, the vas is found and a small section cut out with the remaining ends tied off, and the whole procedure takes about fifteen minutes.

There is usually a little discomfort and swelling of the scrotum for the first few days and, unlike female sterilisation, it is necessary to use alternative methods of birth control until the doctor advises that this is no longer required. This will be judged by examination of at least two semen specimens over a three-month period to confirm the complete absence of sperm. Each surgeon will have his or her own routine of follow-up which should be strictly adhered to.

Contrary to the myths surrounding this operation vasectomy leaves the male genital system unchanged. There is no alteration in the output of hormones or the ability to perform sexually. Erection and ejaculation occur in the same way as before and there should be no change in the amount of semen produced, although of course no sperm are present.

Is Male or Female Sterilisation Reversible?

If only a small section of Fallopian tube in the woman or vas deferens in the man is occluded, it should in theory be possible to re-join the remaining portions of the tubes and restore fertility. However, the overall results of reversal of sterilisation are disappointing. For these reasons doctors usually advise the couple that any sterilisation procedure should be regarded as an irrevocable step.

If a woman who has been sterilised wishes to conceive, the feasibility of reversal will depend largely on which method was used. If the tubes were simply occluded by a clip using the torch method, it is possible to remove the clip and attempt to join up the normal ends, though again the success rate is poor. If the tubes have been removed, then of course the position is hopeless and the only chance of conception is by fertilisation outside the body (IVF).

The success rate of reversing sterilisation in men is higher than in women, though the often quoted figure of twenty-five per cent is probably unrealistic.

A well-motivated couple who understand the principles involved in sterilisation will be happy with the result. Those who have been coerced into asking for sterilisation, or who harbour fears that the procedure will involve an alteration in their sexual feelings, may suffer from psychological upsets largely as a result of guilt.

After Childbirth

If a mother has decided that she would like to be sterilised and the decision has been made earlier in the pregnancy, then it would seem logical to do the operation while she is still in hospital. However, there are a few complications that are commoner if sterilisation is done this early, including a higher incidence of clot formation in the legs, and also a greater chance of failure because the recently pregnant Fallopian tubes are very much thicker and softer than in the non-pregnant state, and therefore there is a higher chance that they may grow together. The best time to sterilise is two to three months after the birth.

If sterilisation has been pre-planned in a woman who needs to be delivered by Caesarean section, then it is simple to perform this at the same time as the delivery. Again it is important that adequate counselling has taken place well before term so that the couple have a chance to discuss the implications fully with the consultant and the decision is not made at the last minute when it could be regretted.

Where to Get Family Planning Advice

Remember that there are a number of different options. Your family doctor may provide family planning or, if not, another doctor in the area is perfectly entitled to give contraceptive advice. The doctors, health visitors and midwives can advise you if you have your baby in hospital. The address of local family planning clinics can be obtained from health centres, hospitals, the telephone directory, or your health authority.

The choice of where you seek advice is entirely yours. It may be that you have a very good family doctor but you feel uncomfortable talking about contraception, in which case any of the alternatives would welcome a visit.

Remember that all these avenues are open to you and cost nothing. There is a list of useful addresses at the back of this book.

Induced Abortion (Termination of Pregnancy)

The higher incidence of unplanned pregnancies and the dangers of malformation following the mother contracting a disease such as German measles in the first few weeks of pregnancy, together with the ability to diagnose abnormalities such as Down's Syndrome with modern sophisticated techniques, make abortion a necessary and integral section of this book.

Inducing an abortion is the oldest known method of population control. For centuries it was widely practised and tolerated in many societies in the world. Following the declaration by Pope Pius IX in the 1860s that all abortions were murder, laws were passed in most Western countries prohibiting abortion unless it was necessary to save the woman's life. It was not for a hundred years, until 1967, that a new Abortion Act became law in the UK legalising abortion under certain well-defined circumstances. According to the Act it is legal for a registered medical practitioner to terminate a pregnancy if two doctors are of the opinion that:

• The continuance of the pregnancy would involve risk to the life of the pregnant woman greater than if the pregnancy were terminated.

• The continuance of the pregnancy would involve risk of injury to the physical or mental health of the pregnant woman greater than if the pregnancy were terminated.

• The continuance of the pregnancy would involve risk of injury to the physical or mental health of the existing children of the family of the pregnant woman greater than if the pregnancy were terminated.

• There is a substantial risk that if the child were born it would suffer from such physical or mental abnormalities as to be seriously handicapped.

Though by no means supported by all, the change towards liberal attitudes to abortion has occurred partly for cultural reasons and partly because so many women suffered irreparable harm and occasionally death following self-induced abortions, or when abortions were procured illegally.

Abortion today is still illegal in certain countries, notably those with a predominantly Roman Catholic faith such as Spain and Italy; legal, under certain circumstances, in the UK and the USA; and obtainable on demand in some countries such as Hungary and Japan. In the UK abortion must be carried out in a place approved by the

Department of Health who carefully monitor the outcome and have the right to withdraw a licence for termination of pregnancy if the regulations are not strictly adhered to.

Methods of Terminating Pregnancies

Legally, the definition of viability is twenty-four weeks and this is based on the assumption that before this time the chances of survival are extremely minute. It is illegal to terminate a pregnancy after twenty-four weeks unless the fetus is so severely malformed that it would not survive if it were born naturally.

The principal methods of terminating pregnancies are surgical, and the methods depend on the stage of the pregnancy.

Termination of Pregnancy before Twelve Weeks

This procedure is similar to a D & C or womb scraping that is commonly performed on the non-pregnant patient. The whole procedure takes only a few minutes and is usually carried out under general anaesthesia. It consists of stretching the cervix so that a small suction tube can be passed into the uterus and the contents evacuated. The procedure is known as vaginal termination of pregnancy and in most NHS hospitals it is performed as a day case.

Termination of Pregnancy after Twelve to Fourteen Weeks

At this stage in pregnancy the uterus is quite large and it may not be possible to remove all the products of conception. The procedure becomes hazardous once the uterus is much over fourteen weeks. The procedure here is to insert a small vaginal tablet or pessary into the vagina containing a hormone called prostaglandin. This has the ability to soften the cervix and start contractions so that in fact the woman has to go through a mini-labour.

Obviously the early pregnant uterus will resist any attempts to empty its contents and therefore, if one pessary does not stimulate labour, the procedure is repeated two or three times. In the majority of instances a mini-labour will ensue and the fetus and the placenta will be expelled. In rare cases, this procedure does not work, in which case an injection of prostaglandin is given abdominally through a needle into the cavity of the uterus, or via a tube into the cervix.

In very rare instances, mainly if all these methods have failed or for medical reasons, termination of pregnancy may have to be achieved through an abdominal operation. Thankfully, this is rarely necessary nowadays.

If there is any doubt that all the fetus and placenta have been passed, a D & C may be necessary under general anaesthetic to ensure that the uterus is quite empty.

Complications of Termination of Pregnancy

The earlier the pregnancy the fewer the complications, and the risks of the procedure up to ten weeks are negligible. Fortunately these days serious infection, which was always the anxiety years ago, is rare following legal abortion. Before the Abortion Act was introduced desperation led many women with unwanted pregnancies to the back-streets and the abortion parlours. Attempts at producing abortions were usually made by unqualified people using unsterile instruments, with the result that infection was introduced into the womb with catastrophic consequences, sometimes even resulting in the death of the unfortunate woman.

It is significant that the number of so-called septic abortions has been dramatically reduced since 1967 and this serious complication is now happily rare. However, even if termination of pregnancy is properly carried out in an operating theatre with sterile instruments, infection can occur and, although it is extremely uncommon for any serious impairment of the woman's health to result, mild infection in the womb may spread to the Fallopian tubes, occasionally resulting in tubal blockage.

Incompetency of the cervix (see pages 200–201) may arise following termination if the pregnancy is over twelve weeks as the cervix necessarily has to be stretched in order to allow the instrument to be passed through. This complication may cause a miscarriage in a subsequent pregnancy.

Other rare complications include prolonged bleeding due to the inability of the uterus to be completely emptied, and occasionally the uterus is accidentally perforated during the procedure, which needs further surgical intervention.

Medical Methods of Terminating Pregnancies

A new drug has recently been developed in the form of a pill which may safely induce bleeding and cause an abortion in very early pregnancy. This drug is under trial in the UK and has not yet been licensed, but the principles of medical termination, with the obvious advantages, are promising.

To most women the end of an unplanned pregnancy is an enormous relief. Some, however, may develop psychological problems, perhaps due to guilt, and with the passage of time attitudes about the pregnancy may change. One estimate based on a large series of women whose pregnancies were terminated in Sweden suggested that twenty-five per cent of them suffered some sort of psychological upset in later life. The ultimate decision as to whether a pregnancy should be terminated must be made by the woman and her medical advisers. Health visitors and medical social workers may give considerable help through their knowledge of any relevant social circumstances, as well as outlining help that may be available to the woman who has decided to keep her pregnancy. There is good evidence to show that the incidence of psychiatric problems that occur following termination can be greatly reduced by skilful and sympathetic counselling beforehand.

CHAPTER 14

The Childless Couple

About ten per cent of married couples in this country are childless. Blame was formerly attached to the female partner, but it is now known that the male is at fault in about thirty-five per cent of cases of infertility, the female in another thirty-five per cent of cases, and in thirty per cent there are factors present in both. Ninety per cent of married couples with no abnormalities should achieve a pregnancy within a year of trying and for this reason the word 'infertility' is reserved for those who have failed to achieve a pregnancy by the end of this time.

Unfortunately, despite considerable research into the causes of infertility, the success rate after treatment of either of the couple remains at the relatively low figure of forty per cent. In order to understand why some couples fail to achieve a pregnancy, it is important to consider some of the factors responsible in both sexes.

Pregnancy will result if the male produces spermatozoa of sufficient quantity and quality, they are deposited in the vagina, and move upwards through the neck of the womb via the body of the uterus to the Fallopian tubes. Although about four hundred million sperm are produced with each ejaculation, by the time they have proceeded along the hazardous course from the vagina to the Fallopian tubes, only a few hundred survive.

Once in the Fallopian tube, they then have to swim for some way up the tube against the normal current. If the timing of the arrival of a single sperm in the tube coincides precisely with the arrival of the egg from the ovary which has been grasped by the tentacles of the tube and wafted down to meet the sperm, fertilisation may occur. This timing is critical because the egg may only survive for thirty-six hours in the tube, and the sperm one or two days.

Once conception has occurred, the fertilised egg has to pass along the tube into the body of the uterus within three to four days. Here it sinks into the already prepared lining of the uterus and hopefully it will then begin to grow and form an embryo.

Unfortunately in about twenty per cent of pregnancies the developing embryo inside the uterus may be expelled and a miscarriage may result. On other occasions the fertilised egg may get stuck in the Fallopian tube for some reason, leading to an ectopic pregnancy (see pages 110–113). With so many factors involved in producing the egg and the male seed, together with the perilous journey that both have to make before meeting, it is really quite surprising how often pregnancies do occur.

Causes of Failure to Conceive

Male Factors

Perhaps no sperm or insufficient sperm are produced by the man, and there are many causes for this. The testicles may have been diseased in childhood or they may have been slow in descending at puberty. Injury to the testicles, or exposure to large amounts of X-ray treatment, or certain drugs, can lower the normal sperm count. It is well known that, if the temperature in the scrotal sac is much higher than normal, the efficiency of the sperm diminishes. This may be due to varicose veins of the testicles, or the wearing of athletic underwear which keeps the scrotal sac at too high a temperature. Excessive alcohol consumption is known to diminish sperm counts and sometimes the passageway carrying the sperm may be blocked.

The testes may be able to produce sperm but ejaculation may not be satisfactory, may occur prematurely, or rarely the testes or penis may develop abnormally. Sometimes sperm may be correctly deposited in the vagina but may be unable to swim due to disease of the male prostate gland which affects their mobility.

Female Factors

A single egg must be produced by the ovary some twelve to fourteen days before the next menstrual period. The Fallopian tubes must be healthy and normal so that the eggs can be conveyed towards the uterus. The lining of the womb must be correctly prepared for receiving the fertilised egg so that implantation and further growth may occur. The neck of the womb must not act as a barrier to the passage of the sperm and should liberate clear colourless fluid at ovulation when the egg is released so that the sperm can travel through into the womb and along to the tube. Simple lack of knowledge of the correct timing of intercourse, ignorance or fear of the sexual act, and a host of emotional factors may all play a part in delaying conception.

Investigation of the Infertile Couple

Just because a pregnancy has not been achieved after one year the couple should not take this to mean that they are infertile, and the initial consultation and examination by the doctor will often do much to remove these fears. It is surprising how often a pregnancy will result once reassurance has been given.

Significant information may be gained from the questions asked at the initial interview. In the man a history of injury or disease of the testicles, drinking habits, the use of particular drugs and the nature of ejaculation may give a clue if there are problems. Examination of the testes may reveal a discrepancy in the size or some abnormality of the penis or enlarged veins in the region of the scrotum.

In the female it is important to know whether the periods are regular and whether the menstrual flow each month is normal. If so, ovulation is almost certainly occurring. Pain with the periods, though a nuisance, does usually indicate that ovulation is taking place. Some women know when they ovulate because of abdominal discomfort midway between the periods, sometimes accompanied by a little blood-stained jelly-like material from the vagina. If the periods are irregular, or the amount of menstrual flow is scanty, ovulation may not be occurring normally.

The frequency and timing of intercourse is important. In order to achieve a pregnancy intercourse must take place two weeks before the next period, and this is so even if the interval between the periods is not exactly four weeks. If the periods come every six or seven weeks the timing of ovulation is still constant and still occurs twelve to fourteen days before the next period.

It is important that frank discussion of sexual habits takes place because it is well known that simple explanation and correction of misconceptions will often help a couple achieve a pregnancy without further investigations.

A general examination then takes place which may exclude any obvious cause for failure to conceive. Perhaps the internal examination may reveal a spasm or tightening of the muscles around the genital organs which may indicate that intercourse is not taking place satisfactorily. Sometimes the womb may be enlarged by small innocent muscle lumps called fibroids which occasionally can cause problems conceiving, or the ovaries may be enlarged and contain cysts. A tilted or retroverted womb is often thought to be a cause of infertility, though it is doubtful whether this is in fact relevant.

Having established that there is no abnormality in either partner and having excluded any existing general disease, the couple can be reassured that a pregnancy should occur. If it fails to happen after eighteen months or two years, or if there is a particular reason to investigate the couple earlier, the following tests are usually undertaken:

Male Tests

Semen Analysis

A specimen of sperm is produced by masturbation and is examined within six to eight hours in the laboratory. Sexual intercourse should be avoided for two or three days before the specimen is produced. The sample, which should be put into a small plastic sterile bottle obtainable from any chemist, should be kept at room temperature and not be excessively hot or cold.

Post-coital Test

This is an alternative method of analysing sperm efficiency and the principle is to examine a fresh quantity of sperm deposited in the vagina after intercourse. The female partner is asked to attend for a visit within twelve hours of intercourse. A sample is painlessly taken from the vagina and examined under a microscope to see how many sperm are present, how active and mobile they are, and how they behave. This test may show that the sperm are not able to swim through the cervix or are killed off in the vagina before reaching the cervix. The normal cervix produces a thin watery discharge at ovulation time which is particularly attractive to the sperm. If this fluid is too thick and not of the correct consistency, the sperm may not be able to enter the cervix. This also occurs if there is any infection in the vagina or if the cervix itself is inflamed. The test is usually timed midway in the female cycle so that it occurs at the time of ovulation.

Female Tests

Tests to Determine Whether the Egg is Shed (Ovulation)

Ovulation testing can be simply done by temperature recordings. The woman takes her temperature with an ordinary thermometer every morning on waking and notes the temperature change that occurs. The temperature in the first twelve to fourteen days of the menstrual cycle is fairly constant, but after ovulation there is a dip followed by a rise and for the second half of the cycle the temperature remains elevated (see the graph on page 17). The temperature change occurs because ovulation causes the hormone progesterone to be liberated by the ovary which raises the body temperature. It is best to continue temperature recordings daily over three consecutive cycles so that a pattern emerges which not only shows whether ovulation occurs but also when.

Alternatively, a blood test can be done around day twenty-one of the cycle which tests the level of the hormone progesterone and this indicates whether ovulation has occurred during that cycle.

There are also more sophisticated tests for ovulation, usually reserved for when the woman is undergoing fertility treatment, by different hormone evaluations. Also, ultrasound scanning can show whether the ovary has caused ovulation.

Home ovulation kits are available which are very simple to use and can be bought from a chemist.

Tests to Determine Patency of the Fallopian Tubes

The Fallopian tubes must be able to suck in the egg from the ovary so that it can pass through the canal and fertilisation can occur. Fertilisation has to occur in the Fallopian tube in the human and the fertilised egg will then proceed upwards towards the uterus where it will grow and will ultimately become a developing embryo. There are a number of instances where part of the Fallopian tubes may be blocked, kinked, diseased, or even absent, so it is vital to find out exactly the state of the tubes.

There are two methods for determining the patency of the tubes, both involving the injection of dye through the neck of the womb: X-ray (salpingogram) or by direct inspection (laparoscopy), whereby the passage of the dye can be traced along the Fallopian tubes and out into the general abdominal cavity. Salpingograms or X-rays can be done without an anaesthetic and are usually quite tolerable. There is some discomfort similar to the insertion of a coil but it has the advantage of being a non-invasive technique with virtually no complications. Laparoscopy (see pages 429–430) involves admission to hospital, usually as a day case. A light anaesthetic is generally required and this method gives more information than a salpingogram as the whole of the pelvic contents including the tubes, ovaries and uterus can be visualised directly through the torch.

The choice of procedure will depend on the policy of the particular hospital, the views of the gynaecologist, and the suitability of the patient.

If dye can be seen to spill out of the ends of the tubes, then no blockage exists. Sometimes the dye will not pass along the inner parts of the tubes or will collect at the outer ends into a blind-ending sac. This will obviously prevent the egg from getting into the tube at all or, if fertilisation does occur, will block the channel leading back to the uterus. If only one of the tubes is shown to be blocked and the other is open, this should not decrease the incidence of a successful pregnancy. Nor is there any decrease in likelihood of conception because both ovaries still continue to shed their eggs alternately and the egg produced by the ovary on the side of the blocked tube is able to find its way across to the opposite normal tube. This fact is well borne out by the frequency of success in achieving a normal pregnancy following an ectopic pregnancy when the tube may have had to have been removed.

Treatment of the Infertile Couple

The Low Sperm Count

An average of 60 to 100 million sperm are present in a normal ejaculate and, although only a single sperm is needed to fertilise the female egg, so perilous is the journey from the vagina to the Fallopian tube where fertilisation occurs, that a sperm count of below 20 million will decrease the chances of conception somewhat and a count below 5 million may seriously impair the likelihood of achieving a pregnancy.

If a low count is found, a second specimen is usually examined after the couple have abstained from intercourse for at least five days beforehand. If the second count remains low, the opinion of a urologist with an interest in infertility may be sought. The testicles are examined to ensure that they are of normal size and consistency and to exclude any visible abnormality such as varicose veins or fluid causing distension of the sac of the scrotum. Both of these conditions are common causes of impaired sperm production and quite easily correctable by surgery.

Sometimes there is an obstruction in the vas tube which can be diagnosed by injection of a contrast dye and taking X-rays. Again, this blockage is usually amenable to surgical treatment with an often dramatic improvement in the sperm count. If no abnormality of the testicles is found, blood tests are done to detect whether the hormones responsible for producing sperm are insufficient and sometimes a small piece of testicular tissue is removed for microscopical examination.

Injections of male hormone (testosterone) or pituitary hormone, produced by the part of the brain responsible for initiating sperm production, may improve a low sperm count but results are not always satisfactory. Artificial insemination with the husband's semen (AIH – see pages 447–448) may be worthwhile.

Complete Absence of Sperm

Orgasm and ejaculation may occur normally but when a specimen is tested no sperms at all are present. Here there is either gross impairment of sperm production, which may be due to a general disease process, or injury to or abnormality of the testes that may have occurred in childhood, but often no cause is found on examination. A specimen containing no sperms is unlikely to be improved by medication and the couple may be forced to consider artificial insemination using donor sperm (AID – see pages 447–448) or adoption.

Failure to Ovulate

If ovulation testing has shown that an egg is not being produced monthly, accompanied by a complete absence of periods, or if ovulation is only occurring occasionally, ovulation can sometimes be stimulated with certain drugs. The commonest and simplest drug in use is called Clomiphene or Clomid. It works by acting as a booster to the ovary that may not be good enough at making eggs properly. It also persuades the pituitary gland in the brain to be more efficient at liberating the hormones necessary for ovulation.

Treatment usually consists of one tablet a day from the second day of the menstrual cycle for five consecutive days and a course of three to four months is usually advised. Temperature charts or blood tests will show whether this treatment has achieved the required result and, if not, the dose may be increased to two or three tablets and the same procedure adopted.

If the woman is not menstruating for any reason, Clomid can re-educate the hormones to work properly and sometimes after a three-month course the pituitary gland is kicked into action and the periods and ovulation recommence. Treatment with Clomid is easy because there are few side effects. Hot flushes may occur and just occasionally the ovaries grow to form cysts which can usually be controlled but sometimes need deflating. Also, there is no need for sophisticated monitoring of how ovulation is occurring.

If Clomiphene fails to produce ovulation, a combination of hormones which are usually liberated by the pituitary gland can be given in the form of tablets or injections. Treatment, however, with these hormones is more complicated and painstaking for patient and doctor. This is because the drugs are powerful and the body's response sensitive, and therefore two or three eggs may be fertilised and twins or triplets are possible. The only way to guard against this is for the dose to be precisely calculated before treatment, and close co-operation is needed between the patient and doctor during treatment by ongoing urine and blood tests. Because this treatment is more complicated and because of the sensitivity, maximum success is usually achieved in specialised centres which have fertility clinics and sophisticated monitoring equipment necessary for the assessments. There are also newer drugs which can stimulate ovulation in certain circumstances.

Blockage of the Fallopian Tubes

It has been estimated that twenty-five per cent of all cases of female infertility are due to Fallopian tube occlusion. Damage to the tubes can occur from infection, from previous surgery and for a number of other reasons. Because the canal of the tube which has to transport the egg is no wider than the diameter of a straw, previous inflammation may cause irreparable damage.

Can Anything be Done to Unblock Fallopian Tubes?

There are no drugs available which can open up tubes that are blocked and therefore the choices lie between a surgical procedure to unblock the tubes, or in-vitro fertilisation (IVF – see page 449).

With advances in surgery, it would seem a relatively simple procedure to operate on the tubes, and cut out the area that is blocked, or to remove a portion of the tube if it is blocked and implant the remaining healthy part into another site in the uterus. Although the surgical technique of any tubal surgery is not particularly difficult, the results are disappointing mainly because the tubes are so delicate that, despite meticulous care during surgery, blockages can re-form. The best results are achieved when the tubes are not actually blocked but just kinked or twisted into an unusual position.

The site of blockage or degree of damage to the tubes is usually assessed by laparoscopy (see pages 429–430) and before surgical reconstruction is attempted all other causes of failure to conceive are completely excluded. Obviously ovulation must be confirmed and the sperm examined before surgery. Many hospitals do not undertake tubal surgery and prefer to refer women to specialised centres where these forms of operations are done with the aid of an operating microscope.

Is it Possible to Transplant Tubes?

Attempts have been made to substitute diseased or blocked Fallopian tubes with healthy tubes removed during, for example, a sterilisation procedure in another woman. In practice this method has not proved successful, mainly because of rejection of tissue by the recipient, and also because the Fallopian tube is not just a channel for transport but also has important functions enabling the early embryo to grow before it passes into the lining of the womb. It has been suggested that a diseased Fallopian tube could be entirely replaced by another tissue, say even a vein, but this to date has also proved unsuccessful for similar reasons.

Artificial Insemination

This involves the artificial transference of semen into the cervix, either using the husband's semen (AIH) or sperm from an unknown donor (AID). AIH may be indicated when there is inability to deposit sperm in the vagina during normal sexual intercourse perhaps because of an anatomical fault of the penis, or if ejaculation occurs too early, if the semen count is low, or if the cervical secretion is hostile, preventing access by the sperm.

There are two ways in which artificial insemination with the husband's sperm can be done. Either a small quantity of sperm produced by masturbation is injected with a syringe through the cervix at the correct time of ovulation, or the couple can be taught how to use a simple cap device which the woman inserts onto the neck of the womb and is connected to a thin rubber tube through which the husband may inject a specimen of his own sperm with a syringe.

AID is indicated if the husband has no sperm at all or when he is known to be a carrier of a certain hereditary disorder. The donor is carefully chosen to match the partner in appearance and to be free of disease. Apart from the emotional, ethical and legal implications of AID, the couple will have to decide whether they would prefer to rear the child of an unknown semen donor rather than adopting a child. The donor is completely unknown and he has no knowledge of who has received his semen.

AIH is a relatively simple procedure and is available in most hospital centres, but AID is not yet widespread in the NHS and your family doctor may be able to suggest where specialist advice can be obtained.

Assisted Conception

Perhaps the most remarkable recent advance in assisted conception is the 'test-tube' baby story (in-vitro fertilisation – IVF). This of course is a misnomer because test-tubes are not actually used in order to grow the fertilised egg. The principle here is that an egg is removed from the ovary just before ovulation, either by laparoscopy or vaginally with ultrasound guidance, and the egg is grown outside the woman's body in the laboratory. Male sperm is then added so that hopefully conception will occur. If conception occurs, the fertilised egg is then either replaced into the womb directly, or into the Fallopian tube. The latter is known as the GIFT procedure.

The theory is marvellously simple but the execution equally as difficult. Success in this country has already been achieved on many occasions and huge advances in techniques and in simplifying the methods have occurred since the first baby was conceived using this procedure and was safely delivered by Caesarean section in 1978.

Results from all over the world with the new methods of IVF are encouraging, but the problem is that there are only a few units in the UK undertaking such a programme on the NHS, largely because of lack of finance. As the technique becomes simplified and the success rate improves, so the indications for IVF expand. Initial programmes were directed only at the woman who had blocked Fallopian tubes, but now many centres are including couples who have not managed to achieve a pregnancy for a number of years with no demonstrable abnormality. Some practitioners believe that the technique has better results than operating on hopelessly damaged tubes.

There are a number of different techniques now used in assisted conception, all employing similar principles but slightly different in their execution.

IVF (In-vitro Fertilisation)

Eggs from the ovary are collected through the vagina under ultrasound control, for which the patient normally needs a light general anaesthetic. Fertilisation with sperm is performed outside the body and the fertilised egg is then re-implanted in the uterus.

GIFT (Gamete Intra-fallopian Transfer)

The eggs are collected by laparoscopy, involving an anaesthetic and a small cut around the navel, with a torch inserted into the abdomen and another instrument inserted lower down to collect the eggs. The best two or three eggs are then collected and two or three re-implanted in the tube with the sperm. The advantage here is that the whole procedure takes place under the one anaesthetic, but it is only suitable for women with normal Fallopian tubes.

ZIFT (Zonal Intra-fallopian Transfer)

The procedure here is similar to IVF. The eggs are collected via the vaginal route, fertilised outside, and then three embryos are replaced a day or two later.

ICSI (Intra-cytoplasmic Sperm Injection)

The procedure here is again similar to IVF except that the eggs are mobilised in a small glass tube or pipette to which is added one sperm which is then injected into the centre of the egg. This procedure is indicated if the sperm count is poor.

SUZI (Sub-zonal Insemination)

This is similar to ICSI where the egg is isolated and ten sperms are deposited into the egg membrane.

Freezing Procedures

Freezing to store sperm and embryos for later use is feasible and eggs from an ovary can be transferred direct to another recipient. However, eggs themselves cannot be frozen or stored.

Many couples who are desperate to conceive may be unable to obtain advanced fertility treatment under the NHS as the centres offering assisted conception are limited. There are, however, many excellent private fertility centres with good results that can be consulted (see addresses on pages 455–456).

CHAPTER 15

Life in the Womb and Beyond

Modern technology has enabled observations of the baby's spontaneous movements and behaviour in the womb and has opened up exciting possibilities of understanding how the baby reacts to external influences. Already we are able to see the baby's mouth opening and closing; swallowing, eye movements, and neck flexion can be seen at nine weeks of pregnancy; the baby is seen to make complete revolutions from sixteen weeks, and to suck its thumb at twenty weeks.

There are studies to show how babies communicate with their mothers from birth which have brought to light patterns of expressions for human emotions. It is known that infants are coherent in the expression of their feelings and responses, integrating communication through all their senses. Newborn babies seek eye to eye contact, listen to each other's vocalisation, and move their hands and face in matching rhythms. A two-month-old infant can join with its mother in cycles of expression, and even in exchange of utterances. Just as adults do when questioning and answering, the infant periodically seeks the eyes of the other, listens and watches, smiles in recognition of their responses and then takes the initiative with vocalisation, lip and tongue movements of rudimentary speech, and gesticulation of hands. The speech of mothers to young infants in different languages has been described as having universality of rhythm, melody and vocal qualities.

Experiments exploring infants' powers of perception for the essential signals of human communication show that they are capable of discriminating key features of emotion by eye, by ear and by touch, all through sensitivity to movements of the body. Newborn babies have been shown to be capable of modifying their sucking to trigger recordings of their mothers' voices and they show preferences for features of the speech that they heard in utero.

The behaviour of newborns in imitating what they see around them shows that they are not responding in a reflex manner without mediating processes. They search for awareness of the parent and imitate in a voluntary testing way. Observations of fetuses with ultrasound images demonstrate the continuity of expressive movements in the last months of gestation.

The reactions of young infants to insensitive or emotionally inappropriate maternal behaviour show that their emotions are ready to signal loss of empathy, sadness, anger, and avoidance or withdrawal. There are experiments to show how infants react to a mother who withholds her natural sympathetic response, or who is depressed. If a young child is cared for by a depressed mother who is unable to provide affectionate companionship, this can have lasting effects on the child's psychological development.

In the third and fourth months, infants gain control over the movements of their arms and can support their heads while exploring with their eyes and ears. Their visual system develops and they reach and grasp objects, linking what they see with what can be felt and heard. Increased awareness of their bodies leads to playful reaction to attempts by parents to lead them into rhythmic games.

Mothers discover that after three months infants listen to and move with songs. The songs and chants that mothers make for infants in the second three months show universal patterns. Communication can even be sustained in an infant who lacks one or more sensory faculties. A blind baby responds eagerly to an affectionate mother's voice and to the way she touches and moves the baby's body. A deaf baby focuses on the mother's face and hands, seeking to overcome the isolation that deafness causes. Thus a mother reaches for full communication with a blind or deaf infant. Also, fetuses have been observed to respond before and after birth to particular music. Young babies react differently when deprived of parental communication. The ability of some babies to seek out alternative sympathetic partners also occurs.

Unlike other types of research into the unborn child, research into fetal behaviour concentrates on the movements of the unborn child during the third trimester of pregnancy. It is precisely during this stage of pregnancy that the movements of the fetus in the uterus provide important indications of the child's well-being, especially if the movement patterns are linked to heart rate recordings. This approach to the study of fetal behaviour is based on the contention that the transition from fetus to baby is a continuing process. The state of the fetus six weeks before birth is almost identical to that of the baby six weeks after. Logically, therefore, the two should not be treated differently.

A fetal behavioural study may be called for if the fetus's behaviour is irregular or baffling, but a study of this kind can take up a complete working day. The mother, for example, begins with an hour's rest during which the doctor is present. Fetal behaviour is normally recorded by the CTG and ultrasound scans but these can also produce false–positive or false–negative results. In other words conclusions drawn from these procedures are often far reaching. Measuring the fetal heartbeat, for example, can be compared with taking a pulse but, if the fetus sucks its thumb, this can generate heart frequency patterns that appear suspect. As a result it may be that Caesarean section is carried out for an unnecessary reason.

In the Nijmegen Centre for Fetal Behavioural Studies in Amsterdam, Director Dr Jan Nijhuis has noticed for some time that the activity and importance of fetal movements can be assessed in different ways. For example there are various behavioural states in the fetus similar to deep sleep. A newborn child, for example, is sometimes in a very deep coma-like sleep which is perfectly natural during the first weeks after birth and mother and doctors accept it as such. This is certainly not the case during the weeks just prior to birth when anxiety is sometimes induced by the fact that the baby does not seem to be moving.

However, fetal behaviour is often difficult to assess. If the mother is active, for example, her movements may coincide with the active periods of the fetus. The same might be true for the periods of rest and therefore it is possible that the pregnant woman may feel nothing for an entire day, which would obviously worry her.

The controversy surrounding the stage at which the fetus develops consciousness is also addressed in fetal behavioural studies. What we know now is that a baby responds very differently six weeks after birth than it does shortly after birth, but it is quite possible that a certain consciousness exists even while the child is in the womb. Reflexes have been identified in the womb, for example, and studies have shown that the neurological development of the child remains unchanged in the period from two weeks before birth to two weeks after.

Fetal behaviour, therefore, has already been accepted as an independent field of research and there have been remarkable developments considering that the first scientific article appeared as recently as 1978. While knowledge is increasing rapidly, the medical profession tends to accept fetal behaviour as an indicator of the unborn child's well-being. In the future, researchers will probably concentrate on pathology in an effort to predict how sick or damaged the fetus may be in relation to various observations.

Useful Addresses

The Active Birth Centre
25 Bickerton Road
London N19 5JT
0171 561 9006

AIMS
163 Liverpool Road
London N1 0RF
0171 278 5628

Association for Postnatal Illness
25 Jerdan Place
Fulham
London SW6 1BE
0171 778 0868

Association of Breastfeeding Mothers
26 Fermshaw Close
London SE26 4TH
0181 778 4769

Association for Spina Bifida and Hydrocephalus
ASBAH House
42 Park Road
Peterborough
Cambs PE1 2UQ
01733 555988

The Birth Centre
7 Waldemar Avenue
London W13
0181 767 8294

Brooks Advisory Centres
Central Offices
153a East Road
London SE17 2SD
0171 763 9660

Caesarean Support Groups
81 Elizabeth Way
Cambridge CB4 1BQ
01223 314211

Contact a Family with a Handicapped Child
16 Strutton Ground
London SW1P 2HP
0171 222 3969

The Compassionate Friends
53 North Street
Bristol BS3 1EN
0117 953 9639

Down's Children Association
4 Oxford Street
London W1N 9SL
0171 580 0511

The Family Planning Information Service
27/35 Mortimer Street
London W1N 7RJ
0171 636 7866

Family Welfare Association
501/505 Kingsland Road
Dalston
London E8 4AU
0171 254 6251

SIDS
35 Belgrave Square
London SW1X 8QB
0171 235 0965

Gingerbread
35 Wellington Street
London WC2E 7BN
0171 240 0953

Health Education Association
Hamilton House
Mabledon Place
London WC1H 9OX
0171 383 3833

The Herpes Association
41 North Road
London N7 9OP
0171 609 9061

La Lèche League
BM 3424
London WC1N 3XX
0171 242 1278

Mama (Meet a Mum Association)
c/o Woolside Avenue
London SE25 5DW
0171 654 3137

Marie Stopes House
108 Whitfield Street
London W1T 6BE
0171 388 0662

The Maternity Alliance
15 Britannia Street
London WC1X 9JN
0171 837 1265

MENCAP
123 Golden Lane
London EC1Y 0RT
0171 454 0454

The Miscarriage
Association
18 Stoneybrook Close
West Bretton
Wakefield
West Yorks WF4 4TP
01924 85515

National Association for the
Childless
c/o 113 University Street
Belfast BT7 1HP
01232 325488

National Childbirth Trust
Alexandra House
Oldham Terrace
London W3 6NH
0181 992 8637

National Council for One
Parent Families
255 Kentish Town Road
London NW5 2LX
0171 267 1361

Patients' Association
8 Guilford Street
London WC1N 1DT
0171 242 3460

Health and Education Board
for Scotland
Woodburn House
Canaan Lane
Edinburgh EH10 4SG
0131 447 8044

SANDS
28 Portland Place
London WIN 4DE
0171 436 5881

Sickle Cell Society
54 Station Road
London NW10 4UA
0181 961 4006

Society to Support Home
Confinements
17 Laburnum Avenue
Durham DHY 4HA
01385 61325

The Spastics Society
12 Park Crescent
London W1N 4EQ
0171 636 5020

Index